T0392607

Debates in Mathematics Education

This new and updated second edition of *Debates in Mathematics Education* explores the major issues that mathematics teachers encounter in their daily lives. By engaging with established and contemporary debates, this volume promotes and supports critical reflection and aims to stimulate both novice and experienced teachers to reach informed judgements and argue their point of view with deeper theoretical knowledge and understanding.

Divided into five accessible sections, this book investigates and offers fresh insight into topics of central importance in mathematics education, with this second edition including new discussions and chapters on:

- Classic and contemporary issues of pedagogy, politics, philosophy and sociology of mathematics education
- International comparisons of achievement
- Digital technologies for teaching
- Mastery in mathematics
- Pop culture and mathematics
- Whether mathematics can be harmful

Designed to stimulate discussion and support you in your own research, writing and practice through suggested questions and activities throughout, *Debates in Mathematics Education* will be a valuable resource for any student or practising teacher, and those engaged in initial teacher education, continuing professional development or Master's level study. This book also has much to offer to those leading mathematics departments in schools and initial teacher education programmes, and to beginning doctoral students looking for a survey of the field of mathematics education research.

Gwen Ineson is a senior lecturer in Mathematics Education at Brunel University London, UK, where she is director of postgraduate research and responsible for the primary mathematics programme.

Hilary Povey is Professor Emerita in Mathematics Education at Sheffield Hallam University, UK, where she is engaged in research, professional writing and curriculum development.

Debates in Subject Teaching
Series edited by Susan Capel

Each title in the Debates in Subject Teaching series presents high-quality material, specially commissioned to stimulate teachers engaged in initial teacher education, continuing professional development and Master's level study to think more deeply about their practice, and link research and evidence to what they have observed in schools. By providing up-to-date, comprehensive coverage the books in the series support teachers in reaching their own informed judgements, enabling them to discuss and argue their point of view with deeper theoretical knowledge and understanding.

Debates in Science Education
Edited by Mike Watts

Debates in History Teaching, 2ⁿᵈ edition
Edited by Ian Davies

Debates in Geography Education, 2ⁿᵈ edition
Edited by Mark Jones and David Lambert

Debates in Computing and ICT Education
Edited by Sarah Younie and Pete Bradshaw

Debates in Physical Education, 2ⁿᵈ edition
Edited by Susan Capel and Richard Blair

Debates in English Teaching, 2ⁿᵈ edition
Edited by Jon Davison and Caroline Daly

Debates in Mathematics Education, 2ⁿᵈ edition
Edited by Gwen Ineson and Hilary Povey

For more information about this series, please visit: https://www.routledge.com/Debates-in-Subject-Teaching/book-series/DIST

Debates in Mathematics Education

Second Edition

Edited by
Gwen Ineson and Hilary Povey

Routledge
Taylor & Francis Group

LONDON AND NEW YORK

Second edition published 2021
by Routledge
2 Park Square, Milton Park, Abingdon, Oxon, OX14 4RN

and by Routledge
52 Vanderbilt Avenue, New York, NY 10017

Routledge is an imprint of the Taylor & Francis Group, an informa business

© 2021 selection and editorial matter, Gwen Ineson and Hilary Povey; individual chapters, the contributors

First edition published by Routledge 2012

British Library Cataloguing-in-Publication Data
A catalogue record for this book is available from the British Library

Library of Congress Cataloging-in-Publication Data
Names: Ineson, Gwen, editor. | Povey, Hilary, editor.
Title: Debates in mathematics education / edited by Gwen Ineson & Hilary Povey.
Description: Second edition. | Milton Park, Abingdon, Oxon ; New York, NY : Routledge, [2020] | Series: Debates in subject teaching | Includes bibliographical references and index. | Summary: -- Provided by publisher.
Identifiers: LCCN 2020008603 | ISBN 9780367074982 (hardback) | ISBN 9780367074968 (paperback) | ISBN 9780429021015 (ebook)
Subjects: LCSH: Mathematics--Study and teaching.
Classification: LCC QA11.2 .D445 2020 | DDC 510.71--dc23
LC record available at https://lccn.loc.gov/2020008603

ISBN: 978-0-367-07496-8 (hbk)
ISBN: 978-0-367-07498-2 (pbk)
ISBN: 978-0-429-02101-5 (ebk)

Typeset in Galliard
by Cenveo® Publisher Services

Contents

List of illustrations   viii
List of contributors   x
Introduction to the series   xvii
Introduction to the volume   xix
Preface   xxi
Acknowledgements   xxiii

SECTION ONE
Debates about international comparisons   1

1 **Learning about mathematics teaching from other countries**   3
 DYLAN WILIAM

2 **Mathematics education in translation: Mastery, policy and evidence**   13
 MARK BOYLAN

SECTION TWO
Debates about social justice   25

3 **The dark side of mathematics: Damaging effects of the overvaluation of mathematics**   29
 PAUL ERNEST

4 **School mathematics as social classification**   43
 PETER GATES AND ANDY NOYES

5 **Ability thinking**   55
 MARK BOYLAN AND HILARY POVEY

 6 Pedagogical possibilities for all-attainment teaching   66
    HILARY POVEY

 7 Should 'teaching for understanding' be the pinnacle
    of mathematics education?   78
    ANNA LLEWELLYN

 8 Mathematics, gender and normativity   89
    MARK MCCORMACK AND LUIS E. MORALES

 9 The financial crisis, popular culture and maths
    education   101
    HEATHER MENDICK

SECTION THREE
Debates about classroom matters   111

10 Planning for the unexpected: Working within symbolically
    structured environments   115
    ALF COLES AND NATHALIE SINCLAIR

11 Effective questioning and responding in the mathematics
    classroom   131
    JOHN MASON

12 Debates in task design   143
    ANNE WATSON

13 Fake news, artificial intelligence, mobile divisions,
    likely futures? Debates on digital technologies
    in mathematics education   155
    KEITH JONES

14 Mental maths: Just about what we do in our heads?   169
    GWEN INESON AND SUNITA BABBAR

15 The role of examples in mathematics teaching   182
    TIM ROWLAND

SECTION FOUR
Debates about mathematics teaching and social content   195

16 Mathematics and politics? Climate change
    in the mathematics classroom   197
    RICHARD BARWELL

17 Mathematical literacy: What is it? And is it important?   210
    HAMSA VENKAT

18 History of mathematics in and for the curriculum   224
    LEO ROGERS

SECTION FIVE
Debates about assessment   241

19 Formative assessment in mathematics education:
    Key debates   243
    ALISON BARNES AND RACHEL MARKS

20 The fitness and impact of GCSE mathematics
    examinations   256
    IAN JONES

21 Choosing the future: Which mathematics?   269
    CATHY SMITH

    Index   282

Illustrations

Figures

10.1	Two 8-dot shapes	116
10.2	Student offers of 8-dot shapes	117
10.3	Information needed for each shape drawn	117
10.4	Sketchpad tools	120
10.5	A triangle	120
10.6	A stretched triangle	121
10.7	A triangle or line?	122
10.8	Diagonals of regular polygons	127
10.9	A concave quadrilateral	127
10.10	The colour calculator	128
12.1	Examples used in a lesson on division (adapted from Kullberg, Runesson and Mårtensson, 2014)	147
12.2	Contrasting 'practice' tasks (from www.ncetm.org.uk/public/files/38491476)	152
12.3	Card-matching simple functions	153
13.1	Projects using a programming/coding environment	157
13.2	OECD average data on computer use for particular tasks in mathematics lessons	158
14.1	Long division algorithm for 2047 ÷ 23	171
14.2	Using chunking for long division	172
14.3	Using decomposition to solve 1001 – 999	175
14.4	One way of using the ENL to solve 53 –26	178
16.1	Annual global mean temperature anomalies (land and sea combined) 1820–2011 (Jones, 2012)	202
17.1	Graph showing the components of the Gini coefficient calculation	215
17.2	Graph showing the figures involved in an example of the Gini calculation	217
17.3	Gini graphs of the Johannesburg data set	219
18.1	Hindu squares	226

18.2   Euclid Book II Proposition 4   227
18.3   Bhaskaracharya's Pythagoras proof   227
18.4   The 'Babylonian Algorithm'   228
18.5   Euclid Book VI, 13 the Mean Proportional   228
18.6   Al-Khowarizmi's equations   229
18.7   Cardano's solution   229
18.8   Cardano's factors   230
18.9   Piero della Francesca's 'Vanishing Point Theorem'   230
18.10 Arithmetic and Geometry: ©Leo Rogers after Theo
       van Doesburg   231
18.11 Tesseract   232
18.12 Le Grande Arche © Lyndon Baker – SumImages   233
18.13 Euler's formula   234
18.14 Liu Hui triangles   234
18.15 Ratio and proportion: historical concept links   237
19.1   The assessment cycle   244
19.2   Number differences   250
19.3   Students forming and testing conjectures and making
       trials (a and b)   251
21.1   Number of Mathematics A-level candidates
       (16–18 year olds entering A2 in English schools and colleges)   270
21.2   Exam questions   274

Tables

1.1   Marks obtained by students on a GCSE question (Jones, 1993)   6
2.1   Shanghai and English primary practices compared.
      Adapted from Boylan et al. (2019)   15
4.1   GCSE mathematics grade and income deprivation
      (cumulative percentages)   46
10.1 A table of results   119
17.1 A 'spectrum of agendas' of the nature of interlink
      between content and context (with some terminology adapted),
      drawn from Graven and Venkat, 2007)   214
17.2 List of Johannesburg occupations developed for the task   218
17.3 Life-related, dialectical and mathematical understandings
      that have been incorporated into the working   220
20.1 Possible components of a broader approach to assessing
      Key Stage 4 mathematics   263

Contributors

Sunita Babbar's teaching career spans 17 years in a variety of roles in the secondary school setting. The experience she gained from her years as a classroom practitioner led to her role as a mathematics consultant for a local authority, which involved focusing on school improvement and developing teaching and learning in mathematics. Another key aspect of her role as part of the local authority advisory team was the provision of professional development, both at departmental and whole school level. She now works at Brunel University London, where she is a subject tutor for the secondary PGCE mathematics. She also oversees Initial Teacher Education at Brunel. Sunita has always maintained a keen interest in mathematics education, in particular curriculum development, transition and the development of problem solving skills in mathematics.

Alison Barnes is a Senior Lecturer in Primary Mathematics Education at the University of Brighton. Prior to this, she taught in primary schools in England and, in her role as a numeracy consultant, supported practitioners' professional development. She has worked on a number of projects with teachers using lesson study to generate knowledge, inform practice and improve outcomes for students and practitioners. She teaches on Master's and doctoral programmes in Brighton and Mauritius, supervising post-graduates researching mathematics education. Her research interests include practitioner enquiry and students' experiences of learning mathematics, in particular the interplay between cognition and affect during mathematical activity.

Richard Barwell is Professor of Mathematics Education and Dean of the Faculty of Education at the University of Ottawa, Canada. His research looks at the role of language in learning and teaching mathematics, as well as at the role of mathematics in relation to environmental sustainability and the planetary ecosystem. He has published research on how teachers use language in their teaching of mathematics, how students use language to think about mathematics, on second language learners or bilingual learners in school mathematics and on how mathematicians use language to talk about mathematics. He has also written about the use of critical mathematics education and how the philosophy of post-normal science can help to define the role of mathematics education with respect to the current planetary emergency.

Mark Boylan is a Professor of Education at Sheffield Hallam University. His background is in secondary mathematics teaching and primary and secondary mathematics teacher professional development and initial teacher education. His research focuses on evaluation of curriculum and professional development projects and critical mathematics education. He led the evaluation of the Mathematics Teacher Exchange: China-England – a key government initiative to promote East Asian teaching approaches in England.

Alf Coles was a teacher of mathematics in secondary schools for 17 years before moving into teacher education at the University of Bristol in 2010. A strand throughout his research has been a focus on engaging with teachers of mathematics and their learning. He has more recently been researching how mathematics education can respond to global and societal crisis, and what such crises mean for both the learning of mathematics and the education of teachers of mathematics. Alf is author of the book *Engaging in Mathematics in the Classroom* and was co-editor of *Teaching Secondary Mathematics as if the Planet Matters*, both published by Routledge.

Paul Ernest taught mathematics in a London comprehensive school in the 1970s. He lectured in mathematics and education at Bedford, Cambridge and Kingston, Jamaica and was appointed to the University of Exeter where he is Professor Emeritus. At Exeter he established the doctoral and Master's programmes in mathematics education, including distance learning versions studied on four continents. His research explores the intersections of philosophy, mathematics and education. Currently he is writing on ontology and on the problems of ethics in mathematics and education. Publications include *The Philosophy of Mathematics Education*, cited in 2500 scholarly publications, and *Social Constructivism as a Philosophy of Mathematics*. He edits the open access *Philosophy of Mathematics Education Journal*, located at http://socialsciences.exeter.ac.uk/education/research/centres/stem/publications/pmej/

Peter Gates qualified as a teacher in 1976, and taught in the United Kingdom and Mozambique in the aftermath of the Portuguese revolution to help strengthen a socialist society. Peter become a Head of Department in Milton Keynes, in a school that was built upon strong equitable relationships that eschewed ability grouping. In 1988 he made a move into higher education and for the next 30 years worked in The Open, Bath, and Nottingham Universities training teachers, researching equity and teaching on Master's and doctoral programmes. Peter established, with Tony Cotton, the Mathematics Education and Society group, which has now been meeting internationally for 20 years. Peter achieved liberation from wage slavery in 2017, but still seems to be doing as much as he ever did (which some say was never that much!). Peter is a member of the ESRC Peer Review College, and the Inner Circle of the Irish Research Council. He is also a member of the Association of Teachers of Mathematics, the British Educational Research Association, English Heritage, and the Campaign for Real Ale. In preparation for a trip to Cuba to celebrate the 60th anniversary of the revolution, he started learning Cuban Salsa and is constantly amazed at the level of mathematics involved in dancing.

Gwen Ineson worked in primary schools in north London for ten years before joining Brunel University London where she is a Senior Lecturer in Mathematics Education. She is responsible for supporting primary student teachers to develop their mathematics for teaching and she chairs the Brunel Partnership mathematics steering group. She is currently the Director of Postgraduate Research and supports a number of doctoral students working in mathematics education. Her research has focused on supporting teachers develop their mathematical understanding.

Ian Jones is a Senior Lecturer in Mathematics Education at Loughborough University. Prior to this he was a Royal Society Shuttleworth Education Research Fellow, secretary of the British Society for Research into Learning Mathematics, and has taught in various schools around the world. Ian is widely published in the discipline of mathematics education and sits on the editorial board of Research in Mathematics Education. He leads a programme of research investigating the application of comparative judgement to the assessment of problem solving and conceptual understanding.

Keith Jones taught mathematics for more than ten years in a number of multi-ethnic inner-city comprehensive schools, including time as a Head of Department. He works at the University of Southampton where his expertise in mathematics education spans the use of technology in mathematics education, geometrical problem-solving and reasoning, and mathematics teacher education and professional development. He is co-editor of the journal *Research in Mathematics Education* and serves on the editorial board of a number of other academic journals. He has taken part in several ICMI (*International Commission on Mathematical Instruction*) studies, including on digital technologies in mathematics education, on geometry education, and on task design in mathematics education. He has served on the international programme committee for several of the ICTMT (*International Conference on Technology in Mathematics Teaching*) conferences and has led and worked on numerous projects. He has well-established research collaborations with mathematics educators in China and Japan. He has published widely; his recent books include *Key Ideas in Teaching Mathematics, Youngsters Solving Mathematical Problems with Technology, International Perspectives on the Teaching and Learning of Geometry in Secondary Schools* and *Broadening* *the Scope of Research on Mathematical Problem Solving.* For up-to-date information, see: www.southampton.ac.uk/education/about/staff/dkj.page and https://twitter.com/KeithJonesUoS

Anna Llewellyn is an Assistant Professor of Education, whose work sits at the intersections between educational, sociology and cultural studies. She is primarily concerned with examining normative constructions within society and culture, with particular regard to marginalisation. Her specific interests are discourses, normalisation, childhood, mathematics, identity, gender, sexuality and policy. Anna has worked at the School of Education, Durham University since 2005, having previously taught mathematics in secondary schools in the United Kingdom. At Durham she has led several programmes of study, including the PGCE Secondary Mathematics, MA Education, and the BA Education Studies.

Rachel Marks is a Principal Lecturer at the University of Brighton. Specialising in primary mathematics, she taught in primary schools across the United Kingdom for five years before entering academia. Her (ESRC) funded doctoral study investigated the use of ability, language and practices in primary mathematics education. Her research interests include ability, equity, assessment and the social context of mathematics teaching and learning. She has been involved in a range of research projects including two Education Endowment Foundation reviews into Improving Mathematics in the Early Years & Key Stage 1 and in Key Stages 2 & 3, and a recent review of conference proceedings for the British Society for Research into Learning Mathematics.

John Mason, having spent 40 years at The Open University supporting people in teaching mathematics, in all phases from kindergarten to tertiary, now spends his time working on mathematical problems, many of which arise from pedagogical situations, in order to provide insights into possible pedagogical actions. This mostly means building applets to help himself, and perhaps others, to enrich concept images and to develop natural powers in the service of mathematical thinking. He continues to conduct workshops and to publish accounts of his investigations, mostly in response to invitations.

Mark McCormack is a Professor of Sociology at the University of Roehampton, London. Prior to this he held posts at Durham University and Brunel University. His research examines how gender and sexuality structure the lives of young people, with a focus on how liberalising attitudes towards sexuality are changing the social dynamics of these groups. He is author of *The Declining Significance of Homophobia: How Teenage Boys are Redefining Masculinity and Heterosexuality,* published by Oxford University Press, and co-author of *The Changing Dynamics of Bisexual Men's Lives.* He is also lead author of an introductory sociology textbook, called *Discovering Sociology,* published by MacMillan Higher Education.

Heather Mendick works as a freelance academic focusing on science, mathematics and technology; equity issues; youth aspirations and choices; and the relationship between learning and popular culture. Her main current collaborative research explores how changing ideas about geeks are impacting on who studies and works in technology. She is the author or co-author of three books: *Masculinities in Mathematics, Urban Youth and Schooling* and *Celebrity, Aspiration and Contemporary Youth*. She has published widely, blogs irregularly on education and politics, and tweets from @helensclegel. She still does a bit of maths teaching, is trying to learn Spanish, is excited by the growing popularity of veganism and spends most of her free time campaigning for socialism.

Luis Emilio Morales is a graduate research student currently based at the University of Winchester. As an early-career researcher, his published work in gender comprises multi-cultural and youth masculinities, primarily in sporting contexts. Luis's work centralises the question of how gendered identities and practices are navigated and negotiated in secularising, globalising, and modern conditions. Further areas of academic engagement include culture, social theory, the social construction of brain trauma, sexualities and pedagogy (particularly within higher-education).

Andy Noyes joined the University of Nottingham in 2001, having previously taught in a secondary school for nine years. Since then he has been Head of School and is now Associate Pro Vice Chancellor for Research and Knowledge Exchange (Social Science). Andy is a founding member of the Centre for Research in Mathematics Education and has a wide variety of research interests, largely focused on mathematics education and 14-19 learner participation, pathways and policy. He convenes a Royal Society working group on post-16 mathematics education and is Chair of the Joint Mathematical Council of the United Kingdom. A former member of the Advisory Committee on Mathematics Education, Andy is involved in a range of consultancy and advisory work.

Hilary Povey worked for the Inner London Education Authority (ILEA) for a number of years as a secondary school teacher, curriculum designer, advisory teacher and Director of the *Smile* project before joining Sheffield Hallam University where she is now Professor Emerita of Mathematics Education. Her research centres on social justice issues in mathematics education. Current research interests include all attainment teaching, transformative learning in mathematics classrooms, the role of historical awareness in combating neo-liberalism and, most recently, on possible interconnections between the concept of global citizenship and the teaching of mathematics for a better world. She is involved in curriculum development and has led a number of projects related to school mathematics, most recently *Mathematics in the Making* (MiMa) (http://mathematicsinthemaking.eu/) and the *Project* *in Citizenship and Mathematics* (PiCaM) (http://www.citizenship-and-mathematics.eu/). She is an Advisory Editor for Research in Mathematics Education and author of *Engaging (with) Mathematics and Learning to Teach: an Integrated Approach to Mathematics Preservice Education* published by WTM-Verlag.

Leo Rogers is a founder member of the British Society for the History of Mathematics and founder of the International Study Group on the History and Pedagogy of Mathematics (HPM). He has taught in primary and secondary schools in England and, as a trainer of teachers, worked with pupils and teachers in a number of European Community school curriculum and university research projects. His principal interests are the historical, philosophical and cultural aspects of mathematics as they relate to the development of curricula, mathematical pedagogies and individual learning. When not involved with mathematics education, he dances the Argentine Tango.

Tim Rowland has spent most of his professional life at the University of Cambridge, UK, where he is now Emeritus Reader in Mathematics Education. His research in the last 20 years has focused on the ways that teachers' mathematics-related knowledge is made evident in their classroom practice. In 2003 he introduced the Knowledge Quartet, a theoretical framework for the analysis and development of mathematics teaching. In August 2012, he was appointed Professor in Mathematics Education at the Norwegian University of Science and Technology (NTNU), in Trondheim, Norway, and Honorary Professor of Mathematics Education at the University of East Anglia, Norwich, UK. He was Vice President of the International Group for the Psychology of Mathematics Education (PME) until 2013, and Chair of the Joint Mathematical Council of the United Kingdom 2012-15. Tim has held Visiting Professor positions in several countries.

Nathalie Sinclair is a Canada Research Chair in Tangible Mathematics Learning at Simon Fraser University and a Professor in the Faculty of Education. She is the founding and current editor of Digital Experiences in Mathematics Education and has authored several books including *Mathematics and the Body: Material Entanglements in the Classroom*, as well as over 70 journal articles. Her primary areas of research include the role of digital technologies in mathematics education, the teaching and learning of geometry and the nature of mathematical embodiment.

Cathy Smith is the Lead in Mathematics Education and a Senior Lecturer at The Open University, UK. After starting her career as a secondary mathematics teacher, then many years in initial teacher education, her current work involves designing and teaching distance-learning courses that deepen pedagogic content knowledge in mathematics. She has a long-standing research interest in pedagogy of advanced mathematics education and in the discourses that give meaning to participation in mathematics, studying the ways that students explain their subject choices as one way of expressing who they are and who they want to be. Her recent work has focussed on schools' strategies for promoting girls' participation in mathematics.

Hamsa Venkat holds the SA Numeracy Chair at the University of the Witwatersrand in Johannesburg – now in its second five year phase of research and development in primary mathematics. The project has involved designing, implementing and studying interventions seeking to improve primary mathematics teaching and learning in government schools in South Africa. Her work in South Africa has been in the areas of Mathematical Literacy and Primary Mathematics. Prior to this, Hamsa was based in England, working initially as a secondary school mathematics teacher in London comprehensive schools, before moving into teacher education at the Institute of Education and research in mathematics education at King's College London.

Anne Watson was a secondary mathematics teacher and then joined Oxford University to teach and research Mathematics Education until retirement. She now works mainly with teachers, teacher educators and advisors with a particular focus on learning key ideas across all ages, and on the aspects of the curriculum that can empower all learners. She has been an advisor to the United Kingdom and Welsh governments on curriculum structure, and she led the study on Task Design undertaken by the International Commission on Mathematical Instruction. Other dimensions of her work can be found at pmtheta.com.

Dylan Wiliam is Emeritus Professor of Educational Assessment at University College London. After a year teaching in a private school, he taught in Inner London for seven years, before joining King's College London in 1984, where he served as Head of the School of Education (1996-2001) and Assistant Principal (2001-2003). In 2003 he moved to the United States, as Senior Research Director at the Educational Testing Service, Princeton, NJ and, from 2006 to 2010, was Deputy Director of the Institute of Education. In 2010 he left academic life to spend more time on research and teaching. He now works with teachers around the world on the use of assessment to support learning (sometimes called formative assessment).

Introduction to the series

This book, *Debates in Mathematics Education*, is one of a series of books entitled *Debates in Subject Teaching*. The series has been designed to engage with a wide range of debates related to subject teaching. Unquestionably, debates vary among the subjects, but may include, for example, issues that:

- impact on Initial Teacher Education in the subject;
- are addressed in the classroom through the teaching of the subject;
- are related to the content of the subject and its definition;
- are related to subject pedagogy;
- are connected with the relationship between the subject and broader educational aims and objectives in society, and the philosophy and sociology of education;
- are related to the development of the subject and its future in the 21st-century.

Consequently, each book presents key debates that subject teachers should understand, reflect on and engage in as part of their professional development. Chapters have been designed to highlight major questions, and to consider the evidence from research and practice in order to find possible answers. Some subject books or chapters offer at least one solution or a view of the ways forward, whereas others provide alternative views and leave readers to identify their own solution or view of the ways forward. The editors expect readers will want to pursue the issues raised, and so chapters include questions for further debate and suggestions for further reading. Debates covered in the series will provide the basis for discussion in university subject seminars or as topics for assignments or classroom research. The books have been written for all those with a professional interest in their subject, and, in particular: student teachers learning to teach the subject in secondary or primary school; newly qualified teachers; teachers undertaking study at Master's level; teachers with a subject coordination or leadership role, and those preparing for such responsibility; as well as mentors, university tutors, CPD organisers and advisers of the aforementioned groups.

Books in the series have a cross-phase dimension, because the editors believe that it is important for teachers in the primary, secondary and post-16 phases to look at subject teaching holistically, particularly in order to provide for continuity and progression, but also to increase their understanding of how children and young people learn. The balance of chapters that have a cross-phase relevance varies according to the issues relevant to different subjects. However, no matter where the emphasis is, the authors have drawn out the relevance of their topic to the whole of each book's intended audience.

Because of the range of the series, both in terms of the issues covered and its cross-phase concern, each book is an edited collection. Editors have commissioned new writing from experts on particular issues, who, collectively, represent many different perspectives on subject teaching. Readers should not expect a book in this series to cover the entire range of debates relevant to the subject, or to offer a completely unified view of subject teaching, or that every debate will be dealt with discretely, or that all aspects of a debate will be covered. Part of what each book in this series offers to readers is the opportunity to explore the interrelationships between positions in debates and, indeed, among the debates themselves, by identifying the overlapping concerns and competing arguments that are woven through the text.

The editors are aware that many initiatives in subject teaching continue to originate from the centre, and that teachers have decreasing control of subject content, pedagogy and assessment strategies. The editors strongly believe that for teaching to remain properly a vocation and a profession, teachers must be invited to be part of a creative and critical dialogue about subject teaching, and should be encouraged to reflect, criticise, problem-solve and innovate. This series is intended to provide teachers with a stimulus for democratic involvement in the development of the discourse of subject teaching.

Susan Capel June 2017

Introduction to the volume

The 21 chapters in this volume cover a very wide range of topics embracing, we believe, the key debates currently informing research and practice in mathematics education in schools. Readers will note that many of the chapters intersect with one another (and some of these intersections are signposted within the chapters themselves). We have grouped the chapters into five sections where we feel that common and interrelated themes are strongest but readers will notice that there are also many significant connections from across sections too.

The first section, *Debates about international comparisons*, contains two chapters. The first addresses the dilemmas and difficulties in general of using international comparisons to inform policy and practice and the second takes the current 'mastery' agenda in England as an exemplar.

Although we believe that social justice issues permeate the whole volume, those chapters which take social justice issues in the classroom as a specific focus are included in the second section, *Debates about social justice*, which contains seven chapters. The section begins with a look at the nature of mathematics itself and warns us of a hidden dark side to the subject both in terms of what it allows us to do and also the sort of thinking which it tends to promote. This is followed by three chapters looking at the processes of classification endemic to mathematics teaching, the first focusing on social class and the second two on 'ability' thinking. Each suggests ways that teachers can be supported to challenge inequitable thinking and practices that are perceived as simply natural, as 'common sense'. The next two chapters take discussion of this normalising process further, the first with respect to 'teaching for understanding' and the second with respect to gender. Both point to the exclusionary thinking and practices which follow. The final chapter in the section looks at mathematics and popular culture, using three fictions – two films and one novel – based on the global financial crisis of 2008 to explore new themes in how mathematics and mathematicians are portrayed.

There are six chapters in the third section, *Debates about classroom matters*. The first contribution discusses the need to plan for the unexpected through symbolically structured environments if the teacher's intention is to inculcate mathematical thinking by encouraging the 'right kind' of answers rather than the 'right' answers. With the same intention, the next chapter considers what the most productive form of teacher question is and argues for questions the answers to which are not known in advance and which are of genuine interest to the teacher. The next two chapters discuss the nature of classroom tasks to prompt mathematical thinking – carefully structured to encourage mathematical reasoning and involving the creative use of digital technologies; but both authors stress that it is what a teacher does with a task rather than the task itself that structures the classroom activity. The last two chapters in this section focus on the nature and use of examples in the mathematics classroom, drawing attention to the need for choice of example to be fit for mathematical purpose. The first of this pair also argues against the current emphasis on standard written algorithms for calculations.

The fourth section, *Debates about mathematics teaching and social content*, contains three chapters. The first two centre on content related to present day political questions, the first on climate change and the second on the Gini coefficient of inequality. In both chapters, the topics are chosen as worthy in their own right but also as exemplifying wider issues. The first argues that politics and mathematics are inextricably and inevitably linked and the second focuses on the mathematics that we all need in order to live lives as educated and informed citizens as well as to cope with daily interactions requiring mathematics. The section concludes with a discussion about the role of the history of mathematics in acknowledging our varied mathematical heritage and in humanising the subject and making it more engaging and accessible.

The final section of the book, *Debates about assessment matters*, contains three chapters. The first debates the use of formative and summative assessment in the classroom. The final two chapters in the book discuss key UK qualifications in mathematics and the extent to which the forms of assessment each uses support problem-solving and reasoning.

Each of these sections begins with a short description of the chapters in the section and then a short overall commentary explaining what we see as the links and connections between them.

We hope that you enjoy reading the book as much as we have in working with our collaborators.

Preface

Welcome to the second edition of
Debates in Mathematics Education

Welcome to this second edition of *Debates in Mathematics Education*. We loved the first edition of this book and feel deeply indebted to its editors, Dawn Leslie and Heather Mendick, both for the way their collection supported us as researchers and teacher educators and for the inspiration it gave us for this new volume. We consider ourselves honoured to be its editors. Some of the chapters are reconsiderations and revisions of chapters from the first edition where the debates which they cover have remained relevant to the current context of schooling. But a significant number are by new authors and cover new topics, reflecting changes since 2014. For most of the chapters, the schooling context in which they are set is that of England; however, the topics debated pertain to many contemporary education systems worldwide.

As with the editors of the first edition, we regard both initial teacher education and the continuing professional learning of teachers to be more than just practical advice for how to proceed in the classroom. Vital though this is, how we act cannot be separated from our aims, values and intentions and from how we understand the nature and purpose(s) of education itself. Such understanding comes into being and is informed by consideration of its history, philosophy, psychology and sociology. It also comes from going beyond current 'common sense' and by interrogating accepted policies and normative practices. As with the previous editors, we intend the book to open up such debates, while keeping them closely linked to practice, and to support the development of educators who are reflexive, politically aware and open to engaging with the social, cultural, ethical and pedagogical issues surrounding the study and teaching of mathematics.

Like the first edition, the book is aimed at all those with a professional interest in mathematics education and, in particular: initial teacher education students learning to teach the subject in secondary or primary school; newly qualified teachers; teachers undertaking study at Master's level; teachers with a subject coordination or leadership role and those preparing for such responsibility; and mentors, university tutors, CPD organisers and advisers to all these groups.

The chapter authors all locate their positions in the debates by reference to, or interrogation of, competing standpoints and by providing commentaries on further relevant reading in selective, annotated, bibliographies. Each chapter is therefore supported by reference to further reading and other reference material which will enable the reader to explore any of the issues in more depth. Some reflective questions are included throughout the text of each chapter. These can be used as a starting point for introspection and reflection and for seminars, research assignments and essays. The chapters are written by active practitioners and researchers who are experts on the topics they are discussing. As with the first edition, the style of writing is relatively informal which we hope will make reading the book enjoyable and engaging (and not too daunting!), while remaining rigorous and carefully argued. Like the pervious editors, we have learned a great deal from this book, reading and re-reading each chapter and engaging with the ideas therein, and we hope you find them similarly thought-provoking, challenging and inspiring.

Acknowledgements

First we should like to thank our authors who have contributed so generously to this volume. We consider the collection to be an outstanding summary of and contribution to the current debates in mathematics education and feel honoured to have worked with such a distinguished group of researchers. In addition, we should like to thank them for their patience when, due to unforeseeable events, things have not gone quite according to plan. We should also like to thank our publishers for similar patience and for commissioning and publishing this book.

In designing the collection, we revisited Peter Gates' edited volume *Issues in Mathematics Education* and, of course, the first edition of *Debates* edited by Dawn Leslie and Heather Mendick. Both were an inspiration to us, at the time they were published and also as we began work on this book. We hope this second edition of *Debates* will share something of these previous successes.

We should also like to thank the people we have met in a variety of mathematics education communities including: the *British Society for Research into Learning Mathematics*; at *Mathematics Education and Society* conferences; the *International Congress on Mathematics Education* through its topic study groups on the social and political dimensions of mathematics education and its philosophy; and the thematic working group focusing on social, cultural and political challenges at the *Congress of the European Society for Research in Mathematics Education*. Without access to the conversations we have had there, the volume would have been the poorer. We consider ourselves very fortunate to be members of such a vibrant part of international educational research.

Section One
Debates about international comparisons

Introduction

Dylan Wiliam considers the role in current policy rhetoric and practice of international comparisons based on, for example, Programme for International Assessment (PISA) and Trends in Mathematics and Science Study (TIMSS) test results. He raises some significant difficulties with this: What exactly is being measured and is that something important? Given, for example, difficulties in translation, are the assessments comparable? And, are the groups of students taking the tests in different countries similar? Even if these technical difficulties are accounted for, how reliably can we identify which of a wide range of factors that vary between countries are key to educational performance? And even if we can isolate the relevant variable, how confident can we be that it will have the same effect when translated into another culture? He concludes that, nevertheless, provided all these difficulties are acknowledged and taken into consideration, international comparisons may help us in setting our own agenda for mathematics education.

Mark Boylan considers teaching for "mastery", a concept and set of practices imported from Shanghai and operating as government policy in England at the time of writing, particularly with respect to primary mathematics. He problematises the concept and illustrates how it is being deployed in quite different ways by different actors on the educational scene. He highlights the ways in which international comparisons, market principles, the use of randomised control trials and political agendas have shaped how mastery has been formulated. He notes some positive outcomes in primary mathematics classrooms from the mastery policy initiative.

Comparing performance between countries has become a key driver of policy in mathematics education in many neoliberal education systems including that of England. Dylan Wiliam takes a careful look at this practice and the associated research and alerts us to a range of difficulties with it. Taking these as a proviso, he nevertheless argues that such comparisons can be valuable in helping us formulate an agenda for mathematics in schools. Mark Boylan provides a specific example of such dilemmas and difficulties at play in mathematics education through the English government's commitment at the time of writing to pursuing a "mastery" agenda imported from Shanghai. He problematises the concept, illustrates the multiple meanings associated with it and shows how the processes of translation and adaptation of the imported practices occur at every level from initial ministerial engagement through to individual teachers' classroom practices.

Chapter 1

Learning about mathematics teaching from other countries

Dylan Wiliam

Introduction

In 2007, the Organisation for Economic Cooperation and Development (OECD) published results from the third round of the Programme for International Assessment (PISA) which, every three years since 2000, has tested the reading, mathematics and science achievement of 15-year-olds in a number of the OECD's member countries and other jurisdictions.

In mathematics, Finland scored 548, joint top with Korea, and the average score of Finnish 15-year olds across the three subjects tested was 553, which was higher than any other country in the world. PISA results are reported on a scale where 500 is the international average, and the standard deviation of the scores is 100, so students in Finland were scoring half a standard deviation higher than the international average. Another way of thinking about this is that, because one year's progress for students of this age is around 0.4 standard deviations (Rodriguez, 2004), Finnish students are about 15 months ahead of the international average, and indeed, about 15 months ahead of students in the United Kingdom, who averaged a score of 495 in the same round.

Predictably, politicians and policymakers rushed to Finland to find out what was behind the "Finnish miracle", and, again predictably, people felt confident that they could identify the features of the Finnish system that had produced these successes. Some attributed Finland's high scores to the fact that Finnish children do not start school until the age of 7, and argued that similar policies should be adopted in their own countries. Some pointed to the fact that almost all Finnish children between the ages of 2 and 7 attend preschool, and advocated that universal nursery schooling was the way forward. Still others attributed Finland's success to its adoption of comprehensive education and lack of grouping students by ability. Policymakers at the Department for Children, Schools and Families in London thought that it was the fact that the vast majority of teachers in Finland had master's degrees that was responsible for these high levels of achievement, and, for a while at least, it was government policy in England that all beginning teachers should be encouraged to study for a Masters in Teaching and Learning at the conclusion of their initial training.

One particular feature of the Finnish system that attracted much attention was the fact that in Finland, teachers enjoy quite high social status (Dolton & Marcenaro-Gutierrez, 2013). Although their salaries are no higher than comparable graduates, one survey found that when asked what kind of job they would most like a life partner to be doing, "teacher" was top of the list. Further evidence of the attractiveness of teaching as a profession is provided by the fact that there are usually ten or more applicants for every place on a teacher education programme (Bonsall, 2015). As a result, many concluded that the high status of teachers and the selectivity of their teacher education programmes were the cause of Finland's PISA success, and concluded that the key to improving education in the United Kingdom was to make teaching more attractive.

> *Reflection question: Are there any other factors that you can think of that might make it difficult to determine why some countries get higher mathematics test scores than others?*

The problem with such an approach is that it suffers from what Jay Greene (2012) calls "selection on the dependent variable" (p. 72). If we only look at what high-performing systems do, we cannot be sure that the variable we have selected is the cause of that high performance. This is why, when doctors diagnose illnesses, they do not just look for which diseases have the symptoms they see in their patients. Instead, they look for a "differential diagnosis" – symptoms that patients with the disease would have and those who do not have the disease do not. And when we apply a similar approach to international comparisons, we find that many, if not most, of the reasons proposed for Finland's success are not plausible. Recruitment into teacher education in Ireland is, if anything, even more selective than in Finland (International Review Panel on the Structure of Initial Teacher Education Provision in Ireland, 2012), and yet its results in most international comparisons are modest. Singapore does even better than Finland in most international tests, and yet it groups students by ability even in primary school.

More importantly, in the four PISA surveys since 2006, Finland's maths results have been declining steadily, scoring 541, 519, 511 and 507. Since the PISA tests are taken by 15-year-olds, they are the result of at least eight years of education, which in turn was the result of policy decisions taken many years earlier. In order to understand why Finland's 15-year-olds did so well in 2006, we should be looking at what Finland was doing in the early 1990s. What has been going on in Finland over the last 12 years is probably lowering educational achievement, not increasing it.

At this point, it would be easy to despair and say that there is nothing we can learn from international comparisons, but in my view this would be too negative. We can get ideas about how to improve education from other countries, but we have to look carefully and critically at the data. In the remainder of this chapter I offer a number of questions that may be useful in considering what we may, and may not, conclude from international comparisons of performance in mathematics.

Are the assessments measuring something we think is important?

One interesting feature of the various international comparisons that have been undertaken over the last 50 years or so is that while the correlations between different measures are reasonably high (typically in the region of 0.6–0.8), some countries do much better on one measure than another. For example, as well as the triennial PISA survey, the International Association for the Evaluation of Educational Achievement (IEA) has conducted the Trends in Mathematics and Science Study (TIMSS) every four years since 1995. In the early days of PISA, students in the United Kingdom tended to do better on PISA than on TIMSS, but in the most recent surveys, this trend has reversed. While the mathematics achievement of UK 15-year-olds on PISA has been modest, with scores of 495, 492, 494, 492 and 502 in 2006, 2009, 2012, 2015 and 2018, respectively, performance on TIMSS has been much better.

In fact, the performance of UK 14-year-olds in maths has improved quite a lot over the last 20 years. In 1995, England's score was 498, and in 2015, it was 518. While TIMSS uses the same scale as PISA, far more developing countries, with lower mathematics achievement, participate in TIMSS, so scores on PISA and TIMSS cannot be easily compared, there is no doubt that the story of mathematics achievement in England painted by TIMSS is much rosier than that painted by PISA.

Why this might be is far from clear, but it does appear that TIMSS focuses more on the maths that students are learning in their maths classrooms, while PISA tends to focus on students' ability to apply their mathematical knowledge to real-world problems. Which of these is more important is a matter of continuing debate, but it seems that PISA scores may be a better indicator of students' readiness for the world of work, while TIMSS measures the readiness of students for further mathematical studies. In this context, it is worth noting that while, in 2006, Finnish students performed as well as students of any other country in mathematics, at around the same time, professors of mathematics in Finland were complaining that the performance of Finnish 18-year-olds in the university entrance examinations in mathematics was declining, and universities were having to run remedial classes for college students (Astala et al., 2005). Before we can draw any conclusions from international comparisons of mathematics performance, we have to be sure that we know what these tests are, in fact, assessing.

Reflection question: What are the advantages and disadvantages of emphasising the role of mathematics as a preparation for the world of work?

Are the assessments comparable?

One of the most significant challenges in comparing the mathematics performance of students in different countries is making sure that we are using similar tests. Where students in different countries speak the same language, this is not too difficult, although care does need to be taken to ensure that the vocabulary used in the tests is familiar to students. For example, what is called a "trapezium" in the United Kingdom is called a "trapezoid" in the United States, and the definition is slightly different too. In the United Kingdom, a trapezium is generally defined as a quadrilateral with one pair of parallel sides, whereas in the United States, a trapezoid is generally defined as a quadrilateral with *exactly* one pair of parallel sides. A square is a trapezium in the United Kingdom, but a square is not a trapezoid in the United States.

When tests have been translated from one language to another, the standard way of ensuring that test questions have been translated correctly is through a process known as back translation. A test is produced in one language, translated into another language and the translated test is then translated a second time back to the original language. If the resulting translation of the translation is close to the original, then this is taken as an indication that the translated version is a good translation. However, this does not prove the items are equivalent. To see why, consider the following example given by Dylan Jones (1993).

He looked at a sample of scripts from students who had taken a GCSE examination in the summer of 1991, and selected 112 students who had taken the examination in the medium of English, and another 112 students, matched in terms of their overall scores on the exam, who took the examination in Welsh. He then looked at the proportion of marks students got on one four-part question, and the results are shown in Table 1.1.

The scores of the students who took the exam in Welsh and in English are comparable for the first three parts of the question, but on the fourth part of the question, students taking the examination in the medium of Welsh did much better.

The reason is that part (d) of question 12 required students to use properties of similar triangles. The Welsh word for *similar* is *cyflun* and this word is only ever encountered in mathematics classrooms (the Welsh word for *similar* in other contexts is *tebyg*). Students who took the Welsh version of the examination were cued to use their mathematical knowledge, whereas many of those taking the examination in English assumed that two triangles that were *similar* merely resembled each other. The important point here is that a "back translation" of

Table 1.1 Marks obtained by students on a GCSE question (Jones, 1993)

	Paper Average	Question part			
		12(a)	12(b)	12(c)	12(d)
Welsh medium	71%	96%	91%	90%	41%
English medium	71%	95%	82%	87%	23%

this question from English to Welsh, and then back from Welsh to English, would suggest that the two versions are perfectly equivalent. The way that words "sit" in a language means that there can never be a perfect translation of any test, and this is especially important in mathematics.

> *Reflection question: Can you think of other examples where the fact that words are used differently in mathematics classrooms from the way they are used elsewhere might cause problems for students?*

Are the students taking the test representative?

In the 1990s, teachers in the United Kingdom were told that students in Germany were much better at mathematics, and in particular, that, at least in mathematics, there was a "long tail of underachievement" in England. The evidence from the Second International Mathematics and Science Study (SIMS) certainly seemed to support this conclusion. German 14-year-olds had higher average levels of performance in mathematics, and the spread of achievement was much smaller, with far fewer students with very low scores.

However, in 1996, the results of the Third International Mathematics and Science Study created quite a stir, especially in Germany, when it was found that there was, overall, no significant difference between British and German 14-year-olds in either the mean achievement or in the spread of scores (Beaton et al., 1996, p. 22). The reason for this was because TIMSS sampled students differently from SIMS.

In SIMS, students in the United Kingdom were sampled from Year 9 classrooms, and this provided a reasonably representative sample of all 14-year-olds in the country. In Germany, a similar approach was used, sampling at random from eighth-grade classrooms, but this did not yield a representative sample of 14-year-olds because of the use of grade retention. In Germany, as in many other countries, students who are not considered ready for the next grade do not progress. Instead, they are retained in their current grade for another year, to give them time to learn the material they need to learn, and as many as 25% of students in Germany have repeated a grade by the time they are 14. The German sample for SIMS was not representative of all 14-year-olds in Germany, because a large number of German 14-year-olds were not in eighth-grade classrooms, but in seventh, or even sixth-grade classrooms. In TIMSS, the sampling was undertaken in such a way that ensured a representative sample of all 14-year-olds in each participating country, and the inclusion of students who had been held back a year or two lowered the average score for German students substantially.

Getting a representative sample of the students being studied is even more difficult in PISA, because the participating students are older, and in many countries, students are able to leave before the age of 15. Even in countries where the school leaving age is 16 or higher, many of the lowest achieving students are frequently absent from school, making a representative sample much more challenging to obtain. This is a particular issue when looking at results from China.

In 2012, the province of Shanghai posted the best results in the world in reading, maths and science (570, 613 and 580, respectively), and, not surprisingly, international attention switched from Finland to China. However, these apparently impressive results are not even representative of Shanghai, let alone the rest of China.

All citizens in mainland China are required by law to be registered as residents of a particular area, and the record of this registration is called a *hukou*. One of the most important consequences of the *hukou* system in modern China[1] is that it is difficult – and quite often impossible – to obtain government services, such as schooling, in a province other than that of one's *hukou*. Parents who move from rural areas to Shanghai for work therefore have to choose between leaving their children with grandparents, or bringing their children with them, and paying often unaffordable fees for their children to attend government schools or finding school places in private schools, which are more affordable, but generally of low quality. According to the OECD's own statistics, only around 73% of the 15-year-olds in Shanghai were sampled for the 2012 PISA survey. If those that were missing scored around 400 (which is reasonable given that, even if they are attending schools, they are likely to be of rather poor quality) then Shanghai's real score would be over 50 points lower. It is also worth noting that Shanghai is not even representative of other large metropolitan regions in China, let alone the whole country. In the 2015 PISA survey, mainland China was represented by Beijing, Jiangsu and Guangdong in addition to Shanghai, and the average score across these four provinces was 514 – a creditable performance, but 74 points lower than Shanghai's average across reading, maths and science three years earlier.

The main conclusion here is that while the results from countries like Singapore, Korea, Finland and other rich countries can probably be trusted as being reliable guides to the achievement of 15-year-olds, for other countries – and China in particular – there are real doubts about the meaningfulness of results on survey tests such as PISA. Unless we can be sure that all 15-year-olds have an equal chance of being asked to take the test – whether they were in school or not – we should be sceptical. Moreover, even when the results of a particular country can be trusted, even when it is clear that student achievement in that country is high, it is really hard to determine the reasons for that success.

> *Reflection question: If we did want to compare the results of Shanghai with results of students in the United Kingdom, which would be the fairest comparison: with Greater London, the southeast or the whole of England?*

Can we identify the factors contributing to educational performance?

For the last quarter century, countries in the Western rim of the Pacific Ocean – Korea, Japan, China, Hong Kong, Taiwan and Singapore – have consistently achieved high scores in international assessments of mathematics achievement.

There has, predictably, been no shortage of people claiming to know the reasons for these high scores. Unfortunately, most of these claims are little more than speculation, and many are just plain wrong.

In the discussion of the results of Finland above, it was highlighted that successful performance in international assessments may depend on policy decisions taken decades earlier, which makes connecting causes to effects very difficult.

There are also differences in how much time students spend studying, although these are smaller than many people imagine. Journalists often report that Finland's students spend less time studying at school than other countries, but at 24 hours a week, a typical Finnish student's working week is not that much shorter than a student in the United Kingdom (26 hours a week) (Organisation for Economic Co-operation and Development, 2016, Table II.6.32). However, when we also include time spent studying out of school, bigger differences are apparent. Students in Finland spend an additional 12 hours out of school each week studying, compared to 17 additional hours in the United Kingdom. While students in Hong Kong and Taiwan spend similar amounts of time out of school on their studies, students in Singapore and Korea spend over 20 additional hours on out-of-school study, and for those in China, it is almost 30 hours (Table II 6.37). However, these figures should be interpreted with caution since they are based on students' self-reports about how much time they are studying, and these are notoriously inaccurate. In addition, the way this out-of-school study is done varies substantially from country to country. In the United Kingdom and the United States, this is likely to be spent at home, doing homework, while in many Pacific Rim countries, much of the time is spent in formal private coaching sessions, and the impact of these supplementary schools can be substantial. In Korea, for example, one estimate suggests that without the effects of private tuition and supplementary schools, achievement would be below that of the United Kingdom (Choi, 2012).

Finally, it is worth noting that cultural factors have a large effect on education achievement. John Jerrim (2014) looked at the scores obtained by Australian students on PISA and found that Australian children of Chinese heritage achieved higher scores than students in Shanghai. Cultural factors may be far more important than the education system that a student attends.

The important conclusion here is that there are far too many variables, and far too few data points, for us to draw any strong conclusions about the reasons behind a country's performance on international comparisons. There may be good reasons to explore particular factors that might be relevant, but there is simply no way to be sure that a particular factor is responsible for the performance of a country.

Reflection question: What cultural factors do you think are likely to have the greatest impact on students' achievement in mathematics?

Even if we figure out why other countries do well, could we do this here?

From the foregoing, it should be clear that it is hard, and probably impossible, to identify exactly why some countries perform better than others in international comparisons such as PISA and TIMSS. But there is an even greater problem with trying to improve education by copying other countries, and that is that even if we are right about the reasons for a country's success, whether the same success could be reproduced in another country is far from clear.

For example, policies that are effective where the status of teachers is high may be less effective where the status of teachers is low. Policies that are effective in systems that grant teachers considerable autonomy may be less effective in systems where teachers are given little choice about how to do their jobs. Policies that are effective when implemented in systems where the mathematical knowledge of teachers is strong may be much less effective in systems where the mathematical knowledge of teachers is weak. Perhaps most important, educational policies often take considerable time to implement, and this can dramatically affect the kinds of changes that are possible.

For example, in Finland in the late 1960s, there was considerable debate about whether secondary education should be selective or comprehensive. In the end, the arguments in favour of a comprehensive system prevailed, and comprehensive schooling was adopted as policy. This is, perhaps, not surprising. What is more surprising, however, is that those who had lost the argument *agreed that they had lost the argument*. The focus shifted from what kind of system there should be to making the comprehensive system work.

Although, for the reasons discussed above, it is impossible to be sure of the reasons for a country's success, similar political stability appears to have been an important factor in the success of Singapore, Hong Kong, Taiwan, Shanghai and Korea. However, it is far from clear whether policies that take a long time to implement would be possible to implement in countries like England, where education is treated as something of a political "football" with policies changing with changes of government, and even changes in ministers of education. Looking at other countries may give us ideas. It will never provide us with solutions.

> *Reflection question: From what you know about mathematics teaching in other countries, are there any practices that you think could, and should, be implemented in the United Kingdom?*

Conclusion

Looking at how other countries are doing has a valuable role to play in helping us decide what to do to improve the teaching of mathematics. We can look at how different factors contribute to, or detract from, student success, we can look at the educational experiments that other countries conduct and see whether the successes might be replicated here. We can also examine whether the failure might have been averted if certain features of the reform had been changed. But the main message of this chapter is that we have to be very careful in doing this because of three main reasons. First, countries that appear to be successful may not be as successful as they seem. Second, even if they are successful, it is not easy, and may in fact be impossible, to determine why the country was successful. Third, even when we are sure of the reasons for a country's success, it may not be possible to reproduce the circumstances that led to that success. Looking at what other countries are doing has its place, but the solutions will have to be home-grown.

> *Reflection question: On balance, do you think that it is worth looking at how mathematics is taught in other countries, or should we just focus on looking at successful mathematics teaching in this country?*

Note

1 The system is actually called the *huji* system, with a *hukou* being an individual record within the *huji* system, but the term *hukou* is now widely used to describe the system as well as an individual record.

Further reading

Crehan, L. (2016). *Cleverlands*. London, UK: Unbound. This is a well-written and highly readable account of an inner-city school teacher's experiences of visiting a number of the world's high-performing educational systems. Unlike most reports of this kind, the book explores the reality "on the ground" rather than just relying on data and policy documents.

Organisation for Economic Co-operation and Development. (2017). *Education at a glance.* Paris, France: Organisation for Economic Co-operation and Development. Each year, the Organisation for Economic Cooperation and Development releases a sourcebook of key educational indicators for its members and a number of other partners. While the exact coverage varies from year to year, it provides a wealth of authoritative and up-to-date information about the education systems of the rich countries of the world.

Ripley, A. (2013). *The smartest kids in the world, and how they got that way.* New York, NY: Simon & Schuster. Written primarily for an American audience, this book compares the experiences of students in the US with those in countries that perform better in international comparisons. Although the author's prejudices and biases lead her to overstate some of her claims, it is useful for the way it shows how a country's education system is a result of economic, cultural, and historical influences.

References

Astala, K., Kivelä, S. K., Koskela, P., Martio, O., Näätänen, M., & Tarvainen, K. (2005, August 31). The PISA survey tells only a partial truth of Finnish children's mathematical skills. *Matematiikkalehti solmu [Knot Mathematics Journal]*. Retrieved December 22, 2016, from http://matematiikkalehtisolmu.fi/2005/erik/PisaEng.html

Beaton, A. E., Mullis, I. V. S., Martin, M. O., Gonzalez, E. J., Kelly, D. L., & Smith, T. A. (1996). *Mathematics achievement in the middle school years: IEA's third international mathematics and science study.* Chestnut Hill, MA: Boston College.

Bonsall, E. (2015, November 3). Recreating the Finnish miracle. *Harvard Political Review.* Retrieved December 6, 2016, from http://harvardpolitics.com/united-states/recreating-finnish-miracle/

Choi, J. (2012). *Private tutoring and educational inequality: Evidence from a dynamic model of academic achievement in Korea.* Philadelphia, PA: University of Pennsylvania.

Dolton, P., & Marcenaro-Gutierrez, O. D. (2013). *Global teacher status index.* London, UK: Varkey GEMS Foundation.

Greene, J. P. (2012). Best practices are the worst. *Education Next, 12*(3), 72–73.

International Review Panel on the Structure of Initial Teacher Education Provision in Ireland. (2012). *Report.* Dublin, Ireland: Department of Education and Skills.

Jerrim, J. (2014). *Why do East Asian children perform so well in PISA? An investigation of Western-born children of East Asian descent.* London, UK: Institute of Education, University of London.

Jones, D. (1993). Words with a similar meaning. *Mathematics teaching* 145, 14–15.

Organisation for Economic Co-operation and Development. (2016). *PISA 2015 results: Policies and practices for successful schools* (Vol. 2). Paris, France: Organisation for Economic Co-operation and Development.

Rodriguez, M. C. (2004). The role of classroom assessment in student performance on TIMSS. *Applied Measurement in Education, 17*(1), 1–24.

Chapter 2

Mathematics education in translation
Mastery, policy and evidence

Mark Boylan

Introduction

The first edition of *Debates in Mathematics Education* did not have a chapter with 'mastery' in the title. Ten years ago, even five years ago, it was a word rarely used in discussion of mathematics teaching and learning. Now, in England, it has become a central focus of government policy. Even if schools and teachers do not buy into the mastery agenda, it is the main reference point when discussing changing mathematics teaching in schools and mathematics teacher professional development.

Mastery is a slippery term and used in different ways (Boylan and Townsend, 2018). The term has gendered origins – 'masters' were traditionally men. So, there is a risk of supporting the belief that mathematics is a masculine trait. Putting that to one side, mastery is one of those words or phrases like 'achievement' or 'high standards' that seem to be unquestionably a good idea. However, there is no agreement on the definition of what it is to 'master' something in mathematics, or how to achieve this. Sometimes the idea of depth or deeper level of learning is put forward. An alternative is to consider the capacity to apply mathematical knowledge in both routine and novel situations and to communicate mathematically (Drury, 2014, p. 9). Depending on what definition or meaning is used, issues arise as to whether the mastery agenda is unquestionably a positive development.

Here are some of the other different meanings of 'mastery' as used in England.

1 A mastery curriculum: sometimes the 2014 English mathematics curriculum (DfE, 2014) is referred to as a 'mastery curriculum', as there is an expectation that all pupils should generally progress together.
2 An approach to learning: it was used by Benjamin Bloom to refer to cycles of teaching, learning and assessment.
3 A type of mindset: Carole Dweck (2006) refers to a mastery mindset – that is a belief of learners or teachers that effort rather than innate ability is central to learning (Dweck's ideas are discussed in Chapter 5, Ability Thinking).

The National Centre for Excellence in the Teaching of Mathematics (NCETM) is funded by the government to promote and implement government policy in mathematics education, and this includes the mastery approach. The NCETM's formulation of 'Teaching for Mastery' (TfM) distinguishes between the aim – mastery –

and how this is achieved – teaching. But in schools and every day teachers' talk, this distinction gets blurred and 'mastery' is often used to refer to a way of teaching.

Central to the current mastery promotion is the idea that mathematics should be taught in ways that are similar to those found in East Asian education systems such as Shanghai and Singapore. These systems do well on international comparative tests such as the Programme for International Student Assessment (PISA) study of 15-year-old school pupils' performance in mathematics, science and reading (though see Chapter 1, for discussion of the need for careful interpretation of these tests).

This chapter has two main aims. First, to examine where the current focus on mastery has come from and how the word mastery is being used. Second, to consider the evidence that what is being promoted in the mastery brand might benefit students and teachers.

> *Cambridge Mathematics has produced an 'espresso' or research digest on mastery. It summarises evidence for the mastery approach including different components of mastery. See https://www.cambridgemaths.org/Images/espresso_16_mastery_in_mathematics.pdf*
>
> *A variety of elements of teaching related to mastery are identified. How far are these elements present or referred to when you hear 'mastery' being discussed?*

English and East Asian mathematics education

The current TfM approach is informed by East Asian mathematics education. Some of the first mastery programmes were informed by Singaporean practices. Since then the government has funded teacher exchanges with Shanghai (Boylan et al., 2019) with the aim of changing practice, initially in primary schools in England to be more like those in Shanghai. Table 2.1 summarises some key differences between Shanghai and England, at least as found before the mastery innovation. Notably, policymakers in England promote East Asian informed classroom practices, but not the very different conditions of service of teachers in relation to the amount of class contact and the amount of time for paid professional development.

> *English and Shanghai mathematics education systems are different in the following ways. Rank these four aspects in terms of how big an influence you think they are on pupil outcomes:*
>
> * *culture and beliefs*
> * *organisation of mathematics teaching (for example, grouping and lesson timing)*
> * *pedagogy, curriculum, resources and assessment*
> * *professional conditions and practices*
>
> *Reflect on reasons for your ranking.*

Table 2.1 Shanghai and English primary practices compared. Adapted from Boylan et al. (2019)

Aspect of mathematics education	Shanghai	England
Teaching approach and purposes	Whole-class interactive teaching, brisk tempo to cover multiple small steps; focus on questioning; mini-plenaries; use of carefully chosen examples with purposeful variation; mathematical talk as an instructional priority; emphasis on correct mathematical language.	Explanation through teacher transmission (quick pace) plus individual practice (slower pace); start from objectives, plenary at end of lesson if at all.
Lesson content and purposes	Lessons start from mathematical content or problem.	Teachers aim to maximise content covered in a lesson.
Materials, models and resources	Textbooks; a variety of mathematical models and visual images used to support teaching; careful choice of examples and practice questions.	Variety of resources and materials, often worksheets, usually one model or visual representation used per topic/concept.
Organisation of mathematics teaching	Daily 35-minute lessons with practice as homework.	Daily one-hour lesson with most practice in the lesson.
Curricula progression	Textbooks that are system wide; whole class progresses together. Content covered in fine detail before progression.	Primary teachers prepare and teach almost a full timetable of different subjects; with a small amount of planning time during the school day. Low-attaining pupils progress more slowly, higher-attaining pupils are accelerated.
Pupil access to the curriculum	All-attainment classes of 40–50 pupils. Daily intervention by class teacher, based on daily assessment of homework.	Mixture of setting, in-class grouping and all-attainment teaching in classes of 30 pupils; differentiated learning objectives; intervention often by teaching assistants to pupils identified for blocks of time – term or year. Weekly homework.
Teacher preparation, roles and professional development	Specialist graduate initial teacher education; extensive study of higher mathematics by both primary and secondary teachers. Teach 2 × 35-minute mathematics lessons a day, teach the same class for a number of years; teacher research groups are embedded; 340–560 hours of collaborative professional development in first five years of teaching.	Generalist primary teachers with some specialist teaching at the end of primary school in some schools; usually teach the same year group for a number of years; limited opportunities for specific mathematics professional development.

The mastery innovation in England

Education seems to have fashions. Perhaps, like with clothing styles, once something has become fashionable it is easy to forget that what is currently the trend was not always the case. Educational ideas come and go and then come back and so have histories that are rooted in particular contexts. Increasingly educational policy is shaped by international forces of global comparisons, market or semi-market orientations, and political ideologies that shape what happens in schools including in mathematics classrooms. This is the case with mastery.

In 2007, the *Maths No Problem* textbook scheme and associated professional development programme was developed based on the translation of a Singaporean textbook series. The scheme was initiated by entrepreneurs who had previously lived in Singapore. In around 2009, a multi-academy trust – Ark – also looked to Singapore for ideas, alongside other places viewed as high performing in mathematics. A multi-academy trust is state funded independent grouping of schools, similar to charter school chains in the United States. *Ark Mathematics* was renamed *Mathematics Mastery* around 2010. As noted above, the word mastery had previously been associated with Bloom's ideas. So, this appears to be the first time it had been used in relation to East Asian mathematics, at least in England.

Interest in East Asian approaches led to two study visits funded by the English Department for Education to Shanghai in 2012 and 2013. By 2014, the NCETM had adopted the word 'mastery' and was writing about mastery approaches (NCETM, 2014). The government funded the first teacher exchange with Shanghai in 2014/2015 (Boylan et al., 2019). From this, the TfM programme developed. The TfM programme consists of a professional development programme to train mastery specialists, support for the specialists to work with groups of teachers from local schools, a subsidy to buy textbooks, as well as further exchanges with Shanghai teachers.

The NCETM has published a one-page document – 'The essence of teaching for mastery' https://www.ncetm.org.uk/files/37086535/The+Essence+of+Maths+Teaching+for+Mastery+june+2016.pdf Retrieved July 2016
Print this document. Using highlighters categorise the different elements of teaching for mastery in the document. Although there are nine bullet points, some of these have a number of different sub-points so there are 12–18 different claims or elements identified. Categorise the claims and elements by the extent to which the meaning is clear and understandable for you. If you are not sure about some of the terms, use the NCETM web pages on mastery to find out more.
How is the NCETM approach similar to or different from other ideas about how to teach mathematics that you are familiar with?

Shaping mastery

The last section provided a brief narrative of the development of the mastery policy. However, the brief history does not explain the forces or reasons why mastery has come to be such a buzz word. Within this narrative there are a variety of implicit or hidden influences. Making these explicit not only helps us to understand the development of mastery but also focuses attention on forces or phenomena that are often present in mathematics education policy or education more generally. Each of these is briefly considered in the order in which they relate to the mastery timeline, rather than in order of importance.

International influences

There is a long history of looking overseas for ideas to improve mathematics teaching in England, for example this informed the National Numeracy Strategy (NNS) (Ochs, 2006). However, this tendency seems to have been accelerated by PISA. Dylan Wiliam addresses the issue of international comparisons in another chapter and urges some caution about how outcomes are interpreted. However, even if, for example the PISA scores were taken as showing reliable differences in outcomes, this does not mean that adopting practices from elsewhere will lead to similar outcomes.

Money, finance and profit

Increasingly, education in England is run on market principles. Whilst state-funded schools do not make profits, other education businesses are part of the overall system. The founders of the *Maths No Problem* textbook scheme describe their motivation in setting up their business as a concern for the quality of mathematics teaching their daughter experienced in England, in contrast to Singapore. Whilst there is no reason to doubt the honesty of this or a public-spirited aspect to their initiative, it is also the case that *Maths No Problem* has grown into an international business.

On a national scale, the decision to undertake an exchange with Shanghai, rather than, for example, Singapore, flowed from the teacher exchange being part of, or related to, a wider bilateral trade negotiation between England and China. This was followed up in 2018, during a visit to Shanghai of the prime minister at the time – Teresa May – who talked of China exporting to England mathematics teaching and England exporting English teaching and Early Years businesses to China (Watts, 2018). Looking outside East Asia, Canada and Switzerland are comparatively successful in international mathematics tests, but they have not been a focus for recent international importation of policy.

Whilst the NCETM is not a profit-making business, one of the organisations within the consortium that runs the NCETM is, one of many similar business involved in education that have grown over the last 20 years. Whether the involvement of private enterprise in education is a bad or good thing is something that can be debated. However, it is important to remember that when people are involved in convincing teachers to adopt certain policies that they may have all sorts of interests in doing so. The current NCETM contract is closely tied to the mastery agenda.

Mobilising 'evidence'

Randomised controlled trials (RCTs) and similar quantitative studies are held up as providing the strongest evidence of effects, including, in the case of RCTs, being able to establish causal relationships. RCTs are much used in medicine. In a trial a group is recruited to take part and then randomly (usually) half of them are assigned to a group who, in education, would experience the new approach and the others would have the usual experience. If there is a difference in outcomes, it is argued that this is most likely the result of the innovation as this is the only systematic difference between the groups. The use of RCTs in education is much debated and controversial not least because of how this way of thinking shapes educational values and priorities. Regardless of these debates, there have now been a small number of studies using quantitative methods to evaluate mastery.

The Education Endowment Foundation (EEF) publishes an online 'tool kit' that aims to summarise evidence from RCTs and quasi-experimental studies. In the past a number of trials were undertaken of mastery learning – of the type promoted by Bloom – and these were found to have a positive effect. When Ark mathematics started to use the term 'mastery' for their Singaporean inspired approach, it meant that the previous evidence for mastery could be used to justify undertaking a trial of their approach. This may or may not have informed the decision to take up the term. Either way, it is this mastery learning evidence that is referred to in the Ark trial report (Vignoles, Jerrim and Cowan, 2015). However, *Mathematics Mastery* was different from the mastery learning approach of Bloom researched in earlier studies. The way evidence is 'mobilised' to pursue agendas is something that is important to be aware of in mathematics education.

The EEF (2017) undertook RCTs of both the KS1 and KS3 versions of *Mathematics Mastery*. At KS1, the outcome was that two month's additional progress was made, and, in KS3, one month's additional progress (Vignoles, Jerrim and Cowan, 2015).

More recently, there has been an in depth three-year study of the outcomes of schools that engaged in the first Mathematics Teacher Exchange (MTE) with Shanghai in 2014/2015. Because randomisation was not possible due to how schools were recruited to take part a comparative study was used. Each school involved in the MTE was matched with 20 other schools that were similar to them before the start of the exchange programme. Outcomes were compared for both Y2 and Y6 pupils after three years (Boylan et al., 2019). This study found no evidence that simply being involved in the exchange led to improvements in outcomes. However, not all the schools involved went on to implement mastery approaches. So, the outcomes were examined of only those schools that had used mastery practices for at least two years with their Y6 and Y2 pupils and this found no effect for 11-year-olds and a small effect for seven-year-old pupils. The size of the effect was similar to the *Mathematics Mastery* trial already noted (Vignoles, Jerrim and Cowan, 2015).

Political agendas

Funding for mastery and its promotion comes from government and so government ministers. Politicians have their own predilections and preferences. The TfM formulation specifies that pupils will face the front. This does fit with what happens in Shanghai. However, in the adoption of Shanghai approaches, as noted earlier, somethings are chosen for 'importation' and others not. The idea of facing the front fits with a particular view of what counts as good teaching. This does not mean schools necessarily adopt these practices. Only a minority of schools implementing changes following the first MTE chose to do this (Boylan, et al., 2019). Nevertheless, the perception of Shanghai teaching fits with a traditionalist approach to learning in which teacher explanation and knowledge is emphasised.

> *Who benefits from the mastery policy in terms of money, power and status or job security? That some people have an interest in the mastery policy is not a reason to simply reject it. Any innovation or set of educational ideas will mean that there are some people who have interests of various sorts in others adopting their ideas. However, this is worth taking into account when assessing the value of educational practices.*

In summary, there are a variety of forces or influences that shape the mastery agenda and how mastery is formulated. Arguably the policy is not based on a careful consideration of evidence.

Mastery may be closer to home than we think

The TfM policy is based on the importation of East Asian practices. However, the relationship between English mathematics education and East Asian approaches is not a simple one. Singapore's mathematics teaching and curriculum was strongly influenced by the 1982 Cockcroft Report – produced by a government appointed committee of inquiry in England that influenced practices in the 1980s, and later the English national curriculum. Thus, there is a link between problem-solving being at the heart of Singapore mathematics education and the 'using and applying' strand of the 1991 English mathematics curriculum, influenced by Cockcroft.

The idea of sequencing learning as concrete-pictorial-abstract is a Singaporean version of Jerome Bruner's (1966) theory of enactive, iconic and symbolic, and the importance of using multiple forms of representations in learning mathematics has been encouraged by English mathematics educators for some time (for example, Haylock and Cockburn, 2013). The variation theory that is seen as a distinctive aspect of Shanghai teaching has been promoted in England by mathematics educators such as Anne Watson (Watson and Mason, 2006) and Mike Askew (2015). The emphasis on teacher-pupil interaction in the description of Shanghai practices above is reminiscent of approaches such as dialogic teaching (Alexander, 2008).

It is important to recognise that educational flows of ideas are rarely only one way. This helps to counter a deficit view of mathematics education and mathematics teachers promoted by some politicians. This deficit view is implicit in the mastery policy – English mathematics teachers need fixing by looking overseas. But some of these 'overseas' ideas originated or were influenced by English mathematics education.

Prospects for change

The ambition for mastery is to lead to systemic change in mathematics teaching. The government has put, what appears to be, a lot of money behind the policy. The current intention is to train around 950 primary mastery specialists over seven years, of whom about half will visit Shanghai. These specialists will be resourced to work with other schools for one day per week for a number of years. Schools that are supported by these specialists will be able to get a subsidy for textbooks. Although the scale of the mastery programme in secondary schools is not as extensive, there is a similar ambition to change practice.

Whilst funding and support for the mastery programme appears generous, it is much less than the last big centralised attempt to change mathematics teaching in England – the NNS in the late 1990s. In its first year alone the NNS was recommended a budget of £51.5 million (equivalent to approximately £90 million in the 2020) for primary schools, with 300 full-time numeracy consultants, and resource for every primary school to receive three days' training for the head teacher, mathematics coordinator and one other teacher, and the mathematics coordinator having a further five days of funding to support their school leadership of the NNS (DfEE, 1998). The TfM programme funding is around £15 million per year. So, it is debatable as to whether the policy ambition will be realised given the model for spreading mastery ideas.

As noted earlier, approaches to teaching in, for example, Shanghai are embedded in cultural and social beliefs and practices. Teachers have very different conditions of service and working lives. These aspects of the Shanghai system are not being adopted. However, the mastery policy is helping the development of greater opportunity for mathematics teacher collaborative professional development. It is also opening up spaces for discussion about mathematics teaching. At best, mastery professional development and the use of problems and resources encourage discussion about critical issues in mathematics teaching and learning. This includes about the use of models and representations or the careful selection of tasks.

In the Mathematics Teacher Exchange, teachers reported increased confidence and knowledge of mathematics and greater understanding of mathematical structures. As noted in Chapters 5 and 6, there is an increase in interest in all attainment teaching and this in part will be influenced by the different approach to dealing with difference in prior attainment in East Asia. Taken for granted ideas about mathematical 'ability' and grouping children have been challenged by engaging with mathematics education in other countries which see these issues very differently.

> *How important is it that the mastery initiative leads to increases in pupil attainment, for the policy to be considered a success?*
> *Why else might it be important?*

Conclusion

The mastery innovation in England has been informed by desire to be as successful as Singapore and Shanghai in international tests. It is a 'messy' innovation, open to multiple interpretations and meanings. It is up for debate about what mastery should mean in practice. For some it means sitting pupils in rows so they can better track the teacher. For others it means carefully selecting tasks, slowing down so all can engage and encouraging greater mathematical talk and thinking. For teachers it has opened up spaces for more collaborative professional development focused on mathematical meaning. Whether the innovation realises the ambitions of policymakers will not be known for a sometime. But regardless of this, it is an example of how mathematics education develops by processes of translation and adaptations as different actors interpret and reinterpret evidence, ideas and practices.

Further reading

Drury, H. (2014). *Mastering mathematics*. Oxford: Oxford University Press. This was the first book setting out a version of the East Asian informed mastery approach written by the developer of the Mathematics Mastery programme.

Boylan, M., Wolstenholme, C., Demack, S., Maxwell, B., Jay, T., Adams, G., & Reaney, S (2019). Longitudinal evaluation of the Mathematics Teacher Exchange: China-England – Final Report. https://assets.publishing.service.gov.uk/government/uploads/system/uploads/attachment_data/file/773320/MTE_main_report.pdf, Retrieved January 2019.

This reports the findings of the evaluation of the Mathematics Teacher Exchange and indicates that the adoption of mastery approaches will not lead to the dramatic changes in pupil attainment that politicians hope for. It also provides detail on Shanghai practices and how these are being adapted and implemented in England.

Boylan, M., & Townsend, V. (2018). Understanding mastery in primary mathematics. In T. Cremin and C. Burnett (Eds.) *Learning to teaching in primary school 4th edition* (pp. 456–469). London: Routledge. Although written for primary teachers, this chapter has much in it for secondary teachers too. It provides examples of the type of mathematical activities commonly used in schools in England adopting a mastery approach.

References

Alexander, R. J. (2008). *Towards dialogic teaching: Rethinking classroom talk* (4th ed). New York: Dialogos.

Askew, M. (2015). *Transforming primary mathematics: Understanding classroom tasks, tools and talk.* Routledge: London.

Askew, M., Hodgen, J., Hossain, S, & Bretscher, N. (2010). *Values and variables: Mathematics education in high-performing countries.* London: Nuffield.

Boylan, M., Wolstenholme, C., Demack, S., Maxwell, B., Jay, T., Adams, G., & Reaney, S (2019). Longitudinal evaluation of the Mathematics Teacher Exchange: China-England – Final Report. Retrieved from https://assets.publishing.service.gov. uk/government/uploads/system/uploads/attachment_data/file/773320/MTE_ main_report.pdf

Bruner, J. S. (1966). *Toward a theory of instruction.* Cambridge, MA: Harvard University Press.

DfE. (2014). *Mathematics programmes of study: Key Stages 1 and 2.* London: DfE. Retrieved October, 2014 from https://www.gov.uk/government/uploads/ system/uploads/attachment_data/file/335158/PRIMARY_national_curriculum_-_ Mathematics_220714.pdf

DfEE. (1998). *The implementation of the National Numeracy Strategy: The final report of the Numeracy Task Force.* London: DfEE.

Drury, H. (2014). *Mastering mathematics.* Oxford: Oxford University Press.

Dweck, C. S. (2006). *Mindset: The new psychology of success.* New York: Random House Incorporated.

EEF. (2017). *Improving mathematics in key stages two and three.* London: EEF.

Haylock, D., & Cockburn, A (2013). *Understanding mathematics for young children.* London: Sage.

NCETM. (2014) Mastery approaches to mathematics and the new national curriculum. Available from: https://www.ncetm.org.uk/public/files/19990433/Developing_ mastery_in_mathematics_oc tober_2014.pdf [Retrieved Jan 2015].

NCETM. (2016). *The essence of mathematics teaching for mastery.* Retrieved July, 2016 from https://www.ncetm.org.uk/files/37086535/The+Essence+of+Maths+ Teaching+for+Mastery+june+2016.pdf

Ochs, K. (2006). Cross-national policy borrowing and educational innovation: Improving achievement in the London Borough of Barking and Dagenham. *Oxford Review of Education, 32*(5), 599–618.

Vignoles, A., Jerrim, J., & Cowan, R. (2015). *Mathematics mastery primary evaluation report*. London: EEF. Retrieved March, 2015 from https://v1.educationendowment-foundation.org.uk/uploads/pdf/Mathematics_Mastery_Primary_(Final)1.pdf

Watson, A., & Mason, J. (2006). Seeing an exercise as a single mathematical object: Using variation to structure sense-making. *Mathematical thinking and learning*, 8(2), 91–111.

Watts, J. (2018). *Theresa May launches £500m education programmes with China*. London: The independent. Retrieved from https://www.independent.co.uk/news/uk/politics/theresa-may-china-visit-latest-education-programmes-expansion-brexit-deal-teacher-exchange-scheme-uk-a8185076.html

Section Two

Debates about social justice

Paul Ernest's chapter is concerned with the nature of mathematics itself. He argues that the importance of mathematics to education is overvalued and also leads to harm for some learners; and that as mathematics educators we tend to be complicit in this. He continues by considering the nature of mathematical thinking – seen as detached and instrumental and as promoting separated values (Gilligan, 1982) – and suggests that this way of thinking is dehumanising, contributing to a view of mathematics and its applications as ethically neutral. Reason and rationality are essential for running modern societies fairly; but the implementation of justice rests on values like equality, freedom and caring. The hidden, dark side of mathematics needs to be acknowledged in order for us to combat its effects.

The chapter by **Peter Gates and Andy Noyes** considers the ways that mathematics education contributes to the classification and ranking of school students and, in particular, the overriding impact that social class has on this process. They look at patterns of attainment and link this to the 'baggage' that individual children bring to schooling and to the effects of setting practices which are almost universal currently in secondary mathematics teaching in England and increasingly common in primary too. They argue that taking action to enhance the experience and attainment of children from disadvantaged communities is a required political act and they offer to the reader some strategies to take as starting points for teacher action.

The negative consequences of 'ability' thinking are the subject of the chapter by **Mark Boylan and Hilary Povey**. They note the way in which it results in 'ability' grouping being seen as common sense in England and draw attention to the resultant exacerbating of disadvantage and to the long tail of underachievement such practices create. The concomitant ranking becomes internalised by learners and, as such, leads to seeing differences in attainment as inevitable and beyond learners' (and teachers') power to affect. They argue that teachers need to combat such beliefs both in themselves and in the children they teach; and that when 'ability' thinking is rejected, possibilities for mathematics education are enhanced.

In her chapter, **Hilary Povey** begins by indicating some of the ways that existing practices in mathematics education are limiting learning possibilities.

She draws on the work of Guy Claxton (2002) to highlight four key aspects of practice to which teachers need to pay attention if they are to succeed in enabling mathematics attainment for all. She then takes four case studies from existing research to illustrate and illuminate these four ways of being in the classroom. She concludes by discussing the intellectual, social and emotional or affective purposes that can act as a guide for practice.

Anna Llewellyn notes that teaching for understanding is regarded as an unquestioned good in mathematics education. The argument of her chapter, however, is that we should question such a truth and investigate how it operates to include or exclude people from mathematics. Within education research, it operates as a normalising concept embracing a romantic notion of the 'normal', 'naturally developing' child; in contrast, in policy terms, it is either absent or used functionally. A single case study of student teacher provides an example of how the tension between these two differing discourses leads to exclusion for some.

The chapter by **Mark McCormack and Luis Morales** focuses on gender issues in mathematics education. They are sceptical towards claims of significant gender differences in formal attainment in mathematics but nevertheless argue that gender remains highly relevant to understanding mathematics classrooms. They discuss how gender becomes inscribed in human bodies and draw attention to the ways in which this social construction of gender is produced in schools and in society more broadly. They argue we should move beyond mono-normativity, discussing how classrooms might become places where heterosexism and other forms of gender stigmatising are challenged through a culture of conversation, making them gender inclusive spaces. They conclude with an interrogation of the ways in which mathematics and knowing mathematics are socially constructed.

Heather Mendick's chapter concerns popular culture and the representations of mathematics and mathematicians, focusing on a new strand of stories related to the global financial crisis in 2008. She uses three financial crisis fictions, two films and one novel, to argue that, unlike traditional images in popular culture, these portray mathematics as possibly fallible and subjective and suggest it may function as democratic rather than as elitist, as collective rather than individual. She links back to the chapter which begins this section, noting the moral urgency of taking responsibility for the harm that mathematics can do and suggests that finding ways to share these fictions in mathematics classrooms can contribute towards doing mathematics differently and more inclusively.

As with the first edition, we have sought to have social justice issues inform every contribution to this volume. Some chapters, however, take issues of equity as a central theme. Paul Ernest begins this section by exploring 'the hidden dark side of mathematics' itself which needs to be acknowledged and its effects combated if the subject is to contribute to a more just schooling and a fairer society.

The effect of social class on the experience and outcome of mathematics education is the subject of the chapter by Peter Gates and Andy Noyes. Social class tends to permeate every aspect of contemporary schooling while, at the same time, remaining invisible. They argue that action is required to overcome the further disadvantages that already disadvantaged children meet in mathematics classrooms and offer some useful starting point for actions teachers can take. Overcoming 'ability' thinking is one such strategy and is the subject of the chapter by Mark Boylan and Hilary Povey. Teachers need to challenge and interrogate such thinking in themselves in order to create classrooms where everybody can engage and learn. In a separate chapter, Hilary Povey offers a framework for thinking about practice which might contribute to achieving such a goal and illustrates the four aspects of the framework by drawing on existing case studies in mathematics education.

The previous three chapters take as read the idea that teaching for under-standing is a good. Anna Llewellyn questions this 'truth' and suggests that, as with any discourse that acts as a normaliser producing the 'ideal child', it will operate to exclude some from mathematics. Normativity also plays a part in the chapter by Mark McCormack and Luis Morales where they discuss how gendered thinking also leads to exclusionary practices in mathematics. They discuss classic male/female discriminatory practice, mono-normative constructions of gender and the gendered social construction of mathematics and mathematics education.

The final chapter in this section returns, in part, to themes opened up in the first. It concerns fictions based on the financial crisis of 2008 which illustrate the harm that mathematics can do. The fictions provide a vehicle for Heather Mendick to discuss how mathematics is portrayed in popular culture and to argue that these particular stories offer a way of thinking about doing mathematics differently and more inclusively.

Chapter 3

The dark side of mathematics
Damaging effects of the overvaluation of mathematics

Paul Ernest

Introduction

A widespread belief is that mathematics is an unqualified force for good in society. In this chapter I challenge this idea and claim that mathematics has a dark side. Although it has undoubted benefits, there is significant damage caused by mathematics. Mathematics is overvalued in society which leads to negative consequences, and I describe three ways in which it causes harm. First, the personal impact of learning mathematics on learners' thinking and life chances can be negative for many students. Second, by serving as a 'critical filter' mathematical certification is an impediment to equal opportunities for all. Third, the nature of pure mathematics itself leads to styles of thinking that can be damaging when applied beyond mathematics to social and human issues. I argue that mathematics and mathematics professionals must first acknowledge this dark side before we can start to act on reducing and countering the harm done in society.

The overvaluation of mathematics in and by society

It might seem unusual to mathematicians and mathematics teachers to claim that mathematics is overvalued in modern society. As mathematicians we are insiders who love mathematics for its precision, power, universality, beauty, simplicity and complexity. Mathematics rightly claims to be one of the crowning glories of human knowledge and culture. But not everybody shares our love or happy experience of mathematics. Indeed, as insiders we are only a tiny percentage of the population.

There are, however, good reasons why mathematics is overvalued, beyond the love and pride we mathematicians feel for our specialism. The ubiquity of mathematics and its applications in modern computerised society are seen as reasons why everybody needs mathematics. Computers, information and communication technologies (ICTs) now underpin the media, business, the functioning of civil society including policing, justice, health, education, pensions and social security, the military, sport, to name just some of the more significant functions. Because society depends so heavily on mathematics and computing it is concluded that everybody needs mathematical knowledge and skills. Further, mathematics is a central feature of rationality as it is used in policy, governance and business, and because such reasoning is vital it is assumed that it is mathematics that really matters.[1] Modern business and government depend on utility. Utilitarianism relies on cost/profit calculations, which are mathematical applications. Also, money is the lifeblood circulating around the body of the modern social world. Money really counts, since it is the medium for employment, trade, consumption and national and international organisation. Since money is an application of mathematics, mathematics really matters too, the argument goes.

The flaw in this argument is that despite societal dependence on mathematics it does not follow that all members of society need high levels of mathematical certification. Most citizens do not programme the applications or use the underlying mathematical models on which the workings of society depend. To run and service the technical mathematical underpinnings of modern society only a tiny minority need high levels of mathematical knowledge and skills. Often what is needed is specialised and not available through schooling to 18 years of age, or even traditional university studies in mathematics. However, there is a separate argument about the nature and depth of mathematical knowledge and skills that are needed for citizens to be empowered as full participants in modern democratic society and its governance addressed below.

Mathematical insiders like ourselves are strong advocates for the high valuation and prestige of mathematics in education. But we are a tiny minority of the public, and it is worth contrasting insider with outsider views. For insiders, mathematics is a love object, fascinating, beautiful and attractive. It is seen as meaningful, useful, powerful and an avenue to personal success in which, unsurprisingly, we insiders are deeply invested.[2]

For mathematics outsiders, that is the general public, there is a wide diversity of views. Many of the public also love or like mathematics, as we do, and are fascinated and enjoy recreational mathematics and popular presentations of the subject. But for at least a significant minority of the public mathematics is seen as cold, hard, unforgiving, masculine, meaningless, joyless, rejecting or frightening (Buerk 1982, Buxton 1981, Maxwell 1989). Success in mathematics is seen as based on the inherited ability of a few, seen as other, and not as related to the effort expended in school. For a significant minority mathematics is seen as an obstacle to educational and career advancement and is feared and avoided where possible.

What are the mathematical needs of society?

This is a question for you to consider.
What do you think are the mathematical needs of society?

In answering this question I find it useful to apply Marx's fundamental distinction between use and exchange value. In economic theory, the difference between use value (cost) and exchange value (sale) is profit. In education, the difference between use value (actual utility) and exchange value (social or opportunity value) is educational obstacle/filter or the educational advantage/privilege afforded. My claim is that the actual use value of mathematics in society is limited and the exchange value is exaggerated. To demonstrate this, I need to show what are the actual mathematical needs of society, that is its use value.

1 All citizens need 'numeracy plus' to be functioning critical citizens in a modern democratic society. They need to have mastery of the mathematics underlying their everyday lives including consumer and economic decisions. As functioning modern citizens, they need to be able to interpret and evaluate the uses of mathematics in social, commercial and political claims in published reports, newspaper and other media presentations, advertisements, financial documents and so on. By 'numeracy plus' I mean elementary or primary school mathematics plus some additional knowledge, such as understanding and skills in data representation and processing, spreadsheets and elementary algebra, probability and statistics, ratio and proportion, reasoning and practical problem-solving. This should include understanding algorithms, Apps and big data in principle if not in detail. Such knowledge needs to empower elementary and everyday applications, rather than being directed exclusively at completing written tasks in external examinations and assessments at 16 years or thereafter (see Chapter 20).
2 Society is evidently highly mathematised and almost all citizens use algorithms in ICTs, including computers and mobile phones, the media and so on. However, as users of Apps and ICT citizens need no deep technical comprehension of the underlying computer logic or mathematics. Unquestionably a highly skilled group of specialists is needed to understand the language of mathematics and algorithms to enable the invention, development, writing and evaluation of software and applications (Apps). However, it is only a tiny minority, far less than 1% of the population, in highly specialised professions that need such technical understanding and capabilities.
3 In between the 'numeracy plus' capabilities needed by all citizens and the highly technical knowledge for this tiny group of specialists, there is the need for additional mathematical knowledge and study. This is for those who need or might need mathematics in further university studies and technical- and science-related professions. These include mathematical sciences, physical and biological sciences, experimental psychology, medicine, engineering, accountancy and so on. This is a small minority which is probably less than 5% of the population.

Overall, at the very least, a substantial minority do not need mathematical knowledge and skills beyond 'numeracy plus'. But in modern society the exchange value of mathematics far outweighs its use value. There is a symbolic function of mathematics in which it serves as a social filtration device. Mathematics certification is a critical filter for entry to almost all higher education and professions. Applicants are required to have successfully completed study of mathematics to 16 or 18 years of age, which must be certificated irrespective of whether they will need or use the knowledge or skills in subsequent study or work. If all students gained knowledge and capabilities from this study, that is demonstrated cognitive benefit, it might be argued that it is a worthwhile component of general education. But many young persons are forced to study mathematics involuntarily and a significant number of these experience some degree of failure or incomprehension, suffer loss of self-confidence and develop negative attitudes to mathematics.

Furthermore, as a critical filter, mathematics in effect performs a fractional distillation of the population. Those who fail to pass mathematics tests are often denied entry to university, further studies or fulfilling occupations. What is to a large extent an arbitrary test deprives many of chances for fulfilling studies and rewarding professions and occupations.

Historically, classics used to have same symbolic role as a critical filter up to the 19th century. Entry to the church, governance, diplomacy, the civil service, law and education, all depended on competency in the classics. Even Shakespeare was mocked during his lifetime as uneducated because he lacked knowledge of the classics. If the job of actor and playwright required formal qualifications, the greatest writer of all time would have been denied entry to his profession.

In addition, success in school mathematics is strongly correlated with the socio-economic status or social class background of students. Although this is true about success in virtually all academic school subjects, mathematics has a privileged status. It is the examinations in mathematics in particular that serve as a fractional distillation device that, to a significant extent, is class reproductive. Talented mathematicians from any background may be successful in life, but the net effect of mathematical examinations remains the grading of students into a hierarchy with respect to life chances. This hierarchy doubly correlates with socio-economic status and social class, understood in terms of both the social origins and the social destinations of students. So, it is not merely raw mathematical talent that is reflected in mathematical achievement. It is also partially mediated by cultural capital (Bourdieu 1986, Zevenbergen 1998).

In summary, the overvaluation of mathematics has three major immediate social costs. First, there is the unjust exclusion of persons who are well able to pursue their chosen studies or careers without mathematical certification, but who are denied the chance because they are the victims who are excluded by the critical filter of mathematics. Second, this critical filter is class reproductive, favouring those with cultural capital behind them. Thus, society is denied the benefits of capable people whose backgrounds lack the resources to enable them to access the career ladder in many areas of life and work.[3] Third, there is the social cost of negative attitudes to mathematics. Many learners and adults are labelled as mathematics failures and lack confidence in mathematics and numeracy skills. Some may fear mathematics and thus have reduced opportunities in study and work. Some may have 'scraped through' but have negative attitudes because of the personal and emotional costs in passing tests. This happens with some trainee primary school teachers, who are required to teach elementary mathematics to young children, while still doubting their own mathematical efficacy. Many other citizens may well be potentially competent, but may be inhibited from using their numeracy plus skills acquired through elementary schooling and are not fully functioning and participating citizens in modern society. Thus, the overvaluation of mathematics leads to the wastage of human power in the workforce, contributes to the reproduction of social inequality and leads to negative attitudes and reduced self-confidence with regard to mathematics, as well as, for some, reducing full participation in our democratic society. Let us not forget that these negative outcomes also include reductions in happiness, well-being and life satisfaction.

As mathematics professionals, we are complicit in this overvaluing of mathematics. It is to our benefit, conscious or not, for we gain by not questioning the overvaluing of mathematics in society. We gain more resources, prestige and the privileged place of our subject in schooling. We do not challenge the argument that its ubiquity in society requires that all must study abstract mathematics to 16 or 18 years of age. At the same time, we accept that not everyone must study to 16 or 18 years any of the arts, literature, drama, classics, languages, psychology, philosophy, politics, geography, history or computing, despite the contribution these can also make to being active citizens and to the good life. These subjects are surely important for the personal development not to mention the employment of young persons. But we choose to leave these subjects optional.

The effects of the study of mathematics on thinking

Beyond the harm caused by mathematical failure and negative attitudes for many, there is the potential harm caused by success at mathematics. Historically, written mathematics begins with number and calculation. These have dominated both the practical uses of mathematics and its educational content for 5,000 years, right until very recently. The inclusion of mensuration and trigonometry does not challenge the fundamentally calculational nature of mathematics in schooling and applications.[4] At the heart of calculation are rule-based general procedures. In these, the overall meaning of numerals, especially the place value meanings signified by relative positioning of constituent digits, is largely ignored during most of the algorithmic processes. In addition, largely as a result of Islamic contributions, algebra emerged in the Middle Ages, and now provides the abstract language of mathematics upon which all modern developments depend. Algebra is generalised arithmetic in origin and as such is subject to generalised arithmetical procedures and rules, and its strength is that specific numerical meanings are detached. This was explicitly noted over 300 years ago by Bishop Berkeley.

> ... in Algebra, in which, though a particular quantity be marked by each letter, yet to proceed right it is not requisite that in every step each letter suggest to your thoughts that particular quantity it was appointed to stand for. (Berkeley 1710, p. 59)

At its heart, algebra is variable based, thus forcing the linguistic move in the language away from specific values and meanings to general rules and procedures. This move has some great benefits, enabling the miracle of electronic computing in which mathematical rules and procedures are wholly automated and no reference to or comprehension of the meaning of mathematical expressions is required or even helpful.

Overall, during the application of algorithms and other permitted procedures in arithmetic and algebra the meaning of expressions can largely be neglected with no detriment to the efficacy of the procedures. Meaning is dispensable. Note that when meaning exits stage left, it takes values not to mention ethics with it.

A further characteristic of school, university and research mathematics is that they are represented in the language and symbolism of mathematics. This employs the sentential form in the standard subject-verb form.[5] Analyses show that the predominant verb form in mathematical language is the imperative mood. Imperatives are orders that instruct or direct actions either inclusively (for example, let us, consider) or exclusively (for example add, count, solve, prove). Imperatives occur more frequently in mathematics than in any other academic school subject (Ernest 1998, Rotman 1993). Thus, a schooling in mathematics is a training in obedience.

Mathematical operations require the precise following of rules. At its most creative mathematics allows choices among multiple strategies and representations, but each of the lines of choice pursued involves strict rule following. These rules are necessary because mathematics is very unforgiving. There is no redundancy in its language and any error in rule following derails the procedures and processes. Thus, students of mathematics must learn to use its language and follow its rules with great precision. The net result of extended exposure to and practice in mathematics is a social training in obedience, an apprenticeship in strict subservience to the text, be it printed or spoken.

One of the most important ways that a social training in obedience is achieved is through the universal teaching and learning of mathematics from a very early age and throughout the school years. The central and universal role of arithmetic in schooling provides the symbolic tools for quantified thought, including not only the ability to conceptualise situations quantitatively, but also a compulsion to do so. This compulsion first comes from without, but is appropriated, internalised and elaborated as part of the postmodern citizen's identity.

We cannot stop calculating and assigning quantified values to everything, in a society in which what matters is what counts or is counted.

The teaching and learning of mathematics in schools, and thus the development of mathematical identity, requires that, from the age of five or soon after, depending on the country, children will (Ernest 2016c):

1 Acquire an object-oriented language that focuses on objects and processes alone without reference to fellow agents or their interests;
2 Learn to conduct operations on these objects without any intrinsic reasons or sense of value, thus operating without meaning or with deferred meaning;
3 Decontextualise their world of experience and replace it by a deliberately unrealistic and stylised model composed of simplified static objects and reversible processes;
4 Suppress subjectivity, and feelings of experiential being in their mathematical operations on objects, processes and models;
5 Learn to prioritise and value the outcomes of such modelling above any personal feelings, values and context meanings.

> *Consider the mathematics teaching and learning resources in your classroom. Do they support these claims?*

Making these expectations explicit reveals how skewed and distorted they are.

King (1982) researched the mathematics taught and learnt in five- to six-year-old infant classrooms. He found that mathematics involves and legitimates the suspension of conventional reality more than any other school subject. People are coloured in with red and blue faces. "A class exercise on measuring height became a histogram. Marbles, acorns, shells, fingers and other counters become figures on a page, objects become numbers" (King 1982, p. 244). Further, in the world of school mathematics even the meanings of the simplified representations of reality that emerge are dispensable.

> Most teachers were aware that some children could not read the instructions properly, but suggested they "know how to do it (the mathematics) without it." … Only in mathematics could words be left meaningless. (King 1982, p. 244)

In the psychology of mathematics education instrumental understanding, defined as knowing how to carry out procedures without understanding, versus relational understanding, which includes in addition knowing how and why such procedures work, is much discussed as a problem issue (Mellin-Olsen 1987, Skemp 1976). It is no coincidence that what is termed instrumental understanding is also a form of the instrumental reasoning critiqued by the Frankfurt School, discussed next.

In summary, many procedures on signs are carried out with abstracted or deferred meanings, and many mathematical texts and tasks with their workings based on calculations, derivations or proofs involve the reader following rule-governed sequences or orders. In education, mathematics is the subject most divorced from everyday or experienced meaning, and the objectification and dehumanisation of the subject are a necessary part of its acquisition.[6]

Although mathematical signs and procedures are detached from meaningful referents in the world and from social contexts as sources of meaning, engagement with mathematics can create an inner world of meanings. Successful mathematicians work within richly populated conceptual universes that are very meaningful to them. Success in mathematics at most levels is often associated with having a meaningful domain of interpretation of mathematical signs and symbols, normally within the closed world of mathematics. In addition, applied mathematicians interpret mathematical models in the world around us so in applications meanings are reattached (these meanings may of course be highly ideological, partial and contested). Likewise, although mathematical language is very rich in imperatives, successful users of mathematics at all levels have certain degrees of freedom available to them, such as which methods and procedures to apply in solving problems, which models to use, as is noted above.

These qualifications notwithstanding, the study of mathematics instils both the capacity to, and the expectation of, meaning detachment during reasoning and calculative procedures. Likewise, it prepares its readers to follow the imperatives in the text during the technical and instrumental reasoning involved in mathematics.[7]

Mathematical thinking as detached instrumental and calculative reasoning

My claim is that the linguistic and semantic characteristics and conditioning indicated above have costs, including unanticipated negative outcomes when extended and applied beyond mathematics. The mathematical way of thinking promotes a mode of reasoning in which there is a detachment of meaning, and reasoning without meanings provides a training in ethics-free thought. Value neutrality and ethical irrelevance is presupposed because meanings, contexts and their associated purposes and values are stripped away and discounted as irrelevant to the task in hand. Furthermore, as is argued elsewhere, there is a widespread perception of mathematics as timeless, universal and imbued with absolute certainty, and hence it is viewed as an objective, value-neutral and ethics-free domain of thought (Ernest 1998, 2016a, 2016b). Such reasoning and perspectives contribute to a dehumanised outlook. For without a backdrop of meaning, values and ethical considerations, reasoning is at risk of becoming mechanical and technical and a 'thing' or object-orientated. These modes of thinking foster what have been termed *separated values* (Gilligan 1982). Separated values foreground rules, abstraction, objectification, impersonality, unfeelingness, dispassionate reason and analysis, and are atomistic and object-centred in focus. The contrasting connected values foreground relationships, connections, empathy, caring, feelings and intuition, and are holistic and human-centred in emphasis. These two value positions can be seen as oppositional. The separated values position applies well to mathematics. Mathematical objects are entities resulting from objectification and abstraction, and mathematical structures are constituted by abstract and rule-based sets of objects and their structural relationships. The processes of mathematics are atomistic and object-centred, based on dispassionate analysis and reason in which personal feelings play no direct contributing part (although they can be the source of joy and wonder). Thus for the majority, separated values fit mathematics very well. Mathematics both embodies and transmits these values.

Separated values and the associated outlooks are necessary, indeed essential, by the very nature of mathematics and their acquisition constitute assets and are undoubtedly beneficial for thinking in mathematics. A separated scientific outlook is also useful in reasoning in other inanimate domains, such as in physics and chemistry, where atomistic analysis, strictly causal relationships and structural regularities yield high levels of knowledge. However, thinking exclusively in the separated mode can lead to problems and abuses when applied outside mathematics and the physical sciences to society. In the human sphere exclusively separated values are potentially harmful, since they discount any human and ethical dimensions. In seeing the world mathematically, the richness of nature and human worlds, with all their beauty, contextual complexity and linkages, and ethical responsibilities are replaced by simplified, abstracted and objectified structural models.

Although mathematical perspectives and models are powerful and useful tools for actions in the world, including the improvement of human life conditions, when overextended they can become a threat to our very humanity. Inculcating these values can lead to a dehumanised outlook if applied to social and human worlds. Separated values extended too far beyond mathematics can also lead to the view that mathematics and its applications have no ethical or social responsibility. While there are legitimate philosophical arguments that pure mathematics is ethically neutral, although I argue the opposite (Ernest 2016b), it is widely agreed that mathematical applications bear full social responsibility for their impacts on the world, just as do the applications of science and technology.

My claim is that subjection to mathematics in schooling from halfway through one's first decade to near the end of one's second decade and beyond if one specialises, structures and transforms our modes of thought in ways that may not be wholly beneficial. I do not claim that mathematics itself is harmful. But when the generalised mathematical outlook is integrated into schooling, society and above all into human and power relations in society, there is a transformation of the human outlook, more, a degradation of our interpersonal relationships. Of course this way of seeing is a historical contingency, a selective construction. It results from the modernist model of rationalist thought into which mathematics has been recruited. Western bureaucratic thinking applies systems thinking and separated values at the cost of empathising (Baron-Cohen 2003) and connected values (Gilligan 1982). Mathematical style is used as the basis for the culture of objectification, a culture of *having* rather than on of *being* (Fromm 1978). This fits well with the current Western free-market culture in which everything has a price and buying and selling is a dominant form of human interaction. Wilde (1907, p. 116) presciently expressed it in his dictum about someone "that knows the price of everything and the value of nothing".

One framework that acknowledges these aspects of the application of mathematics is the critique of instrumental reason and rationality provided by the critical theory of the Frankfurt School. Instrumental reason is the objective form of action or thought, which treats its objects simply as a means and not as an end in itself. It focuses on the most efficient or most cost-effective means to achieve a specific end, without reflecting on the value of that end. Instrumental reason has been critiqued by a range of philosophers including Heidegger who argues that instrumental and what he terms calculative thinking lead us into closed systems of thought with no room for considering the ends, values and ethical dimensions of our actions (Haynes 2008). The central argument is often traced back to Kant's *Grounding for the Metaphysics of Morals* of 1785. There he derives the imperative that you must never treat any person merely as a means to an end, but always as an end in themselves.

A broader-based critique comes from the Critical Theorists of the Frankfurt School (including Adorno, Fromm, Habermas, Horkheimer and Marcuse) who see instrumental reason as the dominant form of thought within modern society (Bohman 2005, Corradetti n. d.). By focusing on technical means and not on the ends of their actions, persons, governments and corporations risk complicity in the treatment of human beings as objects to be manipulated, in actions that threaten social well-being, the environment and nature. This outlook underpins the behaviours of some governments and multinational corporations in reducing costs and chasing profits without regard for the human costs. Such actions by corporations have been termed psychopathic (Bakan 2004). We are now so used to the economic, instrumental model of life and human governance that most persons see it as an unquestionable practical reality, a necessary evil, and are not shocked or outraged by corporations or governments treating persons and animals as objects with no concern for their well-being.

Much of the Frankfurt School critique was prompted by the rise of Nazism in Germany, with its authoritarian leaders (Adorno et al. 1950) and the heartless complicity of ordinary citizens in Germany and occupied territories before and during World War II. The capture, transportation, enslavement and murder of millions of fellow citizens were not simply undertaken by monsters. These wholesale activities would not have been possible without many ordinary citizens unquestioningly doing their everyday jobs as part of this monstrous programme. Arendt (1963) terms this ordinariness, from the actions of Eichmann downward, the 'banality of evil'.

My argument is that mathematics plays a central role in normalising instrumental and calculative ways of seeing and thinking. From the very start of their education children are schooled in these ways of being and seeing. The detachment of meaning and the following of imperatives in mathematical texts and thinking provides the central platform for instrumental thought.[8]

A further factor is the social image of mathematics as objective, ethically neutral, unquestionably certain, with its claims settled decisively as either true or false (Ernest 1998, Hersh 1997). Thus, mathematical study is a training in accepting that complex problems can be solved unambiguously with clear-cut right or wrong answers, with solution methods that lead to unique correct solutions. Within the domain of pure mathematics, problems, methods and solutions may indeed be value-free and ethically neutral. But carrying these beliefs beyond mathematics to the more complex and ambiguous problems of the human world leads to a false sense of certainty, and encourages an instrumental and technical approach to daily problems. This is damaging, for when decision-making is driven purely by a separated, instrumental rationality, then ethics, caring and human values are neglected, if not left out of the picture altogether. Kelman (1973) found that ethical considerations are eroded when three conditions are present: standardisation, routinisation and dehumanisation. Since mathematics as the essence of instrumental reason, has procedures that require standardisation, routinisation and dehumanisation, the concomitant erasure of ethics is no surprise. Thus a training in mathematical thinking, when misapplied beyond its own area of validity to the social domain, is potentially damaging and harmful.

However, I must also acknowledge that reason and rationality are essential for the fair running of modern society, and that depersonalised and objectivised thinking is necessary for all large-scale management. Modern society and institutions cannot be run ethically or fairly, let alone effectively, without abstracted, depersonalised and objectivised thinking, for the following reasons. Governance requires the accumulation, allocation and distribution of resources. Whatever the political and ideological orientation of a government it needs to calculate where resources will most benefit society according to its own values. It is the core of democratic governance that priorities for the distribution of resources will vary with different elected governments. Whatever the priorities and values of a legitimate government, and the social goals to which it aspires, resources need to be allocated to fulfil these goals effectively. We would not be able to pursue the practical meaning of our ethics and principles without working out their rational implications. In addition, systematic and rational record keeping is another necessity for fairness and equity. Thus, calculative reasoning and instrumental thinking in the service of societal values and goals is a modern necessity. However, this is not an alibi for the blind following of orders. In a good society there must always be a place for ethical objections and whistle-blowing, where individual conscience can be exercised, when values or laws are transgressed, or unfairness or injustices are perceived.

When it come to the fair running of society, impersonal reason and rationality are essential. Giving benefits only to those one cares about or empathises with leads to inequality, favouritism and nepotism. As one can argue, against the dictum of the 1960s, love is not all you need, if you seek to be fair and just (Pinker 2012). In a just society you must treat strangers and other citizens as having equal rights and deserving equal treatment irrespective of any personal feelings towards them. However, the implementation of justice rests on values, for example the values of equality, freedom and caring. The good society cannot be based on calculation and logic alone, but needs such reasoning to be based on ethical values. We need to make sure that the teaching and applications of mathematics are never wholly divorced from humane values and ethics.

Conclusion

In this chapter I argue that despite its great benefits and intrinsic virtues, mathematics is overvalued in modern society and that this causes harm. First of all, the personal impact of learning mathematics on learners' thinking and life chances can be negative for many students. Second, the role of mathematics as a critical filter, with its exchange value far exceeding its use value, serves as an impediment to equal opportunities for all, favouring those with cultural capital. Third, the universal training in mathematics leads to an instrumental style of thinking that can be damaging when applied beyond mathematics to social and human issues. There is a fourth dimension of the dark side of mathematics that I have not have had space to develop, namely ethical problems in the applications of mathematics.

One obstacle to raising awareness of these problems, let alone trying to solve them, are the philosophical and ideological positions that state mathematics is neutral, value-free and bears no responsibility for any of its applications. Although there are widespread movements concerned with the social responsibility of science, almost no parallels for mathematics exist.[9] However, the ethically questionable uses of mathematics are widespread all around us. Mathematical algorithms have been used to mine personal data of millions of citizens for commercial advantage and political influence. Money and thus mathematics is the tool for the circulation and distribution of wealth. It can therefore be argued that as the key underpinning conceptual tool mathematics is implicated in the global disparities in wealth and life chances manifested in the human world. Mathematics, science and technology are used in the manufacture of guns, explosives, nuclear and biological weapons, battlefield computer systems, military drones and smart bombs, as well as tobacco products, and other potentially destructive artefacts and tools (Ernest 2018).

Is it exaggerated to claim that mathematics has a dark side? Do you agree that the three hidden effects of mathematics in society are potentially harmful? Do you believe that mathematics is often used without thought about its ethical consequences? What could we do to improve this situation?

My argument is not that we should oppose all of these applications of mathematics or the Western capitalist system overall from the outset. Rather it is that we should to acknowledge the implications of mathematics in all of its widespread and fundamental applications across society, many of which are invisible. Mathematics has a hidden dark side, its uses and applications in education and society have costs and harmful outcomes, as well as the more widely acknowledged benefits. Only when we acknowledge this dark side can we start to plan and act on ameliorating, reducing and countering the harm done. Hopefully, the 'numeracy plus' curriculum for all that I propose will put mathematical tools for comprehending the uses and abuses of mathematics in society into the hands of a well-informed critical citizenry.

Notes

1 Of course mathematics is also used to conceal and justify decisions made largely on ideological grounds.
2 By mathematics insiders I mean mathematicians, mathematics educators, mathematics teachers, mathematics-related professionals and others who have specialised in mathematics in their studies. Mathematics outsiders are everybody else.
3 The notably disadvantaged include white working-class males failed by the school system, as well as West-Indian origin males and some other ethnic groups, usually from low-income backgrounds.
4 In elite education Euclidean geometry has played a role, but this is just a different type of a rule following and so further exemplifies the point I am making.
5 Mathematical sentences employ the more general terms-relation form, where a relation is equivalent to a generalised verb.
6 This includes forced decontextualisation and subtraction of human values, intentions and external motives.
7 In addition, in more advanced study of mathematics in high school or university, students learn to reason and draw inferences from assumptions and postulates that are not necessarily true. Such hypothetical reasoning adds yet another level of detachment from the world we live in, weakening the bonds to reality, values and ethics.
8 Of course the right social circumstances are needed too. A society with values of strong social-conformity and a culture of obedience to authority is needed, as Milgram (1974) showed in his experiments. However, as I have argued, subjection to thousands of hours of school mathematics and schooling in general will contribute to this.
9 There is, however, an emergent network concerned with mathematics and ethics which had its first international conference in 2018 led by Dr Maurice Chiodo at Cambridge University, UK.

References

Adorno, R., Frenkel-Brunswik, E., Levinson, D. and Sanford, R. (1950). *The Authoritarian Personality*. New York: Harper.
Arendt, H. (1963). *Eichmann in Jerusalem: A Report on the Banality of Evil*. London: Faber and Faber.
Bakan, J. (2004). *The Corporation*. London: Constable.
Baron-Cohen, S. (2003). *The Essential Difference: Men, Women and the Extreme Male Brain*. London: Penguin Books.

Berkeley, G. (1710). *The Principles of Human Knowledge*. Reprinted 1962 in Fontana Library. Glasgow: W. Collins.

Bohman, J. (2005). Critical Theory. *Stanford Encyclopedia of Philosophy*. http://plato.stanford.edu/entries/critical-theory/. Accessed on 5 May 2015.

Bourdieu, P. (1986). The Forms of Capital. In J. G. Richardson (Ed.). *Handbook of Theory and Research for the Sociology of Education* (pp. 241–258). New York: Greenwood Press.

Buerk, D. (1982). An Experience with Some Able Women Who Avoid Mathematics. *For the Learning of Mathematics*, 3(2), pp. 19–24.

Buxton, L. (1981). *Do you Panic about Maths? Coping with Maths Anxiety*. London: Heinemann Educational Books.

Corradetti, C. (n. d.). The Frankfurt School and Critical Theory. *The Internet Encyclopedia of Philosophy*. http://www.iep.utm.edu/frankfur/. Accessed on 5 May 2015.

Ernest, P. (1998). *Social Constructivism as a Philosophy of Mathematics*. Albany, New York: State University of New York Press.

Ernest, P. (2016a). Values and Mathematics: Overt and Covert. *Culture and Dialogue*, (Special issue Culture, Science and Dialogue, Guest editor: M. Ovens), 4(1), pp. 48–82.

Ernest, P. (2016b). A Dialogue on the Ethics of Mathematics. *The Mathematical Intelligencer*, 38(3), pp. 69–77.

Ernest, P. (2016c). The Collateral Damage of Learning Mathematics, *Philosophy of Mathematics Education Journal*, 31, p. 5. http://socialsciences.exeter.ac.uk/education/research/centres/stem/publications/pmej/pome31/index.html. Accessed on 26 June 2019.

Ernest, P. (2018). The Ethics of Mathematics: Is Mathematics Harmful? In P. Ernest (Ed.). *The Philosophy of Mathematics Education Today*. Switzerland: Springer.

Fromm, E. (1978). *To Have or To Be?* London: Jonathon Cape.

Gilligan, C. (1982). *In a Different Voice*. Cambridge, Massachusetts: Harvard University Press.

Haynes, J. D. (2008). *Calculative Thinking and Essential Thinking in Heidegger's Phenomenology*. http://wwwdocs.fce.unsw.edu.au/sistm/staff/Heidegger_calculation_essential_March08.pdf. Accessed on 3 May 2015.

Hersh, R. (1997). *What Is Mathematics, Really?* London: Jonathon Cape.

Kelman, H. C. (1973). Violence Without Moral Restraint: Reflections on the Dehumanization of Victims and Victimizers. *Journal of Social Issues*, 29(4), pp. 25–62.

King, R. (1982). Multiple Realities and Their Reproduction in Infants' Classrooms. In C. Richards (Ed.). *New Directions in Primary Education* (pp. 237–246). Lewes, Sussex: Falmer Press.

Maxwell, J. (1989). Mathephobia. In P. Ernest (Ed.). *Mathematics Teaching: The State of the Art* (pp. 221–226). London: Falmer Press.

Mellin-Olsen, S. (1987). *The Politics of Mathematics Education*. Dordrecht: Reidel.

Milgram, S. (1974). *Obedience to Authority: An Experimental View*. New York: Harper.

Pinker, S. (2012). *The Better Angels of Our Nature*. New York: Penguin Books.

Rotman, B. (1993). *Ad Infinitum the Ghost in Turing's Machine: Taking God Out of Mathematics and Putting the Body Back in*. Stanford, California: Stanford University Press.

Skemp, R. R. (1976). Relational Understanding and Instrumental Understanding. *Mathematics Teaching*, No. 77, pp. 20–26.

Wilde, O. (1907). *The Writings of Oscar Wilde*, Uniform Edition (Vol. 10, p. 116). New York: A. R. Keller & Co. Inc.

Zevenbergen, R. (1998). *Language, Mathematics and Social Disadvantage: A Bourdieuian Analysis of Cultural Capital in Mathematics Education*. http://www.merga.net.au/documents/RP_Zevenbergen_1_1998.pdf. Accessed 3 May 2015.

Chapter 4

School mathematics as social classification

Peter Gates and Andy Noyes

We need to talk about ... 'class'

> *Imagine ... you meet up with your teacher friends one evening and start discussing your most challenging group, and some of your most challenging students. How would you describe them?*

Probably in doing that, you will have classified students according to some criteria, comparing some students against others. Classifying students is something that teachers and schools engage in all of the time; ranking, grouping, setting, allowing some onto courses, keeping others out and so on. Classification is not only a fundamental process of mathematical activity, but also is fundamental to mathematics education itself. Yet there is a particular type of classification that is of interest to us in this chapter – sorting students by their social and economic backgrounds. So, we begin by asking the following questions:

- How do young people become classified through mathematics education?
- How do our professional practices (our pedagogy, curriculum, assessment, etc.) contribute to this?
- How might we respond in light of this awareness of our collusion in such classificatory processes?

Why is this tendency towards classification such an issue for mathematics teachers that we need a chapter on it? Paul Connolly's (2006) study of GCSE (General Certificate of Secondary Education) performance highlights that student socio-economic background (rather than gender or ethnicity) is the greatest predictor of learning outcomes. This is not to say that these three social characteristics should be seen as unconnected; all three can be difficult to pin down sometimes and we know that gendered and ethnic identities are complex and can, for some young people at least, be problematic.

Social class is a complex, shifting and contested notion and often goes unrecognised which makes its influence hard to see and to measure. In a study drawing on three large data sets in the United Kingdom, Alissa Goodman and Paul Gregg (2010) reported that "only 21% of the poorest fifth (measured by parental socioeconomic status – SES) manage to gain five good GCSEs (grades A*–C, including English and mathematics), compared to 75% of the top Quintile" (p. 7).

The term 'socio-economic' oversimplifies things somewhat and we find the idea of *'capital'* helpful. Capital is usually thought of as financial resources or *economic capital*, but this was extended by Pierre Bourdieu (1986), a French sociologist, into *cultural capital* (buying into particular, 'cultured' ways of living) and *social capital* (having connections and knowing people with relevant influence).

> *Think about a diverse collection of young people (think of your students if you're working in a school). What can you 'see' as the different forms and levels of economic, cultural and social capital they have?*

Identifying 'class'

> There are an estimated 3.5 million children living in poverty in the UK and this figure is expected to soar by 400,000 in the coming years. A lack of jobs, stagnating wages, increased living costs and spending cuts are placing enormous pressure on families up and down the UK. Children's experiences of poverty and the recession are often overlooked. (Whitham, 2012)

It is quite difficult to provide a simple definition or measurement of someone's social class and we generally use some form of *'proxy* indicator'. We could use *'occupational indicators'*. If we use the terms 'working class' or 'middle class', we could classify by the parental occupation and income if we knew them. These two measures will be closely related but not uniquely so. Some 50 years ago this terminology would not have been too problematic – yet as the economy has become more segmented, fragmented and dynamic, such occupational measures become more difficult to depend on.

We might alternatively use some *'economic indicators'* and use the terms 'poor', 'deprived' or 'disadvantaged' to indicate some sense of being denied some opportunities or economic resources. This too is difficult to measure, but one approximation to being poor is being eligible for free school meals so this is often used as a proxy. This is not foolproof as students can easily move in and out of such categories.

A third approach is to use *'aggregated geographical measures'* which are based upon postcodes and census output areas. An example of this is the UK government's *Income Deprivation Affecting Children Index* (IDACI). This measures the proportion of children under the age of 16 who live in low-income households in a particular area and is used when comparing school contextual achievement.

Finally you can use data on *'consumer spending habits'* or *'geodemographic segmentation'*. The system called MOSAIC has been developed by Experian in the United Kingdom and creates 155 person types aggregated into 67 household types. As with the IDACI this assumes we are like the people we live near, which to some extent we all are.

Making judgements

UK Governments use a number of these proxy measures in their analyses of student progress – and other countries will undoubtedly use similar measures. The weakness of these sorts of measures is that they rely heavily on economic capital and on spatial aggregation and ignore the equally import dimensions of cultural and social capital. So, although there are certain allocation problems for some students (transgender, dual heritage, etc.), analysing educational outcomes by gender and ethnicity is relatively straightforward. However, statistical analyses and classifications made on the basis of socio-economic status (SES) are fraught with problems. Research in the United States shows that the mathematics achievement gap related to *SES* is roughly *ten times* the size of the gender gap (Lubienski, 2002, p. 105). However, although SES is arguably the most important dimension of educational achievement, it is the one most often systematically overlooked. It is tricky to separate out the effect sizes of class, ethnicity and gender and to understand the intersection of these: being a white working-class boy makes you as complex as a Chinese middle-class girl.

Having argued that social class is a problematic and contested construct, it *is* the case that we all classify on the basis of some measure of SES. Indeed, as we have said, everyone is engaged in classifying, at a more or less conscious level, all of the time. Our categories and strategies for doing this are themselves a product of our own social backgrounds and upbringing. Part of the way teachers classify their students is through the assessment of mathematical skills but another part is through implicit and often subconscious judgements of the students' cultural capital, even in the form of their names (Noyes, 2003). Do we picture a Kylie or a Dwayne in the same way as a Katherine or a David? There is never a truly fresh start at school!

> *Think of the time you met one of your classes for the first time. What did you notice about the students? What judgements were you forming and how? Write down some notes, reflect on them and prepare yourself to be surprised by (a) your skills as an amateur sociologist and (b) your prejudices. Then consider the implications of those initial judgements for your future interactions with these students.*

So, whether we like it or not, we are all involved in classificatory practices, and these are probably not fair; they tend to benefit certain kinds of people like ourselves. To talk about 'class' then is to organise the world around us, whether we do this organising and classifying in school or in society more generally. A key sociological idea is that schools are one of the key sites of social reproduction; hence, the use of class as an organising principle in school and society is not at all accidental. Neither is the fact that it remains largely hidden, or at best misrepresented in various ways.

Attainment and class

In an earlier study of GCSE mathematics attainment across the Midlands of England by Andy (Noyes, 2009, p. 177), the relationship between the level of income deprivation and attainment became clear (Table 4.1).

Students from the households in the lowest quintile of IDACI scores (that is the least deprived areas) were over twice as likely to achieve a grade C in GCSE than those in the most deprived fifth of households. This grade C is critical for accessing many education, employment and life opportunities. Students from the least deprived homes were over *five* times as likely to get A*/A grade (now grades 7–9) than those in the most deprived households. These grades are the desired prerequisite in most schools/colleges for progression to advanced level mathematics (see Chapter 21.

When this attainment pattern is combined with the fact that low levels of numeracy have been shown to be the strongest predictor of unemployment (Bynner and Parsons, 1997), and that those who complete an A-level in mathematics are likely to earn more in the future (Wolf, 2002; Adkins and Noyes, 2016), there is a convincing argument that the rankings and classifications undertaken through school mathematics have a great influence on organising social classifications for the future – possibly more so than all school subjects. Pierre Bourdieu puts it quite starkly:

> Often with a psychological brutality that nothing can attenuate, the school institution lays down its final judgements and its verdicts, from which there is no appeal, ranking all students in a unique hierarchy of all forms of excellence, nowadays dominated by a single discipline, mathematics. (Bourdieu, 1998, p. 28)

Table 4.1 GCSE mathematics grade and income deprivation (cumulative percentages)

GCSE mathematics grade	IDACI quintile				
	1 (least deprived)	2	3	4	*5* (most deprived)
A*	5.7%	3.8	2.8	1.7	0.8
A or above	18.9	14.1	10.5	6.6	3.8
B or above	42.5	34.3	27.7	19.7	13.2
C or above	68.6	60.3	52.2	41.6	31.8
D or above	83.5	77.1	69.9	59.1	48.6
E or above	92.9	89.5	84.9	76.7	67.9
F or above	97.3	95.6	93.6	89.1	83.3
G or above	98.4	97.7	96.8	94.7	91.9

(Source: Noyes 2009; National Pupil Database.)

In the light of all this, it is really important that teachers of mathematics think about their own roles, and the role of the education system in social classification. So, who gets what in school mathematics in your school, and in your classes?

Virtual school bags

In a study of disadvantaged young people in Adelaide, Pat Thomson (2002) talked about the '*virtual school bag*' to explore how schooling interacts with the *stuff – the 'baggage'* – that young people bring to school. Rarely do teachers of mathematics get to look into these school bags. If we ignore the different contents of these virtual bags and treat all students equally, we give *de facto* support to those who arrive at school with the right kinds of *kit* that is necessary for success in schools. This kit does not just include a pencil, ruler and pen, it also includes ways of thinking, speaking and writing that are common in schools but not common in all kinds of homes.

> *If you are working in a school, identify two contrasting students in your classes and find out as much as you can about them. If you have access to their postcode use the Department for Education (DfE) site to identify their IDACI measure.*

In a study of two very different children (Caitlin and Cory) attending the same school (Jorgensen, Gates and Roper, 2014), differing learning trajectories in mathematics resulted from the influences of family culture and linguistic capital as well as the attainment group that they were taught in; Caitlin was in the top group, Cory in the lowest. Analysis and experience in schools suggests it is very unlikely that either of them will change group even at an early stage of their secondary education, as this grouping seems in many ways to be a product of much more than mathematical knowledge (see Chapter 5).

> *In your experience, how often do setting decisions get changed and students move between sets? What are the implications for students and teacher?*

Both students lived with their mothers. Caitlin lived in an affluent area, she used similar language and had similar values to her teachers. Her parents have endowed their daughter with much social, cultural and linguistic capital. In the educational field, she has distinct advantages, her capital earns her an enhanced reputation, a comfortable position in the highest set and high attainment.

Cory's progression was not so smooth and he did not achieve the same degree of academic success as Caitlin. Cory and the school system did not fit together as naturally as Caitlin and school seem to. Cory's view of education was narrower than Caitlin's; for him the purpose of school is purely functional and looks at individual skills and knowledge as opposed to the value of an all-round education. This agrees with Andy's findings that "the economically and culturally more well-endowed make the most of moving school" (Noyes, 2006, p. 43).

> *How are students' backgrounds and prior experience integrated into curricular and pedagogic decisions in classrooms where you have taught and learned maths?*

One of the ways in which 'class' works in schools is through language, and a number of researchers have explored how language helps in the classificatory and discriminatory practices of school mathematics. Robyn Zevenbergen (2001) highlights the fact that school language is middle class and therefore presents an obstacle to working-class children who may not have the dispositions tacitly required by schools. This means that those children without the same language competence are disadvantaged in the classroom.

How we organise learners

Consider the issue of ability grouping (part of the 'Ability thinking' discussed by Mark Boylan and Hilary Povey in Chapter 5). It is taken as a given in the United Kingdom that for mathematics we must place students in ability groups. Indeed, it is difficult to find schools in which this has not been the accepted practice for years. By contrast, such an approach is uncommon across Scandinavia. Indeed, it is illegal to set by ability in Finland, Denmark and Norway to name just three countries. The PISA (Programme for International Student Assessment) data highlights how countries with a less differentiated attainment range do better in those tests (OECD, 2010). In addition, setting by ability is recognised as discriminatory:

> Early student selection has a negative impact on students assigned to lower tracks, without raising the performance of the whole student population. In addition, selection exacerbates inequities since students from disadvantaged backgrounds are more likely to be placed in the least academically oriented tracks or groups. (OECD, 2012, p. 56)

So why is ability grouping illegal in Finland, Norway, Denmark and other countries? If ability grouping is so good that it is just impossible for most UK mathematics teachers to even conceptualise what teaching would be like without it, why has Finland come top in international comparisons (OECD, 2004). In Finland, low attainers did better than their compatriots in the United Kingdom and the gap between lower and higher attainers was lower than elsewhere.

The challenge is to try and engage young people more effectively with mathematics rather than focus on structural organisational principles. However, it is not just a professional matter, it is a deeply political and ideological one (Gates, 2006). It is also dependent upon the value that young people place on the mathematics that they encounter.

Karen Pellino (2007) argues that "the social world of school operates by different rules or norms than the social world these children live in" by drawing our attention to some of the characteristics of children in poverty. She found they experience high-mobility, hunger, repeated failure, low expectations, undeveloped language, clinical depression, poor health, emotional insecurity, low self-esteem, poor relationships, difficult home environment and a focus on survival.

Socio-economic disadvantage may have a direct influence on children's development, for example through limited material resources and an increased risk of a range of health and developmental problems, and an indirect influence through parental education, expectations and aspirations. Schools favour middle-class attitudes and expectations – which is why working-class students often get into trouble. Working-class students are too often defined by what they are not or do not have: they have no motivation, have low ability, low aspirations, parents who are not interested.

How will you teach?

The thing about social classification is that it goes on all around us all of the time – quietly and powerfully – and we are both the subjects of and agents of this classificatory social world.

Since we wrote the first edition of this chapter in 2013 the world has changed; populism is on the rise and concerns abound regarding 'fake news'; in 2016 the United Kingdom voted to leave the European Union, in part because of incorrect views about immigrations and globalisation; and Donald Trump was elected President of the United States amid varied claims of misogyny, denial of climate change and so on. In Brazil in 2018 the right-wing Jair Bolsonaro, a vocal opponent of same-sex marriage and homosexuality, abortion, affirmative action and drug liberalisation, was elected President. More generally, at the time of writing Nationalism and Neo-fascism are on the rise across Europe. To date, these discourses have been framing the worlds of the many young people in our classrooms and so the ability to think critically about the often hidden social forces in our societies that we wrote about back in 2013 (about social class) is now more urgent than ever before.

However, taking action to ameliorate the experience of working-class learners and communities is not an act of charity, it is a political act. When teachers endeavour to enhance the achievement of pupils bought up in disadvantaged communities, they must, of necessity, ask difficult questions about how those who have benefitted from an education system that tends to reproduce social privilege then in turn influence that society and its education system. Education is essentially political as reflected in the following two excerpts.

Consider the 'research report' seductively titled "*The achievement-wellbeing trade-off in education*" (Sahlgren, 2018) by the Centre for Education Economics (we leave the reader to investigate the political position and associations of CfEE[1]). The message of this report is that educationalists (termed "progressives" by Sahlgren) have for years been working under the fundamental yet misguided assumption of progressive educational theory that we should care for young people's well-being. Those of us who might be "progressive", he claims, can only conceive of genuine learning taking place when pupils are enjoying the expedience and are energised by it; anything else is seen by us as "*inadequate*". For Sahlgren, "progressive theory"

> has therefore come to highlight the relationship between pupil-led learning, enjoyment, and performance as a virtuous circle. Yet little rigorous evidence has been presented in favour of this assumption. Indeed, the paper presents evidence showing to the contrary that effective learning is often not enjoyable. (Sahlgren, 2018, p. 1)

Sahlgren even suggests that such strategies as homework and "*school competition*" (sic) are built fundamentally on a trade-off between achievement and happiness. In contrast to notions of competition and extra homework (which has been shown to benefit the middle classes who have the social and cultural resources to make the most of schooling outside of school), the OECD report on *Equity in Education: Breaking Down Barriers to Social Mobility* sets out a more inclusive vision for

> ... developing teachers' capacity to identify students' needs and to manage diversity in classrooms, to build strong links with parents, and to encourage parents to be more involved in their child's education. Teachers can also foster students' well-being and create a positive learning environment for all students by emphasising the importance of persistence, investing effort and using appropriate learning strategies, and by encouraging students to support each other, such as through peer-mentoring programmes. Clearly, the most impressive outcome of world-class school systems is that they deliver high-quality education across the entire school system so that every student benefits from excellent teaching. Achieving greater equity in education is not only a social-justice imperative, it is also a way to use resources more efficiently, and to increase the supply of knowledge and skills that fuel economic growth and promote social cohesion. Not least, how we treat the most vulnerable students shows who we are as a society. (OECD, 2018, p. 3)

You will need to investigate these positions further and reflect on why it is that one of these positions resonates more than the other.

The challenge we want to give you is to recognise the part that you play, often unwittingly, and to consider what might be done in response. So, in this final section we invite those of you who are teachers or student teachers to think of the school in which you are teaching or aspire to teach. What it is like? How similar or dissimilar is it than the school(s) you yourself went to? Andy's study of student teachers' decisions about their first teaching posts (Noyes, 2008) highlights the tendency for teachers to take up their first post in a school similar to the one that they themselves attended. Who then will teach in the schools in more deprived areas? It appears the answer to that question is, whoever the school can get. With increasing shortages of mathematics teachers, schools are forced to take drastic action, which results in those pupils, who this chapter has been focusing on, often getting taught by the less experienced and mathematically qualified teachers, especially since the more experienced teaches will invariably be allocated to those year groups (KS4 and 5) following exam courses:

> If maths teaching and learning is not as engaging or tuned to individual needs as might be desired there are significant risks of adverse effects on pupil outcomes and progression in those schools struggling to allocate specialist or experienced teachers for younger year groups. (Allen and Simms, 2018, p. 5)

This "double bind" is felt particularity acutely because it is at KS3 that pupil attitudes towards mathematics are forming. So how might we make maths teaching and learning as *"engaging or tuned to individual needs as might be desired"*? Especially for those young people who lead difficult and challenging lives? Our experience over many years of teaching mathematics in schools, and of reading and researching around the subject (see Perry and Francis, 2010), suggests the following might be a good place to start to raise the attainment of those more economically and culturally disadvantaged young people:

- Encourage working-class young people to feel engaged in the mathematics curriculum and to feel it has a purpose.
- Find something out about vocational transition routes and pay attention to alternatives in your examples.
- Focus on what students know and can do rather than on what they don't know and cannot do.
- Engender positive, respectful social and pedagogic relationships to explicitly foster self-esteem and resilience in working with mathematics.
- Treat low-SES students to the same high expectations, with a demanding and rigorous mathematics curriculum that expects all students to succeed and understand.
- Create and use meaningful tasks involving inquiry and cooperative learning, where low-SES learners have some control and responsibility.

- Recognise and embrace the diversity in the student body, valuing the talents and abilities of low-SES learners, encompassing a respect for different life worlds and their contributions to mathematics.
- Get to know the families and provide differentiated support.

Those final two points have been stressed by the Organisation for European Cooperation and Development, (OECD, 2012, p. 142), one of whose recommendations for improving equity in education is *"prioritise linking schools with parents and communities"*. They provide five pages of guidance on how this might be achieved which recognise the responsibility of the school in establishing meaningful mutually respectful two-way channels of communication. School mathematics department has a particular responsibility here, given the importance of parental attitudes towards mathematics.

Perhaps the greatest challenge for all of us is to see the ways in which school tends to reinforce social *class* differences. More specifically, as mathematics teachers, this is to recognise the influence that SES and poverty has on all aspects of teaching and learning mathematics. Engaging explicitly with class and social differences in learning has been shown to have the potential to open up greater opportunities for higher order thinking (Jorgensen et al., 2011), and for raising the intellectual quality of student cognition (Kitchen et al., 2007). *Class*, in some guise or another, is always a latent variable whose invisibility obscures possibilities for action. We need to not only talk about, but do something about, class.

> Studies have shown that poverty has a stronger influence on achievement than instructional quality, leading to a policy imperative that if we want all pupils to do well "minimizing social inequities must be a fundamental component of education policy". (Georges, 2009)

Note

1 The *Centre for Education Economics* (CfEE) rebranded itself from *the Centre for the Study of Market Reform of Education* (CMRE), an organisation that lobbied for profit-making schools, and greater private sector involvement in education. It has a 'collaborative relationship' with the Institute of Economic Affairs, and the Adam Smith Institute.

Further reading

Boaler, J. (2009). *The Elephant in the Classroom*. London: Souvenir Press. In this book Jo Boaler talks about some of the more enduring problems of mathematics teaching and how to acknowledge and use support from home to make mathematics more exciting.

Noyes, A. (2007). Mathematical marginalisation and meritocracy: Inequity in an English classroom. In B. Sriraman (Ed.), *International Perspectives on Social Justice in Mathematics Education*. Missoula, MT: University of Montana Press. This book chapter presents a detailed account of how two 11-year-olds (Stacey and Edward) experience mathematics together in the same class when they are socially very distant from one another. Their mathematical trajectories are about to diverge quite dramatically and the roots of this divergence can be traced to their social backgrounds and the values and dispositions that have been acquired there.

References

Adkins, M., & Noyes, A. (2016). Reassessing the economic value of advanced level mathematics. *British Educational Research Journal*, *42*(1), 93–116.

Allen, B., & Simms, S. (2018). *How do shortages of maths teachers affect the within-school allocation of maths teachers to pupils?* London: Nuffield Foundation. http://www.nuffieldfoundation.org/reports-and-briefing-papers

Bourdieu, P. (1986). The forms of capital. In J. G. Richardson (Ed.), *Handbook of theory and research for the sociology of education*. New York: Greenwood Press.

Bourdieu, P. (1998). *Practical reason*. Cambridge: Polity Press.

Bynner, J., & Parsons, S. (1997). *Does numeracy matter? Evidence from the national child development study on the impact of poor numeracy on adult life*. London: Basic Skills Agency.

Connolly, P. (2006). The effects of social class and ethnicity on gender differences in GCSE attainment: A secondary analysis of the youth Cohort study of England and Wales 1997-2001. *British Educational Research Journal*, *32*(1), 3–21.

Gates, P. (2006). Going beyond belief systems: Exploring a model for the social influence on mathematics teacher beliefs. *Educational Studies in Mathematics*, *63*(5), 347–369.

Georges, A. (2009). Relation of instruction and poverty to mathematics achievement gains during Kindergarten. *Teachers College Record*, *111*(9), 2148–2178.

Goodman, A., & Gregg, P. (2010). *Poorer children's educational attainment: How important are attitudes and behaviour?* New York: Joseph Rowntree Foundation.

Jorgensen, R., Gates, P., & Roper, V. (2014). Structural exclusion through school mathematics: Using Bourdieu to understand mathematics a social practice. *Educational Studies in Mathematics*, *87*, 221–239. doi: 10.1007/s10649-013-9468-4.

Jorgensen, R., Sullivan, P., Grootenboer, P., Neische, R., Lerman, S., & Boaler, J. (2011). *Maths in the Kimberley. Reforming mathematics education in remote indigenous communities*. Brisbane: Griffith University.

Kitchen, R., DePree, J., Celedón-Pattichis, S., & Brinkerhoff, J. (2007). *Mathematics education at highly effective schools that serve the poor: Strategies for change*. New Jersey: Lawrence Erlbaum.

Lubienski, S. (2002). Research, reform, and equity in U.S. mathematics education. *Mathematical Thinking and Learning*, *4*(2–3), 103–125.

Noyes, A. (2003). Moving schools and social relocation. *International Studies in Sociology of Education*, *13*(3), 261–280.

Noyes, A. (2006). School transfer and the diffraction of learning trajectories. *Research Papers in Education*, *21*(1), 43–62.

Noyes, A (2008). Choosing teachers: Exploring agency and structure in the distribution of newly qualified teachers. *Teaching and Teacher Education*, *24*(3), 674–683.

Noyes, A. (2009). Exploring social patterns of participation in university-entrance level mathematics in England. *Research in Mathematics Education*, *11*(2), 167–183.

Organisation for Economic Cooperation and Development (OECD). (2004). *Learning for tomorrow's world: First results from PISA 2003*. Paris: OECD Publishing.

Organisation for Economic Cooperation and Development (OECD). (2010). *PISA 2009 results: What students know and can do: Student performance in reading, mathematics and science* (Vol. I). Paris: OECD Publishing.

Organisation for Economic Cooperation and Development (OECD). (2012). *Equity and quality in education: Supporting disadvantaged students and schools.* Paris: OECD Publishing. http://dx.doi.org/10.1787/9789264130852-en

Organisation for Economic Cooperation and Development (OECD) (2018). *Equity in education: Breaking down barriers to social mobility.* Paris: PISA, OECD Publishing. https://doi.org/10.1787/9789264073234-en

Pellino, K. (2007). The Effects of Poverty on Teaching and Learning. http://www.teach-nology.com/tutorials/teaching/poverty/print.htm

Perry, E., & Francis, B. (2010). *The social class gap for educational achievement: A review of the literature.* London: RSA.

Sahlgren, G. H. (2018). *The achievement-wellbeing trade-off in education,* Research Report 14. London: Centre for Educational Economics.

Thomson, P. (2002). *Schooling the Rustbelt kids. Making the difference in changing times.* Stoke-on-Trent: Trentham.

Whitham, G. (2012). *Child poverty in 2012. It shouldn't happen here.* Manchester: Save the Children.

Wolf, A. (2002). *Does education matter? Myths about education and economic growth.* London: Penguin.

Zevenbergen, R. (2001). Language, social class and underachievement in school mathematics. In P. Gates (Ed.), *Issues in mathematics teaching.* London: RoutledgeFalmer.

Chapter 5

Ability thinking

Mark Boylan and Hilary Povey

Introduction

> *There are many words and phrases used in schools by teachers and students that refer to or describe mathematical 'ability'.*
> *Make a list of words that you have used or heard others use. If you are working or placed in a school you might keep a record of the different ways teachers and students use ability and other labels.*
> *Which of the words on your list are useful and helpful for teachers and learners and which do you think are unhelpful and damaging?*

This chapter is about an important aspect of the way people in the United Kingdom and in some other countries think about how mathematics should be taught and learnt. We call this 'ability thinking' or more properly 'fixed-ability thinking'. Many people believe that each person has a particular level of mathematical ability that is relatively stable or fixed. Mathematical ability, on this view, is an entity that helps to determine how much mathematics an individual can learn and how fast they can do this. It is seen as determining and so predicting future attainment. It is also claimed that learners with similar levels of attainment and so, it is assumed, ability are best taught together. This idea is the basis for either setting or banding of learners in secondary schools in the United Kingdom (Francis et al., 2017) and in primary schools either the use of within class ability grouping or setting. These grouping practices are outcomes of fixed-ability thinking and also help to produce it because they shape how we think about our own and others' capacity to learn mathematics.

Much of our discussion in this chapter is about setting and grouping as these are the clearest manifestations of ideas of ability and symbolise this way of thinking. However, the lens of ability influences everyday interactions between teachers and learners and the way learners relate to each other. It is the dominant way that teachers, children, parents and policymakers think about attainment in mathematics. It is so dominant that it is often taken for granted as obviously true. Because of this it has rarely been debated, even though a recent international study by the Organisation for Economic Cooperation and Development (OECD) concluded that setting students should be avoided at least until upper secondary education as it has negative effects on overall attainment and is unfair (OECD, 2012). However, recent interest in East Asian approaches to teaching mathematics (Boylan et al., 2017), often referred to under the banner of 'mastery', has led to some signs that there is potential for change, in primary schools at least. For secondary schools, there are signs that a shift in thinking might be beginning to occur, at least for some teachers (see, for example, the network Mixed Attainment Maths at https://www.mixedattainmentmaths.com).

Ability thinking

Consider this statement: Your mathematical ability is something about you that you cannot change very much. How far do you agree?

If you broadly agree with the above statement it is likely that you have an entity or fixed view of mathematical ability. You are likely to think that while people can learn more mathematics, each person has an underlying level of mathematical ability which is the main factor in determining, and so is predictive of, future attainment. It is not surprising if you believe this. It is probably shared by the majority of mathematics teachers in the United Kingdom. If educated here, your own experience of being taught in mathematical sets and being labelled by ability is likely to have shaped your beliefs. Further, evidence from schools appears to support this view. After all, some students do know more mathematics than peers of the same age and do seem to understand new mathematical ideas more quickly.

However, the statistical basis for the fixed view of mathematics ability is fundamentally flawed (Gould, 1981). Success in tests that purport to measure innate mathematical ability is not independent of cultural knowledge or formal and informal education. With practice it is possible for people to increase their test scores which should not happen if the tests were measuring something fixed. Recent studies have also shown a link between intelligence test outcomes and motivation. If you believe that success in a test will lead to a reward you tend to do better (BBC, 2011).

Ability thinking also supposes that mathematical ability is a single entity that is generally disconnected from other human capacities. However, mathematics is much more diverse than the content that is included on tests of mathematical ability. For example, research shows that the depth of imaginative play young children engage in and their creativity is a good indicator of later mathematical attainment (Hanline et al., 2008). The current curriculum has tended to be shaped by what can be easily tested rather than reflecting the diverse ways that mathematics is used in society or important aspects of mathematical activity. Ability thinking entails and is supported by a narrow view of what mathematics is that can exclude these other aspects of thinking mathematically including problem-solving, communicating about mathematics and collaborating with others.

Mathematical labels such as high or low ability are used to predict future attainment outcomes. However, it has long been established that students will tend to fulfil the expectations that teachers and the education system place on them (Rosenthal & Jacobsen, 1968/2003). Ability labels tend to lead to a series of self-fulfilling prophecies, lowering expectations of teachers and students as to what is possible. They tend to narrow and restrict learning objectives. By questioning the idea of mathematical ability, we are not suggesting that there are not differences in people's capacity to do mathematics or to learn mathematics. Clearly, learners are not the same and it is important that teachers understand these differences to inform their teaching. However, we do not believe that these differences are fixed, unchanging and context free. Further, ability thinking can get in the way of understanding and appreciating these differences as it can lead to 'seeing and teaching the label' rather than the student.

Setting and attainment

Consider the following possible purposes a mathematics teacher might have:

- *to enable students to have mathematical skills to be active citizens;*
- *to maximise the highest attainment possible for the highest attaining individuals;*
- *to maximise the number of passes in the school-leaving assessment;*
- *to promote enjoyment of mathematics;*
- *to develop problem-solving skills;*
- *to ensure all students have skills needed for daily life;*
- *to maximise the highest possible attainment for the lowest attaining individuals;*
- *to promote the social cohesion of the classroom.*

Which of these purposes do you think are the most important and which the least important and why?
What tensions might exist between these different purposes?
How might setting in mathematics influence or impact on achieving these purposes?

The most visible outcome of ability thinking in secondary schools is teaching students in sets. Setting has been the dominant form of organisation for mathematics lessons in most secondary schools in the United Kingdom for a long time.

In primary schools it has been more common to place students within the same class in small groups that are seen as having the same ability for mathematics lessons, but many primary schools, especially the larger ones, are now adopting setting practices. In response to the pressure to 'raise standards' and official government encouragement for these approaches, since the start of the century these practices have become even more embedded and accepted in England (Ofsted, 2008). Indeed, in one extreme example students were required to wear different coloured ties to indicate their different perceived levels of attainment (David, 2011).

Although ability grouping and thinking is the norm in England, there are other countries that do not organise mathematics learning in this way. Attainment in England is lower than in those countries that do not segregate learners. Over the last 20 years, comparing mathematics education internationally has become a 'hot topic' for politicians and journalists, as well as mathematics educators, and it is important to be cautious about drawing conclusions (see Chapter 1 of this book). Politicians' declarations that England has gone down the international league tables do not entirely stand up when these studies are critically examined. The actual differences in attainment between all prosperous and relatively industrialised countries in mathematics as measured by international comparison surveys TIMSS (Trends in International Mathematics and Science Study) and PISA (Programme for International Student Assessment) are relatively small (Askew et al., 2010). Most learners in most of these countries have quite similar levels of attainment. The reasons for the differences that do exist between them are complex and multiple and so it is possible to find evidence from international comparisons to support a variety of views on setting. However, no high-performing country groups students by ability in mathematics in the rigid and fine ranked way we often do in England. The jurisdictions that are most successful, such as Finland and Shanghai, generally teach mathematics in all-attainment groups and this is generally true of highly ranked European countries. Teachers in these other countries are experienced in teaching all-attainment groups. Further, they will generally have experienced this way of learning in their own education, and importantly their beliefs about learning mathematics are not constricted by ability thinking. In the United Kingdom all-attainment grouping in mathematics has often been put into practice in a hostile policy context, by teachers with little support from initial teacher education or continuing professional development, and where the assessment regime is based on and backs up ability thinking.

Given this we might expect that in the United Kingdom we would find that setting leads to higher outcomes than all-attainment teaching. However, comparisons of different forms of grouping within the United Kingdom also show that grouping by perceived ability does not generally raise attainment when compared with alternatives. The evidence from various studies is somewhat contradictory due, perhaps, to the effects of other features associated with setting such as different curricula and teaching practices. Some studies have shown that no groups of students benefit from setting or tracking in terms of attainment (for example, Boaler, 1997). Other studies have shown that those who are highest attainment on entry to secondary school may get some limited benefit in terms of attainment outcomes, but that lowest attaining students suffer and do less well when segregated (Ireson & Hallam, 2001). Once placed in a lower set, students usually suffer from lower expectations and a restricted curriculum and may be given less qualified or experienced teachers. Students with very similar levels of attainment when placed in different sets have very different outcomes and in mathematics this can be as much as a GCSE (General Certificate of Secondary Education) grade (Wiliam & Bartholomew, 2004).

Setting practices and teaching

> *Investigate how individuals are allocated to particular sets or groups in mathematics and their educational experience in those sets.*
> *You might reflect on your own experience as well as talk to other people about theirs. If you always were in one type of set, then it is valuable to talk to people who were in different types of grouping.*
> *If you're currently working or placed in a school enquire into the process by which students are placed in sets. What influences those decisions?*

Setting practices are deeply inequitable. Some gain at the expense of others and often the ones who appear to do well out of setting tend to be students who are already advantaged. Teacher beliefs about students rather than attainment evidence can be significant in deciding on sets. Such perceptions can be influenced by cultural stereotypes. This may explain why, for example, a lower proportion of African-Caribbean students are entered for the higher mathematics tier than would be expected on the basis of their prior attainment (Strand, 2011). Because movement between sets is rare (Hart et al., 2004) once allocated to a particular set, educational opportunities may be curtailed for the rest of the student's schooling. Students from groups who experience social and economic disadvantage are more likely to be found in the lower sets (Wiliam and Bartholomew, 2004) as are girls (Brown et al., 2008). Our view, and one we hope you would share, is that mathematics teachers have a responsibility to support all students to achieve mathematically and to develop a positive relationship with the subject.

When students are taught in sets, few students receive an appropriate level of challenge. It is all too easy to teach a class in which the range of attainment is narrowed as if the attainment, motivation and disposition of all students in the class is the same. In top sets the usual assumption is that learners benefit from or need a fast pace and instrumental proficiency even though evidence suggests that many learners, and in particular girls, are alienated in this environment (Boaler et al., 2000). Further, such practices appear to put learners off studying mathematics once the subject becomes optional (Brown et al., 2008). Offering those with the highest previous attainment or with a particular interest or disposition for mathematics, a diet of mathematics in pre-digested bit-sized pieces 'delivered' at pace may also leave them unchallenged.

Those in lower sets in secondary schools will often only be offered material that they have previously encountered and so meet a narrow and restricted curriculum (Watson & De Geest, 2005). Through adherence by teachers and schools to a simplistic theory of learning styles, they may be labelled kinaesthetic and so be required to use practical equipment even when it does not support mathematical learning (Marks, 2014). At the same time, students in high sets may not be offered the opportunity to develop their thinking through engaging with manipulatives, physical models or embodied learning that can stretch understanding and provoke debate about the meaning of mathematical concepts. As discussed in Chapter 4, there appears to be a link to the type of curriculum and learning experiences that are offered, and the patterns of social class background found in different types of set. Groups in which working-class students are more likely to be found are offered a more 'manual' curriculum.

Ability mindsets

Setting and the ability thinking that supports it is unjust and damaging in other ways. It not only creates barriers to attainment – it also can have profound impacts on learners' beliefs about themselves and their relationship to mathematics. There is now extensive evidence of the ways in which children, including from young ages, are highly aware of their relative position in the class or year group (for example, Hodgen & Marks, 2009). The process of measuring and being measured affects how children see themselves and others. For some, including those who appear to gain by being labelled clever or 'top set', it can lead to profound anxiety (Boaler et al., 2000). Mathematics comes to be seen as an elitist activity that only some can do (Nardi & Steward, 2003). One understandable response by teachers of previously low-attaining students is to try to further simplify or reduce the challenge in mathematics – to try to make mathematics easy. Unfortunately, this is counterproductive as it makes learners over reliant on teachers doing the mathematical thinking on their behalf, robs the mathematics studied of meaning and purpose thus making it harder to learn, and makes students unwilling to tackle questions or topics that appear difficult when first encountered, to engage in problem-solving or to apply mathematics in unfamiliar contexts.

The effect on identities lasts beyond compulsory mathematics education. Mathematical anxiety and shame experienced at school can still be felt in adulthood (Bibby, 2002). Boaler (1997) conducted a study in the 1990s of the experience of school mathematics in two schools similar in terms of attainment and socio-economic profiles but which had different approaches to teaching mathematics. In one, mathematics teaching focused on a problem-solving curriculum and students worked in all-attainment groupings. This approach will be discussed in more detail in Chapter 6. In the other school students learnt through a more traditional approach and learning took place in sets. When she later interviewed participants from her original study as adults, she found that those who had learnt mathematics in all-attainment classrooms were more likely to be working in higher paid and more highly skilled occupations. She concludes that setting can limit the aspirations of those who are placed in lower sets. One of her interviewees who had experienced setting reflected on the effects on his peers:

> You're putting this psychological prison around them .... It kind of just breaks all their ambition ... It's quite sad that there's kids there that could potentially be very, very smart and benefit us in so many ways, but it's just kind of broken down from a young age. So that's why I dislike the set system so much – because I think it almost formally labels kids as stupid. (Boaler, 2005, p. 142)

We believe it is not only those who find themselves in lower sets who may experience psychological prisons. There is evidence that not just setting but ability thinking itself damages all learners.

Carol Dweck (2006) and colleagues have done extensive research into the way peoples' self-theories or 'mindsets' about ability influence their achievements. She identifies two contrasting theories or beliefs. One is to see intelligence as 'malleable' or changeable. Learners with this incremental view tend to stick at challenges. They see effort as the key to success. The other theory is at the heart of what we call ability thinking. Here intelligence or ability is seen as an entity and is fixed. The consequence of this mindset when met with challenge or difficulty is often to give up due to a belief that ability equates to being able to do a task straightaway. If the task is challenging, then this, it is supposed, means that the task is beyond their ability. Success for the entity theorists should be effortless and there is little point trying. Carol Dweck has found that learners with the same level of initial attainment given the same learning opportunities but with different mindsets have different outcomes. Those with a fixed view of ability tend to do worse.

Dweck's research is able to explain why, for example, even those who go on to achieve highly in mathematics may still feel insecure about their competence or mathematical identity (Black et al., 2009). We have a culture in school mathematics where if someone is placed in the top set through their effort they are not seen as being as 'bright' as others; achievement in mathematics is supposed to be effortless, thus reinforcing entity theories. Most teachers, of course, encourage their students to try hard and not to give up when meeting challenges. However, this encouragement cannot, on its own, develop or sustain an incremental view if the language of the classroom, the emphasis on measurement, the pedagogy, curriculum and the experience of setting all assert a fixed view of ability. Whatever the form of classroom organisation, often the most significant lesson learnt by students is that in mathematics what counts and is valued is speed, competition and the amount 'covered'.

How far does Carol Dweck's research reflect your own experience or that of people you know?
What are the implications of Dweck's research for how mathematics should be taught and organised in schools?

Alternative mindsets

In this chapter we have discussed the negative effects of the setting practices that flow from ability thinking. However, adopting all-attainment groupings will not by itself create inclusive classrooms where the attainment of all can be fostered. The negative consequences of ability thinking can and do happen in mixed ability classes as well, if the ability mindset is the way teachers and learners are thinking about learning mathematics.

Fortunately, there are other ways to think about mathematical capacity and learning than 'ability thinking'. We have discussed Carol Dweck's concept of malleability emphasising that human cognitive and social capacities are not fixed. Susan Hart and colleagues propose a similar concept of 'transformability' that focuses on the potential for change (Hart et al., 2004). There are many ways in which classroom mathematics can be taught based on the principle of transformability and Hilary discusses a number of these in Chapter 6 of this book.

However it may not be the teaching practices, classroom organisation or curriculum that are most important in supporting success for all learners, but rather the beliefs of teachers and so of learners themselves. We noted above that there are many countries which do not think about mathematical capacities and learning in terms of ability and who successfully support high attainment for the majority. These countries differ in their approaches to teaching mathematics, but what they have in common are:

- high expectations of all students,
- allowing all to access a challenging curriculum,
- valuing current effort rather than previous attainment,
- striving for the achievement of all rather than of a few.

These countries demonstrate what is possible on a national scale. Obviously, individual teachers cannot reproduce their pedagogical approaches or the culture that supports them. However, we can, as teachers, change our own mindsets and strive to teach our students rather than teaching to labels. When we do this remarkable and surprising outcomes are possible (for example, Davis et al., 2008).

Watson & De Geest (2005) point to what is possible for whole classes of what they describe as previously low-attaining students. They identify the principles that underlay the practice of teachers who were particularly successful with such students in spite of the restriction of rigid curricula or prescribed types of lessons. These principles include access to a broad mathematics curriculum; supporting students to develop reasoning and thinking and to become mathematical learners; supporting students' self-esteem through mathematics; giving students freedom to exercise rights and responsibility; taking into account the power of external measures but not being driven by them; and providing extended thinking time and extended tasks. It is principles rather than practices, they argue, that are key. These principles also provide their own challenge to the restrictions generated by ability thinking. When low-attaining, demoralised students are given "more choice, freedom, challenge, responsibility and time" (Watson & De Geest, 2005, p. 230) they are enabled to succeed.

In the United Kingdom there is general agreement on the need to support more learners to be successful in mathematics and to address the disengagement of many from the subject. In 2014 a new mathematics national curriculum was introduced which recommended that most learners should progress together rather than some being 'accelerated' to study content usually addressed at a later age. Instead different learners' needs should be addressed by deepening of content. With the change in curriculum, national curriculum "levels" were abandoned. Levels and sub-levels were previously used as tools to identify narrow diets of mathematical content for specific groups of learners. The move away from levels has opened up possibilities to debate grouping and ability practices. As noted above interest in East Asian mathematics practices has led to many schools engaging with 'teaching for mastery' to review and change their fixed ability grouping practices (see Mark's Chapter 2 on mastery elsewhere in this volume). In many cases, the change has been structural and organisational without any challenge to fixed-ability thinking. The children are still seen as having different, more or less fixed abilities in mathematics: the "able" are no longer segregated to work on more advanced topics but instead are provided with "deeper" challenges and richer opportunities for mathematical thinking. However, in some schools engaging with East Asian practices, the rethinking has allowed changes in fixed-ability thinking and we see signs that the approach to teaching mathematics supports the idea of universality, with the learning of everyone being of equal importance and with all contributing to the learning environment.

> With ability-based teaching, an ethic of 'differential treatment' applies: differences justify and, in some cases require, different treatment. Transformability emphasises *universal entitlement* rather than differences: *everybody* counts, *everybody's* learning is equally important, *everybody* contributes to the learning environment. And so it follows that teachers work constantly to create – and if necessary invent – approaches that allow everybody without exception, to engage in the activities provided, to have the experience of being excited by learning, to gain something worthwhile, and to feel a sense of safety and belonging. (Dixon et al., 2002, p. 9)

Challenging our own and others' fixed-ability thinking offers the possibility of honouring these entitlements.

64   Mark Boylan and Hilary Povey

Further reading

Hart, S., Dixon, A. Drummond, M. J., & McIntyre, D. (2004). *Learning without limits.* Maidenhead: Open University Press. This book is based on a research project which studies the practices of a group of teachers who teach all-attainment or widely attaining classes. They propose the concept of transformability as an alternative to ability. Chapter 2 – 'What's wrong with ability labelling' – is particularly relevant to the ideas we have presented in this chapter.

Marks, R. (2013, January). "The blue table means you don't have a clue": The persistence of fixed-ability thinking and practices in primary mathematics in English schools. In *Forum: For Promoting 3-19 Comprehensive Education, 55*(1), 31–44. This small-scale study of a single classroom is very moving and seems capable of shifting points of view and interrupting usual modes of thinking.

Wiliam, D., & Bartholomew, H. (2004). It's not which school but which set you're in that matters: The influence of ability grouping practices on student progress in mathematics. *British Educational Research Journal, 30*(3), 279–293. This article provides a summary of key research on setting in mathematics as well as evidence from a study that tracked the progress of 950 students. The study showed how setting can affect attainment and teaching practices.

Watson, A., & De Geest, E. (2005). Principled teaching for deep progress: improving mathematical learning beyond methods and materials. *Educational Studies in Mathematics, 58*(2), 209–234. This article reports on a two year action research project with 10 teachers to improve the achievement of previously low attaining secondary students. A key finding was that effective practices were based on common principles. These principles represent, in our view, an alternative to ability thinking.

References

Askew, M., Hodgen, J., Hossain, S., & Bretscher, N. (2010). *Values and variables: Mathematics education in high performing countries.* London: Nuffield Foundation.

BBC. (2011). IQ tests measure motivation – not just intelligence. Available at: http://www.bbc.co.uk/news/health-13156817.

Bibby, T. (2002). Shame: An emotional response to doing mathematics as an adult and a teacher. *British Educational Research Journal, 28*(5), 705–722.

Black, L. Mendick, H., Rodd, M., Solomon, Y., & Brown, M. (2009). Pain, pleasure and power: Selecting and assessing defended subjects. In L. Black, H. Mendick, & Y. Solomon (Eds.). *Mathematical relationships: Identities and participation.* London: Routledge.

Brown, M., Brown, P., & Bibby, T. (2008). "I would rather die": Reasons given by 16 year olds for not continuing their study of mathematics. *Research in Mathematics Education, 10*(1), 3–18.

Boaler, J. (1997). *Experiencing school mathematics: Teaching styles, sex and setting.* Buckingham: Open University Press.

Boaler, J. (2005). The 'psychological prisons' from which they never escaped: The role of ability grouping in reproducing social class inequalities. *Forum, 47*(2 and 3), 125–134.

Boaler, J., Wiliam, D., & Brown, M. (2000). Students' experiences of ability grouping – disaffection, polarisation and the construction of failure. *British Educational Research Journal, 26*(5), 631–648.

Boylan, M., Wolstenholme, C., & Maxwell, B. (2017). *Evaluation of the mathematics teacher exchange: China-England third interim report*. London: DfE. Available at: https://www.gov.uk/government/uploads/system/uploads/attachment_data/file/666450/MTE_third_interim_report_121217.pdf

David, R. (2011). School colour codes students by ability. *The Guardian*. Available at: http://www.guardian.co.uk/education/2011/jul/25/secondary-school-streaming.

Davis, B., Sumara, D., & Luce Kapler, R. (2008). *Engaging minds: Changing teaching in complex times*. New York: Routledge.

Dixon, A., Drummond, M., Hart, S., & McIntyre, D. (2002). Developing teaching free from ability labelling: Back where we started? *Forum*, *44*(1), 7–11.

Gould, S. (1981). *The mismeasure of man*. London: Penguin.

Dweck, C. (2006). *Mindset*. New York: Random House.

Francis, B., Archer, L., Hodgen, J., Pepper, D., Taylor, B., & Travers, M. C. (2017). Exploring the relative lack of impact of research on 'ability grouping' in England: A discourse analytic account. *Cambridge Journal of Education*, *47*(1), 1–17.

Hanline, M., Milton, S., & Phelps, P. (2008). A longitudinal study exploring the relationship of representational levels of three aspects of preschool sociodramatic play and early academic skills. *Journal of Research in Childhood Education*, *23*(1), 19–28.

Hart, S., Dixon, A. Drummond, M. J., & McIntyre, D. (2004). *Learning without limits*. Maidenhead: Open University Press.

Hodgen, J., & Marks, R. (2009). Mathematical "ability" and identity: A sociocultural perspective on assessment and selection. In L. Black, H. Mendick, & Y. Solomon (Eds.). *Mathematical relationships: Identities and participation*. London: Routledge.

Ireson, J., & Hallam, S. (2001). *Ability grouping in education*. London: Paul Chapman Publishing.

Marks, R. (2014). Educational triage and ability-grouping in primary mathematics: A case-study of the impacts on low-attaining pupils. *Research in Mathematics Education*, *16*(1), 38–53.

Nardi, E., & Steward, S. (2003). Is mathematics T.I.R.E.D? A profile of quiet disaffection in the secondary mathematics classroom. *British Education Research Journal*, *29*(3), 345–367.

Organisation for Economic Cooperation and Development (OECD). (2012). *Equity and quality in education: Supporting disadvantaged students and schools*. Paris: OECD.

Office for Standards in Education (Ofsted) (2008). Mathematics: understanding the score. Available at: http://www.ofsted.gov.uk/resources/mathematics-understanding-score.

Rosenthal, R., & Jacobsen, L. (1968/2003). *Pygmalion in the classroom: teacher expectation and pupil's intellectual development*. Carmarthen: Crown House.

Strand, S. (2011). The White British-Black Caribbean achievement gap: Tests, tiers and teacher expectations. *British Education Research Journal*, *38*(1), 75–102.

Watson, A. and De Geest, E. (2005). Principled teaching for deep progress: Improving mathematical learning beyond methods and materials. *Educational Studies in Mathematics*, *58*(2), 209–234.

Wiliam, D., & Bartholomew, H. (2004). It's not which school but which set you're in that matters: The influence of ability grouping practices on student progress in mathematics. *British Educational Research Journal*, *30*, 279–293.

Chapter 6

Pedagogical possibilities for all-attainment teaching

Hilary Povey

Introduction

Current practices in the teaching of mathematics in secondary schools in the United Kingdom do not promote attainment for all. In 2017 approximately three in every ten students failed to obtain a grade regarded as a pass in mathematics at age 16 (Ofqual, 2017). As previously, "all seemed not too far from well at the top, but stubborn problems remained at the bottom" (Cassen and Kingdon, 2007: i). Despite being among the countries with relatively high average educational achievement, the United Kingdom also has high inequality in achievement and the report shows that low achievement correlates significantly with indictors of disadvantage (see Chapter 4 for further discussion).

The interplay between setting by previous attainment and "ability thinking" is discussed elsewhere in this volume in Chapter 5. There it is argued that setting practices and the "ability thinking" on which such practices are based suppress the achievement of those whose current levels of attainment do not earn them a place in the top set, creating the notorious long tail of underachievement while not enhancing the attainment of those at the "top". Thus, the most significant way to begin working towards high attainment for all is to tackle these two interconnected "common-sense" notions: that ability is a given, fixed characteristic inhering in individuals and that grouping learners on the basis of previous attainment raises achievement.

Recent interest in all-attainment teaching in mathematics is encouraging (for example, https://www.mixedattainmentmaths.com/). Re-organising mathematics classes into all-attainment groups is not on its own enough (Hart et al., 2004) – many mathematics teachers in the United Kingdom who accept the desirability of all-attainment teaching feel ill-prepared for the different pedagogical demands that they judge will be required. This is not surprising:

> the search for pedagogical possibilities only *begins* once we have freed ourselves from deterministic notions about existing patterns and limits of human achievement (original emphasis, Hart, 1998: 160).

In this chapter I offer some models of pedagogical possibilities for all-attainment teaching. Of course, how learners are grouped is not within your gift as an individual teacher in a secondary school, although in some primary schools this may be devolved to the class teacher – I hope some of the insights and descriptions of practice which follow will also be helpful if you reject "ability thinking" but nevertheless find yourself teaching setted groups.

Pedagogy encompasses classroom practices, classroom relationships, philosophical understandings of the nature of mathematics and ethical judgements about your purposes in the teaching and learning of mathematics. Pedagogical stances generate and are generated by the culture of the classroom, in itself dependent upon your attitudes, conceptions, beliefs and views of the world; and, perhaps most importantly, your values.

I begin by rehearsing briefly what is known about the ways in which current practices damage and alienate learners. From the work of Guy Claxton, I derive a framework for a pedagogy for attainment for all, drawing on four case studies from existing research. I conclude by considering the notion of 'transformability'.

What doesn't work that we currently do?

We know a great deal about what *doesn't* work – what doesn't work in terms of motivation and engagement and what doesn't work in terms of pupil learning; both of these are damaging to attainment. In England, the head of Ofsted recently complained that many schools were simply focusing on test scores, producing 'hollow understanding' rather than 'rich and full knowledge' (Sellgren, 2017). Mathematics teaching geared towards producing enhanced pupil test scores leads to a high level of fragmentation in the mathematics presented with procedural approaches to the fore. It is known that such a pedagogy does not create learners who can think mathematically; it also leads to alienation, demotivation and disengagement (Nardi and Steward, 2003). In an extended case study, Jo Boaler describes teachers seeming to fracture mathematics to help their students get answers and she notes that "it was the transmission of closed pieces of knowledge that formed the basis of the students' disaffection, misunderstandings and underachievement" (Boaler, 1997: 145). Meaning-making is ignored and a sense of hopelessness is generated. And, ironically, such practices can undermine test scores.

In a rare case of an attempt to compare directly a traditional and an alternative approach to teaching and learning (Bell, 1994), two parallel classes in the same school with the same teacher were taught fractions using two very different methods: one involved carefully and gradually graded exercises including a large number of examples worked through individually and the other involved the students working in groups at fairly hard challenges involving the production mostly of their own examples. Although the groups performed comparably at the beginning with comparable improvement at the end of the nine lessons, when they were tested again after the summer holiday break the attainment of the graded exercise group had fallen off to a lower level than before the work began, whereas the learning of the other group was well retained. The first class went from being highly motivated to bored and lethargic, whereas the interest and involvement of the 'conflict and investigation' class increased.

Conventional approaches to mathematics teaching in the United Kingdom produce fractured classroom relationships (Angier and Povey, 1999). Teacher-centred, test-dominated practices tend to encourage a competitive atmosphere which many learners find alienating: "the students are unwilling to engage in this hierarchical game" (Nardi and Steward, 2003: 359). Teacher-pupil dialogue comes to be framed as question-response-evaluation exchanges generating passivity and a fear of public and private shame (Boylan, Lawton and Povey, 2001). (See Chapter 11 for an alternative model of teacher-pupil dialogue.)

Activity

Reflect on your own experiences of learning, in and out of school, and your observations of contemporary classrooms. Which aspects of your own and others' experiences have caused underachievement and alienation?

A pedagogical framework for attainment for all

So, we know what doesn't work – but we also know quite a lot about what does work. Guy Claxton (2002) makes use of the notion of 'learning power' to help us understand how we can support young people to become effective learners. 'Learning power' refers to the personal traits, skills and habits of mind that enable a person to engage effectively with the challenge of learning – to be someone who knows what to do when they don't know what to do. Claxton highlights four key aspects of practice to which teachers need to pay attention if they are to succeed in enabling attainment for all.

Activity

According to Claxton (2002: 67), there are specific things of which you need to become aware in order to develop learning power:

- *how you talk to your students about the process of learning, the kinds of questions you encourage them to ask, the kinds of follow-up you expect and the visual images, prompts and records on the classroom walls;*
- *the kinds of formal and informal comments and evaluations you make of students' work and how you respond when they are experiencing difficulty or confusion;*

> - *the kinds of activities and discussions which you initiate and what sense of purpose these engender in the learners;*
> - *and, perhaps above all, how you present yourself as a learner – what kind of model do you offer, for instance, when things are not going according to plan or when a question arises that you have not anticipated.*
>
> *All of these considerations are highly relevant to a mathematics pedagogy for attainment for all. For each, describe a practice that would support the development of learning power.*

I take these aspects as an organising structure for the rest of the chapter, with four specific case studies offering examples of alternative practice drawn from the research literature. I attempt to draw out some of the ways in which they exemplify engagement with these four fundamental concerns.

Spenser – what is explicitly valued and shared with the whole class

Spenser School, situated in an urban area of high deprivation, had a predominantly white working-class intake and a very low level of achievement. The department decided to undertake a radical change in the way that they taught mathematics: they knew that research evidence suggested that all-attainment teaching would support their learners and introduced it into the first two years of secondary school. Many of the ways they changed their thinking and their practice promoted the learning power which is vital to generating attainment for all.

Right from the start, the teachers at Spenser knew they needed their pupils to develop a wide range of ways to work on mathematics to promote their thinking and engagement and to lay down habits for future work. They drew on a wide range of existing resources and evolved curriculum planning based on pairs of teachers preparing resources on a topic including a summary of the main activities, games and ways to begin and end lessons; formative assessment activities and probing questions; keywords and mathematical ideas; and anticipated difficulties and misconceptions. Crucially, they then worked on the mathematics together and discussed the associated pedagogy. They expected to spend time together at the end of the day, being around and sharing ideas. They knew they had to re-educate students to work together, to talk, to take risks and to do mathematics in new ways.

Having decided to work in this way, Spenser became the subject of a research project focused on interventions with previously low-attaining students. These students developed and maintained a positive attitude to mathematics lessons and to their own achievements within them (Watson and de Geest, 2010). In addition, Spenser had a dramatic rise in mathematics results in the high-stakes national test (then taken at age 14 though now abolished) not matched by similar increases elsewhere in the curriculum. As well as the move to all-attainment teaching, two replicable key factors relating to this rise in attainment were identified by the researchers. First, with the first-year students, there was to be a focus solely on mathematical methods of enquiry, returning only later to a programme of specific mathematical topics. Second, the teaching was characterised by listening to the learners, building on their ideas and being explicit about valuing and supporting the development of reasoning. Much of this teaching was by "leading the collective thinking of a class through the orchestration of ideas" (Watson, 2011: 149) and, as the project developed, a sense of zeal "for their students to understand key mathematical ideas" (p. 149). Anne Watson writes: "I am convinced that many learners learnt mathematics during those whole class episodes because of the methods of *knowledgeable mediation* used" (p. 149, emphasis added).

There are two facets to the thinking and practice described here that link in with the first learning power focus: *what the teachers explicitly value and discuss with the whole class*. First, the teachers made direct and repeated reference to what kinds of mental activity were important and relevant to learning mathematics. This included some general effort and study skills but crucially also involved a wide range of specifically mathematical characteristics with which, it was made clear, everyone was expected to be able to engage.

Activity

Some of these specifically mathematical characteristics were:

- *visualising without prompting;*
- *being aware of difference and sameness;*
- *volunteering conjectures;*
- *creating examples to explore ideas;*
- *asking good questions;*
- *being aware some methods are more powerful than others;*
- *asking why and why not;*
- *providing answers that voluntarily include reasons;*
- *and taking time to understand mathematical ideas.*

Which of these mathematical characteristics do you want explicitly to share with learners in your classroom?
Choose one and explain why you value it. What might you do as a teacher to make it happen?

Second, the teachers worked together themselves on the mathematical activities they were planning to use with their students. There was a focus throughout on the mathematics and about how to give all their learners access to key mathematical ideas. This developed the depth of their own personal mathematical knowledge and thus their facility with responding to the mathematical thinking of their students as shared mathematical meanings were negotiated in their classrooms. It enabled them to give public praise for the sort of mathematical thinking they were wanting to encourage in their learners and to notice and reinforce such mental activity whenever it occurred; this in turn enabled all their students to become more effective learners.

Railside – talking to groups and individuals about their learning and achievements

Railside School, situated in the United States, had an ethnic and socially diverse intake and was on the "wrong side of the tracks". The mathematics department developed an effective approach to learning that promoted high achievement for all in absolute terms when compared to other schools and, most significantly, also reduced differences in achievement between learners (Boaler, 2008). Learners from all levels of prior attainment did well and substantially better than would be expected as the norm but without opening up the gap between high and low attainers; no "long tail" was produced, and systematic sites of disadvantage – gender, class and ethnicity – were overcome. The department was committed to all-attainment teaching groups. Pupils' self-respect was developed as was their authority as learners and these qualities supported the growth of what Jo Boaler characterised as 'relational equity' (2008), that is pupils' respect and concern for their peers and for cultural and individual difference. Teacher behaviour which offers respect helps students to develop and enhance their self-image and their own expectations, which in turn enhance the students' academic achievement.

Central to the practices of the Railside teachers was a form of structured group work based on 'complex instruction'. They worked in class with mathematical problems having open and accessible starting points, ones which provided many opportunities for success: there were many more ways to be successful and many more students succeeded (Boaler, 2008). The key characteristics of their approach are they supported students to develop and carry out specific roles when working in groups; affirmed the competence of all and had high expectations of all; developed students' sense of their responsibility for each other's learning through classroom practices and forms of assessment including assessing collaborative outcomes; emphasised that success in mathematics was the product of effort rather than ability and all could succeed; and explicitly outlined the type of learning practices that would help students to learn.

Here I report on the practices of one of those teachers, Ms McClure, who was successful in fostering collaborative interactions within groups that promoted the attainment of all. There is not room in this chapter to share all the useful things that can be learnt from Ms McClure's practices (Staples, 2008); rather, here I attempt to draw out how in particular she built the students' learning power by *how she talked to groups and individuals about their learning and achievements.*

When students were working together in groups, Ms McClure expected any individual group member to be able to report the understandings of the group. If, when quizzed, it became clear that an individual did not fully understand the problem yet, she would leave the group explaining that she would come back, re-stating that she wanted everyone to "have it". She did not describe this initial response as 'incompetent or wrong, but rather as work in progress' and 'expected everyone in the group would understand'; she would comment "not that it's wrong, it's just incomplete", prompting groups to continue their thinking and build on the work they had already done (p. 360). The tasks she chose were "group-worthy" and enabled a variety of approaches and solutions. Thus, she was able to value each group's work and position each solution as "evidence of competence and productive mathematical work" (p. 361). She debriefed both on the mathematics and on the group processes, celebrating "engagement, persistence, and good mathematical thinking" (p. 357) always focusing on the whole group's achievement and the mutual responsibility for each other's learning that the groups had:

> Many of you are really thinking hard about how to approach the problem and coming up with great ideas. I'm a little concerned however that not everyone in the group is together always. Sometimes a group member is being left behind. Groups, be sure everyone understands what's going on. And everyone, be sure you ask questions! (Staples, 2008: 357–358)

Thus, we see that Ms McClure's way of talking to the students about their learning and achievements reflected a commitment to the idea that all students are capable of engaging with mathematics and achieving more, especially those whose current attainment is lower. This enabled them to become powerful learners and produced results for all.

Activity

What do you want to be the key characteristics of how you talk to groups and individuals about their work? And what do you most want to avoid?

Phoenix Park – what activities are selected

Phoenix Park was a school studied by Jo Boaler (1997) in which lower attainers benefited significantly and overall attainment at age 16 outshone a socio-economic comparator which used a traditional approach to teaching mathematics. Again, students at Phoenix Park worked in all-attainment classes. The pupils worked on open-ended projects which they explored using their own ideas and mathematical knowledge.

> You're just set a task and then you go about it … you explore the different things, and they help you in doing that. (Boaler, 1997: 17)

Such projects involved problem posing and problem-solving – this creates a classroom in which it is alright to take risks; where questioning, decision-making and negotiation are the norm, where there is an expectation that all have a contribution to make and no-one is offered a restricted and diminished curriculum. The open curriculum and their all-attainment groupings created "can do" learners who could take their mathematics into their lives. They not only thought that they could use school mathematics in real-world mathematical situations, but also thought that school mathematics had equipped them to tackle real-world problems that were not mathematical. When asked about the role of mathematics, a typical response was:

J: Solve the problems and think about other problems and solve them, problems that aren't connected with maths, think about them.
JB: You think the way you do maths helps you do that?
J: Yes.
JB: Things that aren't to do with maths?
J: It's more the thinking side to sort of look at everything you've got and think about how to solve it. (Jackie, Phoenix Park, Year 10) (p. 100)

As noted in Chapter 5, the sense of self revealed by such responses had a long-term impact, spilling over into their understandings of their life chances and their possible trajectories (Boaler, 2005).

Because the students worked on large problems, activities that were mathematically rich, time and intellectual space were generated within which they could make links both within mathematics and between mathematics and other experiences. Mathematics then had the room to grow as an open and creative subject, not restricted to a rule-bound set of procedures, which allowed students the opportunity to change their view of themselves as learners. We know that students, especially working-class students, prefer informal relationships built on a basis of mutual respect (Povey and Boylan, 1998). In setted classrooms these are typically offered only to top-set pupils and, more generally, less to working-class pupils. At Phoenix Park there is a strong sense that these were offered to all, *growing out of the nature of the mathematical activities taking place* (but see also Chapter 12 on task design).

In both these ways, *the activities that the teachers selected* played a key role in building learning power: those activities could be approached in a variety of ways with a wide range of appropriate tools thus providing opportunities for learners to see themselves as active, as choosing, deciding, producing arguments for and against, assessing validity and generating questions and ideas. This sense of self was instrumental in generating productive relationships between teachers and learners and between learners and achievement.

Activity

Choose three such mathematical activities. For each, list what might be gained from using the activity in your classroom and what difficulties you think you might encounter.

A spacious classroom – how learning is modelled

The last case study involves a spacious classroom in which learning power was built by the way in which *learning was modelled by the teacher*. When describing how she worked with her students, Corinne Angier explained, "I was thinking about the students as being apprenticed as learners of maths and of me being a model learner not a teacher". She regarded it as key that, at least part of the time, the teacher and the students were engaged in the *same* activity, that is learning to be mathematicians. This has a powerful effect on how learners think about themselves and of what they think they are capable. Jere Confrey warns us that if we enter the classroom with arrogance about our own understandings, we risk overpowering those of the children. Rather she urges us to:

> promote the exchange of student methods with mutual tolerance and respect, the children themselves become increasingly confident of their contributions and the system becomes self-reinforcing. In both peer relations and in adult-child interactions, the roles of expert, teacher, learner, and novice, are flexibly drawn. (Confrey, 1995: 41, emphasis added)

When the teacher is, at times, a co-learner, the expected source of mathematical authority – the teacher, the textbook and the answer book making up a united authority which needs no specification or justification (Alro and Skovsmose, 1996: 4) – is unsettled. In Corinne's classroom, there was room for the students to have insights she did not already have as they learnt together:

> She treats you as though you are like ... not just a kid. If you say look this is wrong she'll listen to you. If you challenge her she will try and see it your way. (Donna)
> She doesn't regard herself as higher. (Neil)
> She's not bothered about being proven wrong. Most teachers hate being wrong ... being proven wrong by students. (Neil)
> It's more like a discussion ... you can give answers and say what you think. (Frances) (Angier and Povey, 1999: 157)

And all the students interviewed knew that Corinne found passionate enjoyment in the subject they were studying together:

> She loves doing triangles! (Dan)
> She loves it ... she's right interested in it. (Frances) (Angier and Povey, 1999: 151)

Although they smiled and found this strange, they knew it was a key element in their own learning. By modelling her engagement with the subject as one worthy of study, effort, application and the strive for understanding, she offered both the learners and the subject respect and showed her students what it was to learn.

Activity

What difficulties would you experience in teaching a lesson where you did not expect to know all the outcomes in advance? What are the mathematical benefits and problems of unexpectedness?

Conclusion

I have taken from four case studies, each rich in pedagogical possibilities, specific characteristics related to a framework for attainment for all. What they all have in common is a notion of 'transformability' defined as:

> a firm and unswerving conviction that there is the potential for change in current patterns of achievement and response, that things can change and be changed for the better, sometimes even dramatically, as a result of what happens and what people do in the present. (Hart et al., 2004: 166)

As has been noted, it is the belief that learners *can* change which seems to make the difference. The transformability perspective echoes the concept of "learning how to learn" based on the development of learners' resilience, resourcefulness, reflectiveness and reciprocity (Claxton, 2002). It finds support in the work of Carol Dweck (2006) written about in Chapter 5 which offers an alternative, evidence-based view of human capacity, which has been found to improve motivation and attainment.

This pedagogic approach has three interrelated sets of purposes that can guide us in our practice:

- Intellectual purposes which include ensuring everybody has access to a curriculum that it is relevant and meaningful and that thinking and reasoning are enhanced.
- Social purposes which include a focus on the inclusion of everybody and promoting a sense of belonging and community.
- Affective or emotional purposes which include developing learners' confidence, security and control over their own learning.

We need our classrooms to be places where learners set up productive relationships with themselves as learners and with the processes of coming to know mathematics. Studying closely accounts of what teachers who have achieved this have done is both an inspiration and an effective way for us to learn, helping us to understand what more innovative pedagogical practices are available to us. Crucially, they also help us call into question currently dominant ideas about how to support attainment – setting, testing, targeting, differentiated expectations and so on – thus making a vital contribution to debates about how to enhance long-term attainment by creating learners who both believe in their own capacity to learn and deem it to be worthwhile engaging in doing so.

Further reading

Each of the four case studies referred to in the chapter would repay exploring further. Each of them is accompanied by relevant references and I can think of no better further reading than engaging more deeply with these sites of practice.

Also recommended is *Inclusive Mathematics* by Mike Ollerton and Anne Watson (2001), London, Continuum. It is written by two highly experienced teachers both of whom are deeply committed to attainment for all and is based on the principle that all learners are capable of sophisticated mathematical thought. It presents the tools with which we can work to reach all students of mathematics.

References

Alro, H., & Skovsmose, O. (1996). On the right track. *For the Learning of Mathematics, 16*(1), 2–40.

Angier, C., & Povey, H. (1999). One teacher and a class of school students: Their perception of the culture of their mathematics classroom and its construction. *Educational Review, 51*(2), 147–160.

Bell, A. (1994). Teaching for the test. In M. Selinger (Ed.), *Teaching mathematics*. London: Routledge.

Boaler, J. (1997). *Experiencing school mathematics: Teaching styles, sex and setting.* Buckingham: Open University Press.

Boaler, J. (2005). The 'psychological prisons' from which they never escaped: The role of ability grouping in reproducing social class inequalities. *Forum, 47*(2&3), 125–134.

Boaler, J. (2008). Promoting 'relational equity' and high mathematics achievement through an innovative mixed-ability approach. *British Educational Research Journal, 34*(2), 167–194.

Boylan, M., Lawton, P., & Povey, H. (2001) "'I'd be more likely to talk in class if …": Some students' ideas about strategies to increase mathematical participation in whole class interactions. *Proceedings of 25th PME Conference*, Utrecht, July 2, 201–208.

Cassen, R., & Kingdon, G. (2007). *Tackling low educational achievement.* New York: Joseph Rowntree Foundation. http://www.jrf.org.uk/publications/tackling-low-educational-achievement

Claxton, G. (2002). *Building learning power: Helping young people become better learners.* Bristol: TLO.

Confrey, J. (1995). A theory of intellectual development: part III. *For the Learning of Mathematics, 15*(2), 36–45.

Dweck, S. (2006). *Mindset.* New York: Random House.

Hart, S. (1998). A sorry tail: Ability, pedagogy and educational reform. *British Journal of Educational Studies, 46*(2), 153–168.

Hart, S., Dixon, A., Drummond, M., & McIntyre, D. (2004). *Learning without limits.* Maidenhead: Open University Press.

Nardi, E., & Steward, S. (2003). Is mathematics T.I.R.E.D? A profile of quiet disaffection in the secondary mathematics classroom. *British Education Research Journal, 29*(3), 345–367.

Ofqual. (2017). Guide to GCSE results for England. https://www.gov.uk/government/news/guide-to-gcse-results-for-england-2017

Povey, H., & Boylan, M. (1998). Working class students and the culture of mathematics classrooms in the UK. *Proceedings of 22nd Psychology of Mathematics Education (PME) Conference*, Stellenbosch, July.

Sellgren, K. (2017). Teaching to the test gives 'hollow understanding'. https://www.bbc.co.uk/news/education-41580550

Staples, M. (2008). Promoting student collaboration in a detracked, heterogeneous secondary mathematics classroom. *Journal of Mathematics Teacher Education, 11*, 349–371.

Watson, A. (2011). Mathematics and comprehensive ideals. *Forum, 53*(1), 145–151.

Watson, A., & de Geest (2010). Secondary mathematics departments making autonomous change. In Joubert, M. & Andrews, P. (Eds.). *Proceedings of the British Congress for Mathematics Education*, April 2010.

Chapter 7

Should 'teaching for understanding' be the pinnacle of mathematics education?

Anna Llewellyn

'"Do you understand?" is a frequent question in the classroom. While looking rather innocent, this can be a problematic question in, for instance how valid is the answer? If you ask this to a student and they answer 'yes', what have you learnt? That they are compliant? That they have heard you? Or that they think they understand you? Perhaps the question you are really asking is 'do you understand in the manner that I understand?' or 'do you understand in the manner that I want you to understand?' but of course the student may not always know if they do. Even if you can establish that they have understood in the way you intended, what do you mean by understanding? Do you mean that you want them to understand how to do the work or are you hoping for something else mathematically; a spark that suggests something 'deeper'?

By asking these questions we have begun to problematise the concept of understanding. We have questioned the amount it is used and the way it is used. We have queried what people mean when they use that word; we have even begun to consider the value it has and what it does to the classroom. We have also suggested that language, in general, is not transparent, meaning is subjective and created in context. This is essentially what this chapter is about; I want to question an accepted good of the mathematics classroom – teaching for understanding. One key way in which I do this is to examine the subjectivity of language and how it can create meaning.

Teaching for understanding seems to be viewed as the crème de la crème of mathematics education. Indeed, it features as a topic on most teacher education programmes. But why is this? Do we believe this creates better mathematicians or people, or do we believe this is the correct, and only, way to learn mathematics? If we do suppose these things what does that mean for the classroom? Should we blindly pursue teaching for understanding and assume there are only good consequences for all? My opinion is we should not. Instead we should question the truths we are told and examine what effects they have in the classroom. Specifically, whether they include or exclude people from mathematics. In addition, truths are not absolute, they change over time. For instance, 40 years ago many people would have thought that boys were better than girls at mathematics. Indeed, some people may still do so. How can this idea be damaging?

It could be that teachers holding such beliefs deliberately exclude girls or conversely they may praise girls more as they think they need more encouragement, which could exclude boys.

Another example is the idea/notion that 'girls prefer pink'. This is actually a modern concept that has only been around since the 20th century. But how can it be bad to think that girls prefer pink? Well, what if you are a boy who likes pink, does that mean that there is something wrong with you and perhaps you are not a 'real' boy? (See Chapter 8 for more on the problem with dominant ideas about gender). So somewhere, and at some point, this 'truth' was created. I don't mean that someone sat down and thought, 'hey I know what would be good marketing, let's produce everything for girls in pink and for boys in blue'. Instead, I mean that through time and the use of language and practice, we have come to accept something as having meaning. We have internally accepted it as the truth.

Hence to engage with this chapter, I need you to do a few things. First, I acknowledge that many people reading this chapter will probably be committed to working with teaching for understanding. If this is the case, then I ask you to put this on a placeholder and allow some space for other ideas. Next, I want you to look beyond the idea that language describes meaning and instead consider that language creates meaning. Of course, and as discussed, creating meaning is about more than language, it is about the way we act towards something and about how it acts with us. Thus, instead of language I am going to use the word discourse and state that discourses create meaning; they are constructive rather than descriptive (Heather Mendick uses the word 'story' to capture the same idea in Chapter 9).

Discourse is a term I borrow from the work of Michel Foucault; he contends that some discourses are more easily heard than others. For example, what would happen if a teacher acted like they did not want their students to pass their exams? This way of acting and speaking would not be permitted; instead the teacher may be ignored and/or branded abnormal or incompetent. A key theme of this chapter is to unpack what we take for granted as 'normal' with regard to teaching for understanding and show how it is not natural but instead constructed by systems, structures and society. Foucault (1978) calls this process normalisation. I argue that normalisation thrives in education; the conformity of the classroom is constructed to propagate it.

> *Do you agree with me that normalisation thrives in the classroom? What do you think are the positive and negative aspects of this?*
> *Think about the perfect classroom. What would it look like and hence what would be normalised? Think of three things you place importance on, and list the reasons why these things are important. Finally, consider where those ideas come from and hence consider why some things are important and others seemingly not?*

In an attempt to unpack the concept of understanding, I examine it with/in two key contexts: educational research and educational policy. In the initial edition of this chapter, I stressed the role the New Labour government had in shaping education in England. The New Labour government (from 1997 to 2010) introduced a wealth of polices and initiatives that had a significant impact upon English education and the maths classroom. The current Conservative context is different to this, yet has similarities. Education is still framed around results and measurable statistics, and I still contend that decisions are often made without research evidence and teacher support. However, the official rhetoric of the Conservative government is that there should be "more and more schools run – and more and more decisions made – by teachers, not politicians" (Gove, 2014). [1]Thus, the influence of policy is arguably less overt yet I suggest it is still present; in this instance the Conservative government's clever positioning allows for them to remove themselves from consequences, but apply sanctions to schools that do not perform as the government intends.

In the next sections of this chapter, I look at how government policy and educational research work to normalise the mathematics classroom. Specifically, I argue that mathematics education research is preoccupied with exploring teaching for understanding and more often than not develops a blinkered, romantic approach to this concept. I compare this to educational policy where understanding is less of a priority. Then I use an example of a primary education student teacher to show how these positions (or discourses) can be problematic for the teacher, the students and the classroom. Although based around primary education, these arguments are transferable to secondary education.

Unpacking understanding

Discourses of understanding within educational research

In the first instance, though understanding is often presented as a uniform and self-evident concept, different forms are found within academic literature. This includes hierarchical constructs such as (Benjamin) Bloom's taxonomy (1956), which has enjoyed recent popularity in schools; Richard Skemp's (1976) value-laden oppositions of instrumental and relational understanding (as discussed in Chapter 14); and Jean Piaget's influential stages of development. More recently, Patrick Barmby and his colleagues (2009) have constructed understanding as a process of connections and representations. These different constructs are not mutually exclusive; in particular they all rely on one key concept – the 'normal' 'naturally developing' child. This enlightened, naturally curious child has much in common with Rousseau's romantic child as a 'state of nature'. However, Valerie Walkerdine (1997, p. 63) argues that in "child-centred pedagogy, 'the child' is deferred in relation to certain developmental accomplishments ... the very practices that claim to discover them actually produce them". Hence this natural child cannot be found, as they are what is being sought; this child is always already a normalised developing child.

This position is problematic as it can create a divide, where these 'developed' children are given status as they are deemed to produce 'real' understanding and 'real' attainment (Walkerdine, 1998). As Walkerdine points out, this is a seductive fantasy and one that is generally accepted as common-sense wisdom. However, I (and Walkerdine) argue that this naturally curious child, where understanding organically develops from experience, is a romantic fiction. Instead the child is more than this; the child has a context, including (amongst other things) gender, sexuality, culture and race.

To illustrate how this romantic discourse can be persuasive I focus on an influential and seductive piece of research. In the 1990s Jo Boaler carried out a comparative ethnography of two secondary schools with contrasting styles of teaching. In unsophisticated terms one school employed an 'open' (or child-centred) approach to pedagogy, while the other adopted a 'closed' (or transmission) approach. Boaler's conclusions drew attention to differences between mathematics results and attitudes between each school. In short, she argued that open classrooms were more equitable. Her arguments are in many ways typical of other research in mathematics education and are seen as "legitimate classroom practice" (de Freitas, 2013, p. 7). Hence, it is useful to unpack them, which I do from three angles (Hilary Povey offers an alternative take on Boaler's research in Chapter 6).

First, I contend that Boaler creates an unnecessary divide between knowledge and understanding, giving value only to the latter. Such use of binary divisions is prevalent within language; however, it is not natural and should not be left uncontested. In this case, it suggests there is a right way to acquire mathematics, which stigmatises those who acquire mathematics otherwise. It suggests that understanding should come before and be held in higher regard than knowledge when in fact the relationship between the two is more complex. Indeed "for many people the acquisition of information both excites and liberates" (Alexander, 2010, p. 247). This leads onto my second critique, the concept of the 'natural' child.

The child within Boaler's classrooms is not only 'free' but is naturally inquisitive, working furiously in social groups demanding mathematical enquiry. However, Boaler does not "really theorise how subjects are produced – practices" (Walkerdine, 1997, p. 59). Crucially she does not recognise that everyone is a product of discourses; even her 'free' students are part of a manufactured system, one that is controlled through surveillance and normalisation. What is most disquieting is that this surveillance masquerades under the facade of liberation. It supports the dream of the autonomous student and classroom (Ball, 1994), which many educationalists strive towards; hence it is a very attractive fiction (Walkerdine, 1990). However, my concern is that we are only seeing/ hearing what we want to see/hear.

My final point of contention is that Boaler fosters the romantic discourse of understanding by arguing that girls have a 'quest for understanding'. This reductive way of reading gender is also found in her book *Elephant in the Classroom* (Boaler, 2009) and her more recent *Daily Telegraph* article (Boaler, 2014). Boaler contends that girls cannot connect to mathematics in classrooms that are bound by transmission-based pedagogies, and hence they remove themselves from them. She largely bases this on interviews stating that "the girls were clear that their mathematical understanding would have been enhanced if they had been given more opportunity to work in an open way" (Boaler, 1997, pp. 144–145). However, there are many reasons why they may have made such statements and it is too simplistic to take their words literally and assume meaning. In particular, the quest for understanding may be a quest for something else or it may be the correct response for the girls to give. In addition, the presence/absence of understanding may be a myth supported by gendered behaviour in the classroom. Hence, boys may be more easily afforded the presence of understanding through social markers such as activity and rule-breaking (Walkerdine, 1998). Furthermore, girls "threaten the running of the child-centred classroom ... [by] producing the wrong kind of development" (Walkerdine, 1998, p. 33); femininity runs parallel to masculine rationality. This provides a sharp contrast to Boaler's findings, where child-centred pedagogies are viewed as girls' liberation.

> *Let's stop to consider what this means in relation to the maths classrooms. Why do people say the things they do and do they always literally mean what they say? Write down a few things that have been said to you about mathematics, either by people in your maths classroom or by people in general. For example, do people say 'they're stuck'; 'they hate maths' or that 'they are finding things too easy'? It may help to think of one or two specific students or people you have met.*
> *Think of as many reasons as you can why they might say these things.*

In summary I have argued that mathematics education research predominantly draws from a romantic discourse of understanding, where the correct version of the child is one who is autonomous and naturally curious. It is only from this that acceptable pedagogies are practised and 'real' understanding can arise. This romantic discourse of the child, of the classroom and of understanding perpetuates divisions in education and restricts discussion. Next, I examine how this plays out in relation to policy. Showing that policy constructs a functional discourse of understanding.

Understanding with/in policy

Before embarking on my deconstruction of Conservative policy, it is important to be aware of the wider context in which this policy circulates. We live in a neoliberal society which means that a particular model of selfhood as autonomous, psychological and entrepreneurial is normalised (Rose, 1999). However, this freedom is a myth as we are in fact governed through this notion of freedom; we are compelled to be free, to make our own choices and find our own way through life (Foucault, 1978; Rose, 1999). This neoliberal fiction is important to the production of understanding in educational policy, specifically as it is concerned with efficiency and the myth of autonomy.

In the previous edition of this chapter, I argued that the prior New Labour government prioritised skills and where understanding was written, it was ascribed as functional. The current Conservative government arguably replaced skills with a 'knowledge-based curriculum' (Morgan,[2] 2015), based on facts and 'proper' subjects. However, it is very much tied to futurity and the economic success of the nation, "unless major alterations in our mathematics education are made, and quickly, we are risking our future economic prosperity" (Vorderman et al., 2011). As such there is an assumption of being able to do and an assumption of progress of the self, tied to progress of the nation. More specifically, a new version of the curriculum was based around rote and procedure with standardised examples given as exemplars; thus, mentions and notions of understanding were noticeably absent. Instead the *phrase de jour* is 'Mastery' of mathematics that is borrowed from the success of education systems in the East. (See Chapter 2 for more detail).

> in East Asia there is much greater focus on fundamental number concepts, fractions and the building blocks of algebra in primary school ... We should also bear in mind that in Shanghai, they have daily maths lessons and regular tests to make sure that all children are learning the basics.
>
> (Gove, 2011)

We can read this as the government advocating that children 'understand' mathematics, or it may still be about a functional being able to do, as in the New Labour government documents. However, what is clear is that mathematics is based upon fundamental ideas, the basics and testing, it is not based upon enquiry and romanticism notions. "Maths and science, ... [are] focused on fundamental scientific knowledge and essential principles that are not subject to controversy and change every month or year" (Gove, 2011). There is no doubt about what mathematics is, or how it should be practiced. This absolutist way of reading mathematics is perhaps just a different side of a coin to Boaler's romanticism. Both fixed in their diametrically incontestable positions.

So far, I have argued that policy constructs understanding in mathematics very differently to mathematics education research: if it is found at all. However, both of these discourses are based upon the notion of a 'normal' cognitive child. As already discussed, in mathematics education research the child is presented as naturally inquisitive; however, in educational policy the child is more of an automaton: a product of an efficient production line, whether it be tied to functionality or economic prosperity. Furthermore, mathematics is both rational and prescriptive, suggesting a Platonic take on mathematical truths that is bound by certainty and the absolute (Ernest, 1991) rather than an idea of mathematical knowledge as a product of human activity (see Chapter 18).

In the next section I draw on interview data from one student teacher (who studied under the New Labour government) to provide an example of how the tension between these differing discourses can play out. In no way is this meant to be representative of the wider population but instead I use one person's story to give value and consequence to the situation. Specifically, for Jane I argue that the tension between the romantic and functional discourses of understanding results in exclusion from mathematics for some.

What this means for Jane, a student teacher

'I didn't know what I was doing and I couldn't get it. Everyone else was understanding it and I wasn't'. On reading statements such as this one from Jane it can appear that she shares Boaler's girls' quest for understanding and perhaps Boaler's romantic take on understanding. However, as I discussed earlier, there are many reasons to desire understanding and/or to make such statements. For instance, in constructing her identity, Jane notably presents herself as different and as a non-mathematician, despite her higher than average grade B[3] in mathematics GCSE (the current examination taken by most young people at age 16 in England and Wales, see Chapter 20). In addition, she is keen to construct a narrative where 'not understanding' mathematics was not her fault:

JANE: Because I always remember at school thinking every time we did anything in maths "why are we doing this? I don't get it, why are we doing this? Why do we have to do it this way? I don't understand". And it was never explained so when I was doing my maths teaching I always made a point of saying "we're doing it this way because it's easier".

Moreover, the text above demonstrates how Jane's version of understanding is more concerned with efficiency and functionality rather than Boaler's natural curiosity. This is shown throughout her interviews, where understanding is functional – concerned with being able to do. Furthermore, not understanding is conflated with not being able to access the work:

JANE: You never got taught anything, you just worked through a workbook and the workbook was supposed to explain how to do things but I quite often never understood what the workbook meant because there was not very often any example.

Jane constructs a powerful narrative, where understanding is the only way to achieve success in mathematics. This seems to be supported by her university lectures: 'that's why I really enjoyed the lectures about rote learning because it made sense to me that that's the way I'd learned'. Hence she is given a reason for her negative relationship with mathematics and can remove herself of personal blame. This narrative continues throughout her interviews:

JANE: I just used to think well surely if I had an embedded understanding it must have come back somehow and then I realised that in some areas I didn't have an embedded understanding I just rote learned stuff.

However, as I unpack below, this quest for understanding is perhaps fictional; a place that allows her to be separated from mathematics, yet to be normal. For instance, in one interview I try to explain a mathematical concept to Jane, she rejects my attempt. This could be for many reasons; perhaps I am the 'maths person' and Jane is the other:

JANE: You have to put a three down and a one up so you add another one to the tens column, they said "why?" and I was, just like, "well just so you know where it's going" and they were like, "why, why do you put it there? Why can't you just put it somewhere else?" "Well that's just the way we do it".
ANNA: Where else did she want to put it?
JANE: Underneath.
ANNA: Oh, right, ok. In the same column though because it's the column that's the important bit.
JANE: Yeah, I know that but it was still like, well, you know [laughter] I know, you're a maths person [laughter]. It was a question that just completely threw me because I never thought that.
ANNA: Some people do put it underneath.
JANE: Do they?

Conversely to Boaler, I argue that Jane may prefer *not* to understand. Perhaps this is the place which offers the most comfort and self-protection from the romantic discourses, with their high status and the consequent failure. Hence, she places understanding away from her, in a position she cannot access. According to Jane, understanding belongs to mathematicians, which in her classroom translates as the high achievers:

JANE: If like, the higher achievers find a different way of doing it then that's fine but just for the lower achievers to know that, you know, that first thing it should circle the lowest number and then they need to find out how low it is and those were the key bits I wanted them to realise.

This position can result in value-laden pedagogies and certain types of teaching being reserved for some. Though yet again her version of understanding is concerned with being able to do; it is functional.

My interpretation is that throughout her interviews Jane is clear that teaching for understanding is the right thing to do; however, she struggles with this in relation to her emotions and experiences. For instance, she states, 'I think the main thing is to let children explore maths … But I think there will always be that ingrained thing with me that it's either right or wrong'. Hence, she has rationalised expectations, but she also has her own 'irrational' emotions and investments, which tend to be absent from overtly rationalised policy and from most academic discussions. Similarly, Jane struggles with the tension between the complexity of the 'real' child she encounters and the simplicity of the rational child expected in both policy and academia (Llewellyn and Mendick, 2011). Hence, Jane struggles to realise academic versions of understanding and is caught up in the measurable functional world of policy. However, she cannot let the romance go completely, which can lead to her (and the children she teaches) feeling removed from mathematics.

> *What do you think of Jane's story? Do you agree with my interpretation?*
> *How does it compare to how other people talk about understanding mathematics?*
> *Do other people have 'excuses' for not doing maths?*
> *Do they link understanding to functionality?*
> *Do teachers restrict understanding to the more 'able' students?*
> *Has your opinion of teaching for understanding altered at all?*

Conclusion

In this chapter I question a common-sense truth that we often take for granted within mathematics education. This is part of a wider argument that stresses that nothing is intrinsically good or bad and no position is power or problem free.

The pursuit of understanding seems to be one of those intangible debates that perpetually floats around mathematics education. I hope I have showed that placing something on a pedestal does not come without consequences; specifically, for 'teaching for understanding', these can be inequity or dissolution. I am not arguing that understanding is bad or good for the classroom; instead I want to expose what it does and problematise its assumed goodness. As Foucault (2003, p. 172) states:

> A critique does not consist in saying that things aren't good the way they are. It consists in seeing on just what type of assumptions, of familiar notions, of established and unexamined ways of thinking the accepted practices are based.

Instead of being caught in a romantic (re)presentation of the child, the classroom and of mathematics, I ask you to consider things more widely – and not just deeply –when you are in the classroom. Moreover, mathematics education research does not exist in a vacuum but is part of the cultural context of the classroom and society which shapes and is shaped by it. Thus, I am suggesting that all of us – teachers, student teachers and educational researchers – should take off the blinkers and think about how what we do affects everyone. Most importantly, we should always question the fiction that is presented as 'normal'.

Notes

1 Michael Gove was Secretary of State for Education from May 2010 to July 2014. This speech was given under the Coalition (Conservative – Liberal Democrat) government – but the message is consistent with Conservative discourse.
2 Nicky Morgan was Secretary of State for Education from July 2014 to July 2016.
3 Note the grading system has changed. A grade B would now be equivalent to either a 6 or high 5.

Further reading

Ball, S. J. (2008) *The education debate*. Bristol: The Policy Press. An excellent critique of neoliberal government education policies and politics. Stephen Ball takes a sociological approach to examining the changing face of education over the past twenty years.
Boaler, J. (1997) *Experiencing school mathematics: Teaching styles, sex and setting*. Buckingham: Open University Press. Described clearly in the chapter, Jo Boaler carries out a longitudinal study on two contrasting schools exploring 'traditional' and 'progressive' teaching methods. It is worth reading to form your own opinion of her highly respected study.
Boaler, J. (2009) *The elephant in the classroom: Helping children learn and love maths*. London: Souvenir Press. A more recent book, where Jo Boaler updates some of her ideas.
Llewellyn, A. and Mendick, H. (2011) 'Does every child count? Quality, equity and mathematics with/in Neoliberalism', in B. Atweh, M. Graven, W. Secada and P. Valero (eds.), *Mapping equity and quality in mathematics education*. Dordrecht; New York: Springer. Here we unpack the notion of ability very similarly to how understanding is unpacked in this chapter. It offers a more developed debate that questions neoliberal values in education.
Walkerdine, V. (1990) *Schoolgirl fictions*. London: Verso. A brilliantly and imaginatively written collection of past articles and new thoughts that explore how masculinities and femininities are fictions lived as fact.

References

Alexander, R. (ed.) (2010) *Children, their world, their education: Final report and recommendations of the Cambridge Primary Review*. Abingdon: Routledge.
Ball, S. J. (1994) *Education reform: A critical and post-structural approach*. Buckingham: Open University Press.
Barmby, P., Harries, T., Higgins, S. and Suggate, J. (2009) The array representation and primary children's understanding and reasoning in multiplication, *Educational Studies in Mathematics*, 70, 3, 217–241.

Bloom, B. (ed.) (1956) *Taxonomy of educational objectives: Handbook 1, cognitive domain/ by a committee of college and university examiners.* London: Longmans.

Boaler, J. (1997) *Experiencing school mathematics: Teaching styles, sex and setting.* Buckingham: Open University Press.

Boaler, J. (2009) *The elephant in the classroom: Helping children learn and love maths.* London: Souvenir Press.

Boaler, J. (2014) Britain's maths policy simply doesn't add up. Daily Telegraph. Retrieved from www.telegraph.co.uk/education/educationnews/11031288/Britains-maths-policy-simply-doesnt-add-up.html

de Freitas, E. (2013) What were you thinking? A Deleuzian/Guattarian analysis of communication in the mathematics classroom, *Educational Philosophy and Theory*, 45, 3, 287–300.

Ernest, P. (1991) *The philosophy of mathematics education.* London: Falmer Press.

Foucault, M. (1978) *The history of sexuality: The will to knowledge* (Vol. 1). London: Routledge.

Foucault, M. (2003) So is it important to think?, in P. Rabinow and N. Rose (eds.), *The essential Foucault.* New York: The New Press.

Gove, M. (2011) Michael Gove speaks to the Royal Society on maths and science. DfE. Retrieved May 2017, from www.gov.uk/government/speeches/michael-gove-speaks-to-the-royal-society-on-maths-and-science

Gove, M. (2014) Michael Gove speaks about the future of education reform. DfE. Retrieved May 2017, from www.gov.uk/government/speeches/michael-gove-speaks-about-the-future-of-education-reform

Llewellyn, A. and Mendick, H. (2011) Does every child count? Quality, equity and mathematics with/in neoliberalism, in B. Atweh, M. Graven, W. Secada and P. Valero (eds.), *Mapping equity and quality in mathematics education.* Dordrecht; New York: Springer.

Morgan, N. (2015) Nicky Morgan: Why knowledge matters. DfE. Retrieved March 2017, from www.gov.uk/government/speeches/nicky-morgan-why-knowledge-matters

Rose, N. (1999) *Governing the soul.* London: Free Association Books.

Skemp, R. (1976) Relational understanding and instrumental understanding, *Mathematics Teaching*, 77, 20–26.

Vorderman, C., Budd, C., Dunne, R., Hart, M. and Porkess, R. (2011) *A world class mathematics education for all our young people.* London: The Conservative Party. Retrieved from www.tsm-resources.com/pdf/VordermanMathsReport.pdf

Walkerdine, V. (1990) *Schoolgirl fictions.* London: Verso.

Walkerdine, V. (1997) Redefining the subject in situated cognition theory, in D. Kirshner and J. A. Whitson (eds.), *Situated cognition: Social, semiotic, and psychological perspectives.* Mahwah, NJ: Lawrence Erlbaum.

Walkerdine, V. (1998) *Counting girls out: Girls and mathematics* (2nd ed). Abingdon: RoutledgeFalmer.

Chapter 8

Mathematics, gender and normativity

Mark McCormack and Luis E. Morales

Examining the differences in success at mathematics between boys and girls is something that we, as a society, seem to find endlessly fascinating. Whether boys or girls are getting more top grades, even by just one percentage point, takes on a special significance. Yet while we argue that it is vital to think about gender and mathematics, it is also worth highlighting the generally small differences in results between boys and girls at mathematics (and, as Andy Noyes and Peter Gates note in Chapter 4, much smaller than differences by social class). Even so, these results are always seen through a lens of gender difference – of one gender being better than the other.

Until recently, this cultural focus on essential gender differences has proven inescapable in the popular imagination, despite the marginal differences between boys' and girls' results. In the United Kingdom in 2009, boys got more of the top two A and A* grades than girls for the first time in several years. It was this that became the media story; for example, *The Guardian* newspaper proclaimed, "Boys have leapfrogged over girls in mathematics GCSE results, bagging more of the top grades for the first time since 1997 after the government scrapped coursework last year" (Curtis 2009). And yet just two years later, a finding that 6.8% more girls than boys were achieving A* and A grades was seen by the Director of the Joint Council for Qualifications as a "growing divide in performance between boys and girls at the top grades" (Shepherd 2011). In this context, gender differences in mathematics are often framed as an issue of boys versus girls.

Yet this narrative has potentially begun to shift, reflected in a greater reporting on the similarities in boys' and girls' abilities, for example, in recent articles from OZY (Kuper and Jacobs 2019) and *The New York Times* (Miller and Quealy 2018); (for a more comprehensive examination of mathematics in the popular culture, see Heather Mendick's Chapter 9 in this edition). Interestingly, while the OZY piece documents gendered differences in education as potentially more damaging to boys in some contexts, the problems are understood as being the result of cultural and social issues, not innate biological ability. Whether these examples reflect a genuine change in media reporting is impossible to tell.

We are confident, though, that the cultural temptation to pit boys against girls will remain a problematically popular way to understand mathematics and gender.

While we have been sceptical of gender differences in results at school level, it is important to recognise the importance of gender in other ways. Primarily, gender differences persist in the take-up of advanced mathematics courses, as well as regarding numbers of men and women who pursue mathematics-related careers (Gunderson et al. 2012). Furthermore, students' experiences of mathematics – as enjoyable, as interesting, as difficult – are also influenced by gender, and the very idea of mathematics has associations with masculinity (Mendick 2006). These factors will affect peoples' use of and relationship with mathematics throughout their lives (they also, as Anna Llewellyn notes in Chapter 7, highlight the importance of teachers' reflexivity in the classroom). This means that even if gender imbalances in mathematics results at school are minimal, we still have to pay great attention to how we deal with gender in the classroom (McCormack 2011).

> *If you are currently working within a co-educational school context, are there gender differences in the results of the mathematics classes? What could be the reasons for these?*
> *It can be difficult to think about the difference that gender makes to our own life. Do you think that your personal relationship with mathematics has been influenced by your gender? Do you ever see this influence in other people's relationships to mathematics?*

The social construction of gender

When scholars talk about the social construction of gender, the first thing to highlight is that we are not arguing men's and women's bodies are *literally* created socially. Of course, bodies exist, and no amount of social interaction would change this. But the practices, expectations and meanings ascribed to these different types of bodies *are* socially constructed, and this has great impact on how we live our lives (West and Zimmerman 1987). The nature/nurture debate is an extremely contentious one and some gender scholars do appear to endorse a view that gender is entirely socially constructed. Such debates have been termed as social determinism versus biological determinism (that is, it is either all social or all biological). In our view, the reality is somewhere between these two poles – society and biology interact to produce these differences in complex and diffuse ways (see Anderson and Magrath 2019; Fausto-Sterling 2000).

In a classic article on the construction of gender, Don West and Candace Zimmerman (1987) explain how people actively 'do' gender. They write that gender is "not simply an aspect of what one is, but, more fundamentally, it is something that one *does,* and does recurrently, in interaction with others" (p. 140). They highlight that even though the essential characteristics thought to constitute our sex (such as genitalia) are hidden, we are always socially perceived as either male or female. Great emphasis is therefore placed on our *gendered* behaviours – that is on our behaviours that are coded as masculine or feminine. This is because our gendered behaviours are seen to confirm (or alternatively question) the 'true' status of our sex. All our gendered behaviours and the meanings attached to them are thus framed and distilled through this desire to demonstrate a united sexed and gendered self. Combined with our innate need to conform to social norms (Asch 1951), West and Zimmerman argue that our continual quest to maintain an appropriate sex and gender is how we 'do' gender in social interaction.

However, while social interaction is of paramount importance in understanding gender in society, we must also consider the broader construction of gender. Sociological studies of institutions demonstrate that gender is also a form of power that pervades the social structures of society. Joan Acker (1990) explicates the ways in which organisations are gendered, where "advantage and disadvantage, exploitation and control, action and emotion, meaning and identity, are patterned through and in terms of a distinction between male and female, masculine and feminine". Barbara Risman (2004) contends that the organisational construction of gender is important, but that a broader theoretical understanding needs to capture its pervasiveness. She argues that gender should be examined as a social structure, just as the economy, the government and the family structure society.

The notion of gendered organisations also applies to schools. Mairtin Mac an Ghaill (1994) highlighted that schools were 'masculinity-making' institutions, where gender differences between boys and girls are produced and consolidated. From school discourses of sport and competition to interactions between boys and girls, the meanings and behaviours associated with masculinity and femininity are actively produced within schools. Accordingly, when we are examining the gender differences within mathematics education, and when we examine the gendered experiences of boys and girls learning mathematics, it is of fundamental importance to consider the social and institutional contexts that shape these experiences and differences.

Think about your experiences of being in a mathematics classroom, as a teacher or a student – did this classroom construct gender in particular ways?

- *Were there discussions of the uses of mathematics using gendered examples (of finance, shopping, etc.)?*
- *Were boys seen as 'naturally' better at mathematics?*
- *Were pictures of famous male mathematicians on the wall, but not female ones?*

Social factors affecting gender differences

The initial research that found significant gender differences attributable to biology has been critiqued by feminist scientists. Anne Fausto-Sterling (1993), for example, highlights that this research ignored other scholarship that focused on parental attitudes, teachers' attitudes and experiences of mathematics lessons as reasons for gender differences in mathematics; scholarship that showed boys' and girls' experiences of learning mathematics within the same classroom were different (Leinhart, Seewald and Engel 1979). More recent scholarship has continued to examine these issues. For example, Elizabeth Gunderson and her colleagues (2012) highlight that these differences are not the result of biology, or of one single social factor, but they are the result of what they call "early-developing math attitudes" (p. 153). These form from a variety of factors, including aptitude, parental and teacher attitudes, maths-gender stereotypes and expectations of success or failure in mathematics, among many others.

One of the key ways that girls can be put off mathematics is through the patronising behaviours of teachers and parents. Sarah Gervais and Theresa Vescio (2012) highlight the detrimental effects of condescending behaviours and attitudes towards women. Distinguishing this 'benevolent sexism' from more overt forms of gender discrimination, they highlight that even well-meaning acts can have negative consequences if they serve to patronise or belittle women. Accordingly, having equal expectations of boys and girls, praising them in similar ways and not using inappropriate gendered language are of vital importance (see Hilary Povey's Chapter 6 for further discussion of methods and practices with which to facilitate the equitable attainment of an education in mathematics for a diversity of students).

Patronising behaviours can often be unintentional and occur from even the most well-meaning of trainees. For example, observing a teacher trainee in school, whom we call Eli here, it was evident that he was reproducing gender stereotypes through how he praised students. During one of his question and answer sessions, he praised boys and girls differently: 'Good girl, Jennifer', Eli said after Jennifer answered a difficult question. 'Brilliant Sarah, good girl', to another student. And when it came to the boys? 'Brilliant John, good man'. Without realising, and in an effort to encourage the boys in the class, Eli was constructing the boys as adults and the girls as children. When Mark discussed this with Eli after, he was shocked that he was doing it. Eli had never thought carefully about the *gendered* nature of the language he used, and so did not realise the negative effect his teaching might have. Similarly, research shows that even when teachers are trying to give more attention to girls than to boys, they still spend greater time interacting with boys (Younger, Warrington and Williams 1999).

Do you reproduce stereotypes of mathematics and gender in your interactions with others inside and outside of classes?
Do you:

- *say 'good man' and 'good girl'?*
- *give boys and girls equal time in answering questions?*
- *let a student's gender influence your expectations of them?*
- *discuss the same possible mathematics careers with all students?*

Beyond the sex binary

A profound issue in the general debate about boys' and girls' ability at mathematics is the flaws in the idea that sex is a neat, simple binary: that sex is a nominal form of data with two distinct categories. The reality is different. The previous sections focused on social norms related to gender, but we also need to consider how sex is complex and structured by cultural norms.

The assignation of sex to a human is rarely considered outside of gender studies and medicine. For the majority of people, the things that determine sex at birth – primary sexual characteristics such as genitalia – match the gender they are raised as. Thus, when people discuss oppression by gender, the focus is on how women and men are disadvantaged by gender in particular contexts. Yet, it is important to expand this to include people who are excluded by the sex binary itself. As Anne Fausto-Sterling (2000) documents in her book *Sexing the Body*, human bodies often do not fit the categories of male and female.

Intersex is a term for people whose sexual characteristics do not clearly align with typical associations regarding male and female bodies (see Davis 2015). Intersex people are diverse, including people with complete or partial reproductive organs usually associated with male and female sexes; chromosomal arrangements different from the typical XX or XY (for example, XXY) and ambiguous genitals. Fausto-Sterling (2000) documents the energy society exerts to police these bodies into the sex binary, and how these actions often fail with damaging effects on the young person involved. Intersex people demonstrate that a sex binary is not sufficient to recognise the diversity of human bodies. The erasure of intersex people from much debate and policy in education can be understood as one mechanism by which the sex binary is reproduced.

In addition to intersex people whose bodies do not fit the sex binary, transgender people are individuals whose gender does not match the sex category they were assigned at birth. Trans people begin discovering or negotiating the contradiction between their assigned sex and sense of gender at various stages in the life course. Furthermore, trans people have varying manners in which they express their gender identity, from the outwardly discernible to their inclination or financial ability to undergo genital reconstruction surgery, for example. These are private issues which should not interfere with a trans student's educational journey. There are also those who identify as genderqueer or gender non-binary: these terms refer to people who do not experience their gender identity as fitting within the gender norms assigned to them.

You may well encounter trans or genderqueer students and you have an obligation to ensure their welfare and ability to learn mathematics is no different from other students (see Sinclair-Palm and Gilbert 2018). Barriers to entry for trans people in mathematics and STEM are not limited to the representative or the cultural; teachers should remember that trans people are often dealing with medical and social issues that most people do not encounter. One should be sensitive to the significant psychological challenges one might face when living in a body or with gendered expectations one might not feel match the way one feels about oneself, particularly in locales and cultures in which being trans is stigmatised. Furthermore, intersex as well as trans people may at any point be dealing with physical medical issues relatively specifically to their status as intersex or trans. These are all barriers which may keep trans and intersex people under-represented in mathematics and STEM, as long as teachers – as well as structural forces – do not mitigate their representation. It is also important to remember that trans students' experiences are diverse and not solely negative or defined by stigma (McCormack 2012a).

In order to develop trans-inclusive teaching practices, Elizabeth Meyer and Bethy Leonardi (2018) interviewed 26 teachers in the United States who have worked with trans students in schools. They found that these teachers organised learning in two key ways: *pedagogies of exposure* and a *culture of conversation*. Meyer and Leonardi argue that pedagogies of exposure, where teachers share stories about trans youth in mainstream media, are important but insufficient to foster inclusive learning. Rather, they advocate for a culture of conversation where teachers, students, parents and administrators are able to work collaboratively to produce inclusive school spaces. This will require the support of the whole school community and is an important endeavour when seeking to ensure learning environments are open to all.

> *Do you find yourself consciously or subconsciously categorising persons you see into a gender binary – as either male or female? Do you give students a gender they do not use themselves?*
>
> *Are public spaces, especially those around schools, inclusive of trans and non-binary people?*
>
> *How might schools legitimatise or delegitimise gender identities that extend beyond the binary or male and female? What ethos or culture might a school exemplify that would encourage or discourage non-binary or trans peoples to pursue careers in math-related fields?*

Challenging heterosexual assumptions

The presumption of the sex binary discussed earlier has been called mononormativity. Thus, trans and intersex people are excluded to reproduce a sex binary; similarly, bisexual people are excluded to fit a gay/straight binary. The binary of sexuality is also problematic because heterosexuality is particularly privileged in Western societies. This occurs through both overt homophobia, where same-sex sexuality is stigmatised and sexual minorities are marginalised, and through heterosexism – an implicit privileging of heterosexuality (Anderson and McCormack 2016; McCormack 2012b).

Teachers in the United Kingdom have a legal duty to protect sexual minority students from homophobia. Importantly, this does not solely involve responding to acts of homophobic bullying or similar behaviour, it also requires pre-emptive action to ensure that schools are safe spaces for sexual minority youth (see Rivers 2011). This means that as teachers, you must also consider ways in which to challenge heterosexism within mathematics education as well as the broader school.

McCormack (2011) has highlighted how heterosexism can persist even among well-meaning teachers. At a secondary school where he was training as a teacher, McCormack discussed how the head of the English department said there was an informal department policy to discuss homosexuality only if it was brought up by a student. Pragmatic reasons were given, the main being that whenever sexuality was discussed, the students "placed too much importance on it". She gave the example of Lord of the Flies, where "all they end up writing about is the homoerotic overtones, because they think it is a novelty". Yet she admitted that this meant sexuality was very rarely discussed in English lessons, not recognising it was this form of silencing that kept sexuality "novel".

This concern about novelty hinders learning for all students. In a study of how university students responded to an openly gay lecturer, Ripley et al. (2012) found that the use of gay examples within lessons hindered students' ability to learn but *only because* they were novel. Given the social justice impetus for representing sexual minorities students' lives in school curricula, discussing sexual minorities (for example, using gay couples in examples) can be an important way of reducing the novelty of sexuality and enhancing learning of all students (see also Batten et al. 2018).

The social construction of mathematics and mathematics education

Perhaps the prevailing understanding of mathematics in society is that it forms a body of immutable and certain knowledge. Often called the absolutist view of mathematics (Ernest 1998), it is argued that mathematical logic is fundamentally objective and independent of culture and social attitudes. However, such a view has been critiqued. Lakatos (1976), for example, highlighted that mathematics is based on a set of axioms that are not provable and thus all mathematical proof rests upon *contingent* foundations. He also showed how even proof itself is negotiable – what counts as a valid proof has varied in different times and places. Paul Ernest (1998) developed this rejection of absolutism to develop a 'social constructivist' approach to understanding mathematics, where mathematical knowledge is created rather than discovered.

Despite its counter-intuitive nature, this social constructivist approach has been adopted by most scholars of mathematics education. This approach has particular significance for gender, because it opens up opportunities to explore the relationship between the social construction of mathematics and the social construction of gender. Examining the doing of mathematics as a community of practice, Leone Burton concentrated on the implications of the social and contextual elements of mathematics for the people learning it. About this approach, Burton (1995) wrote that

> Knowing mathematics would … be a function of who is claiming to know, related to which community, how that knowing is presented, what explanations are given for how that knowing was achieved, and the connections demonstrated between it and other knowings. (p. 287)

That is, learning mathematics is dependent on the learner and who (in terms of class, ethnicity, gender, sexuality, etc.) that person is, as well as how that person is taught. In other words, not only is mathematics constructed, becoming proficient at it is inherently social.

The learning of mathematics as social has been discussed by feminist mathematics educators (notably, Becker 1995, Burton 1986, Walkerdine 1988). One of the key themes within these discussions has been understanding how the method of teaching mathematics impacts on how it is learned and by whom. Joanne Rossi Becker (1995) emphasises the importance of both making connections between components of mathematical learning and presenting mathematics as a process and not a set of facts. In Richard Skemp's (1976) terminology, this would be privileging relational learning over instrumental learning (this distinction is elaborated in Chapter 14 by Gwen Ineson and Sunita Babbar). Becker argues that the ongoing failure to do this has disadvantaged women, writing,

> the imitation model of teaching, in which the impeccable reasoning of the professor as to 'how a proof should be done' is presented to students for them to mimic, is not a particularly effective means of learning for women. (Becker 1995, p. 169)

Here, she is drawing on ideas that men and women, boys and girls, in general, have different 'ways of knowing' with the former favouring abstract or 'separated' ways of knowing and the latter preferring 'connected' ways of knowing in which knowledge is embedded within human relationships.

Pedagogies supporting women's ways of knowing are more compatible with social constructivist than with absolutist philosophies of mathematics. Picking up on this, Jo Boaler (1997, also discussed in Chapters 6 and 7 by Hilary Povey and by Anna Llewellyn, respectively) showed that girls performed better when taught using investigative pedagogies than in 'traditional' talk-and-chalk classrooms because they had a 'quest for understanding' that the latter could not satisfy, while boys were content to apply rules without understanding why they worked. This work by Becker and Boaler has been hugely influential; however, such approaches in some ways reproduce the oppositional girls versus boys arguments that we saw earlier. As when talking about differences in results between girls and boys, it is difficult here to avoid the tendency to see these differences as 'natural' and to avoid generalising about what all boys and all girls are like, ignoring the in-group differences between boys and between girls, the overlap between boys and girls and the problematic gender binary.

Societal constructions of mathematics and mathematicians

Valerie Walkerdine's (1988, 1990) work invites us to think differently about gender and mathematics. She traces the historical processes through which mathematics became enshrined in the curriculum as being *equivalent* to reason and those through which rationality became conflated with masculinity. She suggests that mathematics fits into a pattern of oppositions that are deeply embedded within Western thought – objective versus subjective, abstract versus concrete, rational versus emotional, etc. Masculinity and mathematics line up with the terms on the left-hand side of these oppositions and femininity with those on the right-hand side (Walkerdine 1990). Following this logic, setting up oppositions between separated and connected ways of knowing and between rule-following boys and understanding-seeking girls can support the reproduction of gender differences in mathematics. Heather Mendick (2006) used these ideas to make sense of gender differences in the take-up of post-compulsory mathematics, showing how the boys she spoke to used mathematics to construct a masculine identity, something which was problematic for girls studying the subject. In additional to the historical patterns Walkerdine analysed, Mendick explored how stereotypes of mathematics and mathematicians in the broader culture reinforce the associations between mathematics and masculinity.

It is necessary to recognise the impact that cultural conceptions of mathematics and mathematicians have on how people experience and learn mathematics. While our own histories shape our conceptions of what a mathematician looks like – for example, McCormack's undergraduate degree in mathematics has left him with the residing image of mathematicians as middle-aged, eccentric Russian men – it is discourses at a *societal* level that have the greatest impact on how we as a general population think of mathematicians.

> *What is your philosophy of mathematics and what approach do you use to learn mathematics? Do you think this impacts on how you teach mathematics?*

Conclusion

In this chapter, we have examined how the social construction of both gender and mathematics results in gendered inequalities. We further examined the social construction of sexuality, and the way in which the existence of diversity in human sexuality and gender disrupts essentialist notions of capabilities in mathematics based on a binary. Emphasising the existence of intersex, gender non-binary and trans people stresses the importance of teachers validating that diversity in their classroom, as well as critically examining the ways in which math education may assume a binary and the problems that may create. Highlighting the compulsive attention we pay to gender differences in results in mathematics, and noting the rather small differences that exist at GCSEs, we also argued that there are serious and damaging consequences to how gender is currently treated in mathematics education. These include fewer women taking mathematics at higher levels and mathematics-oriented careers continuing to be male-dominated. Furthermore, we have argued that these differences are being reproduced within mathematics classrooms – at both primary and secondary levels – and that subtle, nuanced expectations, attitudes and behaviours can result in disparities in later life. Accordingly, it is vital that we consider how we talk about mathematics and gender in order to ameliorate these differences.

Further reading

Anderson, E., & Magrath, R. (2019). *Men and Masculinities*. London: Routledge. This textbook provides an interdisciplinary framework to think about masculinities and the lives of boys and men. There is a chapter dedicated to boys at school, and a review of theories of masculinities in various institutional contexts.

Walkerdine, V. (1998). *Counting girls out*. London: Routledge. This book provides a detailed empirical and theoretical account of the myths, prejudices and theorizing of the gendered body and mind, and how it intersects with gender in the teaching and learning of mathematics.

References

Acker, J. (1990). Hierarchies, jobs, bodies: A theory of gendered organizations. *Gender & Society*, 4(2), 139–158.

Anderson, E., & Magrath, R. (2019). *Men and Masculinities*. London: Routledge.

Anderson, E., & McCormack, M. (2016). *The changing dynamics of bisexual men's lives: Social research perspectives*. New York: Springer.

Asch, A. (1951). Effects of group pressure upon the modification and distortion of judgements. In H. Guetzkow (Ed.), *Groups, leadership and men* (pp. 177–190). Pittsburgh: Carnegie Press.

Batten, J., Ripley, M., Anderson, E., Batey, J., & White, A. (2018). Still an occupational hazard? The relationship between homophobia, heteronormativity, student learning and performance, and an openly gay university lecturer. *Teaching in Higher Education*, 1–16. doi:10.1080/13562517.2018.1553031

Becker, J. R. (1995). Women's ways of knowing in mathematics. In G. Kaiser & P. Rogers (Eds), *Equity in mathematics education: Influences of feminism and culture*. London: Falmer.

Boaler, J. (1997). *Experiencing school mathematics: Teaching styles, sex and setting*. Buckingham: Open University Press.

Burton, L. (1986). *Girls into maths can go.* London: Holt, Rinehart and Winston.

Burton, L. (1995). Moving towards a feminist epistemology of mathematics. *Educational Studies in Mathematics, 28,* 275–291.

Curtis, P. (2009). GCSE results: Boys bag top grades in maths. *The Guardian.* Thursday 27th August.

Davis, G. (2015). *Contesting intersex: The dubious diagnosis.* New York: NYU Press.

Ernest, P. (1998). *Social constructivism as a philosophy of mathematics.* Albany, New York: SUNY Press.

Fausto-Sterling, A. (1993). *Myths of gender: Biological theories about women and men.* New York: Basic Books.

Fausto-Sterling, A. (2000). *Sexing the body.* New York: Basic Books.

Gervais, S. J., & Veschio, T. K. (2012). The effect of patronizing behavior and control on men and women's performance in stereotypically masculine domains. *Sex Roles,* 66(7–8), 479–491..

Gunderson, E. A., Ramirez, G., Levine, S. C., & Beilock, S. L. (2012). The role of parents and teachers in the development of gender-related math attitudes. *Sex Roles, 66*(1), 153–166.

Kuper, S., & Jacobs, B. (2019, January 19). The untold danger of boys falling behind in school. *OZY: A news site you'll actually love.* Retrieved from https://www.ozy.com/fast-forward/the-untold-danger-of-boys-falling-behind-in-school/91361

Lakatos, I. (1976). *Proofs and Refutations.* Cambridge: Cambridge University Press.

Leinhart, A. M., Seewald, A. M., & Engel, M. (1979). Learning what's taught: Sex differences in instruction. *Journal of Educational Psychology, 71,* 432–439.

Mac an Ghaill, M. (1994). *The making of men: Masculinities, sexualities and schooling.* Buckingham: Open University Press.

McCormack, M. (2011). Queer masculinities, gender conformity, and the secondary school. In J. C. Landreau & N. M. Rodriguez (Eds.), *Queer masculinities: A critical reader in education* (pp. 35–46). New York: Springer.

McCormack, M. (2012a). The positive experiences of openly gay, lesbian, bisexual and transgendered students in a Christian sixth form college. *Sociological Research Online, 17*(3), 5. Retrieved from https://journals.sagepub.com/doi/full/10.5153/sro.2461

McCormack, M. (2012b). *The declining significance of homophobia: How teenage boys are redefining masculinity and heterosexuality.* New York: Oxford University Press.

Mendick, H. (2006). *Masculinities in mathematics.* Maidenhead: Open University Press.

Meyer, E. J., & Leonardi, B. (2018). Teachers professional learning to affirm transgender, non-binary, and gender-creative youth. *Sex Education, 18*(4), 449–463.

Miller, C. C., & Quealy, K. (2018, June 13). Where boys outperform girls in math: Rich, white and suburban districts. *The New York Times.* Retrieved from https://www.nytimes.com/interactive/2018/06/13/upshot/boys-girls-math-reading-tests.html?action=click&module=Intentional&pgtype=Article

Ripley, M., Anderson, E., McCormack, M., & Rockett, B. (2012). Heteronormativity in the university classroom: Novelty attachment and content substitution among gay-friendly students. *Sociology of Education, 85*(2), 121–130.

Risman, B. J. (2004). Gender as a social structure. *Gender & Society, 18*(4), 429–450.

Rivers, I. (2011). *Homophobic bullying: Research and theoretical perspectives.* New York: Oxford University Press.

Shepherd, J. (2011). GCSE results 2011: Girls widen their lead. *The Guardian.* Thursday August 25th.

Skemp, R. R. (1976). Relational understanding and instrumental understanding. *Mathematics Teaching, 77,* 20–26.

Sinclair-Palm, J., & Gilbert, J. (2018). Naming new realities: Supporting trans youth in education. *Sex Education, 18*(4), 321–327.

Walkerdine, V. (1988). *The mastery of reason.* London: Routledge.

Walkerdine, V. (1990). Difference, cognition, and mathematics education. *For the Learning of Mathematics, 10*(3), 51–56.

West, C., & Zimmerman, D. (1987). Doing gender. *Gender & Society, 1*(2), 125–151.

Younger, M., Warrington, M., & Williams, J. (1999). The gender gap and classroom interactions: Reality and rhetoric? *British Journal of Sociology of Education, 20*(3), 325–341.

Chapter 9

The financial crisis, popular culture and maths education

Heather Mendick

Introduction

This chapter is about maths and popular culture. So, before you start reading, can you remember any times you've seen maths and/or mathematicians in film, television, advertising, computer games, online, music, books, etc.? How do you feel about them?

In the first edition of this book, Marie-Pierre Moreau and I wrote about how mathematics is everywhere and nowhere in popular culture. Like then, I see learning maths as about more than acquiring a range of skills in arithmetic, algebra, geometry, statistics and problem-solving. Learning maths involves forming a relationship with the subject – of love, hate, pain and/or pleasure. Central to this are the stories people tell about maths and about themselves in relation to it. By 'stories', I mean ways of seeing and understanding the world. Marie-Pierre and I identified four, sometimes conflicting, stories about maths that dominate our media: that mathematicians are born not made, that people who are good at maths are geeky – socially awkward, mostly white and mostly male, that doing maths is a solitary and abstract activity, and that maths is useful in everyday life.

The stories we tell about maths come from a range of places, from school mathematics, other people (including parents, siblings, friends, teachers – not just maths teachers) and popular culture. Children and young people, like all of us, do not see things on TV or in a computer game and then copy them, but the things they see are part of the resources that they use to make sense of who they are and what happens to them. Because popular culture plays a key role in shaping relationships with maths, my view is that, as teachers, we should care about that, rather than ignore it.

What stories do you tell about your own and other people's relationships to maths? Where do these stories come from?

In some ways not much has changed since the first edition of this book in 2013. Stories of natural ability and child prodigies continue to dominate over ones of ordinary folk who achieve mathematically through hard work, reflecting the dominance of what Mark Boylan and Hilary Povey call 'Ability thinking' in Chapter 5. So too do dramas that rely on a tension between the lonely obsessive pursuit of mathematics and embracing a rich and social life. However, there has been a greater focus on difference. Recent films include *Gifted* (2017) the story of six-year old white girl, who like her mother and maternal grandmother, is a mathematical genius, *X+Y* (2014) about an autistic white teenage boy who enters an international maths contest and biopics of the Indian mathematician Srinivasa Ramanujan (*The Man Who Knew Infinity*, 2015), disabled mathematician and physicist Stephen Hawking (*The Theory of Everything*, 2014), gay mathematician Alan Turing (*The Imitation Game*, 2015) and three African American women – Kathryn Johnson, Dorothy Vaughan and Mary Jackson – who worked as 'calculators' at NASA in the run-up to the first moon landing (*Hidden Figures*, 2016). Geek stereotypes too have shifted since 2013 as a string of tech celebrity entrepreneurs have become increasingly popular including Facebook CEO Mark Zuckerberg and SpaceX and Tesla CEO Elon Musk. National and international initiatives have sought to promote coding, sometimes connecting this to maths. So when I considered how to update the earlier chapter, one option was to look at the impact of geek chic or at what difference it makes if a mathematician, albeit still often a troubled genius, is black, female, gay or has a physical disability.

Another recent change has been the expansion of online content. How mathematics appears in popular culture is now less reliant on mass media texts like the films mentioned above than in the past and more open to shaping from below through the heterogeneous spaces of Twitter, Facebook, YouTube and so on. In 2015, young people in England went online to parody and protest an examination question mixing probability and algebra that begins with Hannah selecting sweets at random to eat. One tweeted: "Calculate the area of Hannah's dead body after she choked on her sweets". Others re-subtitled and uploaded videos of Hitler's anger and disappointment from the 2004 film *Downfall* to express their feelings about the exam. We are all now producers as well as consumers of popular culture. Debates about maths education also play out online as more and more educationalists find a platform there. Politics too is happening in cyberspace, with online texts reaching more people than mainstream news outlets. In the midst of anxieties about fake news, many invoke mathematics to garner authority for their position. But maths is increasingly contested. In the 2016 US Democratic Presidential Primary between Hillary Clinton and Bernie Sanders, the blogosphere brimmed with debate on 'delegate math'. In the 2017 UK General Election, politicians getting their numbers wrong in a morning interview became a top news story that ran all day and was recycled in online memes for days or even months afterwards. The failure of opinion polls to predict the outcome of either election generated discussion of statistics and polling methodologies. So, how maths circulates online could also be an interesting direction to take in updating the chapter in the previous edition of *Debates in Mathematics Education.*

But I will leave both these possibilities for others. Instead I'm focusing on a new strand of stories about maths: dramas about the devastating 2008 global financial crisis. As Richard Barwell and Paul Ernest also touch on in Chapters 16 and 3, respectively, mathematical instruments were at the heart of this crash. For example, mathematicians working in finance enabled bad debts to be hidden by devising Collateralised Debt Obligations (CDOs) that bundled together thousands of mortgages and sold them off in slices with precisely calculated risks attached. Yet, what are the stories we tell about the place, power and potential of maths through this crisis? To answer this question I analyse three financial-crisis fictions: the films *Margin Call* (Chandor, 2011), *The Big Short* (McKay, 2015) and the novel *Kapitoil* (Wayne, 2010). All three are critical of the free market capitalist status quo that led to and sustains the ongoing financial crisis. The title *Kapitoil* references Karl Marx's classic analysis of capitalism in *Das Capital*; *Margin Call* and *The Big Short* track that moment when it seems, in the words of the *Manifesto of the Communist Party*: 'All that is solid melts into air' (Marx, 1976; Marx & Engels, 1952). Because of this critical positioning, these fictions introduce alternative ways of viewing mathematics, which challenge its image as objective and elitist. These alternatives can be of value to teachers seeking to engage more people in maths.

Against objectivity: Fallible maths

> *Many people, particularly those who do well at maths, like the idea that maths is either right or wrong and find comfort in its apparent objectivity and certainty. How do you feel about this? Can you think of people you teach who fall into this category and other people who don't like the idea that maths is either right or wrong?*

Typically, films (and television programmes) use two visual techniques to show mathematics. These will be familiar to you if you've watched things like *A Beautiful Mind, Good Will Hunting* and *Numb3rs.* First, there are specific images that stand in for the process of doing maths, usually, people writing feverishly on windows, mirrors and transparent whiteboards. Second, there are scenes that seek to explain maths. These extract you from the normal mise en scène, as images change to depict structure and pattern, and normal speech is replaced by a pedagogic voice-over from a mathematical 'genius'. These scenes naturalise how: "mathematics produces new inventions in reality, not only in the sense that new insights may change interpretations, but also in the sense that mathematics colonises part of reality and reorders it" (Skovsmose, 1994, p. 42, see Richard Barwell's discussion of the formatting power of maths in Chapter 16).

They convey the power of maths and the role of mathematicians in mediating that. Their specific mathematical content is irrelevant to the story. Both these patterns are broken in films and TV series about the financial crisis.

The films *The Big Short* and *Margin Call* centre on (mostly male, mostly white) workers in the US financial services sector. Their central characters notice problems in the derivatives markets before the rest of their sector and seek to profit from these. In *Margin Call*, we spend a night in the offices of an investment bank, which has spotted an existential problem in their trading model. In a series of meetings, employees discuss how to respond, ultimately deciding to sell the assets that they now believe are toxic before a loss of market confidence renders them worthless. Set mostly at night, inside the bank, it has a claustrophobic and eerie feel. *The Big Short* is based on a true story of 'outsiders' who bet against the housing market, years before the bubble burst. We follow the financial crisis through their lives, as they take a risk and finally cash in their investments as the US economy collapses around them. It is self-consciously postmodern with, for example, characters 'breaking the fourth wall', speaking direct to camera, to tell us whether the scenes depicted 'really' happened.

There is no feverish writing in either film. Their visual shorthand for doing maths is typing into computers, as small screens of numbers and graphs flicker across the big screen. This shift, from old-fashioned to contemporary images, arguably makes maths feel more accessible. This is supported by the four scenes explaining maths in *The Big Short*. Three exist outside the main narrative, as in other mathematical fictions, using glamour, celebrity and metaphor to describe the maths of mortgage-backed securities, shorting a market and CDOs. They feature: actor Margot Robbie sipping champagne in a bubble bath; chef Anthony Bourdain preparing food in his restaurant and 'Dr Richard Thaler, father of behavioural economics' and 'International Pop Star' Selena Gomez gambling in Vegas. In a change from the past, the film invites its audience to understand mathematical ideas, which are then integrated into the narrative. The film's narrator, banker Jared Vennett, sets these scenes up in opposition to the confusing use of 'financial jargon' that he describes as a deliberate strategy to exclude by making 'you feel bored and stupid'. This financial jargon is implicitly mathematical.

Beyond this focus on the accessibility of maths we find a challenge to its objectivity. In a key scene, Jared tries to sell the idea of shorting the housing market. He is asked "You're completely sure of the math"? In reply, he points to 'my quant', an East Asian man. Jared explains he speaks no English, is called Yang and came top in a maths competition in China. The film instantly cuts to the 'quant'. Looking directly into the camera, he tells us that he speaks English, is called John, and came second in the competition. This draws attention to stereotypes of Chinese people as 'naturally able' at maths. It also exposes mathematical truth as reliant on social factors for authentication: who makes a claim is more critical than any so-called objective criteria.

In *Margin Call*, similarly, what is important is less the detail of the maths (glossed as an "equation" or "formula") than its meaning. The bank's CEO asks Peter, the young risk analyst who uncovers the problem, to "speak as you might to a young child or a golden retriever". Peter's immediate boss exclaims, "Oh, Jesus. You know I can't fucking read these things. Just speak to me in English". Thus, even those on 'the inside' are exposed as fallible. Uncertainty and questioning echo through the film. The "formula" on which the bank has relied for so long is "worthless. … It's broken". When someone objects, "there are eight trillion dollars of paper around the world relying on that equation", the terse response is, "well, we were wrong". The equally terse response to that is: "No, you mean you were wrong". The film thus starts with a loss of mathematical certainty, that is never resolved. This is symbolised by the CEO's statement that, "one and one no longer makes two". Other characters ask "Do we even know if he's right"? "Is that figure right"? And "You think he's right"? The responses, whether certain or uncertain ("looks pretty fucking right to me", "I don't know, I can't be sure" and "I know he's right"), are never final. There is also ambiguity around the film's use of 'right', which refers both to the 'rightness' of maths and to moral 'rightness'. Different characters take different views on whether the bank should liquidate their position. As one puts it, "in acute situations such as this, often what is right can take on multiple interpretations". While, this is a reference to disputes about what is morally right, given the continuing and parallel questioning of mathematical certainty in the film, it could also apply to maths. Thus, both films draw attention to the power of maths to order the world in its own image, and so they expose it and denaturalise it.

> *Should the fallibility of maths evidenced in the financial crisis change how we teach it?*

Against elitism: Democratic maths

> *Imagine a mathematician – what picture do you get? What picture do you think your students would get if you asked them to do this?*

Typically, as Moon Duchin (2004) shows, in mathematical fictions, people doing maths combine features of the socially awkward geek/nerd and the heroic genius. The gender, race and social class of central/peripheral figures align mathematics with being masculine, white and middle class. Stories about the financial crisis reproduce these clichés, but they also turn them into a problem suggesting we shouldn't leave maths to an expert elite but that, as Richard Barwell argues in relation to climate change, mathematical knowledge is part of the democratic competence we need to hold the powerful to account.

Let's start with examples of the clichés. *Margin Call*'s Peter is a former "rocket scientist" who chooses to stay late at the office doing maths rather than going drinking with his workmates. *The Big Short*'s Michael, who develops the idea of shorting the housing market, wears no shoes in the office and admits: "I don't know how to be funny. I don't know how to work people. I just know how to read numbers". He is one of the "outsiders and weirdos" who saw the "lie at the heart of the economy". Although weird, they are presented as innovators as we're told that the man who invented Mortgage Backed Securities has "changed your life more than Michael Jordan, the iPod and YouTube put together". These characters are simultaneously geeks and geniuses. But they are not heroes as such characters are in most mathematical fictions. They did not and do not save us. As Jared chides us towards the end of *The Big Short*, after his $47M bonus for 2008 is announced, "Hey I never said I was the hero of this story". These characters provoke more alienation than empathy. As critic Roger Ebert (2011) put it, the "long black cars and executive perks" in *Margin Call* are "paid for with what was inescapably fraud. One of the characters has a sick dog. The dog is the only creature in the entire film that anyone likes". Their nastiness and fallibility are a warning that we should not leave finance to an elite and so we need to open up access to maths.

In *Margin Call*, one banker, looking at the city through a car window, justifies his role to another: "If people want to live like this, in their cars and the big fucking houses they can't even pay for, then you're necessary". This can be read as a way of shifting responsibility for the financial crisis from bankers to 'ordinary' people. However, it can also be read as opening up maths, moving away from elitism. Connecting consumption to maths implicates all of us in the crisis so we cannot "pretend [we] have no idea where it came from" (*Margin Call*). Similarly, breaking the fourth wall in *The Big Short* implicates us by placing us inside the action. This is most obvious at the end of the film, when Jared explains: "In the years that followed, hundreds of bankers and rating-agencies' executives went to jail. The SEC [Securities and Exchange Commission] was completely overhauled and Congress had no choice, but to break up the big banks and regulate the mortgage and derivative industries". As Jared speaks we see images representing the events he describes. Then, after a pause, he announces "just kidding", reminding us of the bank bailouts, bonuses and lack of reform. Despite knowing what happened, every time I watch this, I momentarily indulge in the fantasy of economic justice. The scene "moves us beyond what is merely actual and present into a realm of possibility, the not yet actualized or the not yet actualizable" (Butler, 2004, p. 28). It indicates we need democratic accountability in our financial systems, something which would also require a democratic maths, an aspiration most fully realised in the novel *Kapitoil*.

Kapitoil is a first person novel centred on Karim Issar, a young man from Qatar seconded to the Wall Street headquarters of his US employer, Schrub

Equities, to tackle the Y2K bug. The book takes the form of his diary entries from 3 October to 31 December 1999. Although set nearly a decade before the crash and two years before the 'war on terror' began, it can be read as a comment on both the financial crisis and post-9/11 US. We follow Karim as he creates a program (the eponymous Kapitoil) designed to use news reports on the Middle East to predict oil price fluctuations.

Karim's first person narration in *Kaptoil* gives insights into his mathematical way of being. For example, when visiting an art gallery he comments on the paintings of Piet Mondrian: "His lines are perfectly straight like geometric Islamic designs and would extend infinitely if the frames did not restrict them" (p. 16). Mathematical references and analogies recur through his diary. Karim's mathematical approach is also evident in his precise use of language: he lists new words beneath each diary entry and his Kapitoil computer program relies on nuanced distinctions, such as, between "claiming" and "taking" responsibility for terrorism. His distinct voice and approach are labelled Karim-esque and are linked to his mathematical and coding skills, but they are also related to the postmodern in a scene with his girlfriend Rebecca: "musicians like Bob Dylan and Leonard Cohen are also appealing because they sing about subjects that reject binaries and are mysterious in the way math can be mysterious, e.g., sometimes you locate an answer and the universe becomes almost magical because in the middle of chaos there is still order, and sometimes there is no answer, and because of that the universe is even more magical since it has secrets that humans can never understand. I told Rebecca this, and she said, 'You're turning into a real postmodernist'" (p. 272). Connecting maths to the postmodern, via the Karim-esque, suggests a maths beyond certainties, as in *Margin Call* and *The Big Short*, where "sometimes there is no answer". What is different than in the films is that *Kapitol* offers a way to navigate this uncertainty.

In Karim, *Kapitoil* gives us a central character who, as a Qatari Muslim, is other to the West, and to our dominant masculinity, preferring the company of women, and rejecting the laddish culture in his workplace. It is this oppositional positioning that enables the book to critique capitalism. When Karim has "nearly finished" programming his mathematical model in Kapitoil, he "evaluate[s] the big picture of what I am creating" and the morality of leveraging violence for profit. He reasons that such violence will persist independent of Kapitoil. "Therefore, by making money, the program produces at least some positives from a very negative situation. It turns the violence into a zero-sum game, because the money and violence cancel each other out" (p. 42). However, ultimately, he rejects this zero-sum game, hoping for a positive game. He refuses to sell his program to Schrub Equities, sacrificing his right to live in the United States with Rebecca and his family's financial security, to make his code freely available so that it can support global health and development. "The code must be on the open market for the best people to utilize it. And there may be applications we have not thought of" (p. 281). Despite retaining a notion of "the best people", this is largely a democratic vision of a collective crowd-sourced maths, in opposition to the exclusivity of private ownership.

> *How does this idea of maths as a collective rather than an individual endeavour fit with your experience? How does it fit with how you teach it?*

Conclusions

The financial crisis has transformed the world: millions have lost homes, jobs or both. In the countries most affected, rates of suicide, addiction and physical and mental health problems have increased dramatically driven by cuts to essential health and social services. My decision to focus on how maths is represented in financial crisis fictions is due to my conviction that as maths educators we cannot ignore the role our discipline played in the global financial collapse, "when the abstractions of the traders' equations become the reality of some (other) people's hunger" (Barwell, this volume, p. 203). Popular culture provides a way to engage with the crisis as it is here that we find the elitism and objectivity of maths being contested. Here we can find the beginnings of a movement for the social responsibility of maths that Paul Ernest calls for in Chapter 3. Through this we can connect the mathematical to other subjects – politics, economics, film and media studies and literature. Of course we can teach the financial crisis without novels and films. So I end with a different example to make some general points about the power of popular culture in the maths classroom.

Sarah J. Greenwald and Andrew Nestler (2004) describe using an episode of cartoon sitcom *The Simpsons* where one character, Homer, gets transported into a parallel universe that appears to be three-dimensional. Greenwald asks her students to write a letter from 3-D Homer to his 2-D wife Marge explaining his new spatial environment. They discuss whether the original world of *The Simpsons* really has two dimensions and extend the exercise to thinking about the difference between three- and four-dimensional spaces. "Typically a course segment on the geometry of the universe begins with a discussion of *Flatlanders*. The advantage of beginning with *The Simpsons* instead is that students relate to them and find them amusing. This helps students feel more comfortable with challenging material. For example, 2-D Marge feels less abstract to students than a Flatlander … After watching the movie clip, without even being prompted, students immediately argue about whether the Simpsons are 2-D or 3-D" (p. 35).

This approach makes creativity intrinsic to mathematical learning, moving us from ability mindsets to alternative mindsets to use the words of Mark Boylan and Hilary Povey. Skills not normally valued in maths classrooms – communication, creativity, imagination and empathy – are central to the task. Mathematical knowledge is no longer a matter of rights and wrongs with the teacher's role being to correct students' errors. It is negotiable and the teacher's role is to attempt to understand the students. It is often tempting, as a pressed-for-time teacher, to try to extract the maths from a text and abandon the rest. However, this can reinforce the opposition between the mathematical and the everyday instead of disrupting it. In this example, maths is not extracted from *The Simpsons* and then worked on separately, but it is embedded in the characters and their relationships. Popular texts create spaces for learners' own views and so give people alternatives to the current limited range of ways of relating to maths. The patterns of emotional investment and identification with characters and stories make these potentially ways of doing maths differently and more inclusively.

Marie-Pierre and I used this same example at the end of the chapter we wrote for the first edition of this book. But this time more is at stake because we have seen the devastation that can happen when we treat maths as infallible and leave it to the so-called experts.

Further reading

As well as the films and novel analysed in detail, the 2010 book *The Big Short* by Michael Lewis and the 2010 documentary *Inside Job* directed by Charles Ferguson are accessible guides to the financial crisis and *La Casa de Papel* is a recent, entertaining and provocative financial crisis fiction available on Netflix.

If you're interested in more stereotypical images of maths and mathematicians on film and television, you can read the chapter I wrote with Marie-Pierre Moreau in the first edition or my chapter 'Mediated Mathematics: Representations of Mathematics in Popular Culture and Why These Matter' in N. J. Higham, M. Dennis, P. Glendinning, P. Martin, F. Santosa & J. Tanner (Eds.) (2015). *The Princeton Companion to Applied Mathematics*. Princeton, NJ: Princeton University Press.

Appelbaum, P. M. (1995). *Popular culture, educational discourse and mathematics*. Albany: State University of New York Press. Peter Appelbaum uses juxtapositions between popular and school maths to challenge how we think about knowledge and education. He also makes suggestions for incorporating his ideas into the classroom.

simpsonsmath.com: http://mathsci2.appstate.edu/~sjg/simpsonsmath/: This website from Sarah J. Greewald & Andrew Nestler tracks the maths in *The Simpsons* TV animated sitcom and provides ideas for incorporating this into maths classrooms. Sarah has written extensively on using popular culture and living mathematicians to teach maths to undergraduates, see her website: http://mathsci2.appstate.edu/~sjg/.

MathFiction: http://kasmana.people.cofc.edu/MATHFICT/: Compiled by Alex Kasman, this is a vast collection of instances of maths and mathematicians in short stories, plays, novels, films and comic books. There is a description for each entry and ratings of their literary and mathematical quality based on user votes.

References

Butler, J. (2004). *Undoing gender*. Abington, Oxfordshire: Routledge.

Chandor, J. C. (Director) (2011). *Margin Call*. USA: Before The Door Pictures.

Duchin, M. (2004). *The sexual politics of genius*. Retrieved 8 July 2015, from http://mduchin.math.tufts.edu/genius.pdf

Ebert, R. (2011). *Margin Call*. Retrieved 23 August 2016, from http://www.rogerebert.com/reviews/margin-call-2011

Greenwald, S. J., & Nestler, A. (2004). r dr r: Engaging students with significant mathematical content from *The Simpsons. PRIMUS – Problems, Resources, and Issues in Mathematics Undergraduate Studies, XIV*(1), 29–39.

Marx, K. (1976). *Capital: A critique of political economy* (Vol. 1). London: Penguin.

Marx, K., & Engels, F. (1952). *Manifesto of the communist party*. Moscow: Progress Publishers.

McKay, A. (Director) (2015). *The Big Short*. USA: Plan B Entertainment.

Skovsmose, O. (1994). *Towards a philosophy of critical mathematics education*. Dordrecht: Kluwer Academic Publishers.

Wayne, T. (2010). *Kapitoil*. London: Duckworth Overlook.

Section Three

Debates about classroom matters

The chapter by **Alf Coles and Nathalie Sinclair** on planning for the unexpected uses two classroom examples to help us consider what can be planned for in advance and what, inevitably, remains unexpected. They emphasise the opportunities within the first task for pupils to think mathematically and they show that through explicit guidance, pupils can use mathematical language such as 'conjecture', 'counterexample' and 'proof' in their work. Their second task is focused on geometric reasoning. They identify how dynamic geometry software enables consideration of non-prototypical examples, which leads to rich mathematical discussion about properties of geometric shapes and also allows the highlighting of the 'indeterminacy of mathematics'. They identify how students' engagement in mathematical thinking relies on *symbolically structured environments*, where the teacher is listening out for student responses of the right 'kind', within an interplay of that which is constrained and that which allows for creativity.

The chapter by **John Mason** on questioning discusses how utterances which expect a response are used in mathematics classrooms. He presents a range of question types and considers what our expectation is in terms of the learner response to each type of question. Through a series of tasks, he encourages us to reflect on what the learner may perceive in the questions we ask. He notes that teachers tend to be good at funnelling questions to help the students to respond to the specific, and typically fairly closed, question being asked. He encourages his readers to consider a wider range of ways in which a teacher can respond to a student working on a mathematical task, either through asking their own questions or responding to the students' responses. He encourages us to ask questions in which we are genuinely interested to know the answer.

Anne Watson encourages us to problematise the design of mathematical tasks. She begins by encouraging the reader to attempt two tasks which she uses to highlight that it is the *associated pedagogy* involved in the use of the tasks in mathematics classrooms rather than simply the tasks themselves that gives rise to their possible richness. Having said that, she goes on to consider the nature of carefully designed tasks which encourage learners to develop their mathematical reasoning. Through the 'key questions' throughout the chapter,

Anne encourages her readers to identify some of the important considerations when planning a mathematical learning episode, for example, about whether the intention is to generate or apply mathematical relationships. Through engaging with these questions, she hopes readers will critically consider the role that tasks play in their teaching.

Keith Jones debates the extent to which the use of digital technologies improves mathematical outcomes. He considers how technology might be able to enhance the teaching and learning of mathematics, as well as how new forms of mathematical knowledge might be possible. He highlights the potential benefits of using the developing range of 'dynamic mathematics' available, where students can use computer software to explore the interaction between various mathematical topics. He explains that students are required to be able to 'specify the relationships' between the elements they are exploring, but not enough is known about how students come to do this. He talks about the way in which students might come to see the software as 'infrastructural', where they are just as used to using this software as they are with using a pencil and paper. He suggests that the potential benefits of digital technologies are nuanced, highlighting the need to consider aspects such as the role of the teacher and equity of access to these technologies.

Gwen Ineson and Sunita Babbar question the focus on 'back to basic' mental arithmetic in their chapter. They use the current English context to exemplify some of the key debates, including the discussion about balancing the teaching of formal written algorithms with a focus on flexible approaches to calculation, and how this relates to different ways of understanding mathematics. They draw a distinction between focusing on what pupils can do *in* their heads, with what they can do *with* their heads, and they suggest that teachers focus on the latter. The example of $207 \div 23$ is used to prompt debate about different ways of understanding. They argue that this would not be a good example to choose if the focus of the learning was on a standard written algorithm, but it is an excellent way to illustrate why the standard algorithm is not always useful; and they illustrate the alternative approaches to the example that their primary and secondary preservice teachers could (or in some cases, could not) draw on. They highlight the need for a limited reliance on the formal calculation approaches that tend to dominate many classrooms, and which seem to be encouraged in many of the questions at the end of primary school in formal assessments.

Tim Rowland focuses on the different roles that examples can play in mathematics classrooms. He encourages us to consider the purpose of examples, and indeed to ensure that they do have a specific purpose. He uses extracts from three lessons to explore the purpose and effect of the teachers' choice of examples within their lessons. He shows that variation theory can be considered when identifying particular examples to use, so that particular mathematical features within the problem can be discerned. He encourages the reader to explore what is possible to discern in the examples he shares in the chapter, as well as what is not possible to discern, in the case of less appropriate examples. He encourages us to consider the potential benefits of carefully pre-planned examples, as well as learner-generated examples, but notes that, ultimately, it is what the teacher does with their examples that can enhance mathematical learning.

All of these chapters focus in some way on mathematical tasks and the ways that teachers use them. The first two both share an awareness that working with tasks in a way that is open enough to generate mathematical thinking inevitably generates some indeterminacy. Alf Coles and Nathalie Sinclair call for the teacher to respond by 'planning for the unexpected' and to locate tasks within a symbolically structured environment where the specifics experienced will vary but where there is a planned for and shared focus on learner responses being of the 'right' kind, replacing an emphasis on the 'right' answer to predetermined questions. John Mason focuses in particular on the kinds of questions that are likely to prompt responses of the 'right' kind and encourages the use of questions to which the teacher does not already know the answer and for which the teacher is genuinely interested in the learner's response.

In common with these first two chapters, Anne Watson underlines the fact that, while the nature of tasks is important, the choice of tasks benefits from careful planning based on intentions about what is to be learnt. This is an important consideration, given the plethora of resources available online to support mathematics teachers. But, as with Alf Coles and Nathalie Sinclair, she shows that ultimately it is the use teachers make of chosen tasks that is key to the task's effectiveness. This point is taken up by Keith Jones, this time in the context of digital technologies. He draws on cases where students used computer programming to think mathematically and computationally but asserts that the debate about the potential benefits of the new technologies is a nuanced one and, in the last analysis, effective use depends on the role the teacher plays.

The detailed and careful planning of the choice of examples is the focus of the final two chapters in this section. The context for the chapter by Gwen Ineson and Sunita Babbar is primary school number work. The authors challenge the dominant use that is made of standard written algorithms and show that well-chosen examples have the potential to open up spaces for children to think about calculation mathematically though, again, only if teachers are able to exploit these opportunities. Finally, Tim Rowland analyses the different functions that examples play in mathematics. He highlights the need to consider what is intended by any given use of an example and he encourages the choice of examples that are fit for purpose.

Chapter 10

Planning for the unexpected

Working within symbolically structured environments

Alf Coles and Nathalie Sinclair

> *What is your image of an ideal mathematics classroom culture? What kinds of conversation would be taking place? What kinds of tasks would be on offer? What would be the role of the teacher? Take a moment to write down or collect your thoughts.*

We begin this chapter with two classroom examples, including some of the thinking behind their planning, we offer them to provoke thinking about what can be planned and what must remain unexpected, if a teacher aims to "create the conditions in which creative and independent work can take place" (Banwell, Saunders and Tahta, 1986, p. 18). These examples were chosen, one from primary and one from secondary school, to allow the raising of issues related to planning for the unexpected. The phrase 'symbolically structured environment', from the title, is one we will elaborate on after the two examples. It links to common features we have recently become aware of, in the teaching of some key figures of mathematics education from the 20th century (for example, Gattegno, 1974; Papert, 1980) and relates to how we might design tasks for the classroom (see Chapter 12 by Anne Watson).

> *We invite you to read the following two accounts and then consider similarities and differences. We also invite you to engage in the tasks themselves.*

Account 1: Pick's Theorem (secondary)

Pick's Theorem is used to determine the area of a polygon on a square dot grid. It connects three features of polygons. Students can work with multiple relationships, for example, by fixing one feature and varying the other two. The Theorem states that, if A is the area of the shape and I is the number of dots on the inside and O is the number of dots on the perimeter, then $A = \frac{1}{2} O + I - 1$. An entry into work on the Theorem is described in the seminal book *Starting Points* by Banwell, Saunders and Tahta (1986). The classroom account below is reconstructed from work that took place in a Year 8 class (age 12–13) in an English school where Alf used to work. In the school's departmental write-up of the task, the reasons for doing it were as follows:

Possible mathematical content:

- Distinguishing area from perimeter, finding the areas of shapes without counting squares, finding the areas of triangles as half of a rectangle and finding the areas of compound complex shapes.
- Opportunities for mathematical thinking.
- Making predictions about the areas of '8-dot shapes', '9-dot shapes' and so on, making conjectures, testing conjectures, finding counterexample, expressing conjectures using algebra, finding relationships between three variables. (Department Scheme of Work).

Work on this task would typically last over a three- or four-week period (that is, around 10 hours class time, along with related homework tasks each week). An overall aim for the year in this school was explicitly stated to students as being about supporting them in 'becoming a mathematician' and 'thinking mathematically'. The language of conjecture, counterexample and proof was introduced by teachers and used in an explicit way, with the aim that students would use these notions to structure their own work on mathematics.

The teacher (and we are drawing here primarily on Alf's experience of working on this task in school) draws on the board (see Figure 10.1) two shapes and says: "These are both 8-dot shapes. Someone come and draw me another, different, 8-dot shape".

Students come to the board and, without comment about why, the teacher indicates if the shape is 8-dot or not.

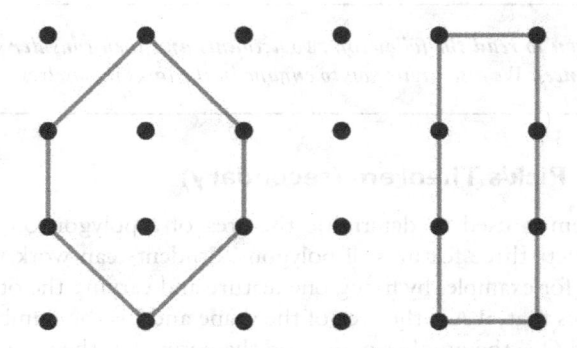

Figure 10.1 Two 8-dot shapes.

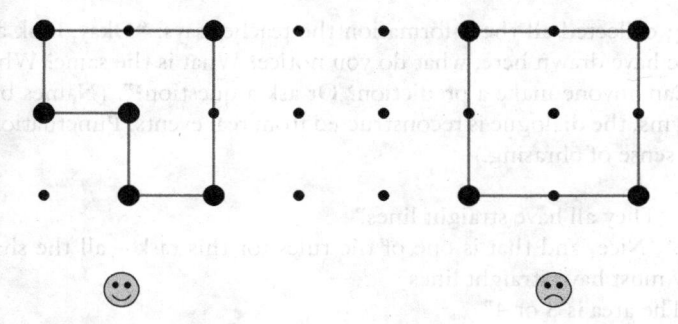

Figure 10.2 Student offers of 8-dot shapes.

The distinction the teacher needs students to make, in setting up this task, is that shapes are labelled by adding up the number of dots inside and on the outside (perimeter). Rather than try to explain this (which would inevitably lead to confusion), the teacher invites students to do something (publicly draw some shapes); the teacher cannot know what students will draw, but can know they will give feedback. The teacher continues inviting new shapes to be drawn until students can explain what makes a shape an '8-dot shape'. The right hand shape in Figure 10.2 is classified as '9-dot'.

The teacher now sets up a structure for the task that, whenever students draw a shape, they need to write next to it, I (for the number of dots 'inside'), O (for the number of dots on the 'outside') and A (for the area of the shape), as in Figure 10.3. Students have met the concept of 'area' before but need reminding about it. The class work together, finding the three values (I, O, A) for all the shapes on the board.

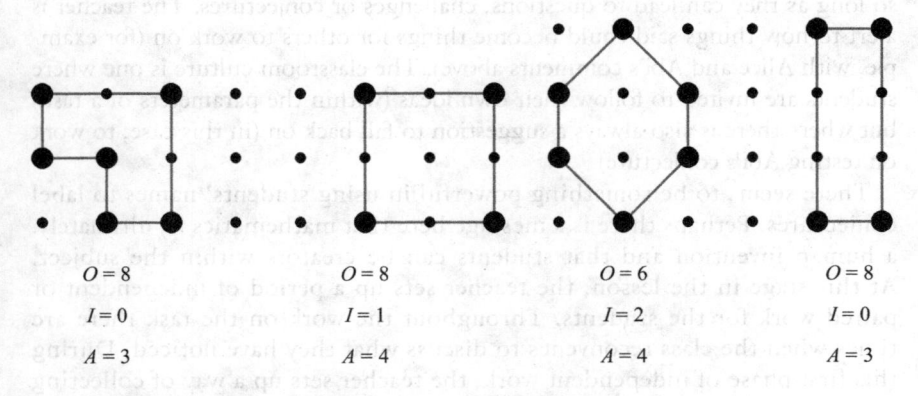

$O = 8$	$O = 8$	$O = 6$	$O = 8$
$I = 0$	$I = 1$	$I = 2$	$I = 0$
$A = 3$	$A = 4$	$A = 4$	$A = 3$

Figure 10.3 Information needed for each shape drawn.

Having collected all the information the teacher says: "Okay, look at all the shapes we have drawn here, what do you notice? What is the same? What is different? Can anyone make a prediction? Or ask a question?". (Names below are pseudonyms, the dialogue is reconstructed from real events. Punctuation is used to give a sense of phrasing.)

JORDAN: "They all have straight lines"

TEACHER: "Nice, and that is one of the rules for this task – all the shapes you draw must have straight lines"

ALICE: "The area is 3 or 4"

TEACHER: "Right, for all the shapes we have here, the area is 3 or 4. So, could someone turn that into a question or a challenge?"

MIKE: "Are the areas always 3 or 4?"

TEACHER: "Lovely, so let's have that as a challenge – can you find an 8-dot shape where the area is not 3 or 4" (writing this on the board)

ABI: "If the inside is zero, the area is 3"

TEACHER: "So, we have our first conjecture on this project. Abi, can you say that again and I am going to write it down, and remember this is just for 8-dot shapes that we are looking at"

ABI REPEATS AND THE TEACHER WRITES ON THE BOARD: "Abi's conjecture: for 8-dot shapes if $I = 0$, then $A = 3$"

TEACHER: "So, how could we test Abi's conjecture?"

The students in the class, by this point in the year, are familiar with what a 'conjecture' means and that they can 'work' on conjectures by trying out if the prediction is correct, for different examples (and examples that do not work are called 'counterexamples', which prompt the need to rework the conjecture). The teacher cannot know what the students will notice, but is confident that there will be some things noticed that allow tasks to be set up for the class, related to the problem. It does not really matter what particular things are said, so long as they can lead to questions, challenges or conjectures. The teacher is alert to how things said could become things for others to work on (for example, with Alice and Abi's comments above). The classroom culture is one where students are invited to follow their own ideas (within the parameters of a task) but where there is also always a suggestion to fall back on (in this case, to work on testing Abi's conjecture).

There seems to be something powerful in using students' names to label conjectures. Perhaps there is a message here that mathematics is, ultimately, a human invention and that students can be creators within the subject. At this stage in the lesson, the teacher sets up a period of independent or paired work for the students. Throughout the work on the task there are times when the class reconvenes to discuss what they have noticed. During this first phase of independent work, the teacher sets up a way of collecting

Table 10.1 A table of results

8-dot shapes		
O	I	A
8	0	3
6	2	4
8	0	3
7	1	3.5

results (see Table 10.1) and students come up to the board to add to it, whenever they find a new shape.

At some point, this table will be organised to support the further noticing of patterns and making of conjectures. Again, the teacher cannot know what shapes students will try out, but can plan to collect results in this way. The structure of the table invites questions such as, what is the greatest number of dots you can create 'inside', with an 8-dot shape?

Once the class have worked on 8-dot shapes for a while, the teacher invites students to try out a different number of dots of their own choosing, following the same pattern of collecting results in a table. All these tables are made visible to all students (what were called 'common boards' in the school) and this visibility invites further noticing of patterns and relationships. Some students get to a general relationship between the three variables.

Account 2: Triangles (primary)

The second task we invite you to read about took place in a grade 2 (aged 7–8) classroom in Canada; the teacher (and we are drawing here primarily on Nathalie's experience of working on this task in school) wants to work on the topic of triangles. Knowing that children of this age often have a prototypical image of triangle, as an equilateral triangle sitting on one of its sides, the teacher wants to engage the children in coordinating the descriptions of triangles with various configurations of triangles. The goal, after all, is to engage in geometric reasoning, and not shape identification and classification, that one might pursue in a biology class. Since dynamic geometric software provides an easy and precise way of generating different configurations of triangles, she invites the children to tell her which of the tools she could use to create a triangle (Figure 10.4), there are three tools: point, circle and segment. The children quickly identify the segment tool as useful and one child instructs the teachers to "make three sides that are connected". The teacher creates the three-sided shape shown in Figure 10.5. The children protest: "that's not a triangle. It's upside down". The teacher responds: "but you told me to make three sides that were connected and that's what I did."

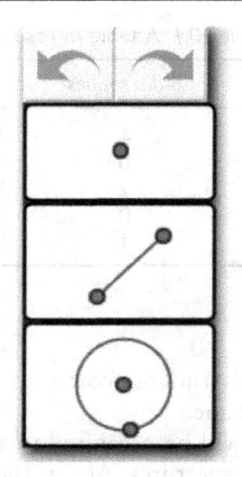

Figure 10.4 Sketchpad tools.

The children are silent. The teacher adds, "You didn't say it had to be right side up." Still more silence.

The teacher announces, "I'm going to move one of the points. Watch what happens." The teacher begins to drag the vertex of the triangle on the screen, producing a range of triangles including one that looks more like 'the triangle' the children are accustomed to seeing. Many children make exclamations of surprise. They are riveted to the screen. One child comments, "You can stretch it out!" Another adds, "It's a triangle." And a third says, "Every shape can be a triangle but it just has to have three corners."

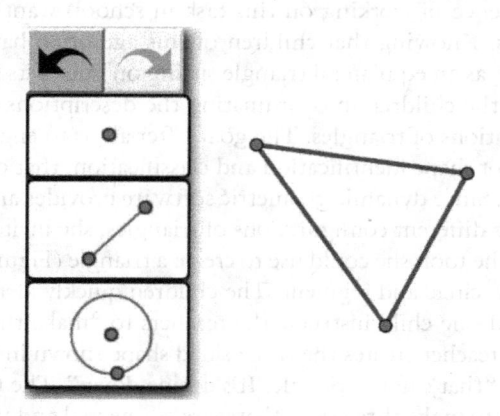

Figure 10.5 A triangle.

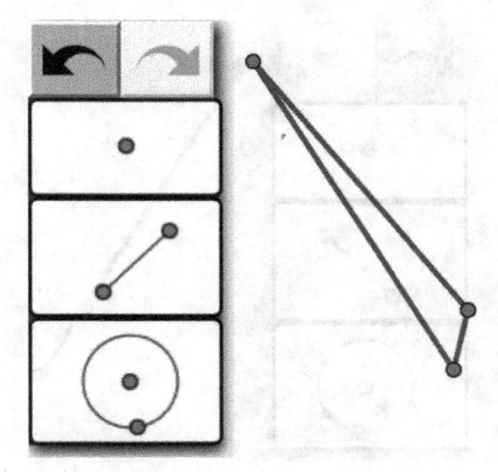

Figure 10.6 A stretched triangle.

Up to this point, the teacher could predict that the children would not count the upside-down three-sided shape as a triangle. She knew that she could make it look more like 'their' triangle. She had also been in many other classrooms, with children ranging from kindergarten to grade 6, in which the act of dragging the triangle had eventually helped the children to coordinate their descriptions of triangles (it has three sides) with configurations of triangles that initially looked strange. Sometimes the children would quickly accept an 'upside-down triangle', but were more reticent with a really long and skinny triangle (Figure 10.6). It could take some more time to get to the kind of definitional statement quoted above. Even though the actual examples might change, as well as the children's comments and reasoning, the teacher's plan was that the children could identify non-prototypical three-sided shapes as triangles.

Now she starts to move one of the vertices around again and this time it lands *on* the opposite side of the triangle. She stops moving it. The children giggle. One child says, "that is *not* a triangle." Another points out that there are still three corners (see Figure 10.7). To this statement, yet another child notes, "but there is no inside". To each of these comments, the teacher nods. By deciding to collapse the triangle in this way, she is braced for the unexpected. Some children react strongly to this degenerate case; already the long, skinny triangle was a stretch, but this monster? Others want to know the right answer, is it, or is it not a triangle? New ideas come up that haven't been mentioned before, like the inside of the triangle. Does every triangle have an inside, or do we really only count the three sides? One child proposes that it should indeed be a triangle, but we are only seeing it head-on and it's actually three-dimensional. What is unpredictable is the valence of the discussion, that is, the emotional reaction the children have, to this shape; whether they accept it into the family of triangles or

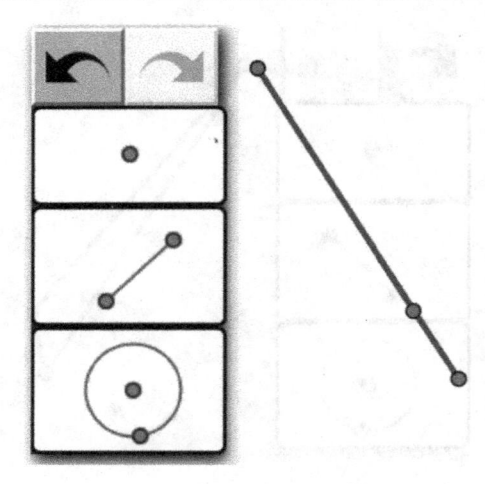

Figure 10.7 A triangle or line?

want to expel it. What is also unpredictable is the direction that the conversation will take. Unlike the upside-down triangle, this degenerate triangle is both a triangle and not a triangle. The definition in play – having three corners – does not discriminate. Indeed, in a pencil and paper environment, this triangle never even comes up for consideration. No plastic shapes have been made that look like this either. And if the children were working with strings or sticks, the configuration wouldn't come up because the sides would have to be lifted off the plane.

In allowing it to emerge, the teacher is drawing attention to the indeterminacy of mathematics itself and to the fact that, sometimes, there is no right answer. If the discussion cannot be resolved by logical means alone, then considerations of aesthetics, in relation to choices, might need to be allowed through the classroom door (Sinclair, 2001). Maybe, since the point can be dragged almost anywhere else and still form a triangle, this flat object should also be counted as a triangle. That would satisfy a penchant for continuity and inclusiveness. Maybe it shouldn't count as a triangle; after all, there's nothing you can do with this triangle: you can't measure its area, you can't find its point of balance, except perhaps abstractly. This somewhat utilitarian view cares less about inclusiveness and more about shapes you can actually do something with. If it's a three-dimensional shape, then are all triangles also to be thought of as being three-dimensional? Does this open up a new path of mathematical activity, or make the current path much too complicated? To work productively with the unpredictability inherent in this task, the teacher must not only listen to the children's ideas, but also help them articulate reasons that may be both logical and aesthetic, both about what they already know about triangles and what they value in mathematics.

This kind of planning for the unexpected might expose children to aspects of mathematics they do not usually encounter. It exposes the very contingent nature of mathematics; the fact that any definition will have counterexamples and even aspects of vagueness; the way in which what initially gets dismissed as nonsense (negative and irrational numbers, parallel lines that meet at a point, quantities bigger than infinity) can later become common sense.

Reflections

> *Looking back over these two descriptions of classroom tasks, what do you notice? What is the same? What is different? What has the teacher planned? What is unexpected and what is not?*

Some of the similarities we see are as follows:

- There appears to be some inevitability, and therefore predictability, in student responses (for example, the noticing of patterns in Pick's Theorem; or the engagement in considering the degenerate triangle) even though the details of responses are unknowable.
- There is some definitional work taking place in both examples; with the triangles, the definition is central to the task, for Pick's Theorem, definitions (for example, of '8-dot shape') are 'held' by the teacher, leading to questions from students.
- We see some of the engagement of students, in both tasks, as arising from the need for them to grapple with deliberately ambiguous definitions ('what is an 8-dot shape?', 'what is a triangle?'). There is perhaps a contrast here to images of mathematics teaching that might value clarity and unambiguous definition. The ambiguity of definition seems significant in creating the space for discussion.
- Students' thinking is made visible to each other with support from the teacher (either through speaking or writing).
- The situations given to students provide them with immediate feedback related to their actions (in Pick's Theorem, in the form of the three numbers they generate for each shape; in the triangle task, via the way the shape responds to moves of a vertex).

> *What else did you notice?*

In terms of what was planned, we consider each account in turn. For Pick's Theorem, we suggest that what had been planned in advance of the lesson included:

1 A process all students will follow (attending to 8-dot shapes only at first; drawing shapes against a criterion, for example, having 8 dots; finding O, I, and A; recording results in a table; looking for patterns).
2 Symbols linked to that process (values for O, I, A).

3   A way of collecting results so that everyone can see them (common boards for O, I, and A, for 8-dot shapes, 9-dot shapes and so on).
4   Complex mathematical relationships (between three variables).
5   A starting point that is accessible to all.

In the triangle task, we observe the following plans:

1   The digital environment to use (in this case Geometer's Sketchpad) that allows actions of transformation (moving the triangle vertices).
2   An image to work with, the image acting as a symbol for a triangle.
3   A way of sharing reasoning (norms for discussion).
4   A digital environment and set of tools that are structured to allow access to the whole of Euclidean geometry.
5   A task that challenges preconceptions.

We have deliberately ordered these features of planning to draw out parallels relating to: (1) an environment that embodies some mathematical constraints and relationships; (2) the way relationships are symbolised; (3) the different ways that students' work is made visible to each other; (4) the importance of the complexity of the mathematical environment, within which a smaller subset of possible relationships is considered as a starting point (5).

And, what was unexpected? We observe:

- The teacher for 'Pick's Theorem' cannot have known what students will notice and therefore what particular conjectures will be worked on by students.
- The teacher in the 'Triangle' lesson cannot have known what arguments students would bring to the 'degenerate' case, nor where the balance of views would lie.

What can allow, then, for both the planning of a lesson and the unexpect-edness of student responses that seems to be so crucial to their engagement in mathematical thinking? We see a key role for the mathematics that is offered. In the next section, we set out our thinking about how tasks can be designed to allow interplay between planning and the unexpected. We conclude this chapter by reflecting on the role of the teacher in planning for the unexpected.

The role of the mathematics: Symbolically structured environments

In both of these examples, we'd like to highlight the ways in which the teach-er's planning for the unexpected has something important to do with the discipline of mathematics. In a sense mathematics itself is a structure with defined symbols and constraints (and thus it is planned) that can nevertheless produce unexpected things. Mathematicians have ways of producing the unexpected such as changing axioms, shifting dimensions, finding counterexamples and building analogies. In doing so, there is a certain arbitrariness in what actually occurs. In the same way, for the Pick's Theorem example, students may come up with a range of conjectures; what matters is that they emerge from the constraints of the 'game' that was offered. In the triangle example, the nature of the arbitrariness is a little different. It seems to relate to the nature of geometric definitions, which the mathematician Coxeter (1987) compared to dictionary entries: when you look up one word, you find in its definition another word that needs to be looked up, which gives a definition of still another word, and so on, *without a real starting point on which all definitions depend.*

In thinking about the environment in which the two examples occurred, and in comparing them to similar kinds of situations, we have found it useful to think of them as 'symbolically structured environments' (SSEs) that are both constrained (by mathematical rules and norms) and generative. We list some features of SSEs, below, and describe how they relate to each of the examples.

a   Symbols are offered to stand for actions or distinctions (unlike a resource such as, say, Dienes blocks, where symbols relate directly to objects).

   TRIANGLE: the task is all about what distinctions come under the label/ symbol 'triangle' and about acting on the geometric objects of points and segments.

   PICK'S: labels of I and O are used to describe distinctions students make about shapes. The label for A is introduced by the teacher, initially linked, perhaps, to splitting a shape into squares.

b   Symbol use is governed by mathematical rules or constraints embedded in the structuring of the environment (rules for symbol use do not need to be memorised but can be enacted and corrected, if needed, with feedback from the SSE).

   TRIANGLE: the way that points move is constrained by the mathematics inherent in Euclidean space (they cannot all of a sudden be split, or move into a hyperbolic plane). A further norm at play is the relation between the particular and the general – there is little interest in defining one particular shape and instead there is a propensity to think in terms of classes of shapes (in this case, classes of triangles).

   PICK'S: the constraint of creating shapes on a square dot grid ensures that there are relationships to be found between the three values that are used on each shape.

c   Symbols or actions can be immediately linked to their inverse (symbols are not taught in isolation and gain meaning from links to other symbols).

> TRIANGLE: an action or transformation of the triangle can be undone.
>
> PICK'S: as a result of putting results in tables, students quickly move from finding the area of shapes they have drawn to the inverse challenge of looking for shapes with particular areas (to fill in missing rows of the table).

d   Complexity can be constrained, while still engaging with a mathematically integral, whole environment (the starting point can become more or less complex, contingent on learners).

> TRIANGLE: only three tools are considered initially and the most simple of closed shapes that can be created.
>
> PICK'S: the teacher constrains attention to only 8-dot shapes initially, before opening up the space to other numbers of dots (but constraining students to focus on a specific number at a time).

e   Novel symbolic moves can be made (creative symbol use does not have to arrive late in the learning process).

> TRIANGLE: moving the third point onto the line connecting the other two; but there is also the potential of working with four-sided instead of three-sided shapes, etc.
>
> PICK'S: new symbolic relationships are noticed by students; the actual shape of the 8-dot polygons can vary enormously (common polygons, concave ones, etc.).

As alluded to in the Introduction, we see these principles as characteristic of some of the work of Caleb Gattegno (1974), who developed a curriculum around the structured use of Cuisenaire rods, and Seymour Papert (1980), who developed 'microworlds' such as Logo, within which children could experience mathematical relationship in a creative and independent manner. We see such spaces as well suited to working with classes that are not grouped by prior attainment (see Chapter 5 by Mark Boylan and Hilary Povey), as there can be opportunity for students to be working on different questions and challenges within the same environment and, the sharing of data or results can allow all students access to pattern spotting and conjecturing.

So, how do you find more of these kinds of spaces? We first address this question by taking each example and trying to vary it a little. For the triangle example, an important trigger involves the tension between precision and ambiguity in geometric vocabulary. How could this be used in a different space? Consider a situation in which students are asked to draw the diagonals of various polygons.

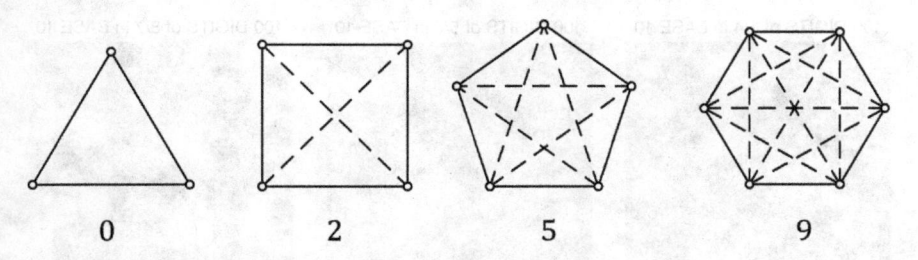

Figure 10.8 Diagonals of regular polygons.

If these polygons are regular, they might propose a certain relation between the number of sides of the polygon and the number of diagonals (Figure 10.8). But the teacher might then propose the concave polygon in Figure 10.9. How many diagonals does it have?

The direction that the task will take depends on how students want to define a diagonal. The teacher might be able to predict that the students will assume all diagonals have to be 'inside' the polygon and therefore be challenged by the concave polygon. Perhaps they make a conjecture that extends the diagonals of regular polygons. The novel symbolic moves thus relate to the way diagonals are drawn and defined. The complexity arises from the opening up of the terrain to non-regular and concave polygons.

For the Pick's example, an important trigger relates to the establishing of a certain entry into the terrain that then has multiple potential directions. The environment was initially constrained to 8-dot polygons, rather than to all polygons. The first few shapes gave a sense of the potential variation, while also hinting at an aspect of invariance or pattern. We might thus be able to imagine a similar kind of unexpectedness in planning a task where students are asked to type the following fractions into the 'colour calculator'[1]: $\frac{1}{4}$, $\frac{5}{6}$ and $\frac{8}{7}$. The display

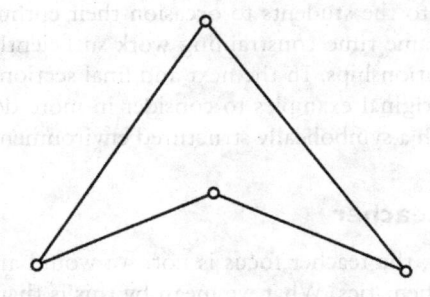

Figure 10.9 A concave quadrilateral.

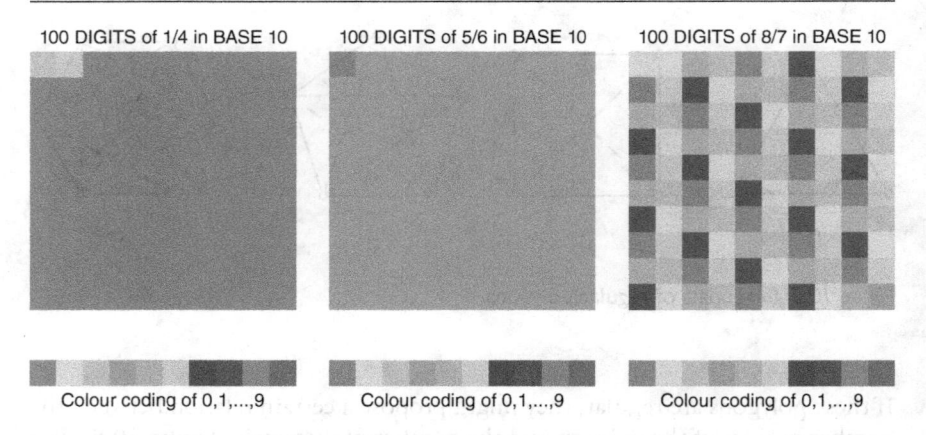

Figure 10.10 The colour calculator.

is a representation of the decimal expansion of any fraction, with the digits 0 to 9 having a unique colour (see key, in Figure 10.10).

The instructions give a sense of the potential variance (the numerator and the denominator can change, the numerator can be bigger than the denominator) and the output provides a hint at what possible patterns might look like. If a student tries $\frac{5}{7}$, the following conjecture might be made: if I use 7 in the denominator, I always get a repeating pattern of six colours. If the student tries instead $\frac{3}{4}$, the following conjecture might be made: with 4 in the denominator there are always three different colours. The concept of fraction is subordinated to the exploration of pattern and the generation of conjectures, just as the concept of area was subordinated in the Pick's example. (Being able to use a concept without paying attention to it would be one way of thinking about what it means to have 'mastered' the concept – see Chapter 2 by Mark Boylan). While the students' prior mathematical experience might help the teacher expect certain kinds of noticing, these are not determined in advance (see Sinclair (2001) for a fuller description of possibilities with the colour calculator).

There is a sophisticated and delicate role for the teacher, in terms of devolving any task sufficiently to the students to occasion their enthusiasm and commitment, while at the same time constraining work sufficiently to ensure a focus on mathematical relationships. In the next and final section of this chapter, we return to our two original examples to consider in more detail the role of the teacher, working with a symbolically structured environment.

The role of the teacher

In the two accounts, the teacher focus is not, we would argue, on the details of the students' mathematics. What we mean by this is that while the students are becoming energised by patterns they notice related to Pick's Theorem, the teacher's attention is on whether students' offers of ideas can be turned into a question or conjecture that others could use to guide their work; or, while students become energised by their own sense of what it means to be a triangle, the teacher's attention is on the form of talk taking place and whether students are reasoning and hearing the reasoning of others.

A requirement of such a focus is that the teacher is able to listen to the detail and subtlety of student contributions. This is no easy task (see Coles and Scott, 2015 for a story of learning and change in relation to listening and the unexpected). In our examples, the teacher is not listening out *for* particular responses (in the sense of a 'right' answer), but perhaps for particular *kinds* of example (the right 'kind' of answer). Familiarity with the environment seems key, in being able to focus attention on the *kinds* of things students say, without needing to worry overly about what might happen next. There is a paradox here. It is hard to work contingently within a symbolically structured environment that is new to you. And yet, the only way to become more comfortable teaching within such an environment is to use it. The teachers in our examples were both experienced at working within those environments, meaning they could take on the role of orchestrating rather than directing events (for example, provoking students with the degenerate triangle or judging when to move students on to looking at other dot shapes and when not).

Having skills to manage classroom talk appears to be a need, for the teacher, across both our examples. Starting to teach, it can seem like an impossibility to generate productive classroom talk. We can split the issue of managing talk into two elements: how to generate some response from students and how to respond to those responses.

In terms of how to generate student responses, we invite you to do the following task:

> *Think back over your own teaching. What are some questions or tasks that generated a buzz of response or conversation? Are there any common features to what you did, or what students were considering?*

When considering how to respond to student responses, we are perhaps straying into the realms of the unsayable. However, a salutary but powerful experience can be to do the following activity:

> *Audio record your interactions with students during a lesson. Listen back to the recording at a later date. Did you hear what was said? What interpretations might be possible of what a student meant, other than the one you assumed?*

Having contrasting examples for students to compare is one suggestion for generating energetic responses (see Brown and Coles, 2000). (In a similar way, we have tried to provide contrasting examples in this chapter, hoping to generate some energetic responses from readers!) From contrasting examples, it is possible to ask "what is the same and what is different?" (ibid) which is a question that can be answered at any level from the most straightforward to the most sophisticated. We hypothesise that a SSE supports students and teachers in answering this question within a mathematical discourse, using the symbols and actions of the constrained space and allowing a creative interplay of the unexpected and the planned.

Note

1   The colour calculator is available online at: http://wayback.cecm.sfu.ca/cgi-bin/ColorCalc/n/maths.cgi/11m/?Eqn=&RawEqn=&nDigits=100&ColourPlotWidth=10&Base=10&do=activity&activity=calc. A similar interface is available here: http://www.sineofthetimes.org/experiments-with-a-color-calculator/

Further reading

Brown, L., & Coles, A. (2000). Same/different: A 'natural' way of learning mathematics. *Proceedings of 24th Conference of the International Group for the Psychology of Mathematics Education, 2*, 113–120. Available at: https://eric.ed.gov/?id=ED452032. This article exemplifies the use of the teaching strategy of setting up tasks where the starting point for students is to answer the question "What is the same, what is different?".

Coles, A., & Scott, H. (2015). Planning for the unexpected in the mathematics classroom: teacher and student change. *Research in Mathematics Education, 17*(2), 121–138. This article charts the change, over a year, of a teacher (Scott) and one of her students, drawing out parallels and implications.

Papert, S. (1980). *Mindstorms: Children, computers and powerful ideas.* London: Harvester Press. Papert's writing about Turtle Geometry (using the programming language Logo (one of whose heirs is Scratch)) proposed a constructionist approach to mathematics education where children learn by making. His vision was of a mathematics education in which students could be creative inventors at the same time as becoming skilled in technique and in problem-solving (through processes such as bricolage and debugging).

References

Banwell, C., Saunders, K., & Tahta, D. (1986). *Starting points: for teaching mathematics in middle and secondary schools.* St Albans, UK: Tarquin Publishers.

Coxeter, H. S. M. (1987). *Projective geometry* (2nd ed.). New York: Springer-Verlag.

Gattegno, C. (1974). *The common sense of teaching mathematics.* NY: Educational Solutions.

Sinclair, N. (2001). The aesthetics is relevant. *For the Learning of Mathematics, 21*(1), 25–32.

Chapter 11

Effective questioning and responding in the mathematics classroom[1]

John Mason

Introduction

Asking learners (especially children) questions is so strongly embedded in our culture that most adults do it when in the company of children, and most children do it when playing 'school' with their friends or by themselves. Furthermore, in these types of interactions, the questioner usually knows the answer, and most children quickly work out that this is the case. They engage in the game for various reasons, including as a way to get adult attention. Questions in school are seen as some sort of testing process, through which learners supposedly learn, and this carries over into adult-child interactions. Many classroom interactions are some variant on "guess what is in my mind". This suggests some issues:

> *How do questions arise in the classroom?*
> *How can we use them effectively?*
> *How can we stimulate learners to ask their own questions?*

These questions are addressed through considering a number of conjectures which cannot be proved as universal:

> There are no rich tasks, only tasks used richly: it is not so much the question which is pedagogically effective, ... but the way the response is handled and the ethos in which it is asked.
>
> Every act of teaching is an intervention in the movement of attention of learners.
>
> The kinds of questions asked, and the way in which they are asked, influences learners' perception of the subject matter as well as their disposition to engage.

How do questions arise?

Not all utterances with a question mark, or with a rising tone at the end, are actually questions, while some assertions are intended to produce a response. For example, "We don't do that in here, do we?" is an assertion not a question, and "Tell me what you are thinking" requires or expects a response. For ease of reference the word *question* will be taken to include any utterance (or gesture or posture) which expects a response. So how do questions arise, particularly in an educational context?

> *Conjecture*: an adult asks a learner a question when the adult, while in the presence of the learner, experiences a shift in the focus of their own attention. The question is intended to reproduce that shift of focus in the learner.

This conjecture has to be tested in your own experience, by trying to catch yourself suddenly asking children or other learners some question. Then ask yourself, where did that question come from? What was the impulse to ask? My experience suggests that questions usually arise when I experience a contrast, or a change in my focus, and without even being aware of it, I use the format of a question to try to direct learners' attention. Furthermore, and this is the important part, I often find that it is only when I hear the learner's response that I am aware that it conflicts with what I then (and only then) realise I was expecting. The response shifts my attention from dwelling in my own focus of attention to recognising that I had something in my head, some expectation.

Thus it seems that questions have the effect of focusing or directing other peoples' attention. They arise from the movements of attention of the asker, and they are likely to be a disturbance to the focus of other people's attention. Unfortunately, that disturbance may not always be welcome.

> *Testing the conjecture: over the space of a week, try to catch yourself asking a question while at the same time noting the origin or arising of that question.*

Vacuous questions

After telling learners something it can be very tempting to ask "do you understand?". However, the audience cannot know whether they do actually understand. All they can judge is whether what has been said seems to make sense. (See Chapter 7 by Anna Llewellyn). Similarly, asking learners "what did you learn today" is unlikely to generate a considered response, because it is rare to be explicitly aware of what has been learned.

Controlling questions

Because it is an accepted cultural norm that questions are supposed to be answered, questioning is one way in which people exert social control, one way in which they assert authority or power (Ainley 1987; Love and Mason 1992). For example "What do we do when we come into the classroom … ?", "We don't do that, now do we?", "Where do we put the equals sign?". This applies especially in a class, where by picking on certain individuals to respond, and by stopping one line of discussion through introducing a new one, the teacher retains control. A natural and frequent occurrence, however, is that not-answering is used by learners as a form of reaction or revolt, even an attempt to grab back some power and influence. This is most likely when learners feel buffeted by questions, or when they detect that questions are being used for control purposes.

Similarly, we retain control over learner attention by asking focusing questions such as "What is in front of the x?", "What is next to the three?", "What do we do with the variable?", "What does the diagram tell us?" Sometimes the question usefully redirects attention and the learner is able to take back the initiative, but in many cases, if the learner had an answer to the question, they would probably not be stuck in the first place!

Cloze technique

Pausing in a flow of statements and expecting students to fill in the missing word is a common format for testing-questions in classrooms. For example, "This shape is called a _____.", and "The next thing we do is to carry down the _____." Note that the missing word is usually at the end of a sentence. The assumption is that students are having their attention directed to the key detail, rehearsing patterns of inner speech that will help them carry out the technique. The production by them of the appropriate label is supposed to reinforce memory so that they will know what to do next time.

> *When (not if!) you catch yourself pausing and expecting children to complete your statements, make sure that you are getting them to fill in the reasoning, rehearsing the commentary as a whole, not simply parroting technical terms.*

Genuine enquiry

Not all questions exert control explicitly. Asking "Why?" or even longer questions starting with "why …" may sometimes be effective in engaging learners (see Chapter 19 by Alison Barnes and Rachel Marks), but it often comes across as an attack, a form of control. By contrast, it is possible to enquire genuinely about what someone is thinking: "How did you get that?", "Can you tell me how to do this type of question in the future?", "How do you know?", or by questioning assumptions (see Chapter 16 by Richard Barwell). Unfortunately, the fact that such a question is being asked by a teacher is likely to lead the learner into believing that the teacher knows the answer and expects the learner to know it too, and/or that what the learner has been doing is not correct or not appropriate. Thus the fact of a question being asked is likely to generate a defensive stance, to be seen as controlling even when this is not intended.

Voice tones together with posture and gesture can be critical for indicating genuineness. A slight change of inflection, a suitable pause and facial movement can make all the difference. It takes time to build up trust and to establish a suitable mathematical environment, a 'conjecturing atmosphere' (see later section).

> *How might your learners distinguish between you enquiring genuinely, and you drawing attention to something that needs adjusting?*

Meta-questions

Meta-questions are questions about the activity which draw learner attention out of the particularities of the current task with a view to making them aware of a process. For example: "What would you have to do next time to answer a similar question?" and "What question am I going to ask you?" are typical meta-questions.

This last question is typical of a range of increasingly indirect prompts used to encourage learners to internalise questions which they could usefully ask themselves. When a particular type of question is proving fruitful such as "Can you give me an example", or "What do you *Know* in this problem and what do you *Want* to find?", the teacher can explicitly refer to the use of these questions, perhaps by asking themselves out loud and replying in front of the learners while working on a problem, then using the same questions with learners, before gently sliding into more meta-questions.

If learners come to rely on the teacher to ask the same question every time, then learners are being trained in dependency, not educated to be independent. After a period of time it is important to become less and less direct and more and more indirect so that learners begin to internalise the question. The aim is that they take the initiative to ask themselves.

The process of moving from *directed questions*, through increasingly *indirect prompts* towards *spontaneous use* by learners, is also known as scaffolding (the direct questions) and fading (increasingly indirect prompts). The term *scaffolding* was introduced by Wood et al. (1976) and used by Bruner (1986) to bring ideas of the Russian psychologist Lev Vygotsky to the West. The effectiveness of scaffolding lies not in the actual scaffolding itself but in the fading, the increasingly indirect prompts so that learners internalise the support (Brown et al. 1989).

> *What might prompt you to begin 'fading' some question type that you have been using?*

Open and closed questions

There is a penchant for classifying questions as being open or closed, or more specifically, open-ended or open-fronted, and closed-ended or closed-fronted. However, questions are just words with a question mark or rising tone: the notion of openness and closedness is more to do with how the question is interpreted than with the question itself. Thus "What is a triangle with three equal sides called?" could be taken as a stimulus to explore the use of the term *equilateral* for other polygons, while "For which polygons does equilateral imply equiangular and vice versa?" could be taken as an instruction to locate and prove a theorem concerning triangles. Thus qualities of openness and closedness are mainly in the eye of the beholder.

> *Take an assertive mathematical question and rethink it so that it opens up enquiry. Take an enquiring mathematical question and see it as asserting what students are expected to do. What in your demeanour encourages learners to enquire and explore, to reconstruct for themselves and to form their own personal narratives?*

Using questions effectively

Questioning is effective if it contributes to focusing learner attention appropriately, not just in the moment, but also in the future. For example, questioning (in its broadest sense) can focus attention on some mathematical possibilities, whether through shifting attention onto a particular detail, onto a relationship or onto some property. It can also draw the learner out of immersion in activity so that attention is directed to the kinds of prompts and questions the teacher is using, helping learners to become aware that they could be using those questions for themselves in the future. (See also Chapter 12 by Anne Watson).

Most importantly, effective questions contribute to building a positive disposition towards the subject as well as immersing learners in the kind of questions the subject addresses. (See also Chapter 6 by Hilary Povey).

Interrogating your own experience

The first thing necessary is to try to catch yourself using questions, in order to try to check any conjectures about questioning, its sources and its effects, for yourself. If you find some agreement with them, if it helps make sense of your past experience, then you may want to work at changing the way you use questions. The rest of this section makes suggestions to this end. If you do not agree with the conjectures, then the rest of this section may provide further food for thought and experimentation. The specific questions are a matter of personal taste and current concerns; the general thrust and ways of working in which they are embedded are what matter.

> *Get a colleague to observe some of your lessons, looking for specific indications of the mathematical ethos or atmosphere. Do the same for them. What is the same and what different about the ethos promoted in the two lessons?*

Reducing the use of questions for controlling

The conjectures put forward imply that all questions asked by a teacher are controlling to some extent, and certainly intended to disturb the learner's flow (or stuck) thoughts. But it is possible to reduce the use of questions for social control and for exerting authority, so as to allow questions to be used for teaching mathematics.

To locate a question asked for the purposes of social control, ask yourself how you would feel if the learners asked the same question of you! What sorts of questions from a learner would be acceptable and what kinds would be seen as impertinent? The impertinent ones are probably the ones used for controlling and norming. The use of 'we' is also characteristic and can be used to catch yourself asking this form of question: when you find yourself about to say 'we', stop and ask yourself who the 'we' is. Notice also that when a teacher reports that in a lesson 'we discussed ...' there is no evidence to distinguish between a norming and controlling sequence of questions and a genuine discussion or enquiry. As a form of interaction, controlling and norming questions are perfectly natural, common and necessary, but they may get in the way of developing a conjecturing, enquiring atmosphere in the classroom. There are other equally effective ways of socialising and controlling learners, such as by making a direct instruction or statement.

> *Where maintaining the power structure is necessary, try using assertions rather than questions. Learners quickly recognise that questions are being used for control purposes, and it merely muddies the water for creating a questioning, conjecturing atmosphere in the classroom which supports rather than obstructs mathematical thinking.*

Funnelling

Asking a learner a question is one thing, but what happens if they do not respond? Perhaps the question is too difficult? Perhaps a more pointed, more focused, more precise question will make it clear? So begins a process of funnelling (Bauersfeld 1995; Wood 1998), of playing the game "Guess what is in my mind".

The teacher keeps asking one or more learners more and more precise and detailed questions in an attempt to find something that they can answer. John Holt (1964) gave a paradigmatic example of funnelling, in which a student steadfastly refuses to answer his questions, which consequently become more and more specific until eventually the question can be answered without knowing anything beyond simple arithmetic.

> *How can you break out of a funnelling sequence? As soon as you become aware that you are playing some form of "Guess what's in my mind" you have the option of admitting to yourself, or even to them, that you do indeed have something in mind. You can go to one extreme, perhaps, and play a quick game of hangman as you indicate the length of the word you are looking for; at the other extreme you can simply tell them the answer, and then perhaps genuinely enquire why they had not thought of that themselves, and how they might learn to think of it in a similar situation in the future.*

Creating a conjecturing atmosphere

A mathematical, or conjecturing atmosphere, is one in which whatever is said is said tentatively as a conjecture in the hope of getting feedback and suggestions for modification. Those who are confident that they 'know the answer' tend to keep quiet, or perhaps ask pointed questions in order to support and assist others, while those who are uncertain take every opportunity to say what they can say, and then get help in extending or completing it. Struggle is valued, even praised. No one says "no that's wrong", they say "I invite you to modify your conjecture".

How might a conjecturing atmosphere be developed? The first essential feature is to adopt a conjecturing stance yourself, treating everything said by you or by others as a conjecture which may require modification, not as an assertion that has to be right or wrong. Second, take opportunities to praise learners for changing their mind, for modifying what they previously said or did. Third, take opportunities to praise learners for making a conjecture (without implying judgement about the quality or aptness of the conjecture). This enables you to attend to the process and ethos of the topic development rather than to the correctness or otherwise of what is said. Try to put the onus on learners to test out what others conjecture. Fourth, especially at the beginning, label conjectures as such. For example, when someone asserts something forcefully, you say "conjecture"; when someone says "no" or "that's not right" to someone else, you invite them to change what they say to "I disagree with your conjecture" or "I invite you to modify your conjecture".

Being genuinely interested

The secret of effective questioning is to be genuinely interested not only in what learners are thinking, but in how they are thinking, in what connections they are making and not making. Genuine interest in the learners produces a positive effect on learners, for in addition to feeling that they are receiving genuine attention, you can escape the use of questions to control and disturb negatively. Instead of asking for answers, which in most cases you probably already know, you can genuinely enquire into their methods, their images and their ways of thinking. In the process, you demonstrate to learners what genuine enquiry is like, placing them in an atmosphere of enquiry which is, after all, one view of what schooling is really intended to be about.

> *Try holding yourself very still when you ask a question, and think about it yourself while waiting for an answer. If no response is forth coming, get the learners to talk to each other about the question for a few seconds, and then ask for contributions. Make it clear that every contribution is valued (for example record everything said on a board). Sometimes a smile with an eyebrow raised while looking (not staring or glowering) at a learner will encourage them to respond.*

Attending to attention

If there is something to the conjecture that questions disturb the flow of attention of learners, then effective use of questions would be built around gaining insight into what learners are attending to, and being aware oneself of how learner attention could most usefully be focused. To do this requires being aware of how your own attention is structured (for more details, see Mason 2006, 2010).

What is the learner attending to?

A teacher is demonstrating how to work through a particular problem. The teacher is aware that this problem is 'only' a particular case of a general class of problems, and sees it that way (seeing the particular in the general having been stimulated, perhaps, to see the general through the particular [Mason and Pimm 1984]). The numbers are merely representative of any (relevant) numbers that could appear, while the structural constants are seen as common to all such problems. But the learners may only be aware of the particular problem being solved. They may be trying to work out what the rules are, what the steps are in solving it, without being aware of generality. They may not be ready to attend to and distinguish what is generic and what is particular in the resolution of the problem.

An important question therefore is what learners are attending to: what features are they stressing and what are they consequently ignoring? Unfortunately, asking them directly is rarely informative: learners usually don't know how to answer. However, there are some less direct ways of revealing something of what they are stressing.

One way is to get learners to read a problem or statement out loud, as they may reveal from voice tones and stress what is meaningful and what not. Another is to get them to 'say what they see' as they look at an expression, a diagram, a picture, a poster, a computer screen, etc. No fancy technical terms are needed, just describing some aspect or feature. What they choose to describe is most informative, as long as you remember that the absence of evidence is not evidence of absence: just because something is not mentioned does not mean that it is not attended to, only that no one has chosen to refer to it. Probably, the most effective way to enquire into what learners are attending to is to get them to construct examples: examples of similar questions, examples of mathematical objects satisfying certain properties or conditions and so on (Watson and Mason 1998).

What do I want the learner to attend to?

In order to use questioning effectively for focusing attention, it is necessary to do more than simply ask a question whenever an idea pops into your head. As a first step, it is necessary to become aware of what features you are stressing, and to make sure that your actions, both overt and covert, serve to stress or highlight those same features. By pausing after saying something significant, by pointing physically and verbally, by getting learners to try to say to each other something you have just said, you can assist them to focus on what you think is central and essential.

> *Try to catch the locus and focus of your attention. Are you discerning details, recognising relationships in some situation or perceiving general properties as being instantiated? What about your students?*

Responding to learners' questions

Suppose a learner asks you how to do something, perhaps a fact or some technique they are supposed to know already. You have a choice: you can decide that it is more important that they make progress on the main topic (and so tell them directly), or you can decide that they need to refresh their skill and reconstruct it for themselves (and so make some suggestion or ask a pertinent question). Answering a question with a question may be attractive, but it can be excruciatingly irritating to a learner seeking information, as many teachers find when their own children get the 'teacher treatment' when seeking help with their homework: "Don't ask me a question, just tell me"! Establishing an overt contract with the learners is valuable in such cases, by finding out what sort of a response they are seeking and then providing it, but making an agreement to work on the issue later if need be.

However, what learners need is not for a teacher to resolve all their uncertainties, answer all their questions or tell them what they do not remember. Rather what they need is to become familiar with *how* to deal with getting stuck: for example, looking for confidence inspiring examples to try out to see what is going on; looking up technical terms in order to check meaning and replace them with something more confidence inspiring and clarifying what they actually know and what they need in order to solve the problem.

If a learner does not understand, they are most likely to ask for a repetition ("could you say that again please?", "could you go through that again please?"). If as a teacher you always accede to this request, you train learners in dependency and you preserve your role of authority. You can choose instead, sometimes, to get someone else to 'say what they think you said', in order to stimulate learners to listen to each other and to learn from each other. It doesn't matter if someone doesn't repeat what you said, or even gets it twisted, because you can then all work on it together, while as a teacher you become aware of some uncertainties in the class. If you can establish a practice in which learners are willing to struggle out loud because they know that others will help them (rather than mock or ignore them), then you and they will find that learning becomes more efficient as well as more satisfying.

> *Try to catch yourself reinforcing learner dependency on your questions, by making use of meta-questions.*

Summary

Although a very common activity, question asking is at best problematic and at worst an intrusion into other people's thinking. By catching yourself expecting a particular response you can avoid being caught in a funnelling sequence of 'guess what is in my mind'. By being explicit at first, then increasingly indirect in your prompts, you can assist learners to internalise useful questions which they can use for themselves to help them engage in effective and productive mathematical thinking. Above all, the types of questions you ask will quickly inform your learners of what you expect of them, and covertly, of your enacted philosophy of teaching.

The key to effective questioning lies in rarely using norming and controlling questions, in using focusing questions sparingly and reflectively, and using genuine enquiry-questions as much as possible. This means being genuinely interested in the answers you receive as insight into learners' thinking, and it means choosing the form and format of questions in order to assist learners to internalise them for their own use (using meta-questions reflectively). The kinds of questions you ask learners indicate the scope and breadth of your concern for and interest in them, as well as the scope, aims and purposes of mathematics and the types of questions that mathematics addresses. For more examples in secondary school, see Watson and Mason (1998), and for the same ideas in primary school, see Jeffcoat et al. (2004).

> *What for you are the hardest aspects of questioning?*
> *What for you is the most salient or striking suggestion in this writing?*

Note

1   This is a revised and truncated version of a reworking of a chapter that first appeared in Mason (2002). I am very grateful to Hilary Povey for suggesting that I rework these ideas.

Further reading

Brown, L. & Coles, A. 2000, Same/different: a 'natural' way of learning mathematics. In T. Nakahara & M. Koyama (Eds.) *Proceedings of the 24th Conference of the International Group for the Psychology of Mathematics Education*, pp. 2-153–2-160, Hiroshima, Japan. This paper describes how over a period of time, a class went from the teacher using "What is the same and what is different about ..." to initiate mathematical activity and discussion, to the students taking over the initiative and suggesting the use of that action.

Brown, M. & Kuchemann D. 1976, Is it an add, miss? *Mathematics in Schools*, 5(5) pp. 15–17. This paper addresses the issue of children waiting until the teacher comes around in order to be told precisely what they are supposed to be doing, rather than working things out for themselves.

Cuoco, A. Goldenberg, P. & Mark, J. 1996, Habits of mind: An organizing principle for mathematics curricula. *Journal of Mathematical Behavior*, 15 pp. 375–402. This paper beautifully describes the kinds of dispositions which, when developed, turn routine behaviour into mathematical thinking.

Watson, A. & Mason, J. 1998, *Questions and prompts for mathematical thinking*, ATM, Derby. This booklet offers dozens of questions and other prompts which can be used with children so that they make use of their natural powers and encounter mathematical thinking.

Watson, A. & Mason, J. 2005, *Mathematics as a constructive activity: Learners generating examples*, Erlbaum, Mahwah. This book develops the strategy of getting learners to construct their own examples as a way to increase engagement and to reveal otherwise hidden aspects of that learners comprehend and appreciate about the mathematical topics they are learning.

References

Ainley, J. 1987, Telling questions, *Mathematics Teaching*, 118 pp. 24–26.

Bauersfeld, H. 1995, "Language Games" in the mathematics classroom: Their function and their effects. In P. Cobb & H. Bauersfeld (Eds.), *The emergence of mathematical meaning: interaction in classroom cultures*, pp. 271–291. Lawrence Erlbaum Associates: Hillsdale, NJ.

Brown, S., Collins A. & Duguid P. 1989, Situated cognition and the culture of learning, *Educational Researcher*, 18 (1) pp. 32–41.

Bruner, J. 1986, *Actual minds, possible worlds*, Harvard University Press, Cambridge.

Holt, J. 1964, *How children fail*, Pitman, London.

Jeffcoat, M., Jones, M., Mansergh, J., Mason, J., Sewell, H. & Watson, A. 2004, *Primary questions and prompts*, Association of Teachers of Mathematics, Derby.

Love, E. & Mason, J. 1992, *Teaching mathematics: action and awareness*, Open University, Milton Keynes.

Mason, J. 2002, Minding your Qs and Rs: Effective questioning and responding in the mathematics classroom, in L. Haggerty (Ed.) *Aspects of teaching secondary mathematics: Perspectives on practice*, pp. 248–258. RoutledgeFalmer, London.

Mason, J. 2006, Micro-structure of attention in the teaching and learning of mathematics. *Proceedings of the mathematics teaching 2005 conference*, pp. 36–41. Edinburgh Centre for Mathematical Education, Edinburgh.

Mason, J. 2010, Attention and intention in learning about teaching through teaching. In R. Leikin &R. Zazkis (Eds.) *Learning through teaching mathematics: Development of teachers' knowledge and expertise in practice*, pp. 23–47. Springer, New York.

Mason, J. & Pimm, D. 1984, Generic examples: seeing the general in the particular, *Educational Studies in Mathematics*, 15(3) pp. 277–290.

Watson, A. & Mason, J. 1998, *Questions and prompts for mathematical thinking*, ATM, Derby.

Wood, T. 1998, Funneling or focusing? Alternative patterns of communication in mathematics class. In H. Steinbring, M. G. Bartolini-Bussi & A. Sierpinska (Eds.) *Language and communication in the mathematics classroom*, pp. 167–178. National Council of Teachers of Mathematics, Reston, VA.

Wood, D., Bruner, J. & Ross, G. 1976, The role of tutoring in problem solving. *Journal of Child Psychology and Psychiatry*, 17 pp. 89–100.

Chapter 12

Debates in task design

Anne Watson

This chapter problematises several aspects of the design and use of tasks to teach mathematics: the nature and role of tasks and the importance of associated teaching strategies; the authorship of tasks: who designs them and why; and differences of intentions and expectations between designers, teachers and learners.

The nature and role of tasks

> *What do you ask your students to do in lessons and for homework?*
> *What impression of mathematics as a subject, and what it means to 'do' it, do they get from these tasks?*
> *What makes a task 'rich'?*

Learning takes place because a learner is or has been engaged in a mathematical task. This could be: listening to or watching teacher or a colleague; performing a procedure in order to calculate; creating a line of reasoning; committing facts and technical terms to memory; working on some mathematics arising in a familiar situation; adapting something to use in an unfamiliar situation; solving familiar or unfamiliar problems; generating data or cases; reflecting on their patterns and behaviours – in other words all the mathematical things that we ask or expect learners to be doing in or out of classrooms. Tasks therefore shape the learning of mathematics and engaging in mathematical tasks promotes learning. They do more than this; they also shape learners' understanding of what mathematics is and what it means to do mathematics. If learners experience tasks that required them to internalise, imitate and perform procedures privately, then the private performance of procedures becomes their view of mathematics and directs their mathematical behaviour. If learners experience tasks that require them to read, interpret, express, manipulate and reason about mathematical ideas, listen to and communicate with others, then those actions become their view of mathematics and their mathematical behaviour. If learners are given tasks that ask them to make something, whether virtually on-screen or a physical object of some kind, they will come to see mathematics as a creative tool. The centrality of tasks in thinking about teaching and learning is evidenced in Chapter 10 by Alf Coles and Nathalie Sinclair. Tasks shape what learners come to see as 'doing mathematics'.

'Task' and 'activity'

In much, but not all, of the literature about task design the word 'task' is taken to imply a particular kind of mathematical activity in which learners are presented with a situation, either within mathematics or in some other context, requiring some interpretation, some unravelling of complexity, application of previous knowledge, adaptation of known procedures and some open-mindedness about other possibilities. To make the distinction between this kind of task and more ubiquitous tasks, such as practising procedures or applying a recently learned procedure to worded contextualised problems, they are often called 'rich tasks'. This serves as a useful search term for finding resources. However I find it more useful to distinguish between the word 'task', meaning anything that the learner is asked or expected to do, and the word 'activity' which is the complex of mental, social, linguistic, physical, emotional and mathematical actions that arise while the task is being done (Christiansen and Walther, 1986). I justify this distinction by referring to two tasks: the first is an exercise from Durrell's Algebra (1911: 28) textbook and the second a well-known type of task that, in various versions, appears in many internet task banks.

Task 1:

  Factor and check:

1   $x^3 - 5x^2 + 6x$
2   $x^3 - 4a^3 x$
3   $2x^3 - 8ax^2 + 8a^2 x$
4   $x^7 - x$
5   $x^4 + 2y - 1 - y^2$

As with any writing about mathematics, it is a good idea to have a go yourself before reading on, so I assume that when you have done that you will have had mathematical experiences and observations. You may have noticed that some of these factorisations could be done by first searching for a common factor and then thinking about what remained once this had been 'taken out'. You may have found that in some of these your recognition of something familiar may or may not have been helpful. For instance, I saw $(x^6 - 1)$ as the difference between two squares before I recognised it as an example of $(x^n - 1)$. In question 3 you may have had to decide whether to deal with x or a. Whatever your experience, discussing it with others, comparing the separate questions, maybe constructing your own questions that are like these in some way, could turn the experience into one that is mathematically rich and that also gives you some insight into how you and others think about mathematics. It is what you do with the task that makes it rich or not.

Enrichment of traditional textbook tasks is a valuable pedagogic skill that teachers can learn, either by using techniques to 'tweak' tasks or by developing a repertoire of probing questions and follow-on tasks that encourage reflection, as suggested above (see also, Bills et al., 2004; Prestage and Perks, 2001; Watson and Mason, 1998).

> *Task 2:*
> *You are building a rectangular pond and think you will make it 6 metres by 2 metres and need to make a path around it with paving slabs that are 0.5 metre square. How many slabs would do you need for a pond of these dimensions?*

A statement of the task introduces a note of doubt about whether these are really going to be the final dimensions or not, so there is an opportunity to explore different dimensions and different numbers of slabs. In an exploratory, investigative, classroom context where teachers and children take opportunities to vary problems and explore relationships this could lead to complex mathematical activity. However, it is also possible for the task to be undertaken in a procedural manner with no discussion, no variety and no exploration and indeed I have seen it done this way. Learners have been given squared paper, told what to draw and how to draw it, what to count and how to count it, how to record the result and how to generalise for other dimensions. The mathematical activity that arises from the task in this scenario is, quite frankly, not very rich and possibly boring.

In the two cases that I have just described what makes the difference is not the task itself but the associated pedagogy (see John Mason's Chapter 11 for elaboration of this idea). Mathematical 'richness' comes from how the teacher engenders curiosity, experimentation and realisations about underlying structure, rather than from focusing on successful completion of final answers. But both are tasks, in that they are intended to prompt some mathematical behaviour and some learning.

Having said that richness ultimately is generated through the pedagogy, some designed tasks support richness more than others. For example, while it is easy to allow learners to work mechanically with a list of similar questions for which answers seem to be the end point, it is less easy to work mechanically if the task is to find out about a hidden idea in an unfamiliar context, such as many of the tasks on NRich (nrich.maths.org). It is also less easy if there are hidden conflicts to be resolved through thinking about properties of mathematical objects, such as is the case for many tasks designed by Malcolm Swan (2008).

Teaching with the 'same' task

Johnson, Clarke and Coles (2017) extend the meaning of 'task' to include the designer's intended purpose, the teacher's intentions in implementation, the students' activity and any associated artefacts (tools, objects, writing and diagrams) as well as the task as stated. Others might see these as components of the learning environment, which would also include the normal habits of the classroom. Where you draw a line between 'task' and 'activity' is up to you, but the main point is to recognise that the 'same' written or designed task, used by different teachers in different classrooms, is not going to result in the 'same' activity or the 'same' learning; it is an illusion to think that a task engenders the same learning wherever and however it is used. If you are able to work with a colleague using the same task and compare what happens in your lessons, you will find that there will be some similarities and some differences in what learners say and do, how you respond, and what you think has been achieved. Kullberg, Runesson and Mårtensson (2014) illustrate this by observing the detail of ways in which two teachers present a co-designed sequence of examples, the shared goal being to counter the assumption that division makes numbers smaller (a detailed discussion of the role and use of examples can be found in Chapter 15 by Tim Rowland). They notice that the teachers gesture differently, thus drawing attention to different comparisons that can be made, and thus also creating two different opportunities to learn.

> *When and why does it matter, if at all, that the 'same' task might lead to different activity and outcomes in different lessons?*
> *In your context, how can you work with others to compare different ways of teaching the 'same' task?*

Here I present the material they planned so that readers can consider how they might use it, what comparisons can be made and what learning might take place. It is also noticeable that there is no task here, in the sense of asking students to do something – the task is developed through teachers' questions – although clearly some 'design' in the sense of this chapter has taken place.

More radical is the idea that a designed resource can be given to learners, and they can raise their own questions from it. For example, the sequence offered by

$$100 \times 20 = 2000 \qquad \frac{100}{20} = 5$$

$$100 \times 4 = 400 \qquad \frac{100}{4} = 25$$

$$100 \times 2 = 200 \qquad \frac{100}{2} = 50$$

$$100 \times 1 = 100 \qquad \frac{100}{1} = 100$$

$$100 \times 0.5 = 50 \qquad \frac{100}{0.5} = 200$$

$$100 \times 0.1 = 10 \qquad \frac{100}{0.1} = 1000$$

Figure 12.1 Examples used in a lesson on division (adapted from Kullberg, Runesson and Mårtensson, 2014).

Kullberg in Figure 12.1, which uses variation theory as a design tool, could be used to raise, rather than answer, questions.

The authorship of tasks: Who designs them and why

Who produces the tasks you use in your lessons?

In the task examples above the question of authority might be raised. The authority for mathematics is always the internal coherence of mathematics itself, I am not going to discuss that here. However, the question of authority in task design is pertinent in the literature. If you take my definition of 'task' as anything a learner is asked to do, then it is obvious that teachers, textbook authors, test writers and anyone who creates resources is in some sense a designer. However, there is a school of thought that claims task design as a specific skill that cannot be done by teachers, because teachers do not have the time or resources to undertake research-informed cycles of design that, following an engineering process, lead most effectively to learning (Wittmann, 1995). This latter argument could suggest that an aim of task design is to produce 'teacher-proof' materials, meaning materials that cannot be 'misused' by teachers. There is some research in the US which points out that some adaptation of tasks in practice is always likely, and researchers found that it was common to reduce the cognitive demand of externally designed tasks when put into practice in classrooms (Henningsen and Stein, 1997). On the other hand, it is also possible for teachers to enhance cognitive demand by using enrichment techniques, as described above in relation to the example from Durrell. Since all school learning takes place within a particular school and classroom culture, it is unlikely that a 'pure' application of a designed task is possible, or even desirable, since teachers can select, order and adapt for particular groups of learners.

Designers often have a particular view about how they expect tasks to be used. Often their aim is to support teaching that enables vibrant and complex mathematical activity. There are several ways in which people who produce mathematical resources, such as textbook authors, curriculum projects teams and so on, try to do this: provision of teaching guides with appropriate strategies; presenting tasks step-by-step fashion towards more complex mathematical ideas; offering scripted question sequences that lead to engagement with the deeper ideas; providing professional development which gives teachers direct experience of the value of complex mathematical activity.

> *What guidance do you find useful for using tasks designed by others?*
> *What would be the difference between tasks that support your way of teaching and tasks that are intended to change your way of teaching?*

Research into the use of teaching guides suggests that many teachers in Europe and North America tend to ignore them, while Pacific Rim teachers tend to take them very seriously as stimuli for collaborative professional development (Ma, 1999). How universal these apparently cultural differences are I am reluctant to assume, but unless teaching guides offer insight into the purpose and appropriate pedagogy of the tasks to achieve those purposes it is hard to understand what they would add to the skills and practices of an experienced teacher who understands the subject. Some teaching guides limit themselves to listing what materials are needed for particular lessons and which parts of the book can be omitted or directed towards particular students. They might explain why a particular order of topics has been chosen. Other published resources explain how the authors imagine a lesson to proceed in terms of classroom management, planning and so on. Some offer lesson scripts (using 'mathematics lesson scripts' as search term accesses several). Few textbooks in the United Kingdom explain why particular examples have been offered, or how mathematical learning of new ideas is expected to take place.

> *When and how could you use the teacher guides that come with textbook series?*

Presenting tasks in a guided step-by-step fashion, thus closing down possibilities to one common pathway, might be seen to absolve the teacher of the necessity to plan and anticipate in advance what variations and structuring of questions might lead students towards harder mathematical ideas. This can limit the possibility for exploration and initiative on the part of the students. Unless step-by-step guidance is research-based, and has been trialled and evaluated, it might not be helpful, and a teacher who knows mathematics well and has attuned their pupils to working thoughtfully with mathematics may not need such guidance. Some experienced teachers might find it patronising for external designers to intend to change their practice. On the other hand, it can be helpful to have well-designed tasks from external sources.

Banks of online tasks designed by teachers can be useful if selected and adapted appropriately. A recent development of this idea is the provision of design templates to help teachers use methods that are supported by research (such as comparison of cases, learner generated examples, structured variation) but, as with all resources, the design intentions and assumptions have to be considered as it is possible to use such a template without a clear mathematical purpose or pedagogic vision.

Teaching through design

> When and why have you created tasks yourself, and what difficulties did you encounter?
> Think about times in your teaching when you have created a task from what learners say and do, or when you had to make something up in-the-moment.

Responsive teaching, that is teaching that takes learners' actions, understandings, reactions and ideas into account, is always going to involve task creation and adaptation. Task design and selection can assume that learners are more than mechanistic learning machines. For example, Ainley, Pratt and Hansen (2006) have identified a need for learners to understand the purpose and utility of mathematics, through the design of tasks. The examples they develop have a constructive element – something has to be made or achieved that has authentic meaning for learners, such as a game, or toy or useful object – which has to be achieved by the application, adaptation or development of a mathematical idea. Thus, while the task has a purpose appropriate for children, it also embeds the utility of a mathematical idea. While individual or groups of teachers could design such tasks, it takes time to do so and it may be more convenient to use externally designed tasks. This approach is more than merely saying that learners need mathematics to be relevant, since 'relevance' is often turned into a suggestion of applications for life outside the classroom, or even for adult life and employment, rather than relevant for those students at that time (see Hamsa Venkatakrishnan's Chapter 17 for a discussion on tasks that can be used to open important debates). The challenge for teachers is then how to draw out the utility of the mathematics in the task and help learners make use of it in the future when appropriate.

Over the last few decades the Freudenthal Institute in Utrecht has developed Realistic Mathematics Education (RME). In this approach it is sequences of tasks, rather than individual tasks, that make a difference for learners. Early tasks in a sequence are contextual in ways that encourage learners to imagine a core relationship (or model) that different contexts have in common. This is called 'horizontal mathematisation' and from this experience learners develop an understanding of that relationship. Then, using this new-to-them relationship as a tool, they are given tasks that are more abstract and symbolic. This is called 'vertical mathematisation' (Freudenthal, 2006). If you think about your own behaviour in mathematical situations, it becomes clear how hard this would be to do through your own task design. Typically, we use a range of *ad hoc* methods depending on the problem so it is important to have a set of initial problems that have a common mathematical structure. Empowerment is achieved through learners constructing common methods in these tasks, then recognising when and how to use them in the future. In RME, the process of moving to vertical mathematisation becomes the culture of the classroom that learners expect. Many textbooks emphasise the reverse process of 'practise an abstract technique and apply it to problems'; RME turns this on its head.

> *When would you use tasks that generate mathematical relationships; when would you use tasks that apply mathematical relationships?*

Another way in which task design relates to learners as active, cognising beings is through the notion of 'emergent' design (Coles and Brown, 2016), in which a teacher or student in a lesson takes an opportunity to craft a task from student responses, so that learning mathematics becomes a sense-making and expanding flow between learners and teacher. This requires teachers to have the sensitivity to decide whether and when to ignore, park or include learners' ideas, and how to manage such inclusion. One way is for teachers to have a repertoire of 'task types' that can be applied in many situations, such as asking learners to construct counterexamples to a conjecture, or to construct extreme cases or to consider two similar but different objects. This is in contrast to teachers responding by making up examples themselves 'on the fly', a skill in which teachers have varying levels of competence. Another way is for a task to emerge through shared enquiry between teacher and learners, or between learners, in a classroom where discussion of mathematical ideas is the normal culture. Obviously emergent, responsive, tasks cannot be designed by external designers. (As contrast, Keith Jones' Chapter 13 describes responsive tasks in a digital environment).

Task designed by learners

> *When, how and why do learners create their own tasks?*

Despite the above examples and discussion, ultimately the mathematical task depends on how the learner engages with it. In a classroom where I took the role of learning support assistant I observed learners adapting the tasks they had been given to make them more interesting or more challenging. In the same classroom there were others looking for ways to streamline their work so they could complete it as easily as possible. For example, students had a blank coordinate grid and a sequence of coordinate pairs to plot, joining the points to make a shape. Most students plotted the points in the given order. Almira restructured the task for herself by identifying adjacent coordinate pairs which would give the same vectors (reported in Watson, 2001: 470).

In that particular classroom these acts were private and individual, but in other classrooms learners' own contributions to design are central. For example, presenting a situation and asking learners to pose their own mathematical questions has been shown to be helpful for the development of problem-solving approaches (Singer, Ellerton and Cai, 2013).

So far I have assumed that 'design' means the production of tasks and materials for teachers to use that are somehow offered to learners. A lone teacher constructing a sequence of practice questions is designing a task, and a curriculum development team working across several countries to produce study packages of complex tasks over a period of several years is also designing tasks. However, it has been argued that an externally produced task does not stop being designed when the teacher chooses it, as when, how, to whom and why it is used is still part of the design. Marton (2014) calls this the *enacted* object of learning. Still further, it does not cease being designed when a learner engages with it. The learner's experience, the *lived* object of learning, is influenced not only by individual cognitive, emotional and social influences but also by expectations about normal language, actions and behaviour in school mathematics.

Different elements of design

> *Think about how you choose tasks, create tasks and implement tasks. What do you have to consider when deciding what to use?*

Whether it is a complete plan, a blueprint for action, to be enacted by the teacher (who may have designed it) or whether it is a process by which the task develops through anticipation by the teacher and participation by learners, every task design activity contains standpoints and choices, explicit or implicit, about several common parameters of mathematics teaching and learning. These can be summarised as: an intended mathematical focus; a theory about learning mathematics; a set of connections between task, teaching, environment and the mathematical focus; a relationship between the focus and general educational aims; anticipations of what learners are likely to do and how their actions and thinking will support their learning and imagination about how uncertainty and dilemmas might be managed (see Mark Boylan's Chapter 2 for these parameters from the standpoint of mastery).

Anyone who designs and uses tasks needs to have some idea of the likely activity that might take place because of the task, and how this activity might support mathematics learning. 'Learning' is a slippery concept and its meaning varies according to the speaker and the context. The meaning of learning that is implied in this chapter so far is mainly about adopting appropriate mathematical behaviour and developing a disposition to act in certain ways in the context of a task. To be more explicit, it includes becoming familiar and fluent with new concepts and new procedures, reformulating and combining known concepts and procedures, knowing more about how and when to apply concepts and procedures and how to adapt and devise procedures, developing mathematical thinking and problem-solving capabilities, and becoming more capable of mathematical reasoning.

Ideally, a good mathematics lesson changes the way in which learners think about a particular mathematical idea by engaging with generalisations, structures, conventional language and symbols, abstraction, vertical mathematisation, variation, co-variation, classifications or domains of applicability. Different assumptions about the relationships between design, teaching, learning and the nature of mathematics show up in the final enacted and lived versions of a designed task.

Figure 12.2 shows an example from Mike Askew of how slight differences in the design of 'practice' tasks can promote very different learning experiences:

Set A suggests that random practice is of some use in learning how to subtract, whereas set B suggests that organised practice can lead to realisations about the concept of difference as an arithmetical structure, and the behaviour of different number combinations, and flexible choice about methods of subtraction.

A very different kind of design is shown in Figure 12.3 from Malcolm Swan (2008) in which discussions about conflicting ideas are used to promote a deep understanding of some simple functions by matching several sets of cards. Each set shows a different representation of functions.

Here are examples from two of the sets:

Set A	Set B
120 - 90	120 - 90
235 - 180	122 - 92
502 - 367	119 - 89
122 - 92	235 - 180
119 - 89	237 - 182
237 - 182	502 - 367

Figure 12.2 Contrasting 'practice' tasks (from www.ncetm.org.uk/public/files/38491476).

Multiply n by two, then add six	Multiply n by three, then square the answer	$\dfrac{n+6}{2}$	$3n^2$
Add six to n, then multiply by two	Add six to n, then divide by two	$2n + 12$	$2n + 6$
Add three to n, then multiply by two	Add six to n, then square the answer	$2(n+3)$	$\dfrac{n}{2} + 6$
Multiply n by two, then add twelve	Divide n by two, then add six	$(3n)^2$	$(n+6)^2$

Figure 12.3 Card-matching simple functions.

Final words

Completion of a task, however well-designed it is, does not itself guarantee the learning of a particular fact, procedure or way of thinking. Johnson, Clarke and Coles (2017) call this the 'illusion' of task design. But learners have expectations and motivations as well and these, too, influence the lived object of learning. In this chapter there has been an opportunity to give tasks central stage in your thinking about teaching and learning. Because they hold this position, it is important to engage critically with aspects of their design and purpose and to avoid assuming that tasks provided by external sources will necessarily lead to desirable learning (in Rachel Marks and Alison Barnes' Chapter 19 you will find more about the learning that might take place). The internet gives access to thousands of tasks; teachers need to ask critical questions about their design, even when the content appears to match their immediate needs. The more agreement there is between teachers and the design team about the elements outlined above, the more likely it is that a task will be used as intended by designers and teachers and will be experienced usefully by learners.

References

Ainley, J., Pratt, D., & Hansen, A. (2006). Connecting engagement and focus in pedagogic task design. *British Educational Research Journal, 32*(1), 23–38.

Bills, C., Bills, L., Watson, A., & Mason, J. (2004). *Thinkers: A collection of activities to provoke mathematical thinking.* Derby: Association of Teachers of Mathematics.

Christiansen, B., & Walther, G. (1986). Task and activity. In B. Christiansen, A. G. Howson, & M. Otte (Eds.), *Perspectives on mathematics education* (pp. 243–307). Dordrecht, Springer.

Coles, A., & Brown, L. (2016). Task design for ways of working: Making distinctions in teaching and learning mathematics. *Journal of Mathematics Teacher Education, 19*(2–3), 149–168.

Durrell, F. (1911). *Algebra: Book 2 with advanced algebra.* New York: Charles Merrill Company.

Freudenthal, H. (2006). *Revisiting mathematics education: China lectures* (Vol. 9). Dordrecht: Springer.

Henningsen, M., & Stein, M. K. (1997). Mathematical tasks and student cognition: Classroom-based factors that support and inhibit high-level mathematical thinking and reasoning. *Journal for Research in Mathematics Education, 28*, 524–549.

Johnson, H. L., Coles, A., & Clarke, D. (2017). Mathematical tasks and the student: Navigating "tensions of intentions" between designers, teachers, and students. *ZDM, 49*(6), 813–822.

Kullberg, A., Runesson, U., & Mårtensson, P. (2014). Different possibilities to learn from the same task. *PNA, 8*(4), 139–150.

Ma, L. (1999). *Knowing and teaching elementary mathematics: Teachers' understanding of fundamental mathematics in China and the United States.* Mahwah, NJ: Lawrence Erlbaum Associates.

Marton, F. (2014). *Necessary conditions of learning.* Abingdon: Routledge.

Prestage, S., & Perks, P. (2001). *Adapting and extending secondary mathematics activities: New tasks for old.* Maidenhead: David Fulton Publishers.

Singer, F. M., Ellerton, N., & Cai, J. (2013). Problem-posing research in mathematics education: New questions and directions. *Educational Studies in Mathematics, 83*(1), 1–7.

Swan, M. (2008) *A designer speaks.* www.educationaldesigner.org/ed/volume1/issue1

Watson, A. (2001). Instances of mathematical thinking among low attaining students in an ordinary secondary classroom. *The Journal of Mathematical Behavior, 20*(4), 461–475.

Watson, A., & Mason, J. (1998). *Questions and prompts for mathematical thinking.* Derby: Association of Teachers of Mathematics.

Wittmann, E. C. (1995). Mathematics education as a 'design science'. *Educational Studies in Mathematics, 29*(4), 355–374.

Chapter 13

Fake news, artificial intelligence, mobile divisions, likely futures?

Debates on digital technologies in mathematics education

Keith Jones

In recent times, the use of digital technologies across many fields has come under increasingly intense scrutiny. Concerns have been growing over data security, cyberattacks, fake news, long-term exposure to wireless devices and digital screens, and the effect of use of social media on mental health and well-being. While there is no doubt that innovations in digital technologies are impacting positively on the tackling of major worldwide challenges from climate change and energy supply to provision of sufficient food and water, the increasingly widespread uses of digital technologies are also continuing to raise significant social and ethical dilemmas.

This chapter examines key debates in the use of digital technologies in the teaching and learning of mathematics. These debates encompass the extent to which the use of digital technologies improves educational outcomes in school mathematics (or whether there is much 'fake news'), the rise of digital 'assistants' and 'tutors' for mathematics education (or whether such 'intelligence' is literally artificial) and whether increasing use of mobile digital technologies in mathematics education helps all learners (or whether it is contributing to an exacerbated 'digital divide'). Across these debates are the issues not only of how the teaching and learning of school mathematics could be conducted in technology-enhanced ways, but also what new forms of mathematical knowledge and practices it might be possible to teach and learn. Given these new forms of mathematical knowledge and practices, the chapter concludes with consideration of the impact of current developments on the likely futures for promising forms of digital technologies for mathematics education.

'Fake' news? Digital technologies and educational outcomes in school mathematics

The use of digital technologies in mathematics education is said to offer the potential for "opening up diverse pathways for students to construct and engage with mathematical knowledge, embedding the subject in authentic contexts and returning the agency to create meaning to the students" (Bray & Tangney, 2017, p. 256). Not only that, but using digital technologies can "help increase collaboration and bring about more of an emphasis on practical applications of mathematics, through modelling, visualisation, manipulation and the introduction of more complex scenarios" (op cit.). All this suggests that the use of digital technologies in mathematics classrooms should improve educational outcomes. Indeed, that the latest digital technology is set to 'revolutionise' and 'transform' education in general, and mathematics education in particular, is the stuff of marketing campaigns and intense selling of technological 'solutions'.

The evidence of the impact of the use of digital technologies on educational outcomes in school mathematics is, however, more nuanced (see Drijvers, 2018; Falck et al., 2018). On top of this, even when there is clear evidence of a positive impact on learning, such as is the case with the informed use of calculators in mathematics lessons, government policy might be to restrict certain uses of the technology such as banning the use of calculators with younger-age children (for a review of the evidence, see Hodgen et al., 2018).

The particular value of the use of digital technologies for mathematics education, and for STEM (science, technology, engineering and mathematics) subjects in general, is "to make the abstract world [of mathematics] more accessible through experiential learning" (Davies et al., 2013, p. 2). This is achieved, Davies et al. illustrate, by enabling students to "manipulate complex ideas – represented on screen as computational objects – to gain a deeper connection with the ideas" (op cit.). An example they give, shown in Figure 13.1, is of a collection of projects created using a particular programming/coding tool that demonstrate, and require, both mathematical and computational thinking.

Reports of innovations in the use of digital technologies in school mathematics, such as those reviewed in Davies et al. (2013) and in Jones (2011), often provide pointers to ways in which such technologies might positively influence educational outcomes in school mathematics. A picture of more widespread use of digital technologies in school mathematics is provided by data from international studies conducted by the Trends in International Mathematics and Science Study (TIMSS) and the Programme for International Student Assessment (PISA). As part of the 2012 PISA study, for example, students were given a list of seven possible mathematics tasks and asked whether they (or their classmates) had used a computer for the tasks during the previous month, whether their teacher had demonstrated the tasks using a computer or whether they had not encountered the task at all. The results of this are shown in Figure 13.2.

As the data in Figure 13.2 shows, a minority of students across the Organisation for Economic Cooperation and Development (OECD) countries reported that computers were used during the preceding month, either by themselves or by their teacher. While student scores on the PISA mathematics tests can be related to their use of (or exposure to) digital technologies, any relationship cannot be said to be causal because allocation of digital technologies to students and schools in the PISA studies is not random. This means that any difference in mathematics test scores by students who use computers more than students in other places, or use them less, cannot be attributed to differences in computer

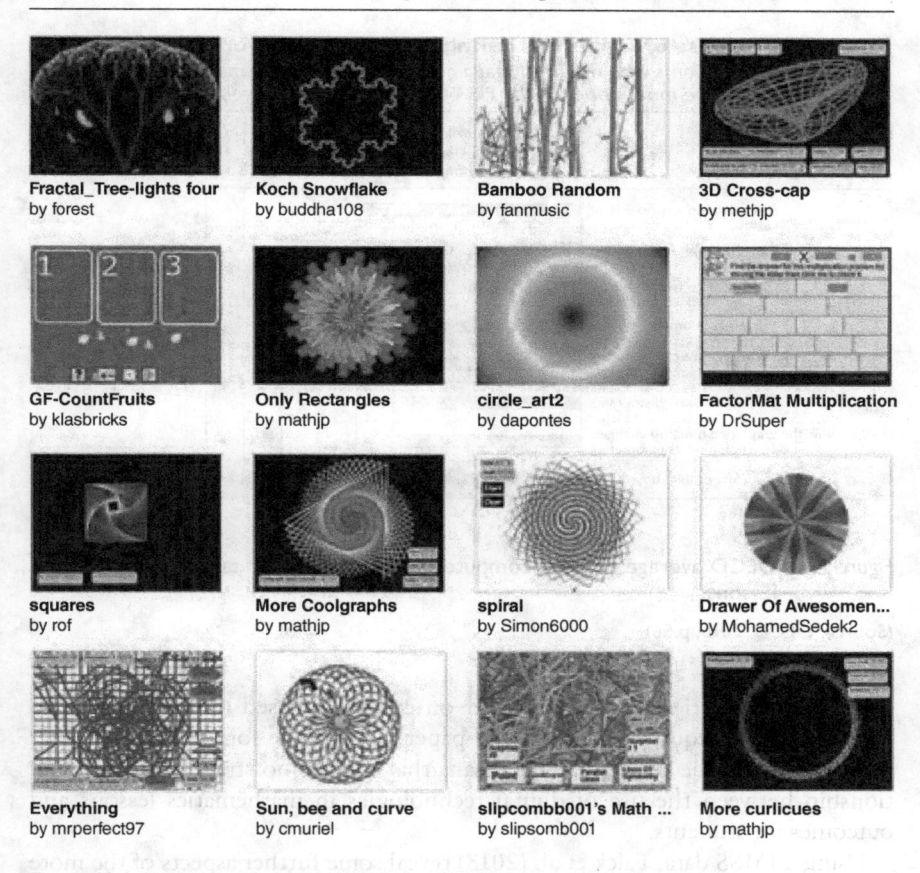

Fractal_Tree-lights four
by forest

Koch Snowflake
by buddha108

Bamboo Random
by fanmusic

3D Cross-cap
by methjp

GF-CountFruits
by klasbricks

Only Rectangles
by mathjp

circle_art2
by dapontes

FactorMat Multiplication
by DrSuper

squares
by rof

More Coolgraphs
by mathjp

spiral
by Simon6000

Drawer Of Awesomen...
by MohamedSedek2

Everything
by mrperfect97

Sun, bee and curve
by cmuriel

slipcombb001's Math ...
by slipsomb001

More curlicues
by mathjp

Figure 13.1 Projects using a programming/coding environment.

(Source: Davies et al., 2013, p. 9)

use as, inevitably, there are a host of other influences on the test scores (for more on international comparisons, see Chapter 1 by Wiliam). What the OECD report (2015, p. 146) concludes is that the relationship between computer use at school and test performance is more of a "hill shape" in that "limited use of computers at school may be better than no use at all, but levels of computer use above the current OECD average are associated with significantly poorer results".

No doubt, the sorts of mathematics tasks that students tackle with digital technologies, the level of teacher knowledge and form of teacher input and the general classroom environment are all important factors that affect student learning of mathematics with digital technologies (Jones, 2012). On top of this are issues to do with the validity and reliability of tests of educational outcomes in school mathematics. In testing students in mathematics using both pencil-and-paper tests and computer-based tests, the OECD (2015) report shows that students

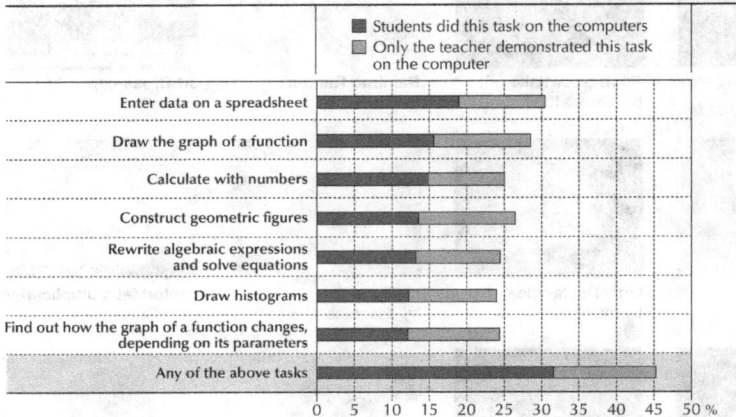

Use of computers during mathematics lessons

Percentage of students who reported that a computer was used in mathematics lessons in the month prior to the PISA test, by task (OECD average)

Figure 13.2 OECD average data on computer use for particular tasks in mathematics lessons.

(Source: OECD, 2015, p.56)

from some countries performed better on computer-based tasks compared to their success on equivalent pencil-and-paper tasks, while for students in other countries it was the opposite. This means that there is no straightforward relationship between the use of digital technologies in mathematics lessons and outcomes for students.

Using TIMSS data, Falck et al. (2018) reveal some further aspects of the more nuanced impact of the use of digital technologies on educational outcomes in school mathematics. Their analysis indicated that the impact of using digital technologies depends on whether the use of the digital technologies replaces less productive, or more productive, existing uses of teaching time; in particular, they suggest that "classroom computers are beneficial to student achievement when used to look up ideas and information but detrimental when used to practice skills and procedures" (p. 29). This finding is worth bearing in mind in the sections that follow, and especially in the final section of this chapter on likely futures for promising forms of digital technologies for mathematics education.

To what extent has the 'digital revolution' been overhyped as something that can cure all teaching ills in mathematics education?
Why is it not straightforward to determine the 'impact' of the use of digital technologies on educational outcomes in school mathematics?

'Artificial' intelligence? Digital 'assistants', 'tutors' and curriculum for mathematics education

An increasingly evident type of digital technology in mathematics education is in the form of resources to augment mathematics teaching. One popular form of digital resource for mathematics education consists of repositories of online video clips. As Davies et al. (2013, p. 33) explain, the "rationale, motivation and potential" behind such repositories is that "the information and tutoring available is independent of time and place, and (assuming it is of the highest quality) allows precious face-to-face time between teachers and students to be invested in more meaningful activities in the classroom". This approach, in which students tackle learning material before the lesson and classroom time is then allocated to 'deepening' learning through discussion and problem-solving, is commonly referred to as 'flipped learning' (or the 'flipped classroom') as the conventional approach to teaching and learning is inverted. Of these online video resources, an increasing number are including interactive question-and-answer activities where students can test their knowledge.

Another increasingly available resource that can be used in the classroom, or for self-study, is the electronic book (or e-book). This is a digital resource that usually goes beyond a digital version of the 'hard copy' book in that the e-book might feature interactive tools and tasks that are embedded in the resource. As with using online video clips to 'flip' learning, digital (or 'smart') e-textbooks can enable different forms of interaction and provide adaptive tasks that are tailored to an individual student based on their responses. Here there can be formative feedback to the student in 'real time' (through forms of digital diagnostic assessment) together with digital records for the teacher. There may also be possibilities for teachers to edit, or fully author, e-book components (see, for example, Bokhove et al., 2014, 2015) in order to further personalise provision and support their own, and their students', creativity (Bokhove & Jones, 2018).

Digital curriculum resources can also be of the form of augmented reality (AR) or virtual reality (VR). As an example of the former, Davies et al. (2013, p. 43) envisage a student in their home or community using an AR app on their digital device to "see the mathematics in the shape of a car, or the molecular structure of their cereal, or the algorithm behind the traffic-control system, or to capture and improve the design of a backpack". While augmented reality does not attempt a fully immersive experience, VR aims at simulating the real world, or an imaginary world, which, when viewed through a head set, places the user in that 'world'. For example, Jones et al. (2010, p. 58) foresee a VR version of Edwin A. Abbott's classic 19th century novel Flatland in which the learner "might take part as one of the 'creatures' in Flatland and experience (in 'virtual reality') what it is like to 'live' in a flat land".

In parallel to the development of digital curriculum resources (such as online video clips, e-books, AR and VR), another form of technology-enabled development is 'Adaptive Tutoring' using so-called Intelligent Tutoring Systems (ITSs), an application of Artificial Intelligence (AI) in education. In mathematics education, such systems are designed to provide individualised 'assistance' to students as they work on mathematical problems and/or provide an environment for collaborative learning across locations (and time zones) that can involve large numbers of students. While existing implementations have been primarily targeting procedural tasks (and may feature problem-solving tasks that are heavily structured), research is continuing on expanding "the range of intelligent support for students working in exploratory learning environments by tracking, analysing and responding to their actions and choices" (Davies et al., 2013, p. 32; see also Jones et al., 2013; Miyazaki et al., 2017). For example, one way in which research on 'agent' technology is continuing is into learning environments where students learn through 'teaching' an avatar.

It is unclear whether the strand of development into digital 'assistants' and 'tutors' may eventually lead to pedagogic 'robots' that could, at some point, supplant human teachers. Current work on such innovations utilise not only AI but also educational data mining (EDM) techniques to 'track' the work of each student in order to provide both challenge and support. What such systems attempt to offer is 'just-in-time' guidance to shape learning. With such 'just-in-time' guidance for students, and, for their teachers, comprehensive reporting on their progress, there rises the possibility of avoiding (or minimising) the need for the 'stop-and-test' approach to assessment that characterises much current assessment practice (for more on assessment see Chapters 19 and 20 by Alison Barnes and Rachel Marks, and by Ian Jones, respectively). Nevertheless, challenges in fully realising the potential of such technological advices remain; especially in terms of something better than the 'content' being 'hard-coded' into the tutoring software, and something better than current ways that tutoring software have of diagnosing, and responding to, students' 'incorrect' responses. As such, attention continues on approaches to 'blended learning' and the appropriate balance between teacher-led and technology-led features (Fujita et al., 2018).

One emerging driving force for developments in AI in education is the shortage of teachers, especially teachers of mathematics, in many parts of the world. The Global Learning XPRIZE, for example, has set a challenge to develop an open source, and scalable, software solution that can enable children in developing countries to teach themselves basic arithmetic. There may be other reasons for supplanting human teachers in more developed parts of the world, even if only to provide respite in instances of acute short-term teacher shortage.

What can digital technologies provide in the mathematics classroom that the teacher cannot, and, conversely, what can the mathematics teacher offer that digital technologies cannot?

How might the use of digital technologies support the better assessment, both formative and summative, of learners of mathematics?

'Mobile' divisions? Access to, and via, digital technologies for mathematics education

In many current initiatives, digital technologies are being designed to enable all learners to access mathematics learning resources that are optimal for their needs and that may provide tailored feedback. Such resources can be accessible via a multiplicity of devices and be utilised offline as needed, with access increasingly being via personal devices (tablet computer, smartphone or similar). In many ways, such developments can be seen as 'democratising' access to forms of mathematical knowledge that, historically, have been accessible mainly to a relative few. What is more, digital technologies can bring mathematics learning opportunities for learners with special educational needs, learners who are visually impaired, hard of hearing or have physical mobility challenges, and learners who may be in geographically remote and underserved communities. All this can mean that the use of digital technologies and digital learning resources can help to reduce educational inequalities.

Yet, at the same time that digital technologies can provide unprecedented educational opportunities, inequalities in access to and knowledge of how to use, digital technologies may lead to the exacerbation of existing inequalities or the creation of new educational inequalities (for more on issues of equity, see Chapter 4 by Gates & Noyes and Chapter 8 by McCormack & Morales). With the increasingly widespread availability of handheld mobile devices, issues to do with access to and knowledge of how to use, digital technologies apply not only to classroom use in schools but also beyond-school access in the wider community (Carreira et al., 2016). Unequal, or skewed, patterns of home and school access to digital technologies may spur the creation of the 'digitally privileged' and the 'digitally disadvantaged'. For the latter, it can be a 'double-bind' in that the digitally disadvantaged may lack not only access to digital technologies but also that this lack of access worsens a lack of knowledge of how to use the latest digital technologies.

Evidence of a 'digital divide' is changing and is becoming more nuanced. The OECD report (2015, p. 124), using PISA data, indicates that digital technologies that "were once exclusively available to the most wealthy fraction of the population tend to become universally available" and that, as a consequence, "many gaps in access close". Nevertheless, the very latest digital technologies "are almost invariably marketed only to the most wealthy, thus reinforcing, at least initially, the privilege of more advantaged populations" (op cit.). Overall, the OECD (2015, p. 125) concludes that "By 2012, in most countries and economies that participate in PISA, socio-economic differences were no longer associated with large divides in access to computers" but that "gaps previously observed in the quantity, variety and quality of ICT tools available, as well as in the mastery of them, persisted". Even with such disparities, the OECD (2015, p. 138) found that, in terms of mathematics education, "on average, students who attain a certain score in PISA mathematics perform equally well in the paper-based and computer-based assessments, regardless of their socio-economic status".

Needless to say, this 'average' does mask discrepancies. While the OECD report (2015) indicates that digital resources "tend to be as good in those schools that serve predominantly disadvantaged students as in more advantaged schools" (p. 132), out-of-school use of digital technologies differs across socio-economic groups in that "disadvantaged students tend to prefer chat over e-mail, and to play video games rather than read the news or obtain practical information from the Internet" (p. 135). Such out-of-school learning with digital technologies is becoming increasingly important. In a project in which they studied youngsters engaged in mathematical problem-solving using digital technologies of their choice, and to which they had personal access, Carreira et al. (2016, p. 232) report that, while the youngsters they studied were "surrounded by digital technologies", the young people displayed "some weak skills in using technology as a means for learning, tending to be more resourceful in uses related to social communication and retrieving online content for fun and recreation". In particular, they found that the youngsters they studied "have domain over a set of general-use digital tools, but it appears that they are less aware of the digital resources with a stronger association with mathematical knowledge and procedures" (op cit.). They conclude that, while the youngsters they studied were able to use "several digital tools they have access to for addressing and expressing their solutions to non-routine mathematics problems" (p. 236), a key issue for further research is "how these mathematical activities beyond the school, which welcome and favour technology usage, can be harnessed and help to promote the success of youngsters in mathematics in our digital era" (p. 237). All this points both to the educational opportunities of out-of-school use of digital technologies, and also how inequalities in access to, and knowledge of how to use, digital technologies might continue.

While Governments sometimes ban the use of certain technologies by certain students (such as banning younger students using calculators), the increasingly widespread use of personal mobile technologies (such as 'smartphones') by school students is beginning to result in Governments banning use of such devices during school time (France is an example). Where Governments do not ban, schools are banning students from using such devices. Concerns about irresponsible use of mobile devices is on the one side; on the other is the teaching and learning opportunities of students being able to use a digital device with which they are familiar and which they can use out of school. This latter thinking about the teaching and learning opportunities of personal mobile technologies underpins the idea to Bring Your Own Device (BYOD) or Bring Your Own Technology (BYOT). As with informed use of calculators in mathematics lessons, the BYOD/BYOT argument is for responsible use of personal mobile devices for mathematics education. Nevertheless, there are a number of challenges to BYOD/BYOT, including, especially, the extent to which students unable to BYOD/BYOT would be disadvantaged.

> *To what extent do all teachers and learners of mathematics have access to the latest digital technologies for mathematics education, and to what extent are all teachers and learners of mathematics aware of how to make the best use of digital technologies for mathematics education?*
> *What are the pros and cons of allowing learners to bring their own digital devices for use in the mathematics classroom?*

Likely futures? Promising forms of digital technologies for mathematics education

These debates over the impact of digital technologies on educational outcomes, the rise of digital 'assistants', the 'digital divide', arise not only in mathematics classrooms but across education in general. In mathematics education, the development of new digital technologies is resulting in new forms of mathematical knowledge and practices. As such, it is crucial to give consideration to likely futures for promising forms of digital technologies for mathematics education.

Hoyles (2018, pp. 211–212) categorises six forms of digital tool for mathematics teaching and learning:

- *dynamic and graphical tools* that allow mathematics to be explored in diverse ways, from different perspectives;
- *tools that outsource processing power* that previously could only be undertaken by humans, to change the focus of attention;
- *tools that offer new representational* infrastructures *for mathematics* to change what can be learned and by whom;
- *tools that offer connections between school* mathematics *and learners' agendas and culture*, bridging the gap between school mathematics and the students' world;
- *tools that exploit high-bandwidth connectivity to support mathematics learning* opening new opportunities for students to share knowledge construction and their evolving solutions both within and between classrooms;
- *intelligent support for the teacher* to reduce the burden of scaffolding the diverse solutions generated when students engage in exploratory learning with digital technologies.

Considering these in turn, in terms of dynamic and graphical tools, one example is the form of digital tool generally called 'dynamic geometry' but increasingly called 'dynamic mathematics'. With such a tool, students can construct not only geometric figures but also graphs, charts and other plots, by specifying relationships between elements used in the construction (Jones, 2011, 2012). This 'dynamic mathematics' has extended to calculus tools, statistical tools and computer coding tools. Across these dynamic and graphical tools, questions remain about how students learn to specify the necessary relationships between the elements they used in their construction and what students understand from complexly moving diagrams, graphs and charts.

Tools that outsource processing power encompass not only four-function calculators but graphing calculators, computer-algebra systems and apps for specific tasks. Here, questions remain about the development of, and mastery of, mathematical skills and fluency (for more on skills and fluency, see Chapters 2 and 7 by Boylan, and by Llewellyn, respectively).

A category that overlaps with the above two categories is that of tools that offer new representational infrastructures for mathematics. The latter comprise tools that offer "such a new representational infrastructure" that the new representations "change and shape a learner's language of interaction with mathematics and the ways mathematical ideas are expressed" (Hoyles, 2018, p. 216). The example given by Hoyles is that of dynamic geometry systems (such as Cabri Express, Sketchpad Explorer or GeoGebra). If these were 'infrastructural', in that students were just as familiar using these systems as they are using a pencil, then this raises questions about what is known about mathematics teaching with digital technology that promotes explanation of the dynamic geometry system output as students are tackling mathematical problems with that technology (Komatsu & Jones, 2019).

Tools that offer connections between school mathematics and learners' agendas and culture are associated with the emergence of design software and three-dimensional printers, linked to the development of a 'Maker' culture. While activities connecting school mathematics and learners' agendas and culture may, in the past, have been prohibitively expensive, or possibly unsafe, such activities can now be tackled at relatively low cost and with increased safety. Such activities raise the possibility that students' mathematical studies provide intellectual reward for students, as well as an important qualification (for more on this, see Chapters 3 and 21 by Ernest, and by Smith, respectively).

Tools that exploit high-bandwidth connectivity to support mathematics learning have the potential to lead to "sharing solutions, problem solving strategies and knowledge construction" (Hoyles, 2018, p. 219). Such possibilities raise a host of questions about synchronous, asynchronous and 'just-in-time' learning that are only just beginning to be tackled.

Intelligent support for the teacher is subtly different to 'Adaptive Tutoring' using so-called ITSs, mentioned above. Here the phrase to be emphasised is support for the teacher that can "reduce the burden of scaffolding the diverse responses generated when students engage in exploratory learning with digital technologies" (Hoyles, 2018, p. 220). Here, the issue remains how "to design support in ways that provide students with 'enough' freedom so they could actively engage in their construction task, yet with adequate constraints so as to be able to generate feedback that assists students in achieving the planned mathematical goals" (op cit.).

On top of all the issues raised above, and across all these digital technology innovations, questions remain about the most appropriate forms of professional development for teachers. There are also questions for school leaders and for Government officials and for politicians with responsibility for, and influence on, educational policy on curriculum and assessment.

> *To what extent is digital technology enabling mathematics teachers to use or create more interactive, engaging and flexible learning materials?*
> *What changes could be made to the school mathematics curriculum that might more fully utilise the potential of digital technologies for mathematics education?*

Conclusions

Increasingly, major digital technology companies and online platforms are being portrayed as threats to truth and the democratic tradition. Alongside this are concerns about data security, long-term exposure to digital screens and the effect of use of social media on mental health and well-being. One potential benefit of this so-called techlash is that efforts are made to go beyond the digital technology 'revolution' or 'tech wreck' headlines to the more nuanced evidence. Among the issues raised in this chapter are the extent to which the digital 'revolution' has been overhyped as something that can cure all teaching ills in mathematics education, and why it is not necessarily straightforward to determine the 'impact' of the use of digital technologies on educational outcomes in school mathematics.

Other important issues are determining what digital technologies can provide in the mathematics classroom that the teacher cannot, and, conversely, what the mathematics teacher can offer that digital technologies cannot. In addition is the issue of how the use of digital technologies might better support the assessment, both formative and summative, of learners of mathematics.

Equity issues remain of key importance, including the extent to which all teachers and learners of mathematics have access to the latest digital technologies for mathematics education, and the extent to which all teachers and learners of mathematics are aware of how to make the best use of digital technologies for mathematics education. In addition there are the pros and cons of allowing learners to bring their own digital devices for use in the mathematics classroom.

Finally, there is potential for digital technology to enable mathematics teachers to use or create more interactive, engaging and flexible learning materials. This might necessitate changes being made to the school mathematics curriculum so that it might be more possible to utilise more fully the potential of digital technologies for mathematics education.

All these things place demands on teachers and raise questions about the most appropriate forms of professional development, be these face-to-face or online or a combination. Such things, in turn, raise questions for school leaders and for Government officials and for politicians.

Across all these issues is the central question of not only how the teaching and learning of school mathematics could be conducted in technology-enhanced ways, but also what new forms of mathematical knowledge and practices it might be possible to teach and learn. This entails being clearer about the less effective existing practices in mathematics education, be these be in teaching, in curriculum specification and in assessment practices.

Further reading

Ball, L., Drijvers, P., Ladel, S., Siller, H.-S., Tabach, M., & Vale, C. (Eds.) (2018). *Uses of technology in primary and secondary mathematics education*. Cham, CH: Springer. doi: 10.1007/978-3-319-76575-4. This book provides international perspectives on the use of digital technologies in schools around the world. The chapters provide both a snapshot of the current situation in using technologies in school mathematics, and outlines how technologies might impact school mathematics in the years from now.

Drijvers, P., Ball, L., Barzel, B., Heid, M. K., Cao, Y., & Maschietto, M. (2016). *Uses of technology in lower secondary mathematics education*. Cham, CH: Springer. doi: 10.1007/978-3-319-33666-4. This book provides an overview of the current state of the art in technology-use in lower secondary mathematics education (up to the age of 15 or 16). The book examines how teachers can integrate physical and virtual experiences with technology to promote a deeper understanding of mathematics. The book is free to download.

Hegedus, S., Laborde, C., Brady, C., Dalton, S., Siller, H., Tabach, M., Trgalova, J., & Moreno-Armella, L. (2017). *Uses of technology in upper secondary mathematics education*. Cham, CH: Springer. doi: 10.1007/978-3-319-42611-2. This book provides an overview of the current state of the art in technology-use in upper secondary mathematics education (from age 15 or 16). The book reviews which technologies to choose for which purposes for this age-group, and how to integrate the technology into teaching so as to maximise benefit for students. The book is free to download.

Roschelle, J., Noss, R., Blikstein, P., & Jackiw, N. (2017). Technology for learning mathematics. In J. Cai (Ed.), *Compendium for research in mathematics education* (pp. 853–876). Reston, VA: National Council of Teachers of Mathematics. https://www.nctm.org/Store/Products/Compendium-for-Research-in-Mathematics-Education/. This chapter provides a comprehensive survey and critical analysis of the use of technology for teaching and learning mathematics. The chapter is structured around three pedagogical purposes: to do mathematics, to practice mathematical skills and to learn mathematical concepts.

References

Bokhove, C., & Jones, K. (2018). Stimulating mathematical creativity through constraints in problem solving. In N. Amado, S. Carreira, & K. Jones (Eds.), *Broadening the scope of research on mathematical problem solving: A focus on technology, creativity and affect* (pp. 301–319). Cham, CH: Springer. doi: 10.1007/978-3-319-99861-9_13.

Bokhove, C., Jones, K., Charlton, P., Mavrikis, M., & Geraniou, E. (2014). Authoring your own creative electronic book for mathematics: The MC-squared project. In K. Jones et al. (Eds.), *Proceedings of the International Conference on Mathematics Textbook Research and Development (ICMT-2014)* (pp. 547–552). Southampton, GB: University of Southampton. https://eprints.soton.ac.uk/367609/

Bokhove, C., Mavrikis, M., & Jones, K. (2015). The potential of authoring creative electronic mathematics books in the MC-squared project. In N. Amado, & S. Carreira (Eds.), *Proceedings of the 12th International Conference on Technology in Mathematics Teaching (ICTMT12)* (pp. 547–549). Faro, Portugal: University of the Algarve. https://eprints.soton.ac.uk/380856/

Bray, A., & Tangney, B. (2017). Technology usage in mathematics education research: A systematic review of recent trends. *Computers & Education, 114*, 255–273. doi: 10.1016/j.compedu.2017.07.004.

Carreira, S., Jones, K., Amado, N., Jacinto, H., & Nobre, S. (2016). *Youngsters solving mathematical problems with technology: The results and implications of the Problem@Web project*. Cham, CH: Springer. doi:10.1007/978-3-319-24910-0.

Davies, P., Kent, G., Laurillard, D., Lieben, C., Mavrikis, M., Noss, & Price, S. (2013). *The impact of technological change on STEM education*. London: Royal Society. https://royalsociety.org/~/media/education/policy/vision/reports/ev-6-vision-research-report-20140624.pdf

Drijvers, P. (2018). Empirical evidence for benefit? Reviewing quantitative research on the use of digital tools in mathematics education. In L. Ball et al. (Eds.), *Uses of technology in primary and secondary mathematics education* (pp. 161–175). Cham, CH: Springer. doi: 10.1007/978-3-319-76575-4_9.

Falck, O., Mang, C., & Woessmann, L. (2018). Virtually no effect? Different uses of classroom computers and their effect on student achievement. *Oxford Bulletin of Economics and Statistics, 80*(1), 1–38. doi: 10.1111/obes.12192.

Fujita, T., Jones, K., & Miyazaki, M. (2018). Learners' use of domain-specific computer-based feedback to overcome logical circularity in deductive proving in geometry. *ZDM: Mathematics Education, 50*(4), 699–713. doi: 10.1007/s10763-018-9892-0.

Hodgen, J., Foster, C., Marks, R., & Brown, M. (2018). *Improving mathematics in key stages two and three: Evidence review*. London: Education Endowment Foundation. https://educationendowmentfoundation.org.uk/evidence-summaries/evidence-reviews/improving-mathematics-in-key-stages-two-and-three/

Hoyles, C. (2018). Transforming the mathematical practices of learners and teachers through digital technology, *Research in Mathematics Education, 20*(3), 209–228. doi: 10.1080/14794802.2018.1484799.

Jones, K. (2011). The value of learning geometry with ICT: Lessons from innovative educational research. In A. Oldknow, & C. Knights (Eds.), *Mathematics education with digital technology* (pp. 39–45). London, GB: Continuum. doi: 10.5040/9781472553119.ch-005.

Jones, K. (2012). Using dynamic geometry software in mathematics teaching: A revised research bibliography. *Mathematics Teaching, 229*, 49–50. https://eprints.soton.ac.uk/348619/

Jones, K., Geraniou, E., & Tiropanis, T. (2013). Patterns of collaboration: Towards learning mathematics in the era of the semantic web. In D. Martinovic, V. Freiman, & Z. Karadag (Eds.), *Visual mathematics and cyberlearning* (pp. 1–21). London, GB: Springer. doi: 10.1007/978-94-007-2321-4_1.

Jones, K., Mackrell, K., & Stevenson, I. (2010). Designing digital technologies and learning activities for different geometries. In C. Hoyles, & J-B. Lagrange (Eds.), *Mathematics education and technology: Rethinking the terrain: The 17th ICMI study* (pp. 47–60). New York: Springer. doi: 10.1007/978-1-4419-0146-0_4.

Komatsu, K., & Jones, K. (2019). Task design principles for heuristic refutation in dynamic geometry environments. *International Journal of Science and Mathematics Education*, *17*(4), 801–824. doi: 10.1007/s10763-018-9892-0.

Miyazaki, M., Fujita, T., Jones, K., & Iwanaga, Y. (2017). Designing a web-based learning support system for flow-chart proving in school geometry. *Digital Experiences in Mathematics Education*, *3*(3), 233–256. doi: 10.1007/s40751-017-0034-z.

OECD. (2015). *Students, computers and learning: Making the connection.* Paris: OECD. doi: 10.1787/9789264239555-en.

Chapter 14

Mental maths
Just about what we do in our heads?

Gwen Ineson and Sunita Babbar

Introduction

Mental mathematics has, for many, negative associations with timed times table tests or questions fired out to be solved quickly, but they have little memory of the explicit teaching of specific approaches to mental calculation. In this chapter, we unpick what we mean by 'mental mathematics', how it relates to mathematics as a subject and how it is conceptualised within the teaching of mathematics. We provide an overview of the English context below to exemplify the tensions and dilemmas we discuss throughout the chapter.

The English context

In the current version of the National Curriculum, developed while Michael Gove was Secretary of State for Education, the status of arithmetic has been raised. In a letter to the National Curriculum Expert Panel, the then UK Education Minister Michael Gove (DfE, 2012) wrote:

> In mathematics there will be additional stretch, with much more challenging content than in the current National Curriculum. We will expect children to be more proficient in arithmetic, including knowing number bonds to 20 by [age 7] and times tables up to 12×12 by [age 9]. The development of written methods – including long multiplication and division – will be given greater emphasis, and children will be taught more challenging content using fractions, decimals and negative numbers so that they have a more secure foundation for secondary school.

Michael Gove was determined to have a primary curriculum in place, which demanded what he thought of as the highest of standards and which had gleaned best practice from the most successful schools, both in this country and abroad. However, his plans were met with strong opposition from the mathematics education community who stressed the importance of developing flexible approaches to calculation. Where to place the balance between teaching algorithms (for everything from addition to – the oft-dreaded but symbolically important – long division) and teaching such flexible approaches has been an ongoing debate within mathematics education.

Indeed, just a year before Gove's comment, the England schools inspectorate, Ofsted (2011, p. 1, although now withdrawn) advocated a very different approach that identified the key aim of the teaching of calculation as developing mathematical understanding:

> It is … of fundamental importance to ensure that children have the best possible grounding in mathematics during their primary years, number, or arithmetic, is a key component of this. Public perceptions of arithmetic often relate to the ability to calculate quickly and accurately – to add, subtract, multiply and divide, both mentally and using traditional written methods. But arithmetic taught well gives children so much more than this, understanding about number, its structures and relationships, underpins progression from counting in nursery rhymes to calculating with and reasoning about numbers of all sizes, to working with measures and establishing the foundations for algebraic thinking. These grow into the skills so valued by the world of industry and higher education and are the best starting points for equipping children for their future lives.

Here we see a distancing from Gove's and the public's focus on calculation. And, although we might want to argue for purposes of mathematics education beyond preparing students for industry and higher education, clearly it is important that we give young people access to these fields. Also, research by Laurie Buxton (1981) and others on mathematics anxiety shows what a damaging long-term impact not feeling comfortable with numbers can have on people. (See Paul Ernest's Chapter 3 for further discussion about the potential harm that mathematics can do).

These two positions on calculation, represented here by Gove and Ofsted, reflect different underlying philosophies on mathematics education. Paul Ernest (1991) identified five such positions: industrial trainers, technological pragmatists, old humanists, progressive educators and public educators. Gove is typical of the 'industrial trainers' following a New Right ideology that sees mathematics as a set of absolute truths and rules to be learnt and so prioritising a drill and practice pedagogy that aims for "'Back-to-Basics' numeracy and training in social obedience" (p. 139). Indeed a further development of this position is the new times table tests to be statutory from 2020. However, Ofsted, along with many mathematics education researchers, represents a 'progressive educator' position that sees mathematics as a set of absolute truths but "with great value … attached to the role of the individual in coming to know this truth" (p. 182) and so advocating a child-centred process-oriented pedagogy that aims for creativity and self-realisation. Our own sympathies lie with this position based on connection, care and empathy between humans. Thus, in this chapter, we will argue for an informal approach to mental mathematics as a way of developing 'relational understanding' of mathematics. We begin by unpacking what we mean by relational understanding.

What do we mean by understanding mathematics?

> *Consider the problem 2047 ÷ 23. Take a moment to solve this problem. How did you do this? Did you use the long division algorithm to solve this? Consider the steps that you took – how would you explain these to someone else? Do you feel that you understood what you did?*

The problem in more formal classrooms would be written as in Figure 14.1 and the mantra heard would go something like this:

23 into 2, doesn't go
23 into 20, doesn't go
23 into 204 .... hmmm how many 23s are there in 204? [and would then proceed to write down multiples of 23 discretely on the back of a piece of paper].

An alternative approach, which has been used in schools more recently, is that of chunking. This encourages teachers to promote relational understanding (see below and Anna Llewellyn's Chapter 7 for further discussion about this) as there is no prescribed approach – pupils are encouraged to relate division to repeated subtraction where 'chunks' (multiples of the divisor) are subtracted from the dividend. The sizes of the chunks subtracted are not predetermined, unlike the formal long division algorithm where the largest multiple of the divisor must be subtracted. A number of chunks subtracted are totalled to find the solution. Figure 14.2 illustrates two different approaches to using chunking for long division. The first is a rather cautious approach, subtracting relatively easy multiples of 23. However, what is formally recorded in this illustration is what is often surreptitiously recorded on scraps of paper. The second

$$
\begin{array}{r}
8 \quad 9 \\
23 \overline{\smash{\big)}\ 2\ 0\ 4\ 7} \\
1\ 8\ 4 \quad \downarrow \\
\hline
2\ 0\ 7 \\
2\ 0\ 7 \\
\hline
0
\end{array}
$$

Figure 14.1 Long division algorithm for 2047 ÷ 23.

Figure (a):

```
                8   9
2   3 | 2   0   4   7
      -   2   3   0        (10x23)
          1   8   1   7
      -   2   3   0        (10x23)
          1   5   8   7
      -   2   3   0        (10x23)
          1   3   5   7
      -   2   3   0        (10x23)
          1   1   2   7
      -   2   3   0        (10x23)
              8   9   7
      -   2   3   0        (10x23)
              6   6   7
      -   2   3   0        (10x23)
              4   3   7
      -   2   3   0        (10x23)
              2   0   7
      -   1   1   5        (5x23)
                  9   2
      -       6   9        (3x23)
                  2   3
      -       2   3        (1x23)
                      0
```

(a)

Figure (b):

```
                8   9
2   3 | 2   0   4   7
      -   2   3   0        (10x23)
          1   8   1   7
      -   1   1   5   0    (50x23)
              6   6   7
      -   4   6   0        (20x23)
              2   0   7
      -   2   0   7        (9x23)
                      0
```

(b)

Figure 14.2 Using chunking for long division.

is slightly more sophisticated in that larger chunks are subtracted. The numbers in bold are the number of chunks being subtracted from the dividend, which are totalled at the end.

Figures 14.1 and 14.2 illustrate some familiar (and maybe some unfamiliar!) strategies for 'long division'. Some people (including industrial trainers like Michael Gove) would consider this approach long-winded, ineffective with potential for errors, and resulting from 'vague generic statements of little value'. However, although we too feel that there is a significant difference in efficiency between Figures 14.1 and 14.2, we disagree. For us, the first appears to treat numbers as digits, rather than holistically and operates algorithmically, whereas the second figure builds on a knowledge and understanding of mathematical relationships, for example, the relationships embedded in place value and those between multiplication and division and between division and subtraction. Perhaps speed for calculations such as this was important in the 19th century, for example, for clerks working in commerce, but in today's society there is no real need to emphasise efficiency. We would however argue that there remains a need for pupils to *understand* their calculations. We see this approach to calculation as being about 'mental mathematics' since there is some mental work required to select the appropriate number of chunks to subtract. Research has shown that children are often very successful in coming up with their own idiosyncratic calculation strategies which they understand (Thompson, 1994), but that they encounter problems when they try to make sense of these within the more formal written methods encouraged in school.

It is useful to draw on the distinction that Richard Skemp made between instrumental understanding of mathematics and relational understanding. He wrote about pupils developing an 'instrumental' understanding of mathematics who would follow 'rules without reasons' (Skemp, 1978). The alternative approach is to develop 'relational' understanding, which encourages pupils to know *both* what to do with a calculation *and* why. A useful analogy to illustrate the difference between these two types of understanding is a comparison between someone who only uses the underground to travel around London and a London taxi driver. Let us say that the underground traveller is attempting to navigate between Buckingham Palace and the Science Museum. They would be able to use the underground (tube) map to get themselves between the two, but they would struggle if the tube trains were not running. The London taxi driver, however, would be aware of numerous possible routes between the two landmarks and further, would be able to cope with finding alternative routes due to traffic restrictions or jams. The underground user is like the pupil with instrumental understanding; able to follow rules to go between different concepts within mathematics – for example, able to follow an algorithm to solve long division. The London taxi driver on the other hand is the pupil with relational understanding – able to navigate in a multitude of ways between different mathematical concepts. Using the long division example – a pupil with relational understanding would be able to solve the problem in numerous ways, make a reasonable estimate of the solution and know how to check their solution.

Do we always have to teach so that pupils have relational understanding? Consider some examples, such as multiplication of negative numbers, division of fractions and the angle sums of polygons. What does relational understanding mean to you in each case?

Deciding what constitutes relational understanding of any aspect of mathematics is a complicated (perhaps impossible) business. However, we are not trying to claim that there is a clear-cut distinction between relational and instrumental understanding. For example, in our example above, the taxi driver has probably acquired their knowledge of London through 'rote learning' and the underground user's understanding of the underground network is functional and is likely to be based on a deeper understanding of urban transportation. However, just as the taxi driver and tourist have different relationships to space and different feelings about navigating London, we would suggest that how a pupil understands mathematics affects their relationship with the subject and the distinction between relational and instrumental understanding is helpful in discussing this.

We conducted a study to compare the approaches to long division of primary and secondary student teachers (Babbar and Ineson, 2013). They were asked to solve the problem (207 ÷ 23) themselves, then outline how they would support a pupil encountering difficulty in solving it. Secondary student teachers were found to be more secure in the approaches that they used themselves, but struggled to think of alternative ways to support pupils in developing approaches for long division. Their favoured approach was that of an algorithm, even when the numbers involved were near multiples of 10. Although most secondary student teachers recognised that $23 \times 10 = 230$, which is near 207, nevertheless, their initial response was to write down the algorithm. Primary student teachers, on the other hand, were found to be less likely to be able to find the accurate solution but could suggest a range of alternative approaches for supporting learners. This raises questions about the kind of understanding the secondary student teachers had and how they would teach division. These are questions that we explore through focusing on mental mathematics in the rest of this chapter.

What is the place of mental mathematics in the mathematics curriculum?

Think back to your own experiences of mental mathematics: What memories do they conjure up. Do you remember mental mathematics tests? What impact did these have on you? Do you remember any other aspect of mental mathematics? While considering these questions, how would you define mental mathematics and what does this mean to you?

Before we consider current explanations of mental mathematics, it is useful to first provide some background. For over a century there has been concern over the 'standards' achieved by school leavers in the United Kingdom and less than favourable international comparisons. In addition to this, educationalists have been alarmed by the apparent over-reliance on formal algorithms for relatively simple problems. For example, when faced with problems such as $1001 - 999$, pupils tended to write these numbers out vertically then laboriously use formal written methods involving decomposition to find the solution (illustrated in Figure 14.3). Because of this over-reliance on formal strategies (sometimes described as 'comfort blankets') pupils failed to consider the numbers involved and whether, therefore, there was another more effective strategy.

A Task Group was set up in 1997 to explore the possibilities of raising mathematical achievement through the review of research and theory and

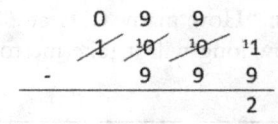

Figure 14.3 Using decomposition to solve 1001 – 999.

although concerns were expressed in professional corners about the range and scope of the Task Group's review, it led to the establishment of the National Numeracy Strategy (NNS) in 1998. This strategy emphasised the development of mental calculation in primary schools and the approach advocated in this document was radical. Prior to the implementation of the NNS, the basis of teaching about calculation in primary schools was the formal written approaches illustrated in Figure 14.3. This in itself gives rise to another question: why the need to change and focus on mental calculation? The new emphasis placed on mental computation was therefore of considerable significance. For example, the NNS stated that pupils should not be taught a standard method of written calculation until they could reliably use addition and subtraction mentally for any pair of two digit numbers. This flexibility in using mental calculation strategies is what is lost in Gove's proposed new primary mathematics curriculum.

In the previous primary framework, teachers were asked to focus on encouraging these skills in their pupils:

- remembering number facts and recalling them without hesitation;
- understanding and using the relationship between the 'four rules' to work out answers and check results: for example, $24 \div 4 = 6$, since $6 \times 4 = 24$;
- drawing on a repertoire of mental strategies to work out calculations like $81 - 26$, 23×4 or 5% of £3,000, with some thinking time;
- solving problems like the following mentally: "Can I buy three bags of crisps at 35p with my £1 coin?" or "Roughly how long will it take me to go 50 miles at 30 mph?" (DfEE, 1998, p. 6).

Following the establishment of the NNS in 1998, the Secondary National Strategy was developed to support with progression from primary to secondary. In the secondary framework, the following examples are given as ways of building opportunities to develop mental mathematics skills:

- remember number facts and recall them without hesitation;
- draw on a repertoire of mental strategies to work out calculations such as $326 - 81$, 223×4 or 2.5% of £3,000, with some thinking time;
- understand and use the relationships between operations to work out answers and check results: for example, $900 \div 15 = 60$, since $6 \times 150 = 900$;
- approximate calculations to judge whether or not an answer is about the right size: for example, recognise that 1/4 of 57.9 is just under 1/4 of 60, or 15;

- solve problems such as: "How many CDs at £3.99 each can I buy with £25?" or: "Roughly how long will it take me to go 50 miles at 30 mph?" (DfEE, 2001, p. 10).

> *Consider the progression in mental mathematics in the primary phase to the secondary phase – does this seem appropriate?*

Liping Ma (1999) carried out research to explore the way in which effective mathematics teachers understand mathematics. She came up with the term Profound Understanding of Fundamental Mathematics (PUFM) to describe the type of understanding that effective teachers had. This included seeing the connections between different mathematical concepts (for example, the relationship between decimals and fractions, or the number operations), the ability to be flexible when calculating and recognising the coherence of the mathematics curriculum. So, in considering the place of mental mathematics in the mathematics curriculum, we suggest that almost all of mathematics could be described as 'mental' in the sense that engaging in a mathematical task involves thinking. Mental mathematics is about more than the recall of facts; it is about having the confidence and competence to deal with numbers. Ma would emphasise the teacher's ability to be flexible when calculating in order to encourage flexibility in their pupils. Many of the examples of skills listed above for both primary and secondary pupils are about developing flexible strategies for calculating. This reflects the views of those Paul Ernest called 'Progressive Educators', that mathematics education should allow pupils to gain confidence and not rely solely on formal procedures.

As research shows, promoting mental mathematics is not without dangers (Beishuizen, 1999; Denvir and Askew, 2001). On the one hand, the NNS suggests that the development of mental capability is more than drill and practice, procedural understanding and memorising number facts; teachers are also encouraged to promote pupils' understanding. On the other hand, research studies also consistently show that there is a tendency, when carrying out daily mental work (as encouraged in the NNS) for teachers to emphasise the procedural at the expense of understanding (Gray and Tall, 1994; Denvir and Askew, 2001). Denvir and Askew (2001) explored the behaviour of pupils during numeracy lessons and found that teachers tended to emphasise the need for speed and accuracy, rather than mathematical thinking. They suggested that these pupils were 'participating' rather than 'engaging' in the mathematical activities. In these and similar contexts, an emphasis on rote memory to recall number facts often has a negative effect, compounding the problems faced, in particular, by those who we construct as lower-achieving pupils, who initially have difficulty in remembering and so develop a reliance on counting strategies, rather than developing a flexible approach to calculation (Gray and Tall, 1994).

We revisit now, Gove's quote at the beginning of the chapter, and his suggestion that pupils should be "more proficient in arithmetic … including knowing the times tables up to 12×12 by the end of year 4". Despite the research evidence about the negative impact on the emphasis on rote memory, Gove has had his way and a new times table test, which becomes mandatory in 2020, will be taken by all 8/9-year-olds. This will be an on-screen test and will check whether pupils have quick instant recall of the multiplication tables, up to 12×12. While few would argue with the need for pupils to learn their multiplication tables, many have voiced their concern about the emphasis, through this assessment strategy, on instrumental understanding.

> *How do you feel about mental mathematics being tested in this way? What kind of understanding do you think this promotes?*

We feel that this promotes the industrial trainer approach, which sees mathematics as a fixed body of knowledge which is best tested in this way. It also reflects the status of mathematics and its power to act as a gatekeeper. However, we feel that there is a distinction to make when working mentally and in this situation the emphasis is on working *in* the head, rather than *with* the head. So, for example, focusing on quick recall or memorising of number facts focuses on *in*-the-head thinking, whereas some of the strategies that were discussed earlier such as using facts (for example, 20 times a number to solve 19 times a number) encourage *with*-the-head thinking. This would not be a 'known fact' but we could use our heads to find the solution, without reliance on an algorithm. While there are clearly benefits of quick recall of number facts, it is also important to focus on the importance of developing strategies – *with* the head (Beishuizen, 1997). This has parallels with Skemp's concern over instrumental understanding, which has a tendency to focus on *in*-the-head work. Research has shown that pupils who have a large bank of known facts (that is, those that they can instantly recall) are able to make use of these for more derived facts (Gray, 1991). Conversely, the same researchers found that pupils who rely heavily on counting strategies (usually because they do not have a bank of quickly recalled known facts) are likely to be slower and less accurate in their solutions (Gray, 1991).

We end this chapter by using the example of the empty number line (ENL) to illustrate this tension between the *in*-the-head and *with*-the-head ways of thinking.

The empty number line: Encouraging with-the-head thinking

As mentioned previously, mental mathematics is not just about what is done *in* the head. In both primary and secondary settings, informal jottings are very much encouraged and these usually draw on visual images that pupils have built

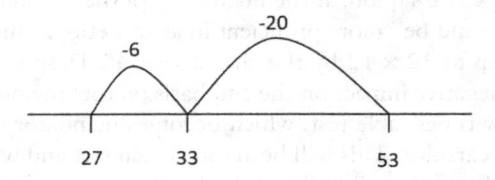

Figure 14.4 One way of using the ENL to solve 53 –26.

up from an early age. The ENL was introduced as a model in schools in the Netherlands, which helped pupils visualise the quantity value of numbers. Ian Thompson (1999) makes the useful distinction between the *quantity* value of numbers and the *column* value of digits. He suggests that it is important for pupils to understand the relative size of numbers, rather than focusing on which column the digits are in. The ENL replaced the practice of partitioning using base ten that encouraged pupils to concentrate on the column value of numbers.

The ENL is exactly what its name describes; a line which is empty. The emptiness is significant because it discourages pupils from counting in ones (which we identified above as unhelpful) and provides the scope for flexible approaches. It is also a useful image on which to record calculation steps. Figure 14.4 uses the ENL to solve 53 – 26.

In this example the 'take away' approach to subtraction is illustrated (rather than the approach which would focus on the 'difference' between the two numbers). The pupil has started with 53 and counted back first 20, then a further 6. Beishuizen (1999) explains that the benefits of this approach in terms of general mathematics competence are that this supports pupils' understanding of number and operations: "dealing with whole numbers supports pupils' understanding and insight into number and number operations much more than the early introduction of vertical algorithms dealing with isolated digits" (p. 159).

In another study by Gwen (Ineson, 2019), primary student teachers were encouraged to use the ENL to solve simple numerical problems in a variety of ways in preparation for teaching in primary schools. They were encouraged to use the ENL as a model to visualise the relationship between the numbers involved in specific calculation problems and as a tool to note steps in their calculations – so that they were working *with* their heads. Initially many student teachers were sceptical about the benefits of such an approach as they felt comfortable and confident using the more traditional approaches to calculation that they had grown up with. However, after spending time in school, many reported that they found that pupils were using the ENL well to support their approach to calculation and were beginning to change their opinion about it. Some even claimed to be using the ENL to support their own calculations. However, during one activity focusing on using the ENL for different approaches of subtraction one student teacher was heard to say, "I'm confused, which numbers do I write on the line?" This suggests that the student teacher was beginning to use the ENL approach as a procedure, or algorithm, rather than as a conceptual model and was focusing on working *in* the head. This may have been because he was so unfamiliar and uncomfortable with an alternative approach to calculation that his only way to embrace it was to 'learn' it as an algorithm because that is how he had become used to operating within mathematics. Given the level of anxiety that mathematics creates for people, it is not surprising that they will seek the apparent security of algorithms.

> a *Have you seen the empty number line being used in the primary classroom? Can you think of alternative ways to use the ENL to solve 53 – 26? Can you think of examples where it could be used to support calculations in secondary classrooms? What alternative jottings have you seen secondary pupils use to support their calculations?*
> b *How would you solve 2001 – 999? It was pupils' perceived over reliance on formal written methods for problems such as this that was one of the prompts to a focus on mental calculation. Thinking about the arguments in this chapters, how important is it that teachers emphasise alternative approaches to formal written methods?*

Summary

In this chapter, we have investigated some of the debates surrounding mental mathematics, including what it is, its place in the curriculum and how pupils might be encouraged to engage with it. We offer the viewpoint that it is important for secondary teachers of mathematics to understand and build on the approaches taken to calculating in primary settings. Furthermore, it is important for them to be fluent in the strategies that pupils are likely to make use of so that they can encourage them to adopt a more flexible approach, ultimately enabling them to develop relational understanding, without an over-reliance on formal written algorithms. Being taught, and subsequently being able to use, specific strategies for mental calculation equip pupils with the ability to make choices and have a 'toolkit' at their fingertips. So even if they have learnt facts and can recall them (*in* the head), they feel sufficiently confident that they are able to apply what they have learnt to unknown situations (*with* the head).

To conclude, we would like to bring the debate back to where we started, with the current National Curriculum. The emphasis on rote learning times tables, as well as specific *approved* formal written algorithms, suggests a move towards industrial training. Primary and secondary mathematics teachers are tasked with the job of ensuring that children and young people leave school with relational understanding of at least some concepts through an emphasis on what they are doing *with* their heads.

Further reading

Ma, L. (1999) *Knowing and Teaching Elementary Mathematics*. Mahwah, NJ: Lawrence Erlbaum. This book has quickly become a classic in mathematics education. Through a comparative study of Chinese and North American primary school teachers, Liping Ma develops her theory that they need a Profound Understanding of Fundamental Mathematics.

Plunkett, S. (1979) 'Decomposition and all that rot', *Mathematics in School*, 8, 3, 2–5. Ever thought about how/why we teach decomposition? A classic article querying the teaching of algorithms.

Skemp, R. R. (1978) 'Relational understanding and instrumental understanding', *Mathematic Teaching*, 77, 20–26. This provides further distinction between these two different ways of understanding mathematics from the originator of the terms.

Thompson, I. (2010) 'Subtraction in key stage 3: which algorithm?', *Mathematics in School*, 39, 1, 29–31. Ian Thompson has written prolifically about mental mathematics but this article continues the debate started in this chapter about algorithms and instrumental understanding.

Murphy, C. (2011) 'Comparing the use of the empty number line in England and the Netherlands', *British Educational Research Journal*, 37, 160, 147–161. This article explores the reason for introducing the ENL as a model to support mathematics education in the Netherlands as part of the Realistic Mathematics Education programme. Carol Murphy critiques the way in which this has been adopted in England and suggests that this has led to an algorithmic approach to teaching mental calculation.

References

Babbar, S. and Ineson, G. (2013) 'Mental mathematics: a comparison between primary and secondary trainee teachers' strategies', paper presented at British Society for Research into Learning Mathematics. Bristol University, UK. March 2013.

Beishuizen, M. (1997) 'Mental arithmetic: mental recall or mental strategies?', *Mathematics Teaching*, 160, 16–19.

Beishuizen, M. (1999) 'The empty number line as a new model', in I. Thompson (ed), *Issues in Teaching and Numeracy in Primary Schools*. Buckingham: Open University Press.

Buxton, L. (1981) *Do You Panic About Maths?* London, Heinemann.

Denvir, H. and Askew, M. (2001) 'Pupils' participation in the classroom examined in relation to "interactive whole class teaching"', *Proceedings of the British Society for Research into Learning Mathematics (BSRLM)*, 21, 1, 25–30.

Department for Education (DfE) (2012) *National Curriculum for Mathematics Key Stages 1 and 2' (Draft)*. London: DfE.

Department for Education and Employment (DfEE) (1998) *The NNS Framework for Teaching Mathematics from Reception to Year 6*. London: DfEE.

Department for Education and Employment (DfEE) (2001) *Framework for Teaching Mathematics: Years 7, 8 and 9*. London: DfEE.

Ernest, P. (1991) *The Philosophy of Mathematics Education*, London: Falmer.

Gray, E. M. (1991) 'An analysis of diverging approaches to simple arithmetic: preferences and its consequences', *Educational Studies in Mathematics*, 22, 6, 551–574.

Gray, E. M. and Tall, D. O. (1994) 'Duality, ambiguity and flexibility: a proceptual view of simple arithmetic', *Journal for Research in Mathematics Education*, 25, 2, 115–141.

Ineson, G. (2019) *Using the empty number line to support elementary pre-service teachers develop number sense* (in preparation).

Ma, L. (1999) *Knowing and Teaching Elementary Mathematics: Teachers' Understanding of Fundamental Mathematics in China and the United States.* Mahwah, NJ: Lawrence Erlbaum Associates.

Office for Standards in Education (Ofsted) (2011) '*Good practice in primary mathematics: evidence from 20 successful schools (Report Summary)*'. Available at: http://www.ofsted. gov.uk/resources/good-practice-primary-mathematics-evidence-20-successful-schools (accessed 7 January 2013 – although now withdrawn).

Skemp, R. R. (1978) 'Relational understanding and instrumental understanding', *Mathematics Teaching*, 77, 20–26.

Thompson, I. (1994) 'Young children's idiosyncratic written algorithms for addition', *Educational Studies in Mathematics*, 26, 4, pp. 323–345.

Thompson, I. (1999) 'Implications of research on mental calculation for the teaching of place value', *Curriculum*, 20, 3, 185–191.

Chapter 15

The role of examples in mathematics teaching

Tim Rowland

This chapter is about some of the ways that teachers use examples in mathematics teaching and aims to raise your awareness of the importance of choosing and using them with care.

> *Imagine that you are planning a lesson on pie charts as a way of representing relative frequency. Your objective is that the students will be able to construct pie charts from a frequency table. You decide to explain with a worked example; but which one? The options available to you are limitless. What will you choose? Why choose these numbers for your data? Perhaps a second worked example would be good as well – what will it be?*

For nearly 20 years, together with various colleagues, I have been observing and analysing mathematics lessons to see how teachers make use of their mathematical knowledge as they teach. We identified about 20 general factors connecting this knowledge to what teachers do in the classroom. It turned out that the most prevalent factor, present many times in every lesson, was the choice and use of examples. But different examples play different roles and are used for different purposes. The aim of this chapter is to describe and explore these roles and purposes.

Ways of using examples

Quite a few teachers introduce the focus of the lesson by asking for a definition: "What is a pie chart?", "What is a fraction?" And "What is symmetry?" Sometimes, rather than asking for a definition – of a fraction, for example – it can be more productive to invite students to offer *examples* of fractions, to see what variety they produce. A fruitful approach is to ask for one example, then another, and another ... each one being in some way different from the last one. This teases out the range of things that they would count as fractions, and what they believe can be varied while remaining within the concept of fraction. Does anyone offer an integer (for example, 3)? Or a decimal number (for example, 0.137)? What do you think about these two examples? Do they 'count' in your opinion? Why? This discussion could go a long way – if you do allow decimal numbers, then what about infinite decimals?

Teachers mainly use examples in mathematics teaching in two ways. The first is in connection with teaching mathematical concepts and procedures. The second is in the provision of exercises for students. These two kinds of use are different and may require different choices. Most of this chapter is focused on these two purposes, but examples fulfil two more important roles: as counterexamples and 'generic' examples. These will be discussed towards the end of this chapter.

Teaching concepts and procedures

In order to teach something, we often provide students (or ask them to provide) examples *of* the thing to be learnt. The 'thing' is *general* in character (for example, the notion of rotational symmetry, or a procedure for solving a quadratic equation); the examples are *particular* instances of the generality. The fractions example was chosen to illustrate an approach to *teaching a concept*. When Jason began a Year 2 lesson by asking "What is a fraction?", George replied "It's a number, a line and then another number". You might think about the adequacy of George's definition, and about alternative definitions. For example, do you want to distinguish between rational numbers and fractions? Do you consider $\frac{2}{3}$ and $\frac{4}{6}$ to be equal fractions, or the same fraction? Do you want to emphasise particular *representations* of fractions in your definition (a number of equal parts of a whole, say), or fraction *notation* (which is also a representation) referring to numerator and denominator (as George did)? Do you want to restrict to 'vulgar' fractions, or include decimal fractions? Do you want to include negative fractions, or 'improper' factions such as $\frac{7}{5}$?

In any case, as indicated earlier, some of these considerations would arise if you asked for examples of fractions. Likewise, if the target concept were 'factor', you would want to find examples of pairs of whole numbers such that one is a factor of the other, like 7 and 21. The pair 13, 611 might be less helpful as an introductory example, because the effort to determine whether 13 divides into 611 'exactly' might become a distraction. On the other hand, the same example might be ideal as an assessment or practice exercise.

Similarly, we *teach a general procedure* by a particular demonstration of that procedure. For example, if we were going to teach solving two simultaneous linear equations by elimination, we could choose two linear equations (in two variables), and demonstrate how to construct equivalent linear equations sharing one variable with the same coefficient. Typically, if we want pupils to see *why* the procedure works, we build in a kind of commentary with the demonstration, to explain what is going on, and to draw attention to potential difficulties and pitfalls. If you started with this example:

$$3x + 10y = 22$$

$$x + 2y = 6$$

you would probably realise that it fails to demonstrate what to do in some other cases (for example, with one or more coefficient(s) negative), and feel that you ought to do one or two more demonstration examples before setting exercises for the class. In your earlier consideration of examples of pie charts, you may have considered that four or five categories (sectors) would keep an introductory example reasonably simple; and that having the sum of the frequencies equal to a factor of 360 will assist understanding to begin with.

Eddie Gray and David Tall (1994) pointed out that the learning of concepts and the learning of procedures are not unrelated. Many concepts grow out of familiarity with a procedure. They capture this duality in the word *'procept'*: a procept is both an abstract mathematical 'thing', or concept, and also a procedure intimately associated with the concept. Anna Sfard (1991, 2008), using different language, observed that abstract mathematical notions can be viewed both *operationally*, as processes, and *structurally*, as objects. In this way, something that we 'do' (like multi*plying*) becomes a 'thing' (in this case, multi*plication*) whose properties and characteristics we can discuss. She uses the word *reification* to describe the mental transition from the process to the object. When we speak of addition and subtraction being 'inverse operations', we have certainly reified both addition and subtraction.

The second major use of examples in teaching is usually directed towards familiarisation and practice, *after* a new idea or a method has been introduced. Examples in this instance are often called *exercises*. Exercises *are* examples, usually selected from a wide range of possible examples. Suppose you had taught a class how to solve simultaneous linear equations in two variables, by elimination. After your introduction, you might well want the students to try some exercises themselves, perhaps in groups, and a few more for homework, to assist retention of the procedure by repetition, then to develop fluency with it. Sometimes such exercises are also a means of assessment, from the teacher's perspective. Practice does not need to be drudgery: sometimes it can lead to different kinds of awareness and understanding. Again, the selection of such examples is neither trivial nor arbitrary. Why choose some of them in preference to others?

Propose about five examples of simultaneous linear equations, in sequence, which you could use when introducing solution by eliminating variables.

Summing up, my main point is that examples are used all the time in mathematics teaching, and for several different reasons. But whatever their purpose, the examples provided by a teacher ought, ideally, to be the outcome of a careful process of *choice*, a *deliberate* and informed selection, because some are simply 'better' than others. Now I want to introduce and consider in detail one particular lesson, thinking about the teacher's choice of examples, and setting out some principles for choosing.

John's lesson: Quadratic functions

John was in the later stages of an initial teacher education (PGCE) secondary mathematics course, and a participant in a research project looking at how teachers use their mathematical knowledge in the classroom. For this lesson, John was teaching a Year 9 class (age 13–14) in a non-selective state school.

The focus was on quadratic functions (polynomials), and finding equivalent expressions by completing the square (CTS). The aim was to apply CTS, which they had met in a previous lesson, in two ways: to solve quadratic equations and to find the minimum point of quadratic functions. These two techniques were then to be used to sketch graphs of quadratic functions. CTS is not usually introduced this early in the United Kingdom, but these students were following an accelerated mathematics course, and John judged that they were 'ready'.

John began by reminding the class about the procedure for CTS by working an example, showing that $x^2 + 6x + 8 = (x + 3)^2 - 1$. Then he gave the pupils these five expressions to try CTS for themselves:

$$x^2 - 8x + 14, x^2 + 2x - 8, \ x^2 + 6x + 5, \ x^2 + 3x - 1, \ 2x^2 + 4x - 2.$$

Later he worked through each example on the board, interacting with ideas from the students.

Following this introduction, John demonstrated solving the equation $x^2 + 8x + 14 = 0$ by CTS, then asked the students to find the zeros of the original expressions. While they were busy, he attempted to activate a graphing package on his laptop, but without success, so later he reviewed some of the examples 'manually', without the graph-sketching software.

John then proceeded to explain how to sketch $y = x^2 + 6x + 8$, finding the minimum value using CTS. The zeros of the function, −2 and −4, had been found earlier, and these were used to identify where the graph intersects the x-axis.

He set the students $y = x^2 + 6x + 5$ to sketch as an exercise, and 'went over' it later. The lesson concluded with sketching $2x^2 + 4x - 2$, when John invited as many students as possible to contribute to a collaborative solution.

> *Look at John's examples. Do you think they were well-chosen? Why? In what ways might you have chosen differently, and why?*

John's choice of examples

John used six expressions as examples. I knew that John had selected them in advance, because they were listed in his lesson plan. So why these examples?

After school, the same day, we looked at some episodes from a video of the lesson with John, and I asked him:

TR: What made you pick those six examples?
    John's was able to articulate reasons for his choices.

JOHN: They all have real solutions was the first thing, umm, so that when sketching them they can use the whole "oh I have got two solutions, it crosses twice, it's a U-shape" ... got one odd coefficient of x, cos they had had a bit of practice of that and if the focus was going to be on sketching there's no need to have sort of overly complicated, umm, squaring point fives and stuff in there cos they can already do that.

    Umm, and the bottom example $[2x^2 + 4x - 2]$ was chosen because you can take a factor of 2 out, and I thought that might be good for when we were talking about the difference between an expression and an equation; because if you are solving that you'd say "I'll divide both sides by two", whereas if you're just putting it into a completing the square form as an expression, you can't say that and so you have to take 2 out as a factor.

TR: So if you like, you kind of invented these, with those factors in mind.

JOHN: Yes.

TR: OK. So what, what made you pick on the $x^2 + 6x + 8$ for this particular ...

JOHN: That's the only one, the only one that factorises, I think. Well I know it factorises but I'm not sure if any of the others do. That factorises so that you get the solutions −1 and −5, which means that they will be able to draw the graph more easily, sketch it more easily, rather than getting a daft surd, to try and draw on their x-axis, just to make ... ease the drawing on their own for the first time.

> *How does John's explanation of his choice of examples compare with your own analysis of them? Did he consider any factors in addition to the ones that you identified? Did you take into account any factors that John doesn't mention?*

Dimensions of variation

Before continuing with John's lesson, I want to introduce a way of thinking about examples proposed by Ference Marton. Marton's Theory of Variation proposes that humans learn by becoming aware of the different ways in which things can vary, and therefore variation needs to be experienced by the learner. In essence, we learn from discerning variation, and what varies in our experience influences what we learn. The provision of examples must therefore take into account the 'dimensions of variation' (Marton & Booth, 1997) inherent in the objects of attention. Anne Watson and John Mason (2005, p. 108) explore this position, from the perspective of mathematics teachers:

> Marton proposed that we learn from discerning variation in simultaneous situations. What varies in a lesson is an important influence on what is learnt. The provision of examples becomes an exercise in deciding how to vary the examples so that learners will learn what we hope they will learn, and trying to minimise other variations which are irrelevant or distracting.

Learning the concept of 'square', for example, is marked by growing awareness of the various ways that squares can vary (dimensions of variation, such as side-length, orientation and colour), and the variants that do not qualify as squares (those that cannot vary, such as the number of sides, relative side-lengths and angles).

John's examples

Now look at John's six quadratic functions again and his reasons for the choice, this time through the lens of variation theory. We can think about a quadratic function in various representations, principally its symbolic expression (the 'formula') $ax^2 + bx + c$, but also its visual representation as a Cartesian graph – a parabola of some sort. In the symbolic form, the 'parameters' a, b, c correspond to dimensions of variation.

The choice of the variable 'a' contributes to the complexity, or otherwise, of CTS. When $a > 1$, the factor a needs to be taken out, rewriting the expression as $a[x^2 + b'x + c']$ first. In fact all of John's examples have $a = 1$, except the one they did together at the very end. He probably judged that in their very first encounter with CTS, this dimension of variation would best be left fixed, but doesn't comment on it in the interview. Permissible variations for 'a' also include $a < 0$ and a is not an integer, both probably best delayed to another lesson.

Notice that John also comments on his last example, $2x^2 + 4x - 2$, in terms of the students' learning to distinguish between *expressions* (formula for functions) and *equations* (statements satisfied only by the zeros of the function). When he divides $2x^2 + 4x - 2$ by 2, the expression changes but the solutions of the equation stay the same.

Suppose, like John, we fix $a = 1$, and consider the variable 'b'. The complexity of CTS is significantly reduced when b is even. When b is odd CTS involves, in John's words "squaring point fives and stuff", and the arithmetic is just a bit more messy. The first four of John's examples have even values of b. The sign of b is another dimension of variation, and his second example introduces a negative (but even) value.

In the final example, when $a = 2$, b is chosen to be 4. This has the advantage that the coefficient of x remains an even integer after the factor 2 has been taken out of the expression.

The choice of the variable 'c' does not affect the complexity of CTS so much, but John includes positive and negative values of c in any case.

In the interview, John begins by referring to the *graphical* representation of the quadratic functions when explaining his choices. He is thinking about the dimensions of variation of the graph, and how these affect the complexity of the task of sketching it. His approach to sketching quadratics in the lesson was: (a) decide whether the parabola is a 'U' or an upside-down 'U', by reference to the sign of the coefficient 'a'; (b) find where the graph intersects the x-axis, corresponding to the solutions of the quadratic equation; (c) find the minimum (or maximum, if $a < 0$) value of the function by CTS, and check that the x-coordinate of this point is halfway between the x-intercepts. John's first concern, in the interview, was that the roots of the equations should be real, so that the x-intercepts could be found and used in the sketch. He also says that he chose $x^2 + 6x + 8$ for the first sketch because it factorises, and so the x-intercepts will neatly be at integers on that axis, "rather than getting a daft surd". You may have observed that his roots of -1, -5 in the interview are incorrect, and that two more expressions factorise, but this does not undermine his reasoning.

An experienced teacher in Turkey

Research on mathematics teachers' choice and use of examples is now taking place in several countries around the world. Let's make a brief visit to the class of one participant in the research of Ramazan Avcu (2014) in Ankara, Turkey. We'll call the teacher Berat. Berat had studied mathematics at university, and he now has been teaching for 14 years. In a sequence of lessons with a grade 5 class (student age 10–11), he introduces five methods of ordering fractions, in order to encourage flexible thinking. These methods are labelled: common denominator approach; common numerator approach; residual approach; benchmarking and equating the number of decimal digits by adding zeros. The common denominator approach is likely to be most familiar to readers of this book. So $\frac{5}{6}$ and $\frac{7}{8}$ can be compared by finding equivalent fractions with denominator 24, and then comparing the numerators 20 and 21. But a common numerator account would compare the equivalent fractions $\frac{35}{42}$ and $\frac{35}{40}$, in the knowledge that $\frac{1}{42} < \frac{1}{40}$. Or, using the residual approach, the two fractions $\frac{5}{6}$ and $\frac{7}{8}$ fall short of 1 by $\frac{1}{6}$ and $\frac{1}{8}$, respectively, so $\frac{7}{8}$ must be greater than $\frac{5}{6}$. In his explanation of these three strategies, Berat first compared $\frac{17}{2}$, $\frac{19}{3}$ and $\frac{35}{6}$, explaining in his planning that "It is very difficult to equate the numerators, but it is easy to equate the denominators". In this way he 'directed' his students towards the common denominator approach rather than the common numerator approach. (Of course, if these three fractions are expressed as mixed fractions $8\frac{1}{2}$ etc. the comparison is very straightforward!). His explanation of 'benchmarking' compared $\frac{1}{7}$, $\frac{4}{5}$ and $\frac{8}{19}$, and his planning included "$\frac{1}{7}$ is close to 0, $\frac{8}{19}$ is close to $\frac{1}{2}$ and $\frac{4}{5}$ is close to 1. Therefore $\frac{1}{7} < \frac{4}{5}$ and $\frac{8}{19} < \frac{4}{5}$".

The 'equating the number of decimal digits by adding zeros' approach is designed to address a common error/misconception in the ordering of decimal numbers – the 'decimal point ignored' (DPI) error was documented in a study by the Assessment of Performance Unit in the United Kingdom (APU, 1982), Berat explains it to his class: "If you are asked to compare 2.545 and 2.55 you cannot [...] simply say that 545 > 55 so 2.545 > 2.55. [...] You should first equate the number of digits after the decimal points. [...] we can write 2.55 as 2.550. Now we can compare the decimal numbers. 550 is larger than 545 so 2.550 is larger than 2.545 and finally 2.55 is larger than 2.545". (Avcu, 2014, p. 280). In this lesson he uses the 'adding zero' method to compare 0.21, 0.2001 and 0.201.

Now Berat will have taught this topic many times in his 14 years in the classroom, whereas it would be John's first experience of teaching quadratic equations. Berat is very clear about the comparison strategies that he sets out to teach, and he justifies his choice of instructional examples convincingly. One could argue that his benchmarking rationale would be improved with the observation that $\frac{8}{19}$ is close to and less than $\frac{1}{2}$, and $\frac{4}{5}$ is greater than $\frac{1}{2}$. But it is very clear that he chose his examples with care, and for good reasons, demonstrating pedagogical content knowledge of the DPI error.

Examples to avoid

A 'dimensions of variation' analysis of a concept or process identifies a few key, independent variables in any mathematical situation (such as the three coefficients in a quadratic expression). When choosing examples to *introduce* a topic, it is usually wise to keep the values of these different variables *distinct* in one example.

Kirsty was reviewing the topic of Cartesian coordinates with her Year 7 (age 11–12) pupils. She began by asking the children for a definition of coordinates. One student volunteered that "the horizontal line is first and then the vertical line". Kirsty then checked the students' understanding of this convention by asking them to identify the coordinates of some points on a grid.

Kirsty's first example was the point (1,1), which would seem to be entirely ineffective in assessing the students' grasp of the significance of the order of the two elements of the pair. This is an example of 'confusing the role of variables', and it happens surprisingly often, though not as blatantly as in Kirsty's coordinates. It is useful to be aware of the possibility of confusing the role of variables in your own choice of examples (for some other types of best-avoided examples see Rowland, 2008).

> *By reference to dimensions of variation, give a sequence of about five examples that might have worked well for Kirsty.*

Interlude: Whose examples?

In discussing the lessons of John, Berat and Kirsty, my emphasis was on the examples that *they*, the teachers, chose, why they chose them, and whether they chose them well. As I remarked earlier, teachers *do* choose and use examples a great deal in mathematics teaching. However, I also began by speculating what responses would be forthcoming if *students* themselves were invited to offer examples (of fractions, in that case), what their responses might reveal, and what opportunities for teaching these responses might afford. In their book, Anne Watson and John Mason (2005) develop both the theory and the practice of such *learner-generated examples* (LGEs), building on the variation theory (Marton & Booth, 1997) mentioned earlier. So is it better to develop a 'student-centred' pedagogy based on LGEs rather than a 'teacher-centred' approach in which the teacher chooses the examples? I would say that this implied association between pedagogies and the sources of examples is unhelpful, and that both approaches are valuable, depending on the intended purpose. As I have already demonstrated, and as Watson and Mason explain at length, the LGE approach is especially valuable in exploring the scope and limitations of concepts with students. See also the discussion of learner-designed tasks in Chapter 12 by Anne Watson. On the other hand, if (like Berat, for example) we set out to teach the ordering of fractions, it is almost certainly better to be aware of the possible strategies and to have prepared a sequence of examples in advance, progressively introducing the various possible complexities that arise. This is more or less what John did in his selection and sequencing of quadratic expressions. This is not to be confused with a 'didactic', transmission-type teaching style, however. Whatever tasks we offer students to do, they often respond in ways that we had not expected or planned for – and student-centred (and mathematically comfortable) teachers investigate students' thinking by following up such responses as they occur.

Proving and disproving: Counterexamples and generic examples

There are two additional uses of examples, which support and challenge students' mathematical reasoning in important ways.

Sometimes a mathematical enquiry leads to an interesting and/or unexpected finding. Take this one, for example. Try it yourself first.

> How many ways are there of ascending a flight of stairs if you can take one or two stairs at a time? For three stairs, for example, there are 3 ways: 111, 12 and 21.

Students can soon find how many ways there are for one stair (one way!), two stairs, four and so on. The sequence of numbers-of-ways is 1, 2, 3, 5, 8, 13, ... Students usually readily see 'a pattern', and point out that $1 + 2 = 3$, $2 + 3 = 5$

and so on. This is the Fibonacci sequence, of course. If they have listed all the possibilities for the first five cases, they usually predict that there are 13 ways for six stairs and may check that this is correct. By then most students are convinced that it continues, 21, 34, ..., and have no appetite for further checking. But at this point, the belief that every term is the sum of the previous two, has the status of a *conjecture*. In mathematics we never know general truths – in the sense of being completely sure that there are no exceptions – on the basis of examples, no matter how many we try.

To establish that a conjecture like the one above is true, we need to *prove* it. To show that it is false, we need a *counterexample*, one case where the conjecture turns out not to be true. If the number of ways for eight stairs turned out to be 35, not 34, then the claim about always summing the previous two terms could not be true in general.

Applying this to the 'stairs' Fibonacci-conjecture: we don't have a counterexample yet, so could we show that it is always true, to explain *why* each term is the sum of the previous pair? I find that very often a student volunteers an explanation, and that a feature of these accounts is that they are invariably grounded in a particular value of n. Following some group discussion, one student, Jenny, expressed it something like this.

> Suppose we've done flight-lengths 1 to 5 by listing all the ways. Now consider ascending 6 stairs. The first step must be 1 or 2. If it is 1, then 5 stairs are left, and we know that there are 8 ways to ascend them. If it is 2, then 4 stairs are left, and we know that there are 5 ways to ascend them. This exhausts all the possibilities, so there are 5 + 8 ways of climbing the 6 stairs.

This particular example then became a window through which other students could see what would happen in other cases (say from 8, 9 stairs to 10 stairs), and indeed beyond particular cases to the general. Jenny's example, with 4, 5 and 6 stairs, is called a generic example, and her argument, displayed above, is a *proof by generic example*. This kind of explanatory insight, achieved by 'talking through' a *single* example, needs to draw attention to the *structure* of that example, in the way that Jenny did. This helps others to see why the same, or analogous, reasoning would work just as well in other cases. This kind of 'seeing' is seeing *through* the particular example, as if it were a window onto a world of things analogous to it.

> *Suggest a generic example to show why the sum of any three consecutive integers is a multiple of 3.*

You can read more about proof by generic example in Rowland (2001) and the NRICH March 2012 issue (see Further reading). An interesting search for a counterexample is given on pp. 131–132 of Rowland et al. (2009).

Conclusion

This chapter has been about the ways in which examples are used in mathematics teaching. Examples play an essential role in the teaching of concepts, in the teaching of procedures, and as exercises through which students become familiar with new ideas, and fluent in the use and application of procedures. Through consideration and careful examination of some actual lessons, I have argued that the examples used in mathematics teaching should be chosen with care, keeping in mind their intended purpose, and the possible dimensions of variation within a particular example. I concluded with two rather different uses of examples, in determining the truth or falsehood of some general mathematical claim. A suitable counterexample can demonstrate that such a claim is false, thereby disproving or refuting it. The normal procedure for establishing mathematical truth is by general proof, but insight into the nature of such a proof can often be achieved by means of a carefully structured argument based on a *generic example*. Thoughtful choice of examples, in advance of teaching where possible, pays dividends.

Further reading

Watson, A. & Mason, J. (2005) *Mathematics as a constructive activity: The role of learner generated examples*. Mahwah, NJ: Lawrence Erlbaum Associates.
This book brings together many years of reflection and enquiry by the authors into ways that teachers can work with students with a focus on examples. It is an eminently 'practical' resource for teachers, securely underpinned by theory, and probably the next thing you should read if you found this chapter relevant and helpful.
Rowland, T. (2008) The purpose, design and use of examples in the teaching of elementary mathematics. *Educational Studies in Mathematics* 69(2): 149–163.
This research paper has a section on some classroom situations in which examples were not well-chosen by teachers, and analyses why this was so. Three types of examples are identified which, for different reasons, do not achieve the intended pedagogical purpose.
Special Issue 69(2) of *Educational Studies in Mathematics* on exemplification.
In this collection of papers, researchers from the UK, North America and Israel consider the use of examples from several perspectives and within different mathematics topics.
NRICH Issue on Generic Examples, March 2012 http://nrich.maths.org/.
Every teacher should know this great website, a resource of interesting mathematical problems for students of all ages. The March 2012 edition features generic examples, with problems, notes for teachers, and an article by myself.
Bills, L., Dreyfus, T., Mason, J., Tsamir, P., Watson, A. & Zaslavsky, O. (2006) Exemplification in mathematics education. In J. Novotna, H. Moraova, M. Kratka & N. Stehlikova (Eds.) *Proceedings of the 30th conference of the international group for the psychology of mathematics education*, Vol. 1, pp. 126–154. Prague, Czech Republic: Charles University.
A readable and useful insight into the scope of the topic, including a historical overview of the way examples have been seen in mathematics education, and accounts of issues relating to teachers' and learners' use of examples.

References

Assessment of Performance Unit (APU) (1982) *A review of monitoring in mathematics 1978-1982*. London: DES.

Avcu, R. (2014) *Exploring middle school mathematics teachers' treatment of rational number examples in their classrooms: A multiple case study*. Unpublished Doctoral Thesis, Middle East Technical University, Ankara, Turkey.

Gray, E. M. & Tall, D. O. (1994) Duality, ambiguity, and flexibility: A proceptual view of simple arithmetic. *Journal for Research in Mathematics Education* 25: 116–140.

Marton, F. & Booth, S. (1997) *Learning and awareness*. Mahwah, NJ: Lawrence Erlbaum.

Rowland, T. (2001) Generic proofs: Setting a good example. *Mathematics Teaching* 177, 40–43.

Rowland, T. (2008) The purpose, design and use of examples in the teaching of elementary mathematics. *Educational Studies in Mathematics* 69(2): 149–163

Rowland, T., Turner, F., Thwaites, A. & Huckstep, P. (2009) *Developing primary mathematics teaching: reflecting on practice with the knowledge quartet*. London: Sage.

Sfard, A. (1991) On the dual nature of mathematical conceptions: reflections on processes and objects as different sides of the same coin. *Educational Studies in Mathematics* 22: 1–36.

Sfard, A. (2008) *Thinking as communicating. Human development, the growth of discourse, and mathematizing*. New York: Cambridge University Press.

Watson, A. & Mason, J. (2005) *Mathematics as a constructive activity: The role of learner generated examples*. Mahwah, NJ: Lawrence Erlbaum Associates.

Section Four

Debates about mathematics teaching and social content

In common with other authors throughout this volume, **Richard Barwell** argues that mathematics and politics are inextricably and inevitably linked. He uses the example of current debates about climate change to explore two related ideas: *politics is mathematical* and *mathematics is political*. He argues that politics is mathematical in the sense that it involves data, statistics, projections and so on, and the democratic competence required to be a citizen includes mathematical thinking; and that mathematics is political in the sense that it shapes our lives and our societies. Both of these points are illustrated with detailed examples drawing on the mathematics of adverse changes to climate and the resulting damage inflicted on ecosystems. He concludes by discussing three stages in the way teachers might respond: through accommodation where climate change topics occur in the curriculum; through reformation where a degree of critical thinking is promoted; and through transformation where the politics of mathematics education itself is acknowledged.

Hamsa Venkat's chapter asks: What do we teach mathematics for? She discusses the concept of mathematical literacy in general and then focuses on the large-scale implementation in South Africa of a mathematical literacy curriculum. She explores the tension between approaches to the curriculum which prioritise mathematical goals with contexts chosen for the degree to which they address mathematical topics and those which have life situations as their primary driver where contexts matter in their own right. She calls for a spectrum of agendas: context driven by learner needs; context and mathematical content connecting dialectically; mainly mathematical content driven; and wholly mathematical content driven. She argues for including them all while focusing on the first two. Her arguments are illustrated through a detailed account of working with Postgraduate Certificate in Education (PGCE) students on a newspaper article on the Gini coefficient.

Leo Rogers' chapter is also concerned with the role of context. He argues that much mathematics teaching is currently not addressing the affective needs, beliefs, attitudes and emotions of students and that the opportunities for learning lack any social context. He advocates including topics from the history of mathematics to engage students by acknowledging our mathematical heritage.

Drawing on a wide range of historical cultures, he provides detailed examples of topics that could feature in the secondary mathematics classroom including geometric constructions, algorithms and algebra and the interconnections between them; and ratio and proportion. He also discusses different historical approaches to abstraction and rigour. He recommends opening up opportunities for students to pursue their own historical enquiries to help make the subject human.

The three chapters in this section all consider the ways in which the content of what is studied in mathematics classrooms can open up wider social awareness and cultural and political understandings. The chapter by Richard Barwell makes the argument that mathematics and politics are linked together whether we like it or not. If the connection is unacknowledged that itself is a political act. He discusses how the topic of climate change might feature in the mathematics classroom and uses this as an example of how teachers might respond to the challenge of doing so – through accommodation, reformation or transformation. Similarly, Hamsa Venkat takes a particular topic and how it might feature in the mathematics classroom – in her case, work on the Gini coefficient, widely used as a measure of inequality – to discuss the wider issue of mathematical literacy. She argues that, alongside acknowledging the need to keep in mind the mathematics required to be taught, the emphasis in choosing topics with social content should be to explore those which learners need to interact and engage with in their lives and to use mathematics to achieve this. The final chapter in this section, rather than looking at contemporary issues, suggests that taking an historical perspective on the mathematics being taught in the classroom supports the affective needs and thus the engagement of learners, leading to less exclusion from the subject. Leo Rogers includes a number of examples to illustrate how this might be done.

Chapter 16

Mathematics and politics?

Climate change in the mathematics classroom

Richard Barwell

Wait. Are you thinking 'Teaching mathematics is not political – this chapter has nothing to do with me'? You are probably in a hurry to get to something that sounds more practical. I want to challenge the idea that teaching mathematics is not political. I don't mean Political (capital P) – I don't want to know who you vote for. By political, I mean that there are links between mathematics, the way society is organised and the way things get decided. Mathematics teaching can help students be aware of these links and participate in democratic debate and social action.

An example: climate change is, whatever you think about it, one of the top political issues of the 21st century. Its increasing significance and urgency is apparent in the now tangible changes to the climate in every part of the globe. The summer of 2018, for example, was marked by heatwaves in multiple regions, wildfires in Sweden, Greece, California and on Saddleworth Moor, near Manchester in the United Kingdom. Every year this century has been one of the hottest ever recorded. Sea level is rising, glaciers and ice caps are melting, island nations are disappearing. The UN-organised Intergovernmental Panel on Climate Change (IPCC) issues regular reports and calls for urgent action (for example, IPCC, 2018) and underlines the causal link between atmospheric carbon pollution (mainly carbon dioxide and methane). Meanwhile, it is business as usual in our daily lives, in our society and in political debates. In particular, humans continue to rely on extracting fossil fuels to make and transport ever increasing amounts of stuff, while pumping greenhouse gases into the atmosphere. Regardless of what you think about this issue, it is certainly important and involves plenty of mathematics.

> *What is the role of mathematics in public debates about climate change?*

In this chapter, then, I use the political debates relating to climate change to illustrate how mathematics and politics are linked. How does mathematics shape what we know about the world? How does mathematics shape our lives? And how, as mathematics teachers, can we engage with how mathematics is used in our society and what it is used to do? To respond to these questions, I present two related ideas: *politics is mathematical* and *mathematics is political*. Each idea is explained in general terms, followed by some illustration based on the issue of climate change.

Politics is mathematical

Politics is mathematical in a fairly simple sense: there is hardly a single political debate that does not involve data, statistics, projections and other mathematical information. Debates about unemployment include jobless totals, unemployment rates expressed as a percentage of the working population, costs of unemployment benefits and so on. Debates about transport policy include trends in car, train or plane use, data on greenhouse gas emissions or economic costs associated with road congestion. Debates on health include cancer cure rates, life expectancy data and figures demonstrating the benefits of exercise and a balanced diet. Debates about wars involve claims about costs and the calculation of the number of civilian deaths. And the world of politics is obsessed with opinion polls, voting intentions and demographics. The presence of mathematics in political debate is fairly simple to observe but has serious consequences. It means, in particular, that in a democratic society, citizens must be able to engage with mathematics in order to participate.

Our society is now so complex and so technological that participation in democratic processes is no simple matter, whether at the level of national politics or at a very local level. This participation requires what is sometimes called *democratic competence*, which can be understood as what citizens need to know and understand in order for the 'ruling class' to be held to account (Skovsmose, 1994, p. 34). If no-one understands what the rulers are doing, they can act in their own interests and not in the interests of society at large. By 'ruling class' I am referring not just to politicians but to scientists, civil servants, the judiciary and so on, that is anyone with significant societal power and influence. Moreover, the same arguments apply at the local level, even within a school, for example, where the ruling class would be the head teacher and staff. For democracy to be democratic, then, it is not enough simply to have elections; citizens need to monitor what their elected governments are doing and challenge them when their actions are problematic. Given the ubiquitous presence of mathematics in political debate, as well as in technology and the instruments of government, it is clear that democratic competence must involve some level of mathematical understanding. Citizens need to be able to interpret the mathematical information used in political debates and need some sense of where this mathematical information comes from, of how it is produced. Indeed, with complex, uncertain, risky situations like climate change, mass extinctions or widespread plastic contamination of our ecosystem, citizens will increasingly need to participate in formulating solutions.

The mathematical dimension of democratic competence has been compared to the role of literacy in empowering citizens to participate in political debate and action. By becoming literate, citizens do not simply gain access to information, they are able to question, to challenge and to make the case for alternative courses of action (Freire, 1972). This perspective is known as *critical literacy*, since it includes critique as a key aspect of literacy. Mathematics can play a similar role: Skovsmose (1994) proposes the term *mathemacy* to capture the sense that mathematics, too, can be empowering. Mathemacy can "help people to reorganise their views about social institutions, traditions and possibilities in political actions" (p. 26). This view of mathematics goes beyond 'the basics' and implies a mathematics education that is about more than providing numerate workers for the labour market. It suggests that mathematics education should empower students to participate in the democratic process through a critical understanding of the mathematical aspects of political debate (Skovsmose, 1994, 2011; see also Chapter 17 by Hamsa Venkat).

Mathematics and climate change

The issue of climate change is replete with mathematics. In fact, it is difficult to say anything very specific about climate change, or even to be sure that climate change is occurring, without mathematics. So what kind of mathematics might be included in the democratic competence necessary to participate in debates about climate change? First, it is helpful to understand the role of mathematics in climate change research.

The mathematics of climate change can be divided into roughly three areas: *description*, *prediction* and *communication* (Barwell, 2013). The mathematics involved in describing climate change includes the measurement and recording of things like temperature, sea level, glacial mass, the onset of spring, greenhouse gas emissions and so on. It also includes the statistical treatment of this kind of data to describe the climate or emissions and to identify trends. This mathematics is not particularly advanced: key concepts include statistical mean, distribution and some basic statistical tests. The huge volume of data does, however, introduce considerable complexity.

For example, the calculation of global mean temperature involves compiling data from weather stations around the world. In fact, scientists do not simply average all this data, since such an average would be meaningless – it does not make much sense to average the temperature in the Arctic with the temperature in Cape Town. Instead, scientists proceed in a number of steps – those shown below are about the annual mean temperature, but the same general method applies for monthly or daily means or means for any other period.

1 For each weather station, they work out a long-term annual mean over a selected 30-year period.
2 For each station, for any given year, they work out the mean temperature.

3 They then work out the difference between the mean temperature for the given year and the long-term mean. This difference is known as a temperature anomaly.
4 The global temperature anomaly for any given year is the mean of the temperature anomalies for all the weather stations.

The global temperature anomaly is, in effect, the average difference in temperature from the long-term mean around the world. Some stations may have been below average, others warmer than the long-term average. If this figure is above zero, it means that, on average, the world is warmer than the long-term mean. This is a simplified account, but it gives a good idea of the mathematics involved (means) and the complex nature of the data.

The prediction or projection of climate change involves much more advanced mathematics, the most fundamental of which is the creation and use of mathematical models of the climate. These models use sets of equations to model different aspects of the climate – the seas, the atmosphere, land surfaces and so on. These equations are all linked together and tested by simulating past climates for which we have measurement data. If the model can simulate the past in a way that fits well with this data, then the assumption is made that it will simulate the near future with a similar degree of accuracy. Climate models are different from weather forecasts in at least one key respect: they are not precise. They offer 'projections' rather than predictions, giving a broad sense of likely trends over the coming decades. Other areas of mathematics that are involved in predicting climate change include differential equations, non-linear systems and advanced probability.

Finally, mathematics is used to communicate climate change, whether in a television news report or in a scientific article. The communication of climate change includes both the production of information about climate change and the consumption of that information. Both production and consumption require an understanding of graphs, tables and other forms of graphic presentation, as well as an understanding of the mathematical processes involved in describing and predicting climate change, though not necessarily at the level of an expert. For example, it is important for citizens to understand how the climate modelling process works, even if few will ever learn the advanced mathematics that this modelling entails.

Mathemacy and climate change

There are many political debates related to climate change. Many of them are about how to respond to climate change, when, for example, formulating energy policy or transport policy or planning where to build new houses. At international level, debate is fierce on what agreements should be put in place to reduce as much as possible the future warming of the planet. The first such agreement, the Kyoto protocol, appears to have had a limited impact on global warming. There are, of course, also claims and counterclaims about whether human-induced climate change even exists. This last debate is a good example with which to illustrate how mathemacy is an important aspect of democratic competence.

In an example from the recent past, Nigel Lawson emerged as a sceptical voice on climate change. In 2008, Lawson published a book setting out his thoughts, which he also expressed in interviews and other public appearances. One of the claims he advanced was that "global warming ... is not at the present time happening" (Interview in *The Guardian*, 3 May 2008). In his book, he stated that "there has, in fact, been no further global warming since the turn of the century" (p. 7) and supported this claim with some data. Specifically, he listed the global mean temperature anomalies for the years 2001–2007. They were, in degrees centigrade, 0.40, 0.46, 0.46, 0.43, 0.48, 0.42 and 0.41. He also mentioned that the anomaly for 1998 was 0.52°C. He summed up the situation as follows:

> the 21st century standstill (to date), which has occurred at a time when CO_2 emissions have been rising faster than ever, is something that the conventional wisdom, and the computer models on which it relies, completely failed to predict. (p. 7)

These claims are related to all three aspects of the mathematics of climate change mentioned above. The reference to recent global temperature data is an example of the description of climate change. The comment in the quotation about computer models refers to the prediction of climate change. And the whole text, including the selection and presentation of some data, involves the communication of climate change.

The information presented by Lawson is, despite the simplicity of the arguments, mathematically non-trivial. A key mathematical idea that is rather implicit in these arguments is the notion of trend. Lawson argued that, although there was a clear warming trend from 1970 to 2000, since that time the warming had stopped. This position assumes that global warming should be a smooth process, with a clear, linear trend. For example, global temperature anomalies would increase by a steady amount from one year to the next. His position also assumes that seven data points are sufficient to establish a counter-trend. Figure 16.1 shows global mean temperature anomalies since 1850, based on the same data set cited by Lawson. It is clear from the graph that global temperature, even averaged over a planet for a whole year, is not smooth in its behaviour – there are peaks and troughs from year to year. Hence, for example, the 1950s were relatively speaking, a little cooler than surrounding decades. But set against the long-term trend, this cooling is of limited duration. So the seven years referred to by Lawson appear to be part of the general fluctuation in global temperature that goes on all the time.

My point, here, is not that Lawson was wrong (although I believe he was), but that, in order to critically engage with what he is saying, a degree of mathematical

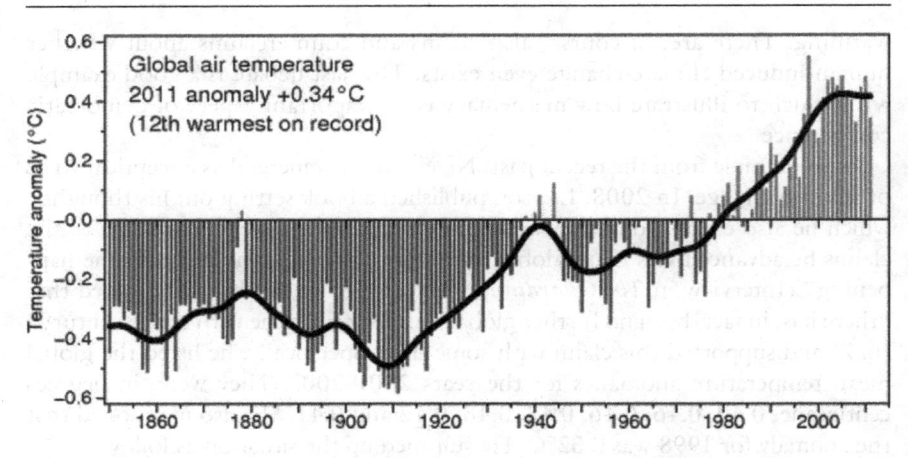

Figure 16.1 Annual global mean temperature anomalies (land and sea combined) 1820–2011 (Jones, 2012).

sophistication is required. Moreover, the mathematics that forms part of the democratic competence to participate in such a debate is not simply an understanding of average, of measurement and of ideas about trends. Such mathematics must also include the capacity to ask questions, to think about the author's agenda and the way mathematics is used in support of that agenda.

The example of climate change I have elaborated illustrates how mathematics is vital to understand and participate in political debate. Given that mathematics is so prevalent in political discourse, democratic competence must include an element of critical mathematics – the capacity not just to make sense of mathematical information, but to question, to challenge and interrogate how that information has been shaped by different agendas. Moreover, the nature of many of the most challenging problems facing our society is too complex to leave to experts, even when we have elected them or they are appointed in our names. Issues like swine flu, plastic contamination, nuclear power or, for that matter, climate change are so complex that developing a response requires the participation of engaged citizens from the start of the process. Mathematics education, therefore, has a role to play in preparing students to participate actively and critically in these debates (Barwell, 2013). For me, this means that simply teaching mathematics well is necessary but not sufficient. Our students not only need to be able to do mathematics, but to think critically with mathematics.

Consider a couple of political issues that interest you. What mathematics do they involve? How could this mathematics be drawn on in your teaching? Should it?

Mathematics is political

If politics is fairly clearly mathematical, in the sense that political debate makes widespread use of mathematical information, the converse is less obvious, but no less important. Mathematics is political because of its role in organising our society and our lives. Mathematics is used to take decisions that affect us. Indeed, mathematics can be seen to have a direct though often invisible effect on our daily lives. This idea runs contrary to the view of mathematics as a neutral activity that has little to do with everyday life, beyond a bit of basic numeracy (see Chapter 3 by Paul Ernest).

As a brief illustration, consider a weekly supermarket run. Supermarkets are organised around highly mathematical systems of distribution, stock control and checkout procedures embedded in IT systems, scanners and barcodes. These systems are mathematical because they are built around mathematical algorithms that model the production and consumption of hundreds of products or that enable detailed tracking of products and customers. They have changed our lives in numerous ways. Shopping is more efficient than ever, we have access to a wider range of products and costs are kept low. On the other hand, much supermarket work is increasingly unskilled and involves ever less interaction with customers (think about self-service checkouts). Mathematisation of stock control is also mathematisation of workforce control. So there is a link between mathematics and such basic aspects of our lives as shopping.

Skovsmose (1994) highlights the role of mathematics in shaping our lives by giving it a name: he calls it the *formatting power* of mathematics. How does mathematics format our society and our lives? Partly through technology, such as the supermarkets' IT systems; but technology is in many respects, simply the vehicle for human designs. These designs are expressed mathematically in the form of algorithms, models and computer code. In mathematical form, human designs are abstract in nature. Once they are embedded in technology, they start to become real. For example, commodities like wheat or oil are traded on international markets. When they are traded on futures markets, they appear as variables in sophisticated differential equations. When the prices fluctuate, however, they can affect the price of a loaf of bread and, in extreme situations, lead to hunger. So the abstractions of the traders' equations become the reality of some (other) people's hunger.

It is in this sense that mathematics is political. Many aspects of our lives are shaped by mathematics, generally embedded in IT systems. Think, for example, about the mathematics involved in mortgages, insurance, medicine, transportation, health care, banking, gambling, communications and so on. Or, closer to the classroom, think of how mathematics is used to process children's scores on national tests, in order to rank children, teachers and schools. On the whole, we pay little attention to this mathematics – after all, it makes our lives easier. The problem is that this mathematics *does not do itself*: someone is creating the algorithms, writing the software and selecting which variables to include and which to leave out. And these someones are largely invisible. Another aspect of democratic competence, then, must be the ability to hold to account the people who are making decisions that affect us. And this ability involves mathematics. Of course, society is not *only* organised using mathematics; my point is simply that mathematics is one important way in which society is organised. As a result, mathematics education needs to empower students to participate in the democratic process, not just through a critical understanding of the mathematical aspects of political debate, but also through a critical understanding of the role of mathematics in shaping our society and our lives (Skovsmose, 1984, 1994).

Mathematical formatting and climate change

The political role of mathematics in the issue of climate change comes from its formatting power. This formatting power has two slightly different but inter-related effects. Both are fairly subtle. First, there is a chain of interconnection from mathematics, via technology, to a globalised consumer society. Much of the basis for this society lies in fossil fuels. Here is an illustration of the UK government's point of view at the time of writing (this position is similar to every other government's since the 1970s):

> New exploration in the North Sea will be supported by a £5 million UK government fund for 2018/19, Philip Hammond announced today (25 September) during a visit to Aberdeen and Dundee. The funding will be used by the Oil and Gas Authority (OGA) to survey under-explored areas of the UK Continental Shelf to find potential new deposits.
>
> The announcement came on the same day that the Oil & Gas Technology Centre in Aberdeen, which the Chancellor visited and is part-funded by the UK government, said its work with industry on new subsea technologies could help unlock 400 million additional barrels of oil and gas from the North Sea and £3 billion of additional value to the industry.
>
> UK Energy Minister, Richard Harrington, said: "North Sea oil will continue to fuel growth and jobs across Scotland and the rest of the UK, with an estimated 10–20 billion barrels still remaining."
>
> (HM Treasury, Department for Business, Energy and Industrial Strategy, News Story, 25 September 2017)

Twenty billion barrels of oil is difficult to imagine and yet in global economic terms, 20 billion barrels is a modest quantity. There is, of course, a direct link between the use of fossil fuels, like North Sea oil, and climate change. Use of fossil fuels results in greenhouse gas emissions, increasing concentrations of these gases in the atmosphere and, thanks to the greenhouse effect, higher temperatures. Fossil fuels, however, are not, on the whole, simply burned to keep us warm. Between the extraction of fossil fuels and the emission of greenhouse gases lies our global consumer society. And, as I have argued already, this global consumer society relies on mathematics embedded in technology. This embedded mathematics is extremely powerful: it enables us, as a species, to do things like control and eliminate diseases, provide clean water and sanitation, and produce all the comforts of modern life. It also enables us to have a huge impact on our environment.

Mathematics helps to hide the human role in making decisions that shape this global consumer society and the environmental impact of these decisions. To return to the supermarket, the mathematics of stock control and of international communication means that we can eat fresh apples in February, imported from South America. The apples are marked with a barcode – just scan and eat! The barcode is the tip of a mathematical iceberg that links your apple to a producer in Argentina, via trucks, planes and automated distribution centres, all for an amazingly low price. The barcode hides the role of mathematics. But it also hides the decisions made to sell apples in February, to source them from South America, to set price levels and shipping times and so on. You do not see all these decisions because they are embedded in the algorithms and models that run the technology. IT systems do not make decisions, they simply move them out of sight.

So when the Chancellor of the Exchequer talks about the prosperity that North Sea oil brings, he is talking about our global, consumer society, a society that depends on mathematics, embedded in technology, which hides its worst effects. I am not suggesting that oil is bad or that mathematics is bad. Rather, I am arguing that if citizens are to participate in finding a way to deal with climate change, they need to be aware of much that is hidden.

The second link between the formatting power of mathematics and climate change concerns our understanding of climate change itself. One of the challenges of climate change is that it is a global phenomenon. It is difficult for any individual to really experience climate change on a global scale. We can only develop a clear picture of climate change by collecting measurements around the world and analysing these data, as shown in the example about mean annual global temperature. This kind of work is important, but it does have a kind of side effect. Climate change is formatted in a particular way, as a quantified, mathematical phenomenon. For example, the communication of climate change includes graphs or charts or references to averages or extremes, whether of temperature, sea level, storm frequencies or other indicators. This mathematisation of climate change does not easily capture the qualitative nature of climate change – the loss of habitat, the subtle changes to ecosystems and the dislocation of climate refugees.

For example, one effect of climate change in the United Kingdom is the desynchronisation of ecosystems. In spring, birds and animals produce offspring to coincide with an abundance of suitable food. Climate change, however, interferes with the behaviours of different parts of this delicate system in different ways. Some creatures may produce offspring earlier, while food sources may move to cooler locations, or new predators may move in. Changes can interfere with the interrelated life cycles of different species so that some struggle to find food. While all this can be documented statistically (for example, Thackery et al., 2010), mathematics does not capture suffering, or the ethics of human-induced species loss, or the intrinsic value of an ecosystem.

In this respect, an awareness of the formatting power of mathematics includes an awareness of its limitations. Mathematics is a powerful way of manipulating our environment and of representing the world. But it leaves out some important things, including ethics, beauty, relationships or values. Mathematics education, therefore, has a role to play in teaching students not only the power of mathematics and the effects of mathematics, but also the limitations of mathematics.

> *Consider two or three aspects of modern society that you particularly appreciate in some way (Your car? Central heating? …). What mathematics is hidden in your choices? What does this mathematics enable? What issues does this raise? How might these issues be addressed by your students?*

Conclusions

Mathematics plays a key role in our society, but this role is often overlooked. In this chapter, I have shown how *politics is mathematical* and how *mathematics is political*. As mathematics teachers, we have the possibility of preparing our students to participate in political debate, to look at our society critically and to be aware of the role of mathematics in shaping their lives. As teachers, therefore, we must decide whether to respond to issues like climate change in our teaching. Indeed, for some, we have a *responsibility* to respond to such issues (d'Ambrosio, 2010). But what kind of response? To address the two themes described in this chapter, mathematics teaching needs to address both democratic competence and the formatting power of mathematics.

Renert (2011) describes a useful framework designed to link mathematics teaching with sustainability, which can be adapted to think about the political dimension of mathematics teaching more generally. The framework involves three levels or stages: accommodation, reformation and transformation. An *accommodation* approach aims simply to pass on knowledge. As mathematics teachers, we would address social and political issues in our teaching largely through using them as examples or contexts with which to teach particular mathematical concepts. In the case of climate change, for example, students might learn about the planetary temperature changes discussed above, as part of work on data handling. Climate change simply provides a convenient context to do some work on averages. This approach is informative, but does not have a strong critical dimension – it does little to promote democratic competence and nothing to highlight the formatting power of mathematics.

A *reformation* approach aims to promote a degree of critical thinking. Students are invited to consider values (ethics, beauty, etc.) as well as knowledge (averages, data handling, etc.) and to think about ways to make the world better – without necessarily questioning underlying assumptions. In particular, students are encouraged to use mathematics to think about how to reform the way things are, but only within existing parameters. For example, students might use carbon calculators to think about how to reduce their greenhouse gas footprints, without going so far as to question the consumerist nature of our economy. Or, to give a different example, they might use data and calculations relating to the Gini coefficient[1] to debate the issue of national and global inequality, without considering why such inequity arises in the first place (see Chapter 17 by Hamsa Venkat). A reformation approach is different from an accommodation approach in its greater attention to social and political issues. In the accommodation approach, such issues are secondary to mathematics curriculum content – climate change is a convenient context through which to teach averages. In the reformation approach, the assumption is still that mathematics will be learned, but a parallel goal is to deepen understanding of social and political issues. The reformation approach, therefore, does address democratic competence, through a focus on social and political issues.

A *transformation* approach is perhaps more challenging to achieve, since it includes a recognition that education itself is part of the equation and may need to change. Not only, then, can we say that politics is mathematical, and that mathematics is political, we must also recognise that *mathematics education* is political (see Chapter 4 by Peter Gates and Andy Noyes for some of its effects). Teaching mathematics has a political dimension (even if we choose not to recognise it). The transformation approach to teaching mathematics will include aspects of the accommodation approach and reformation approach. Students still need to learn mathematics and critically relate mathematics to particular contexts and issues. The transformation approach, however, goes beyond these goals. Renert (2011) argues that such an approach includes the awareness that "teachers are not the only source of ingenuity in mathematics classrooms, and that deconstruction and critique ought to be followed by innovation and transformation" (p. 23). He goes on to give an example of how the topic of 'large numbers' might be tackled from a transformational perspective. Rather than simply teaching the key ideas and, perhaps, using a topic like climate change to provide some context, students could be provided with the following prompt:

> How would you explain the meaning of some large numbers (for example, the number of kilograms of carbon emitted daily into the atmosphere) to adults in your life in order to move them to action? (Renert, 2011, p. 23)

This kind of task requires students to think about the nature of large numbers and the way they are represented, but it also requires them to think about the political meaning of these numbers in the context of climate change, and in particular, the role of mathematics in communicating and formatting climate change.

Of course, a transformation approach is risky. We cannot know the kinds of responses students will generate and some responses may be provocative and challenging. In working on climate change, for example, students may challenge the way their class or school is managed. And as teachers, there is a fine balance to be struck between promoting critical thinking and promoting a particular agenda. In a world in which mathematics, politics and education are interrelated, we need our students to be critical thinkers and we must trust them to use the democratic competence we foster to transform their world.

What kind of approach to teaching mathematics will you adopt?

Note

1 https://www.bbc.com/news/blogs-magazine-monitor-31847943

Further reading

Coles, A., Barwell, R., Cotton, T., Winter, J., & Brown, L. (2013). *Teaching Secondary Mathematics as if the Planet Matters*. Routledge. This book, written for teachers, proposes ways to teach mathematics for global sustainability. It presents key concepts and many examples. One half of the book starts from sustainability, and includes chapters on climate change, biodiversity and economics. The other half starts from mathematics, and includes chapters that look at number, probability and algebra in relation to sustainability.

Gutstein, E. (2005). *Reading and Writing the World with Mathematics: Toward a Pedagogy for Social Justice*. New York: Taylor and Francis. Gutstein, a mathematics teacher and educator in Chicago is a leading advocate of the power of mathematics teaching to give students the tools to engage with the mathematics of political issues. Indeed, he sees mathematics teaching as a way to awaken an awareness of political issues which are directly relevant to students. This book provides both a framework for implementing this kind of approach and many useful examples of what it can look like in the classroom.

Renert, M. (2011). Mathematics for life: Sustainable mathematics education. *For the Learning of Mathematics* 31(1): 20–26. This article proposes a framework for thinking about sustainability issues in mathematics education. Parts of the framework are referred to in this chapter but the article elaborates on these ideas and gives some examples of how it might be used to inform mathematics teaching.

Skovsmose, O. (1984). Mathematical education and democracy. *Educational Studies in Mathematics* 21: 109–128. One of the first articles to relate mathematics education with political issues and the origin of ideas like mathemacy and democratic competence in mathematics.

References

Barwell, R. (2013). The mathematical formatting of climate change: Critical mathematics education and post-normal science. *Research in Mathematics Education* 15(1): 1–16.

d'Ambrosio, U. (2010). Mathematics education and survival with dignity. In *Critical Mathematics Education: Past, Present and Future*, H. Alrø, O. Ravn, and P. Valero (eds.). Rotterdam: Sense Publishers, pp. 51–63.

Freire, P. (1972). *Pedagogy of the Oppressed*. Harmondsworth: Penguin.

Intergovernmental Panel on Climate Change (IPCC). (2018). *Global Warming of 1.5C (Special Report 15) Summary for Policymakers*. Geneva: IPCC.

HM Treasury, Department for Business, Energy & Industrial Strategy. News story: North Sea exploration funding announced. Retrieved from https://www.gov.uk/government/news/north-sea-exploration-funding-announced (accessed 4 August 2018).

Jones, P. (2012). Information sheet 1: Global Temperature Records. Retrieved from http://www.cru.uea.ac.uk/cru/info/warming/. 29 February 2012.

Lawson, N. (2008). *An Appeal to Reason: A Cool Look at Global Warming*. London: Duckworth Overlook.

Renert, M. (2011). Mathematics for life: Sustainable mathematics education. *For the Learning of Mathematics* 31(1): 20–26.

Skovsmose, O. (1984). Mathematical education and democracy. *Educational Studies in Mathematics* 21: 109–128.

Skovsmose, O. (1994). *Towards a Philosophy of Critical Mathematics Education*. Dordrecht: Kluwer.

Skovsmose, O. (2011). *An Invitation to Critical Mathematics Education*. Rotterdam: Sense Publishers.

Thackeray, S. J., Sparks, T. H., Frederiksen, M., Burthe, S., Bacon, P. J., Bell, J. R., Botham, M. S., Brereton, T. M., Bright, P. W., Carvalho, L., Clutton-Brock, T., Dawson, A., Edwards, M., Elliott, J. M., Harrington, R., Johns, D., Jones, I. D., Jones, J. T., Leech, D. I., Roy, D. B., Scott, W. A., Smith, M., Smithers, R. J., Winfield, I. J. and Wanless, S. (2010). Trophic level asynchrony in rates of phenological change for marine, freshwater and terrestrial environments. *Global Change Biology* 16(12): 3304–3313.

Chapter 17

Mathematical literacy
What is it? And is it important?

Hamsa Venkat

Introduction

The debate at the heart of this chapter is centred on what we teach mathematics for. One reason given for teaching mathematics is to lay the ground for the future learning of mathematics – for A-level Mathematics in England, and post-compulsory/tertiary mathematics more generally in many parts of the world. Another argument for teaching mathematics is that it provides experiences of the skills and reasoning needed to function productively in a world that brims with quantitative data – data that needs to be made sense of for effective participation in everyday life. People with these latter competences are sometimes described as 'mathematically literate'. In this chapter, I explore the tensions between these two positions.

At the centre of this chapter is a contextualised task based on a newspaper article drawn from the weekly South African broadsheet *The Mail and Guardian*. Penned by journalist Keith Levenstein (Levenstein, 2010), the article – entitled 'Let the Gini out of the bottle' – describes ongoing inequality in South Africa. In the middle of the article, this sentence appears:

> In any country some people are wealthier than others. This is represented by the income distribution curve. Recent reports ... show that South Africa's Gini coefficient, which represents income inequality, is the worst in the world.

As recently as March 2018, Paul Noumba Um, noted in a World Bank report that "South Africa remains the world's most unequal country" with a Gini coefficient of 0.63 (World Bank Group, 2018). To me, being mathematically literate means being, or becoming, willing and able to engage with such claims and what they are based on. As a mathematics teacher, it means providing opportunities for learners to become mathematically literate as well – and that means looking for ways to turn issues drawn from everyday life into tasks to work with in mathematics classrooms.

In this chapter I share the ways in which I have used this newspaper article to learn about and use the 'Gini coefficient' – a widely used, but contested, measure of inequality, in a Postgraduate Certificate in Education (PGCE) course for secondary mathematics teachers. Students' work on the task provides a basis for discussing the idea of mathematical literacy. I describe how the task has been presented, including examples of questions asked that allow a range of agendas – some more mathematical and some more life-competence focused – to emerge.

Arguments for why it is important to work across the range of goals associated with mathematical literacy in mathematics classrooms (rather than limiting oneself to traditional mathematical goals) are discussed at the end of this chapter. I take a critical advocacy position for mathematical literacy that calls for the 'literate learning of mathematics' as well as 'mathematical literacy' as a life-related competence.

Mathematical literacy – how is it described?

The term 'mathematical literacy' is associated with a range of descriptions. In some descriptions, the need to understand the situation, or to solve a problem in context, drives mathematical selections, while in other descriptions, the situations are just 'vehicles' on which specific mathematical content/processes are carried. Eva Jablonka and Mogens Niss point out in their 2014 overview of definitions of mathematical literacy, the tensions in moving between: "unspecialized context-based considerations and problem situations that employ specialized mathematical knowledge" (Jablonka and Niss, 2014). Dealing with a range of situations that require mathematical thinking is a life-related competence, so the trajectory here is into adult lives and citizenship. On the other side, where contexts are selected to 'surface' particular mathematical ideas, the trajectory is into further mathematical learning.

In England, Mike Tomlinson's report (Tomlinson, 2004) called for education in the 14–19 age range to prepare students for 'participation in a full adult life' while also providing openings for specialised discipline-based trajectories matched to individual "interests, aptitudes and ambitions" (p. 4). The 'core' component included the need for 'Functional Mathematics', which was aimed at supporting students to "succeed and progress in learning, HE, employment and adult life" (p. 29).

In the United States, Lyn Arthur Steen (2001) supports what he terms 'quantitative literacy' – summarising the ways in which it differs from traditional school mathematics:

> Whereas the mathematics curriculum has historically focused on school-based knowledge, quantitative literacy involves mathematics acting in the world. Typical numeracy challenges involve real data and uncertain procedures but require primarily elementary mathematics. In contrast, typical school mathematics problems involve simplified numbers and straightforward procedures but require sophisticated abstract concepts. The test of numeracy, as of any literacy, is whether a person naturally uses appropriate skills in many different contexts. (p. 6)

Steen (2004) argues that in an era where data and technology abound, quantitative literacy, involving a "uniquely modern blend of arithmetic with complex reasoning", is required by all citizens for full participation in society (p. 3). In this view, mathematical working is conducted in service of the situation under consideration rather than for its own sake. Behind his advocacy is evidence from many countries that traditional mathematics courses may not provide the experiences needed to manage the quantitative demands of life. In England, the 2011 Skills for Life survey found an increase between 2003 and 2011 from 5.5% to 6.8% in the proportions of adults with 'poor' or 'very poor' numeracy skills (DBIS, 2012).

Bernard Madison points to school mathematics' presentation of highly restricted problem types – "very sanitized template exercises" (Madison and Steen, 2009, p. 5). The routine nature of traditional mathematical problems is criticised as figuring within students' lack of experience with working with the complex and emphatically non-routine nature of problems in real-life situations.

While the English and US terrain have seen small-scale attempts to incorporate mathematical literacy with one or other, or both orientations, a large-scale implementation occurred in South Africa with the national introduction of a subject called Mathematical Literacy into the post-compulsory phase curriculum in 2006, as an alternative option to 'Mathematics'. (I use the capitalised 'Mathematical Literacy' to refer to the South African subject and the small 'mathematical literacy' to refer to the general concept described in different ways in the international literature). Mathematical Literacy in the revised South African Curriculum and Assessment Policy Statement (DBE, 2011) is described thus:

> The competencies developed through Mathematical Literacy allow individuals to make sense of, participate in and contribute to the twenty-first century world – a world characterised by numbers, numerically based arguments and data represented and misrepresented in a number of different ways. Such competencies include the ability to reason, make decisions, solve problems, manage resources, interpret information, schedule events and use and apply technology. Learners must be exposed to both mathematical content and real-life contexts to develop these competencies. Mathematical content is needed to make sense of real-life contexts; on the other hand, contexts determine the content that is needed. (p. 8)

Here, the rhetoric points to mathematics as a tool with which to understand real-world situations and solve problems. Progression across the three grades (grades 10–12, learner minimum age range 15–18) occurs in terms of mathematical content and processes, and contextual complexity. Like the Tomlinson report, the South African Mathematical Literacy curriculum requires teachers to incorporate mathematical development alongside competence in real-world-related problem-solving.

Some writers question whether 'juggling' between mathematical and situational problem-solving goals is (a) desirable and (b) feasible. Essentially, this juggling can be reduced to asking: Should life-related mathematical literacy figure within the goals of the mathematics curriculum? Proponents argue that the confidence and competence to deal with the multitude of ways in which quantitative data and mathematical models 'format' our lives (see Skovsmose and Yasukawa, 2009, for a detailed discussion, and Chapter 16 by Richard Barwell) is imperative for constructive and critical citizenship. Detractors point to mathematical goals being disrupted if the need for 'relevance' predominates within mathematics curricula (for example, Gardiner, 2008).

A feature that unites more mathematical and more life situational orientations to mathematical literacy is the incorporation of contextual tasks. For advocates of more mathematical orientations, contexts are springboards for 'mathematising' activity – moving from contexts to their mathematical descriptions (Freudenthal, 1983). The contexts selected within this framework are chosen for their potential to 'surface' particular mathematical content and processes – and contexts can be contrived for this purpose. In contrast, within the life situation orientations to mathematical literacy, contexts matter in their own right, even though they may be 'trimmed' in the earlier stages of learning. The nature of the context selected (or at least, the degree to which it is trimmed from real life) often provides clues about the orientation being followed. Subsequently, the extent to which the context remains within the frame of problem-solving is also a key indicator of the orientation.

In South Africa, empirical studies have led to the development of frameworks for thinking about teaching that promote mathematical development *and* real-life-related problem-solving using mathematics as a tool.

Drawing from our studies of Mathematical Literacy teaching, Mellony Graven and I (2007) proposed a 'spectrum of agendas' that we saw at work in classrooms. This spectrum explores differences in the nature of links between content and context within, and across, the teaching we observed. The 'spectrum of agendas', with some terminology adapted, is summarised in Table 17.1.

In the first two agendas, the context retains importance in its own right – in the first agenda, from a life relevance/citizenship perspective, and in the second agenda, in a dialectical perspective, where the need for mathematical development is retained alongside the need for contextual understanding. I think it is sometimes necessary and useful to work in agendas 3 and 4, while maintaining an overall emphasis on the first two agendas.

> *Think about a 'best buy' problem relating to buying a cell phone. What questions could you ask related to the four agendas in Table 17.1?*

I now share the ways in which I have used the article on socio-economic inequality in South Africa to promote discussion and understanding of mathematical literacy. In this work, some episodes indicate more mathematical orientations

Table 17.1 A 'spectrum of agendas' of the nature of interlink between content and context (with some terminology adapted), drawn from Graven and Venkat, 2007)

Driving agenda	*1 Context driven: by learner needs*	*2 Content and context dialectic driven*	*3 Mainly mathematical content driven*	*4 Mathematical content driven*
Description	To explore contexts that learners need to interact and engage with in their lives (current everyday, future work & everyday, and for critical citizenship) and to use maths to achieve this.	To explore a context so as to deepen maths understanding and to learn maths to deepen understanding of that context.	To learn maths and then to apply it in some contexts.	To give learners a second chance to learn basic maths.

(agendas 3 and 4) and some push towards the need to understand the situation that is described (agendas 1 and 2). I show that the two orientations can be linked, and then present an argument for why this linking might be useful to incorporate more often within mathematics teaching.

Working with the Gini coefficient newspaper article

The task drawn from the newspaper article (which has been used several times now with PGCE student groups) deals with a topic of recurring interest in South Africa – the ongoing presence, and indeed, exacerbation of socio-economic inequality in the post-apartheid terrain. Some figures about South Africa's economic situation provide background for this discussion:

- Population (mid-year 2018 estimate): 57.4 million.
- Official unemployment rate (first quarter 2018): 27%.
- Mean monthly earnings (first quarter 2018 figure): R19850.

These opening questions kick off the process of engagement:

Have you seen this article? [Some nod]. Have you seen other articles like this? [Many more nod]. Do you think South Africa does have the worst income inequality in the world? [Some nod their heads, some shrug their shoulders, some mention that Brazil and India also have many poor people]. And have you heard of this Gini coefficient before? [Most shake their heads. In some years, one or two say they heard about it in Economics courses as undergraduates]. But most of you said you have read articles like this before. And I know that many of these articles do mention the Gini coefficient like this one does. Did you just ignore those words? [Some laugh, many nod, some say that this is how most people read newspapers – that you often come across things you don't know about, and you just read "over" them].

I note that this reading 'over' makes it quite hard to come to an informed decision about whether the claim in the article is true, so I then ask:

Might it be possible to find out about the Gini coefficient? [Most nod vaguely, some say: "Yes, Google it"].

So this is what we do, noting that being a mathematically literate citizen involves the inclination and the ability to understand the indices we read about. In some years, I say at this stage that I have already done this, and share some pages of explanation about how the Gini coefficient is defined, and how it is calculated – drawn from internet pages. There are variations, but centrally, all definitions rest on two hypothetical scenarios – 'perfect equality' in a society and 'perfect inequality'. One version of a graph involving the Gini coefficient is shown in Figure 17.1.

We talk about this graph to see if we can understand the three lines/curves that are named. The X-axis represents the cumulative population percentage. The Y-axis represents the cumulative income percentage arranged in order from highest income to lowest income. Students start to see that 'perfect equality' is based on a situation in which 10% of the population (10% on the X-axis) takes home 10% of the total income (10% on the Y-axis), and cumulatively, 20% of the population takes home 20% of the total income and so on. In this situation,

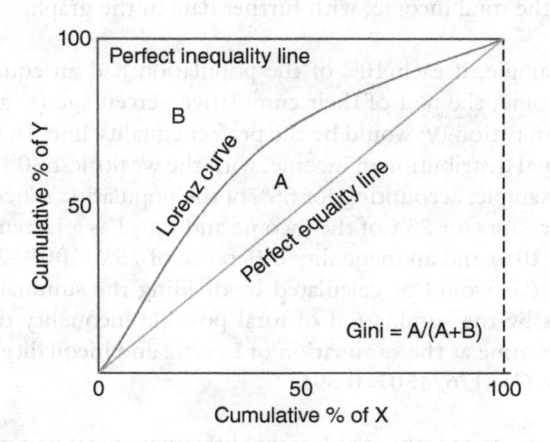

Figure 17.1 Graph showing the components of the Gini coefficient calculation.

(Source: https://transportgeography.org/?page_id=9236)

there is no 'poorer' or 'richer' – everyone takes an equal share of the total income, and that is why it is called 'perfect equality'. This means that the 'perfect equality' scenario can be represented as a straight line graph that connects (0, 0) to (100, 100).

In contrast, 'perfect inequality' is a hypothetical situation in which the highest earner (first earner on the X-axis) takes the total income (100% on the Y-axis), and everyone else takes home nothing. In cumulative terms, this can be represented as a straight line that connects (0, 100) to (100, 100).

The actual situation in any population sits somewhere between these two scenarios. In real populations, the richest 10% might, for example, take home 25% of the total income of that population – so we plot (10, 25). If the next 10% takes home 18% of the total income of that population, then cumulatively, this would mean that the richest 20% of the population takes home 43% of the income, so we plot (20, 43). Continuing like this produces the 'Lorenz curve' – a graph representing the actual cumulative income of the population. This graph always lies somewhere between perfect equality and perfect inequality.

The Gini coefficient value compares the total of the differences between the Lorenz curve and the perfect equality scenario, and the total possible inequality (represented by summing the differences between the equality and inequality lines). Summing can be done in a number of ways: integration can be used, but we can also just measure and total the differences – between the equality value at a range of points and the Lorenz curve value at the same points – and between the inequality and equality lines. The measuring method involves the 'elementary mathematics' that Steen describes as a feature of the mathematical literacy needed for an informed citizenry. An example using this measuring method is given in Figure 17.2 for a population that starts with the income distribution described above: the richest 10% taking 25% of the total income, the richest 20% taking 43% of the total income, with further data in the graph.

> In this example, if each 10% of the population had an equal share of the overall income, the plot of their cumulative percentage (x) and cumulative income proportion (y) would be the perfect equality line. In this case, there is an unequal distribution of income, with the wealthiest 30% of the population, for example, accounting for 55% of the population's income. The richest 10% accounts for 25% of the income and thus has a Lorenz difference of 15% (25%–10%) and an inequality difference of 75% (100%–25%). The Gini coefficient (G) would be calculated by dividing the summation of Lorenz differences by the summation of total possible inequality differences (the latter is the same as the summation of Lorenz and inequality differences on the graph). G = 176/450 = 0.391.

In this graph, adding together the Lorenz differences gives us a measure of how 'far' from equality the actual situation is. Adding together all the Lorenz and inequality differences tells us the total amount of inequality that is possible.

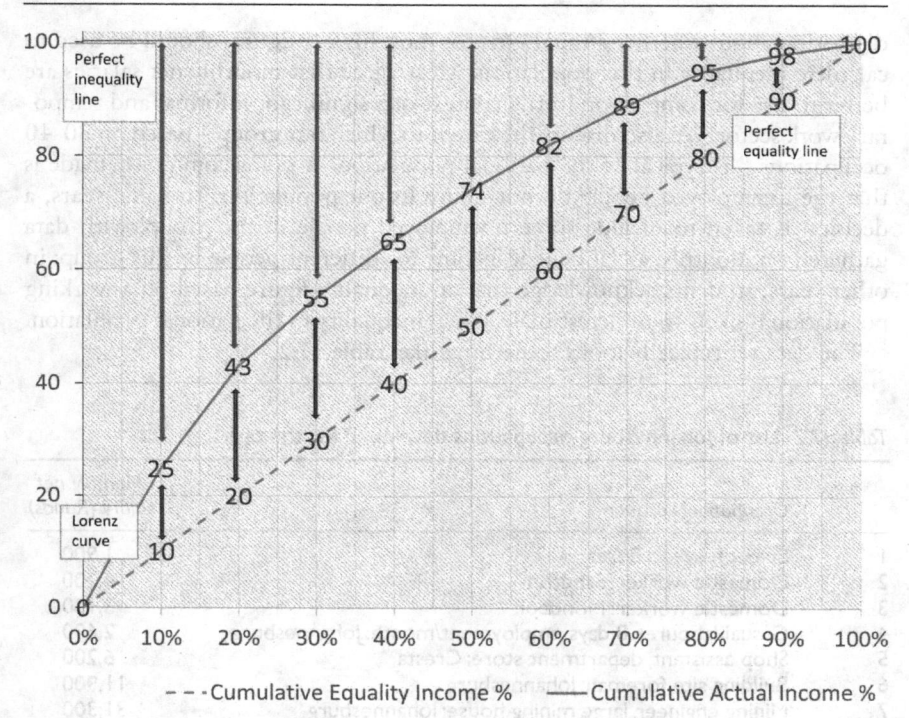

Figure 17.2 Graph showing the figures involved in an example of the Gini calculation.

Comparing these two totals in a fraction gives us the Gini coefficient value, and it is usually stated in decimal form.

Over the years I have found that it usually takes at least a couple of reads to make sense of the mathematical models and calculations. After some reading, I ask the following questions to check student understanding – you can use them to check your own understanding at this stage too.

So how is total equality viewed within the Gini coefficient calculation? And total inequality?

Can you follow how they got the answer given in the scenario above?

I then present the class with a precursor task. Each student in the group is given an 'occupation' – one that occurs in the context of the city we live in (Johannesburg, in our case): shop assistant, domestic help, television producer, newly qualified teacher, financial executive, etc. Students are asked to find out typical annual gross and monthly net salaries – by speaking to people in these jobs or by looking up available data sources. With this data in, we have a discussion about whether annual gross or monthly net figures should be used to calculate inequality in this population. Most agree that monthly net salaries are better to use for comparison in the context of a significant informal and temporary work sector. We also discuss the extent to which our group – based on 30-40 occupations – is typical of the national population. A point commonly made is that the unemployed people do not figure in our population. In some years, a decision is taken to include some unemployed people in the group, with data gathered on monthly social benefit income for different people in this group; in other years, students acknowledge that an inequality figure based on a working population is likely to underestimate actual inequality in the national population.

The data set typically looks something like Table 17.2.

Table 17.2 List of Johannesburg occupations developed for the task

	Occupation: Location	Monthly net salary (Rands)
1	Street hawker: Berea	1,900
2	Domestic worker: Sandton	4,200
3	Domestic worker: Mondeor	3,100
4	Casual labourer, 8 days employment/month: Johannesburg	2,600
5	Shop assistant, department store: Cresta	6,200
6	Building site foreman: Johannesburg	11,900
7	Mining engineer, large mining house: Johannesburg	31,300
8	Journalist – Sowetan	21,800
9	Car mechanic – Alex	10,700
10	Newly qualified school teacher – Soweto	13,400
11	Nurse – public hospital	9,400
12	Hardware store manager – Glenvista	18,800
13	Security guard: CBD	7,700
14	Junior lecturer – university	19,600
15	Power company executive	94,500
16	Homeless magazine seller	900
17	Dancer: Independent theatre group	9,000
18	Administrative assistant – university	8,400
19	Executive PA: Mining company	21,200
20	Junior accounts clerk	16,900
21	Waiter: Rosebank restaurant	9,100
22	Architect: Johannesburg	35,600
23	NGO fieldworker: Diepsloot	11,200
24	Junior doctor: Johannesburg General Hospital	18,200
25	Government department worker	11,400
26	IT support desk worker – engineering company	16,700
27	Airport security personnel	12,900
28	Factory packaging worker	7,700
29	Parking attendant	6,900
30	Mining executive	88,600
31	Partner – accounting firm	68,800
32	Electrician's assistant	8,600

Are you persuaded that we have an authentic data set here?
Do you have any comments on the figures? Are you surprised at some of the figures,
and some of the differentials – or lack of differential – between professions?
So if we wanted to look at inequality in this data set, how might we describe it?
What kind of statistical tools can we use here?
And can we use the reading we did to calculate the Gini coefficient for this data
set – there is data available on Gini coefficients across many countries that we
can compare with?
What agendas from my research with Mellony Graven do each of these questions
fall into?

In answering these questions (which move from Agenda 1 to Agenda 3), students note that we could calculate the range or the interquartile range; others say we can express the highest salary as a multiple of the lowest salary, or variations on this idea – we can calculate the mean of the lowest quintile or decile, and compare this to the mean of the highest quintile/decile. They suggest calculating the values derived from similar lists from other countries/parts of South Africa and representing the inequality with mean and standard deviation values, or in a box and whisker plot. Student groups proceed in a range of ways, some using pen/paper and calculators, and others working on Excel, entering formulas based on the Gini calculation (Agenda 4). Entered on Excel, the working based on the 32 data points can be used to produce an associated Gini graph (see Figure 17.3).

Each group presents their Gini coefficient result and calculation processes. Some argue that the formula has not been applied 'correctly' in the above instance as 32 points have been plotted with 32 differences added up rather than working at 10% intervals as in the example above. Others argue that dividing the population into 32 groups (based on the 32 values in the data set) uses the same idea, and is therefore okay. Apart from errors, most groups end up with

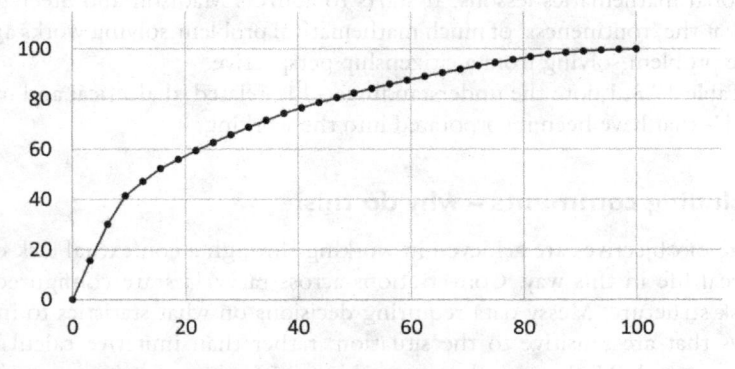

Figure 17.3 Gini graphs of the Johannesburg data set.

Table 17.3 Life-related, dialectical and mathematical understandings that have been incorporated into the working

Life-related competences	Dialectical competences	Mathematical competences
Learning about net salaries across a range of professions – in a context of significant inequality; considering the consequences of this for lifestyle choices. Encouraging conversations with people 'different' to ourselves.	Decision-making around what constitutes 'appropriate' data to use; understanding the implications of these decisions. Ways of measuring inequality – developing understanding of creating mathematical formulas and processes that can be put to use in the social world, critiquing these models – is the Gini model appropriate? What about the simpler ratio-based model? And rather than using 'total equality' as the baseline for comparison, could we use a different baseline model – a normal distribution for example? How might we do this?	Working through a given formula, looking at the calculation structure and sequence. 'Applying' the given formula to a new data set. Discussing 'unusual' cumulative frequency graphs – the equality line in the Gini calculation is actually a cumulative frequency curve, produced with unit increases. Linking the mathematical structure of the equality line with the $y = x$ equation. Summations leading into integration. Representing data distributions. Creating measures of data set distribution.

Gini values of around 0.5, but methodological/rounding differences produce different answers in this region (Agendas 2–4 figure here, but the overall frame is Agenda 2). This figure can be compared with the international Gini coefficient figures available through a range of sources online (for example, en.wikipedia. org/wiki/List_of_countries_by_income_inequality).

This working, while constrained by my questions, is clearly more open, more non-routine, and 'messier' than many of us have seen and experienced in more traditional mathematics lessons. It starts to address Madison and Steen's criticism that the 'routineness' of much mathematical problem-solving works against flexible problem-solving from a citizenship perspective.

In Table 17.3, I note the understandings – life-related, dialectical and mathematical – that have been incorporated into the working.

Concluding comments – why do this?

A range of objectives are achieved in working through a contextual task drawn from real life in this way. Conversations across race/class are configured into the task structure. Messy data requiring decisions on what statistics to include in ways that are sensitive to the situation, rather than imitative calculations, is incorporated. Mathematical sense-making/critiquing of existing models of situations is encouraged, alongside openings for seeing basic mathematics in new ways – for example, a straight line graph as a cumulative frequency graph in a situation of complete equality. Mathematical content from a range of curriculum areas is integrated within the need to understand the data set – number work, graphs and data handling. Flexible and efficiently integrated application of mathematics is often described as a hallmark of 'mathematical proficiency' (Kilpatrick, Swafford and Findell, 2001) and is viewed as central to developing problem-solving competence – the 'predilection to quantify and model' in Alan Schoenfeld's (1992) terms. Additionally, the certainties commonly associated with more traditional mathematics are disrupted here – models of inequality are 'created' and existing models are adapted and critiqued. Anne Watson notes in Chapter 12 that the nature of tasks set in classrooms can change the 'impressions' of mathematics that students construct, and that is part of the aim here.

Mathematical tools gain 'breadth' in this working – useful beyond the 'chapters' in textbooks where they usually surface. Above all, the walls that traditionally make mathematics an enterprise that is restricted to mathematics classrooms start to be chipped at. Evidence suggests that such experiences help to create a disposition to bring mathematical sense-making to bear on mathematical and extra-mathematical situations, replacing the 'reading over' acknowledged by my students and the more serious avoidance and phobia that have been widely documented.

Note, we are not economic experts at the end of this activity; we are using public information, not all of which may be accurate. Some argue that this makes the activity spurious. The dangers are there, but I would argue from a citizenship perspective that such activity starts to enable us to become more informed consumers of information, and in this, lays the ground for more active citizenship. At school level, we have evidence of such work providing openings for participation in social conversations and practices that students were previously locked out of by lack of awareness and understanding (Venkat and Graven, 2008). Thus, such work marks possibilities for greater participation, and for demanding more information and explanation from the 'experts' whose models format significant aspects of all of our lives.

Further reading

DBE. (2011) *Curriculum and Assessment Policy Statement: Grades 10–12, Mathematical Literacy.* Available at: http://www.thutong.doe.gov.za/Default.aspx?alias=www. thutong.doe.gov.za/mathematicaliteracy. It is worth glancing into this curriculum specification document to see how mathematical literacy has been configured into a curriculum. It is also worth noting that the Mathematical Literacy curriculum specification and assessments have been criticised as well. From a mathematical perspective, critics focus on the level of the mathematics being dealt with. From a life-related perspective, critics argue that contexts are artificial and that students' working is too heavily scaffolded to support the development of real-life competence.

National Numeracy.org.uk: http://www.nationalnumeracy.org.uk/home/index.html: This organisation takes a strongly life-oriented view of numeracy. The website provides detail on the organisation's aims, some links to research findings on numeracy levels amongst the adult population, and some reports on the associations between 'innumeracy' and economic consequences for individuals. It is quite interesting to look at their claims and the ways in which they present their data, given the organisation's position on numeracy.

Skovsmose, O. and Yasukawa, K. (2009) 'Formatting power of 'mathematics in a package': A challenge for social theorising?', in P. Ernest, B. Greer and B. Sriraman (eds.), *Critical Issues in Mathematics Education*. Charlotte, NC: Information Age Publishing. This chapter notes the multitude of ways in which mathematics 'formats' our everyday lives – at home, in the workplace, and in society. It tells the story of a particular case of mathematical formatting – encryption software systems, briefly detailing the mathematics underlying these systems. It also details the commercial and political ramifications of Phil Zimmerman's creation and free distribution of a particular software encryption package, in a context where 'packaging' of mathematics into commercial products can be highly lucrative. With mathematical models permeating so much of society, the authors call for mathematically literate investigations to interrogate not just the mathematics within packages, but to ask further: 'What is in the package?', 'Whose package is it?' 'What technical effects does the package have?'

Venkat, H. and Graven, M. (2008) 'Opening up spaces for learning: Learners' perceptions of Mathematical Literacy in Grade 10', *Education as Change*, 12(1): 29–44. In this paper, the experiences of Mathematical Literacy students in one school are discussed. In a situation where the majority of these learners had come into Mathematical Literacy with mathematical histories populated with failure, central findings related to the ways in which working with everyday problems supported both their ability to make sense of problems and solve them, and in turn, supported their participation in social conversations and practices related to the post-school environment.

References

DBE (2011) *Curriculum and Assessment Policy Statement: Grades 10–12*, Mathematical Literacy. Pretoria: Department of Basic Education.

Department for Business, Innovation and Skills (DBIS) (2012) *The 2011 Skills for Life Survey. A Survey of Literacy, Numeracy and ICT Skills in England*. London: DfES.

Freudenthal, H. (1983) *Didactical Phenomenology of Mathematical Structures*. Dordrecht: Reidel.

Gardiner, A. (2008) 'What is mathematical literacy?', *Proceedings of the 11th International Congress on Mathematical Education (ICME)*, Monterrey, Mexico, July.

Graven, M. and H. Venkat (2007) 'Emerging pedagogic agendas in the teaching of mathematical literacy', *African Journal of Research in Mathematics, Science and Technology Education*, 11(2): 67–86.

Jablonka, E. and Niss, M (2014) Mathematical literacy, in S Lerman, B Sriraman, E Jablonka, Y Shimizu, M Artigue, R Even, R Jorgensen and M Graven (eds.), *Encyclopedia of Mathematics Education*. Dordrecht: Springer, pp. 391–396.

Kilpatrick, J., Swafford, J. and Findell, B. (2001) *Adding It Up: Helping Children Learn Mathematics*. Washington, D.C.: National Academy Press.

Levenstein, K. (2010) 'Let the Gini out of the bottle', *Mail and Guardian*. Available at: http://mg.co.za/article/2010-02-04-let-the-gini-out-bottle (accessed 7 January 2013).

Madison, B. L. and Steen, L. A. (2009) 'Confronting challenges, overcoming obstacles: A conversation about quantitative literacy', *Numeracy*, 2(1): 1–25.

Schoenfeld, A. H. (1992) 'Learning to think mathematically: Problem solving, metacognition, and sense-making in mathematics', in D. Grouws (ed.), *Handbook for Research on Mathematics Teaching and Learning*. New York: MacMillan.

Skovsmose, O. and K. Yasukawa (2009) 'Formatting power of 'mathematics in a package': A challenge for social theorising?', in P. Ernest, B. Greer and B. Sriraman (eds.), *Critical Issues in Mathematics Education*. Charlotte, NC: Information Age Publishing.

Steen, L. A. (2001) 'The case for quantitative literacy', in National Council on Education and the Disciplines and L. A. Steen. (eds.), *Mathematics and Democracy*. Washington, D.C.: The Mathematical Association of America.

Steen, L. A. (2004) *Achieving Quantitative Literacy: An Urgent Challenge for Higher Education*. Washington, D.C.: The Mathematical Association of America.

Tomlinson, M. (2004) *14–19 Curriculum and Qualifications Reform: Final Report of the Working Group on 14-19 Reform*. Annesley: DfES.

Venkat, H. and M. Graven (2008) 'Opening up spaces for learning: Learners' perceptions of Mathematical Literacy in Grade 10', *Education as Change*, 12(1): 29–44.

World Bank Group (2018) *An Incomplete Transition: Overcoming the Legacy of Exclusion in South Africa – Systematic Country Diagnostic*. Washington, D.C.: World Bank.

Chapter 18

History of mathematics in and for the curriculum

Leo Rogers

Introduction

We teach mathematics because it is part of our common heritage. It is important for managing our lives, the daily actions of individuals, communities, corporations and governments. Mathematics has evolved in many contexts; it has been and will continue to be a tool for the solution of human problems (see Chapter 3 by Paul Ernest for further discussion on the mathematical needs of society). These problems come in many forms, from the earliest social practices to managing the contemporary economy. Mathematics is about ideas and their development, and it is also about people, societies and cultures. The history of mathematics traces the genesis and development of ideas that have had a major impact on our society.

In learning our language, we study the contexts, authors, literature and poetry, and can relate past literature with its relevance to contemporary problems. Similarly, history gives different perspectives on our culture. But what do we know about the culture of mathematics? Few students ever experience anything of the variety and extent of mathematics, of its styles, its contexts, the people who made it, their problems and achievements. It is a tragedy that such an important part of our culture is unknown to many of our students.

Few people realise that most of the mathematics taught up to age 16 in England and Wales was developed by other cultures and not brought into Western Europe until the late 15th century. Probability and statistical techniques began as rules of inheritance in Jewish and Arabic legal practices, while Mediaeval Arab scholars completed most of advanced school trigonometry. Even some basic ideas of the calculus are found in 14th century in China, India and Arabia. Our 'Western' school curriculum is the result of a transmission of ideas whose origins have been completely hidden. We live in a multicultural society, and students deserve to know about the contribution that past cultures played in the development of school mathematics.

There are many reasons why students who do not continue with mathematics after 16 have negative perceptions of mathematics: it is irrelevant to their lives, disconnected, elitist and de-personalised; they complain about uninteresting teaching, no connections between different areas of mathematics and meaningless rote application of formulas. Even successful students decide to leave for other subjects that are more interesting and creative. (Chapter 21 by Cathy Smith has an analysis of students' choices to opt into or out of mathematics at A-level.) With curriculum and textbooks based on assumptions that mathematics is hierarchical and students' progress necessarily linear, it is unfair to assume students cannot succeed, or that they are incapable of more challenging work (Brown, Brown and Bibby, 2008).

These perceptions are attributed to emphasis on 'teaching to the test', and not enough on engaging and inspiring students. The essence is that *mathematics teaching is not addressing the affective needs, beliefs, attitudes and emotions* of students, and lacks any social context in the opportunities for learning. These aspects are inextricable components of mathematical performance and known to increase confidence, encouraging positive learner identities (Nardi and Steward 2003, Lange and Meaney 2011).

Teaching mathematics requires attention to the *quality of pedagogy* and to *student engagement*. Engagement in mathematics is necessary to go beyond procedure following, by making connections with concepts in active discussions. Recent studies of attitudes of 11–14 year-olds show that *interest* is a key aspect of effective mathematics teaching. The NRICH website (https://nrich.maths.org/) offers interesting contexts where mathematics has regularly contributed to our scientific and cultural well-being. We can engage students' interests and provide accessible problems by enabling *access to historical material that is directly related to the curriculum we teach*. We have to produce good educational material so that history of mathematics becomes part of this enterprise.

We do not have to be experts. We can make links between the mathematics of the past and our present contexts, but *we must be aware that the mathematics of the past is not the same as mathematics today*, even though it may appear so when described in contemporary notation. As teachers we can pass on our *heritage* by exploiting links between the content of the curriculum and what we know of the history of mathematics. So, it becomes possible to describe events in the history of mathematics in terms that students can understand without making impossible demands on our own capabilities or teaching time.

Culture and heritage

Knowledge from the stars

Mathematics has arisen wherever people have begun to settle and organise production of food, measuring land, building storage facilities, irrigating fields and so on. Not only did they deal with their basic needs, but also organised their activities based on the movement of the sun, moon and stars. The constellations rotating about a fixed point in the sky led to more precise regulation of the seasons. Linking the natural with the supernatural established ritual practices, and timing these was crucial, so the need for precise observation was born. Astronomy has been a powerful motivation for developing mathematics from earliest times.

By 2,300 BCE Egyptian priests had divided the ecliptic into 36 sections of 10 degrees each. About 1,600 BCE Babylonians adopted 360 days for the length of the year and established 360 degrees in a circle by observing that the sun moved 1 degree daily relative to the fixed stars. From about 700 BCE they developed a theory of planetary motion, and the 12-constellation zodiac appeared about 500 BCE, corresponding to their year of 12 months of 30 days each. The earliest Chinese calendars appear about 2,000 BCE showing a 12-month year with an occasional 13th month. They became aware this calendar was unreliable and in the 5th century CE the scholar Zu Chongzi was the first to correct the problem.

From about 1500 BCE the Vedic people in Northern India developed simple geometrical constructions with peg and cord that enabled them to build ritual altars and their transformation rules for preserving areas, provided the basis for much of the geometry that appears in Euclid Books II and III.

> *It is easy to combine the equal small squares to make the large square of their combined areas. Figure 18.1(a). For the unequal squares in Figure 18.1(b), can you draw one line in the diagram to show the side of a square equal to the combined areas of these two squares?*
>
> *Move the point of intersection of the perpendiculars in Figure 18.2 along the diagonal. What do you observe about the areas created? Are there other points on the diagonal where a square and rectangle become equal in area?*

In the 12th century CE, Bhaskaracharya gave his well-known proof-diagram for the Pythagorean relation shown in Figure 18.3; *how can this be justified?* Activities like these provide students with the essential experiences of *visualisation and justification* before we attempt formal proof.

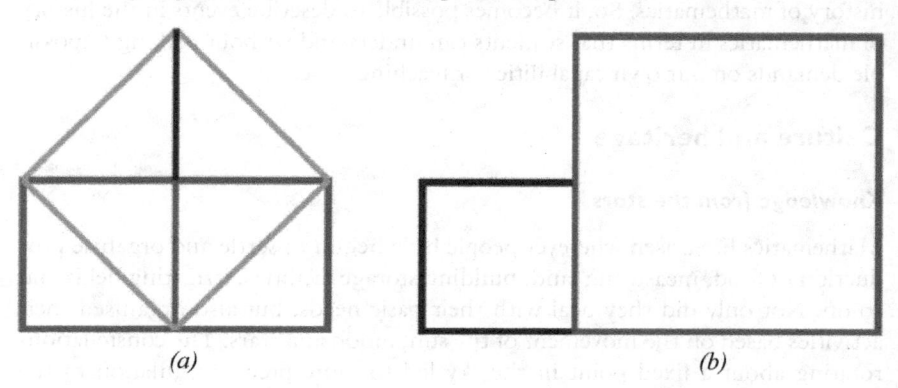

(a)   (b)

Figure 18.1 Hindu squares.

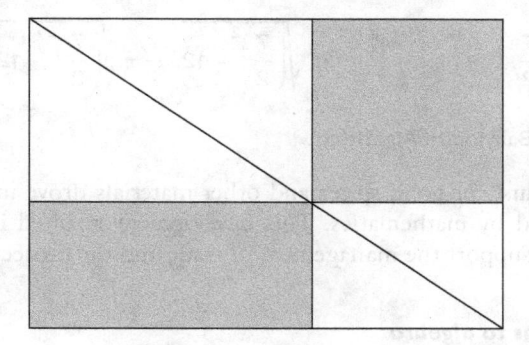

Figure 18.2 Euclid Book II Proposition 4.

In the 8th century CE, Arabian emissaries went to collect knowledge from the known world for the 'House of Wisdom' in Baghdad. By this time, both Chinese and Hindus had begun the investigation of infinite series for the calculation of sines by using differencing techniques, and the evaluation of the ratio *perimeter*: *diameter* for the circle. The Arabs inherited both Babylonian and Greek traditions, improved Ptolemy's *Almagest* and, in the 10th century, Abul Wafa produced new trigonometric tables to an accuracy of 5 sexagesimal (8 decimal) places.

Within the Mediterranean navigation was relatively easy compared with the voyages of the Portuguese to Africa and India in the 15th century. Finding one's way across the open ocean was a much more difficult task, but by the early 15th century the Chinese had established trading posts in Atlantic and Pacific America and in 1421–1423 had circumnavigated the globe. Expansion

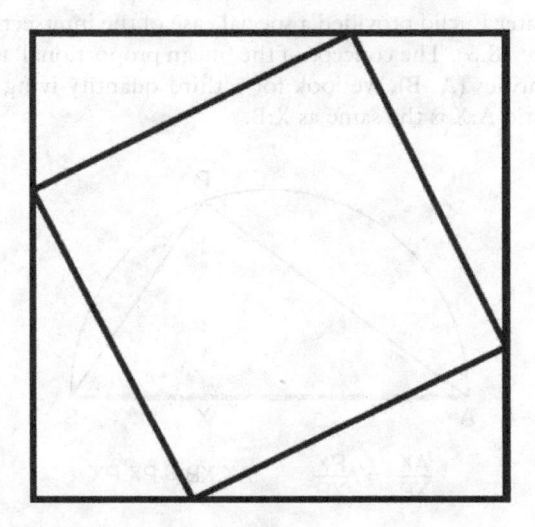

Figure 18.3 Bhaskaracharya's Pythagoras proof.

$$\frac{7}{2}; \left(\frac{7}{2}\right)^2; \left(\frac{7}{2}\right)^2 - 12; \sqrt{\left(\frac{7}{2}\right)^2 - 12}; \frac{7}{2} \pm \sqrt{\left(\frac{7}{2}\right)^2 - 12}$$

Figure 18.4 The 'Babylonian Algorithm'.

of empire, the lust for gold, spices and other materials drove improvements in navigation aided by mathematics. This development resulted in sophisticated instruments to support the management of trade and the prosecution of war.

From algorithms to algebra

The algorithms developed in Mesopotamia from simple land measurement came to us through the discovery of clay tablets. By about 500 BCE these procedures were standardised in Middle Eastern oral tradition for solving various problems. Typically, 'given a *sum* of two numbers and their *product*, find the two numbers involved'. The algorithm is:

> Take half the sum, square it, from this square subtract the product, find the square root of the result, and add or subtract this result to half the sum, to find the two numbers.

For some simple arithmetical values (such as sum, 7 and product, 12), using this 'Babylonian Algorithm', we can illustrate the procedure as in Figure 18.4.

Here, 7 represents the semi-perimeter of a rectangle and 12 is its area. This algorithm reappears in various forms over the years and is the basis of the quadratic equation today. The Hindus had solved this problem geometrically (see Figure 18.2). Later Euclid provided a special case of the intersecting chords theorem (see Figure 18.5). The concept of the 'mean proportional' is shown where, given two quantities (A, B), we look for a third quantity lying between them such that the ratio A:X is the same as X:B.

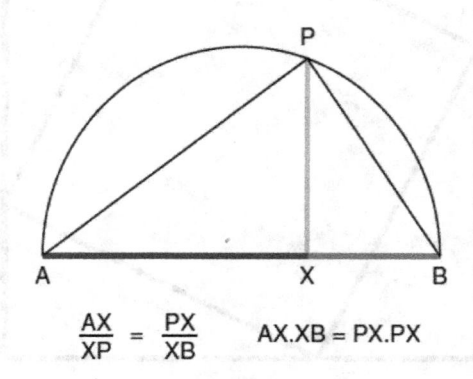

$$\frac{AX}{XP} = \frac{PX}{XB} \qquad AX.XB = PX.PX$$

Figure 18.5 Euclid Book VI, 13 the Mean Proportional.

$$ax^2 = bx \qquad ax^2 = n \qquad bx = n$$
$$ax^2 + n = bx \qquad ax^2 + bx = n \qquad ax^2 = bx + n$$

Figure 18.6 Al-Khowarizmi's equations.

In contrast to the arithmetic approach, this geometrical construction is quite general and can reveal the non-rational situations that Euclid dealt with in his Book X. The ratios show that AX.XB is a rectangle, and PX.PX is the square equal in area.

This information was adopted in the early days of the Arab empire, where scholars were preoccupied with the possible *combinations* of word-forms in standardising the language for a new nation, and debating the religious meaning of the 'knowable unknown' (Rashed, 2009, pp. 16–30). These influences led to Al-Khowarizmi's proposal for finding the 'knowable unknown' and the six classical forms of algebraic equations, given the three elements *mal* (x^2), *jidhr* (x) and *'adad* (n):

> *Using the 'Babylonian Algorithm' in Figure 18.6, develop a series of 'sum' and product' examples for use in the classroom. Compare these with the equations above. What opportunities can you find for developing solutions to your problems and what variations are possible? (You may find it helpful to look back to the discussion of variation in Chapter 15 by Tim Rowland).*

Impressed by Euclidean logic, scholars sought to demonstrate the consistency of this algebra geometrically. By the 9th century CE, Thabit ibn Qurra had shown that each algebraic form could be modelled by a consistent geometrical proof.

Fibonacci's Book of the Abacus, containing the mathematical knowledge of the 12th century Middle East, has practical problems used for training merchants, but also holds the traditional recreational puzzles and the problems that became the basis for the development of number theory and algebra. Mediaeval algebra lacked a notation and dealt only with special cases that gave solutions within an integral-geometric context. Dealing with surd numbers was possible but extremely awkward, resulting in a number of clever but disparate techniques. In the Renaissance, when algebraic notation was beginning to appear, breaking out of the geometric mould was difficult. In 1545 Cardano used the Babylonian Algorithm and showed that (in spite of serious misgivings) square roots of negative numbers could give a sensible answer. Without any algebraic notation, he demonstrated that '*if the sum of two numbers is 10 and their product is 40*', as in Figure 18.7, the result yields two parts of 10 which, when multiplied together confirm the product, as in Figure 18.8.

$$\left(\frac{10}{2}\right); \ \left(\frac{10}{2}\right)^2; \ \left(\frac{10}{2}\right)^2 - 40; \ \sqrt{\left(\frac{10}{2}\right)^2 - 40}; \ \frac{10}{2} \pm \sqrt{\left(\frac{10}{2}\right)^2 - 40}$$

Figure 18.7 Cardano's solution.

$$\left(5 + \sqrt{-15}\right)\left(5 - \sqrt{-15}\right)$$

Figure 18.8   Cardano's factors.

He drew a geometric diagram to explain and asked his readers to imagine a negative side of a square, *but he had achieved the result by following the algorithm into unknown territory.*

Arts, sciences and engineering

The invention of the crane in the 6th century BCE by Greek engineers and the introduction of the winch and pulley led to the theoretical mechanics of Archimedes, and by the first century CE, Hero's *Mechanica* described the mathematical basis for many ingenious machines. In 1901, a remarkable object constructed by an unknown technician was recovered from a shipwreck. Dated about 150 BCE, the 'Antikythera' is a mechanical model of the geocentric planetary system, with over 30 gears. It demonstrated the position of the planets with respect to the Earthly observer.

The creation of depth in paintings led to ingenious devices in the Renaissance where architects like Brunelleschi and artists like Piero della Francesca were involved in developing perspective that evolved into projective geometry in the 17th century.

Figure 18.9 from Piero's *De Prospectiva Pingendi* (c. 1480), the first treatise on perspective, shows his converse of Euclid's theorem which established the transitivity of similarity (*Elements* VI. 21):

EUCLID: Figures which are similar to the same rectilinear figure are also similar to one another.

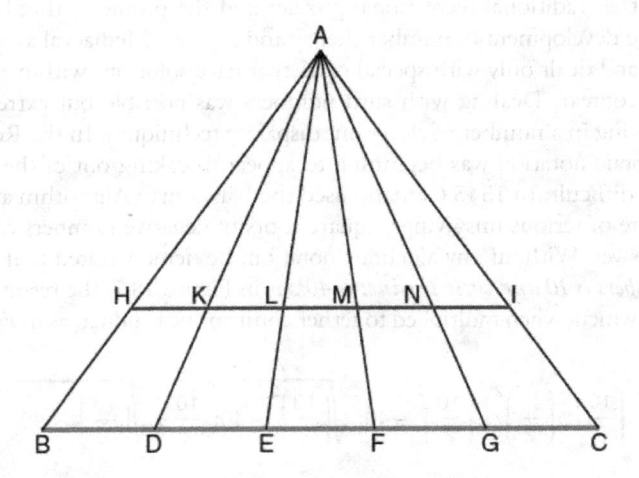

Figure 18.9 Piero della Francesca's 'Vanishing Point Theorem'.

PIERO: If above a straight line divided into several parts a line be drawn parallel to it and from the points dividing the first line there be drawn lines which end at one point, they will divide the parallel line in the same proportion as the given line.

Thus, for a pair of unequal parallel segments divided into equal parts, the lines joining corresponding points converge to a vanishing point. Later, comparing the number of points on parallel lines is considered by Galileo in his *Two New Sciences* of 1638. The theory of the real line may have its roots in Euclid and Piero but does not appear formally until the 19th century.

Theo van Doesburg, an important figure in the Avant-Garde movement, created his *Arithmetic Composition*. Figure 18.10 is an extension of his theme and has many interesting possibilities for classroom exploration. Careful analysis of this picture shows that there is a connection with the principles of proportion in Euclid Book V.

> *Explore the picture in Figure 18.10. What arithmetic and geometric investigations could be devised for students in Y7 and Y10?*

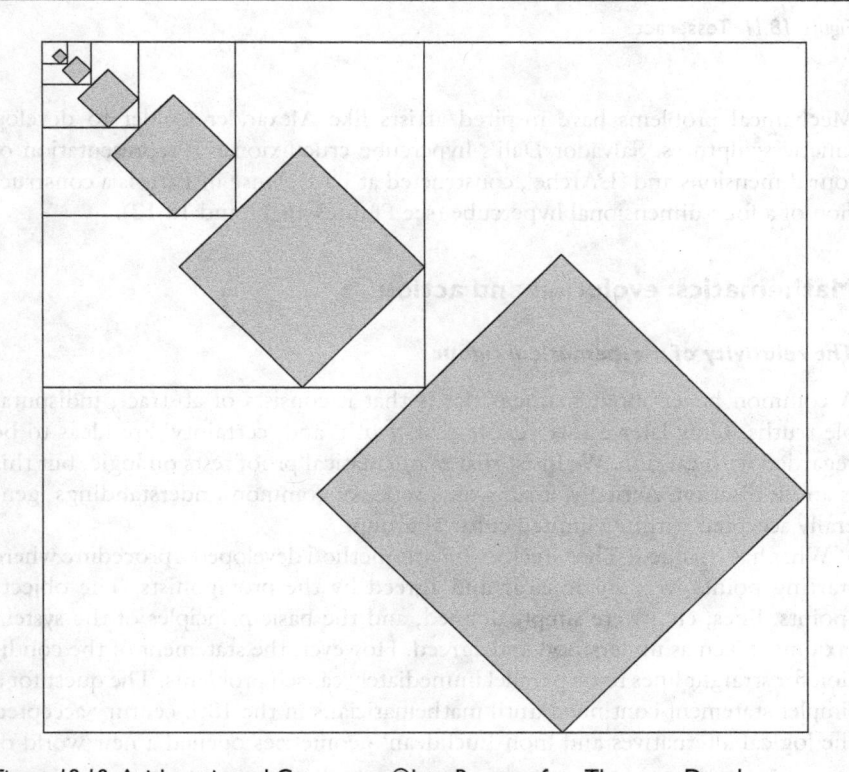

Figure 18.10 Arithmetic and Geometry: ©Leo Rogers after Theo van Doesburg.

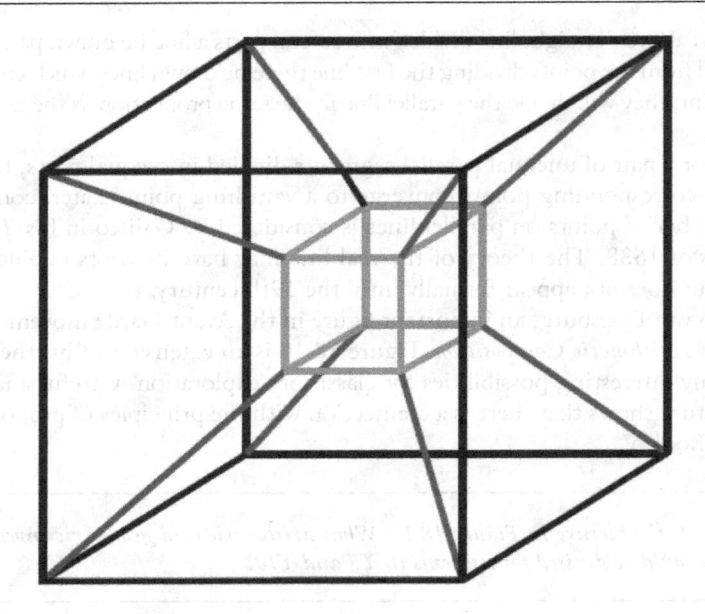

Figure 18.11 Tesseract.

Mechanical problems have inspired artists like Alexander Calder to develop kinetic sculptures. Salvador Dali's hypercube crucifixion is a representation of four dimensions and 'L'Arche', constructed at La Défense in Paris is a construction of a four-dimensional hypercube (see Figures 18.11 and 18.12).

Mathematics: evolution and action

The relativity of mathematical rigour

A common belief about mathematics is that it consists of abstract, indisputable truths. Only later do we realise that 'truth' and 'certainty' are ideas to be regarded with caution. We insist that mathematical proof rests on logic, but this is an idealisation. Actually, it rests on a series of common understandings, generally accepted within a limited cultural group.

What has changed? The Greek axiomatic method developed a procedure where starting points were made clear and agreed by the protagonists. The objects (points, lines, etc.) were simply defined, and the basic principles of the system (axioms) taken as understood and agreed. However, the statement of the condition for straight lines to be parallel immediately caused problems. The quest for a simpler statement continued until mathematicians in the 18th century accepted the logical alternatives and 'non-Euclidean' geometries opened a new world of

Figure 18.12 Le Grande Arche © Lyndon Baker – SumImages.

theory and applications. Imre Lakatos demonstrated the difficulties involved in his *Proofs and Refutations* (1976) where 'proofs' of Euler's formula (shown in Figure 18.13), describing relations between faces, edges and vertices of a poly-hedron, are disputed.

Lakatos showed how choices had to be made. Exceptions were either excluded, or if accepted, the concepts changed. Bringing different tools to the problem suggest different results and change the conceptual basis of the procedure. Each generation sees problems differently, and consequently finds it necessary to rede-fine, re-justify or reject earlier hidden assumptions.

> *During problem-solving activities, how often do we help students to bring out hidden assumptions, extend ideas and generate their own examples?*

$$f + v = e + 2$$

Figure 18.13 Euler's formula.

Those who have accepted this challenge have built up many examples and techniques based on classroom experience that encourage teachers to develop students' learning with tools that mathematicians employ regularly. See, Anne Watson and John Mason's (2005) *Mathematics as a Constructive Activity.*

Cognitive and affective opportunities

Research shows that other cultures had a very different approach to justifying mathematical processes, and that 'Euclidean-style proof' is not the only way to display consistency, validity and generality of mathematical procedures. Writing *about* mathematics began with explaining the work of mathematicians by critically examining their text.

There is now a better understanding of the reasoning behind the mathematical arguments of Indian and Chinese mathematicians who have provided new evidence of perspectives on the concepts of proof, truth and validity. There was no single set of rules for logical demonstration of mathematical statements. Instead, we find a *style of reasoning quite different from Euclid's*. This is important because it aims for *deeper understanding* rather than 'proof' and *generalisation* rather than abstraction.

Figure 18.14 is adapted from the commentary on the *Nine Chapters* by Liu Hui written during the 3rd century CE. Here is a circle touching all three sides of a right triangle. This is the starting point for exploring the properties of the figure that might be extended to cover the general case.

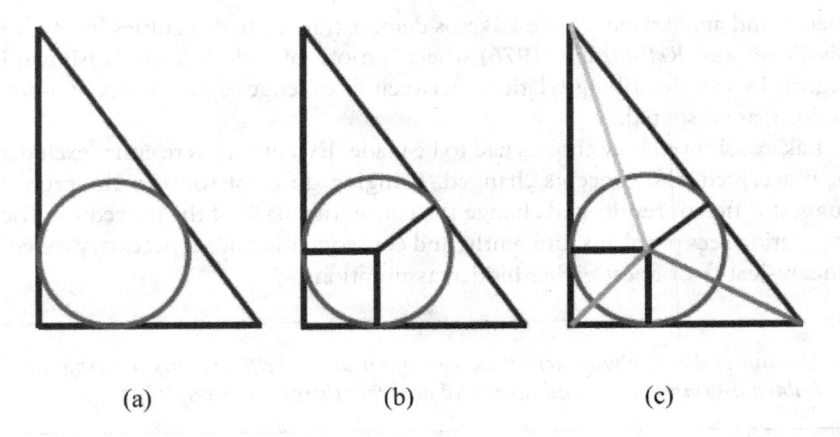

(a)   (b)   (c)

Figure 18.14 Liu Hui triangles.

> *Regarding Figure 18.14 what are the simplest properties of the figure you can deduce from the information given in the diagram?*

Assuming the circle is tangent to all three sides of the triangle, we arrive at Figure 18.14(b). From the symmetries in the object we deduce Figure 18.14(c). Other properties can follow. Use the radius of the circle as a common measure. By rearranging the smaller triangles into rectangles, they all have one dimension in common, and so we find an expression for the area of the original triangle.

> *By using Figure 18.14(a) as a generic example in this way, a teacher can gradually help students to discover, confirm, extend and establish new properties.*
> *If the dimensions of the triangle are integers, does this property apply to all Pythagorean triangles? Can this idea be extended to isosceles and other triangles?*

Classroom practice: maps, narratives and orientations

Concept Maps are graphical multilayered tools for organising and representing knowledge. They have advantages over text, to support collaborative development of knowledge, sharing of vision and understanding, and enhancement of other levels of mathematical thinking (Rogers, 2011). Most textbooks present information as a linear sequence of facts, procedures and exercises, restricted to some arbitrary 'level' of students' competence. Given a *Concept Map*, a user would need a guide (the *Narrative*), that provides information on the general context and background of the Map, and an *Orientation* that describes the activities proposed for students to use among the ideas presented.

A Map is a *virtual environment* where the arrangement of concepts, objects, events, proposals and actions may be partially ordered and multilayered, thus breaking up a linear sequence and juxtaposing different ideas. No Map is ever complete. The principal concept(s) chosen at one stage can be rearranged according to the needs of the learning, and the individuals involved. To be relevant and useful, Maps are best developed collaboratively with a group of teachers, or a teacher and students can share knowledge and combine their visions. In this way both students and teachers can be offered Maps to explore and interpret; organise ideas in particular ways, and examine possible links between ideas in a visual display. Maps can be used as plans for teaching, and scaffolding for learning, leading us to new connections between ideas.

Visualising and representing objects, manipulating them in the mind, brings out hidden properties and relations. Adapting a Map to explore links through the curriculum to historical contexts can act as a knowledge structure for integrating aspects of our mathematical heritage into a teaching programme. *The history then becomes integral to the exploration of the mathematics.* A Map enables teachers to have the freedom to develop their own Narrative. It can throw light on problems, suggest different approaches to teaching and generate new questions.

A practical example

One of the most fundamental concepts in mathematics with a wide range of applications in mathematics science, and daily life is ratio and proportion.

Figure 18.15 shows a Concept Map with some of the main ideas in their historical contexts. It is constructed to relate to the school curriculum, offering an exercise for teachers to make their own map of the relevant contents of their school curriculum.

> *Where does the knowledge and use of ratio and proportion occur in the school curriculum? How could these interconnections appear in a curriculum plan? Where and how are they placed in the textbook? Is there a necessary sequence for learning these ideas? How can these be realised in practice?*

Historical narrative

The definitions are found in Euclid Book V, but the experiences leading to this idea arose when people appreciated a relation between the shadow of a stick and the time of day. Once a proportional relationship between sides of similar right-angled triangles was formalised, new developments became possible. Pyramids symbolise engineering achievements, but the proportional relationship is also found in the solution of linear equations in problems 24–29 of the Rhind Papyrus. As the relation between numerical and geometrical measures was quantified, the techniques of inverse proportion and alternation appear. Here we see mathematical relations enabling advances in practical life, long before any theoretical basis emerged.

The Pythagorean relation was common practical knowledge for ancient peoples, and independently shown to be theoretically true by Indian and Chinese mathematicians, while the intersecting chord theorems stating relationships between segments and angles led to the family of trigonometric ratios. The Mean Proportional (Figure 18.5) was used by Viete in the 16th century in his formulation of quadratic equations, and the same construction shows how it is possible to transform a rectangle into a square of equal area, now easily achieved using algebra. The algebra conceals the problem of *precisely measuring the side of the square*. The *existence of the square and its diagonal* is obvious; but a common measure is impossible and symbolising the diagonal by $\sqrt{2}$ omits a great opportunity to discuss an approximation made some 4,000 years ago.

The ratio of the circle diameter to its perimeter became problematic. The statement that 'Archimedes' value for π was 3.1429' neglects many opportunities for engaging with important mathematical ideas. These examples show

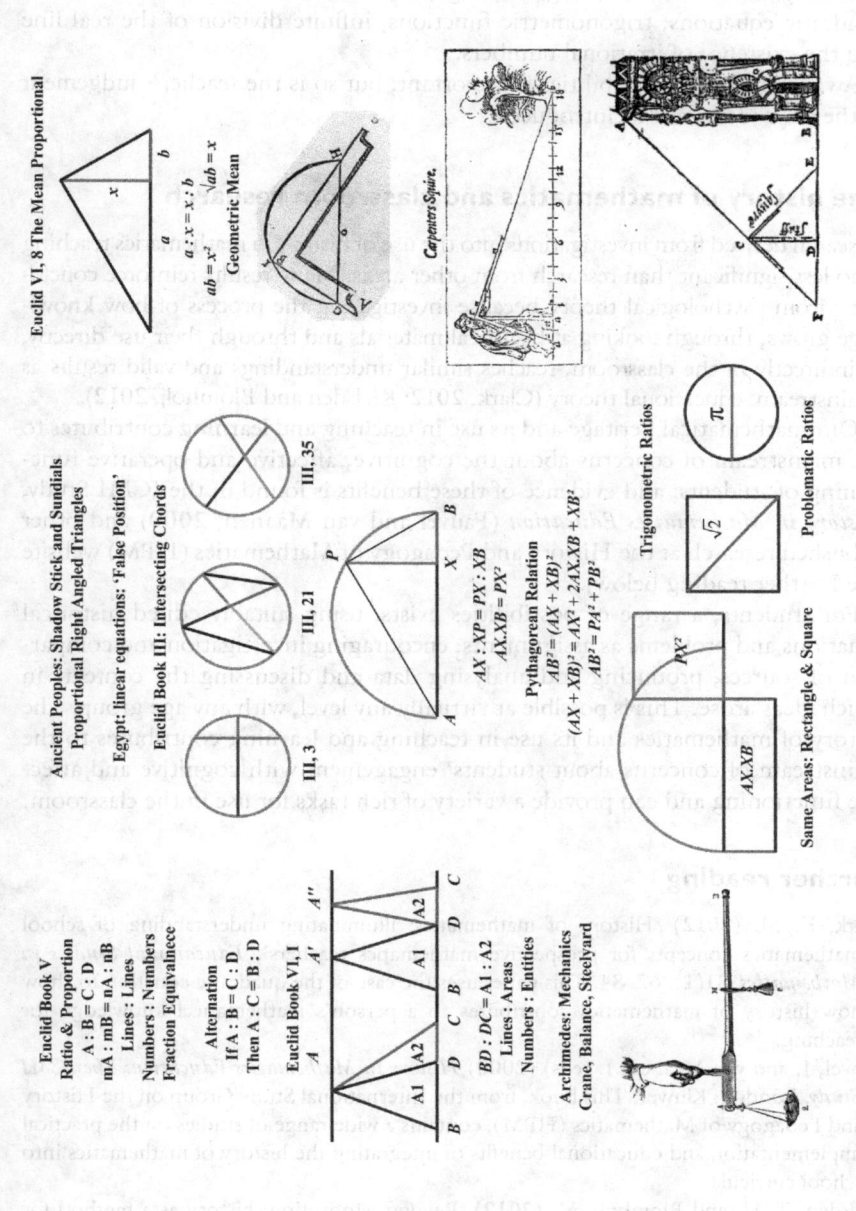

Figure 18.15 Ratio and proportion: historical concept links.

how ratio and proportion underlie the most essential ideas in elementary mathematics. They demonstrate equivalence relations, links between arithmetic and geometry, algorithms evolving into algebra, fundamental ideas of linear and quadratic equations, trigonometric functions, infinite division of the real line and the existence of irrational numbers.

Awareness of the possibilities is important, but so is the teacher's judgement of the ways ideas may be introduced.

The history of mathematics and classroom research

Research derived from investigations into the use of history in mathematics teaching is no less significant than research from other areas. Many results reinforce conclusions from psychological theory because investigating the process of how knowledge grows, through looking at historical materials and through their use directly, or indirectly in the classroom, reaches similar understandings and valid results as 'mainstream' educational theory (Clark, 2012; Kjelsden and Blomholj, 2012).

Our mathematical heritage and its use in teaching and learning contributes to the mainstream of concerns about the cognitive, affective and operative functioning of students, and evidence of these benefits is found in the ICMI Study, *History in Mathematics Education* (Fauvel and van Maanen, 2000) and other published research at the History and Pedagogy of Mathematics (HPM) website (see Further reading below).

For students, a range of possibilities exists, using suitably edited historical situations and problems as assignments, encouraging investigation and comparison of sources, producing and analysing data and discussing the contexts in which ideas arose. This is possible at virtually any level, with any age group. The history of mathematics and its use in teaching and learning contributes to the mainstream of concerns about students' engagement with cognitive and affective functioning and can provide a variety of rich tasks for use in the classroom.

Further reading

Clark, K. M. (2012) 'History of mathematics: illuminating understanding of school mathematics concepts for prospective mathematics teachers', *Educational Studies in Mathematics*, 81(1): 67–84. This paper uses the case of the quadratic equation to show how history of mathematics contributes to a person's mathematical knowledge for teaching.

Fauvel, J. and van Maanen, J. (eds) (2000) *History in Mathematics Education: The ICMI Study*. London: Kluwer: This book, from the International Study Group on the History and Pedagogy of Mathematics (HPM), contains a wide range of studies on the practical implementation and educational benefits of integrating the history of mathematics into school curricula.

Kjelsden, T. H. and Blomholj, M. (2012) 'Beyond Motivation: history as a method for learning meta-discursive rules in mathematics', *Educational Studies in Mathematics*, 80(3): 327–349. This analysis of students' project reports on historical topics shows how reflecting upon the actual historical process contributes to the development of their own understanding and ways of managing mathematical reasoning in the classroom.

Lakatos, I. (1976) *Proofs and Refutations: The Logic of Mathematical Discovery*. Cambridge: Cambridge University Press. This is the classic text on the evolution of mathematical concepts in the pursuit of proof, and the pitfalls of attempting precise definitions.

Rogers, L. (2011) 'Mapping our Heritage to the Curriculum: Historical and Pedagogical Strategies for the Professional Development of Teachers', in V. Katz and C. Tzanakis (eds.), *Recent developments on introducing a historical dimension in mathematics education*. Washington, DC: MAA. This text describes in detail the philosophy, educational approach and practical principles of using of Concept Maps in the classroom.

Watson, A. and Mason, J. (2005) *Mathematics as a Constructive Activity*. London. Laurence Erlbaum. Here, teachers and students together develop mathematical creativity. This is an outstanding contribution to practical, effective pedagogy.

Online resources

History and Pedagogy of Mathematics (HPM) at http://www.clab.edc.uoc.gr/HPM/. This is the site of the International Study Group on the Relations between the History and Pedagogy of Mathematics. There are copies of many Newsletters with accounts of teachers using history of mathematics in their classrooms.

The MacTutor History of Mathematics Archive at http://www-history.mcs.st-and.ac.uk/history/. This is the principal website in the United Kingdom where you can find biographies of mathematicians and histories of many mathematical topics.

The Mathematical Society of America provides a wealth of resources to help teach mathematics using its history, for example, Congruence at http://mathdl.maa.org/mathDL/23/.

NRICH is a mathematics enrichment website. Teachers Experiences of using NRICH at http://nrich.maths.org/6537 offers pedagogical principles, advice and project work by teachers. Some of my own relevant NRICH topics, created for teachers and students and accompanied by notes and pedagogical discussion, are:

A Brief History of Time Measurement: http://nrich.maths.org/6070
Development of Astronomy and Trigonometry: http://nrich.maths.org/6843
Development of Algebra 1: http://nrich.maths.org/6485
Development of Algebra 2: http://nrich.maths.org/6546

References

Brown, M., Brown, P. and Bibby, T. (2008) '"I would rather die": reasons given by 16 year olds for not continuing their study of mathematics', *Research in Mathematics Education*, 10(1): 3–18.

Clark, K. M. (2012) 'History of mathematics: illuminating understanding of school mathematics concepts for prospective mathematics teachers', *Educational Studies in Mathematics*, 81(1): 67–84.

Fauvel, J. and van Maanen, J. (eds.) (2000) *History in Mathematics Education: The ICMI Study*. London: Kluwer.

Kjelsden, T. H. and Blomholj, M. (2012) 'Beyond motivation: history as a method for learning meta-discursive rules in mathematics', *Educational Studies in Mathematics*, 80(3): 327–349.

Lakatos, I. (1976) *Proofs and Refutations: The Logic of Mathematical Discovery*. Cambridge: Cambridge University Press.

Lange, T. and Meaney, T. (2011) 'I actually started to scream: emotional and mathematical trauma from doing school mathematics homework', *Educational Studies in Mathematics*, 77(1): 35–51

Nardi, E. and Steward, S. (2003) 'Is Mathematics T.I.R.E.D? A Profile of Quiet Disaffection in the Secondary Mathematics Classroom', *British Educational Research Journal*, 29(3): 345–367.

Rashed, R. (2009) *Al-Khwarizmi: The Beginnings of Algebra*. London: SAQI.

Rogers, L. (2011) 'Mapping our Heritage to the Curriculum: Historical and Pedagogical Strategies for the Professional Development of Teachers', in V. Katz and C. Tzanakis (eds.), *Recent Developments on Introducing a Historical Dimension in Mathematics Education*. Washington, DC: MAA.

Watson, A. and Mason, J. (2005) *Mathematics as a Constructive Activity*. London. Laurence Erlbaum.

Section Five

Debates about assessment

Alison Barnes and Rachel Marks highlight how many mathematical assessment activities can be used formatively or summatively. They suggest that one's view of mathematics influences the assessment approaches likely to be adopted and that assessing mathematical thinking, for example the extent to which the learner is able to make conjectures, is not straightforward. They take us through a variety of learner and teacher responses to an open and unstructured problem to consider the ways that assessments were, and could have been, used and they identify potential barriers to effective formative assessment. They use this example to highlight the opportunities to focus formative assessment on the mathematical processes that students use, but this involves teachers having secure and confident subject knowledge to be able to respond in the moment to provide feedback.

Ian Jones raises questions about the appropriateness of the General Certificate of Secondary Education (GCSE) examinations by providing a brief history of mathematics examinations taken at age 16. He outlines the debates about how these examinations have been viewed over time, ultimately resulting in a recent change to the grading structure. He also identifies the way that the current examination structure does not provide an opportunity to assess the coherence of the subject for the learner; ease and reliability in marking by setting questions with a limited number of possible correct answers has been prioritised. He points out that because of the number of marks available on GCSE papers from short answer questions, much of the teaching involving preparation for these examinations tends to focus on this kind of approach, something which Ofsted have identified as a problem. He concludes by inviting us to consider alternative modes of assessment, and who might be involved in doing the assessment.

The chapter by **Cathy Smith** on post GCSE mathematics discusses the range of potential options (although not in all cases!) available to post 16-year olds in relation to mathematics. She highlights the differences between two courses of study – Core Maths and Mathematics A-level – in terms of content and structure and in the way that results of GCSE examinations relate to the different options available to students. She encourages the reader to consider learner motivation for different post 16 choices, and how this is related to the learners' mathematical identity. To do this she unpacks issues such as equity, perceptions about mathematics, enjoyment and challenge.

All three of these chapters focus on *what* is being assessed. In the case of the first, the authors look at what is possible to assess through formative assessment, while Ian Jones explores what mathematics is assessed in GCSE examinations and what sorts of mathematical knowledge attracts the highest marks. Cathy Smith looks at the different questions on Core Maths and applied Mathematics A-level papers and shows how these have different requirements in terms of mathematical knowledge.

Each chapter also comments on the extent to which it is possible to assess mathematical understanding and whether summative assessments in England and Wales currently attempt to do so. Alison Barnes and Rachel Marks describe an episode of learning as moving from what was not known to what is now understood; but they argue that assessing understanding is not necessarily straightforward. Historically, the summative assessment of mathematics has tended to focus on problems with only one possible correct solution which can be marked correct or incorrect. They argue that it is more complicated to assess how students think about particular mathematical problems or what their conjectures might be since these cannot be marked in this way. Ian Jones also emphasises the difficulty in the assessment of mathematical thinking but notes that recent changes to the final assessments at GCSE have involved ensuring that over a quarter of the available marks must be awarded for problem-solving, defined in a very broad way. In the final chapter in this section, Cathy Smith discusses a new qualification that involves a focus on the application of mathematics in real life, authentic situations. She shows, through comparison of examination questions, that this qualification requires a degree of reasoning about such situations which involve mathematics, whereas questions on the traditional (and better regarded) qualification have tended to focus more on abstract concepts. However, she also points out that since the recent changes to post 16 qualifications, more attention has been paid to using problem-solving questions in both examinations, questions that require students to think mathematically.

Chapter 19

Formative assessment in mathematics education

Key debates

Alison Barnes and Rachel Marks

Formative assessment and the assessment cycle

The intention of assessment is to tell us something about a student's attainment and consequently it is at the heart of learning. We can model learning in many ways. One way we find useful is to view an episode of learning as a gap to be bridged between what was not known and what is now understood. This learning must start from where the student is and must allow them to reconstruct and reformulate their current understanding, rather than laying new knowledge on weak foundations (Hodgen & Wiliam, 2006). The teacher has a vital role to play in identifying individual students' starting points and supporting them to construct or reconstruct ideas. This is why assessment is so vital. Assessment forms part of the continuous learning process, hence being described as an assessment cycle (Figure 19.1).

Broadly, assessment may be categorised as summative or formative. Summative assessments include examinations and the traditional marking or testing at the end of a piece/unit of work, while formative assessments include activities that provide feedback for developing the next stages of teaching and learning. However, assessment is more nuanced, and both forms may be used together for different needs; virtually all assessment activities, even final examinations, have both a summative and a formative element as we'll discuss below. Traditionally, mathematics has tended to have more formal, and often summative, approaches to assessment. This may be, in part, a result of a persistent view of mathematics as a set of hierarchical procedures with one correct answer. However, views of mathematics are changing and we are seeing a concurrent change in teaching and learning approaches and also in assessment. Teachers use assessment to support learning but do not always see their activities as assessment, particularly if they are not 'formal'.

In this chapter we briefly explore the background to, and current debates within, Assessment for Learning (AfL), formative assessment and feedback in mathematics education. We examine key understandings of these concepts, how these might fit within the current curriculum and practice, and the important role of the teacher within them. We illustrate the issues raised through

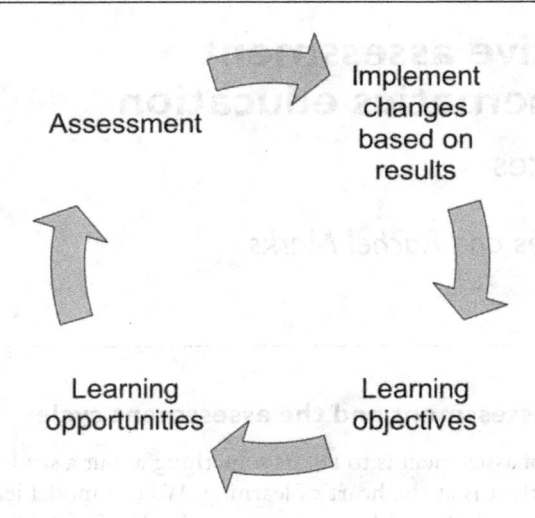

Figure 19.1 The assessment cycle.

examining what these ideas might look like in practice when applied to non-routine mathematics learning; students' reasoning in mathematics. Our proposal is that to assess beyond mathematical subject knowledge content and move towards including assessment of mathematical thinking processes, we need to have the student, and the learning intentions, as explicit and central foci of the assessment cycle.

What do we mean by formative assessment?

Some assessment practices are clearly summative – end of course certifications and assessments conducted to fulfil accountability measures, for example – but others are intended to impact more directly on learning. In your practice you may have encountered different terminology for such assessment, particularly the terms AfL, formative assessment, feedback and self-assessment. There is some debate as to the exact definition of each; they may be used interchangeably, be taken to mean the same or different things and represent a range of practices. AfL is usually taken as the broadest of these concepts (Mittler, 1973; Wiliam, 2018), but even implementation at this level is variable and may diverge distinctly from the original intentions (Harrison, 2018). AfL may include practices that support students – such as test practice – but which do not have a direct bearing on conceptual learning. To be considered formative assessment, which we suggest sits within AfL, the practice or its outcome must lead to the adaptation of future learning or practice – for students or teachers – in either the short or longer term with the intention of better meeting students' needs (Black et al., 2004). We base our discussion in this chapter on this definition.

Formative assessment involves many approaches that might simply be considered good classroom practice and are known to support students. While these approaches include practices as diverse as promoting classroom discussion through to supporting self-regulation, it is feedback which is usually central to discussions of formative assessment and the most common formative assessment practice seen in classrooms. Feedback is a useful example of how broad the terminology is: the Education Endowment Foundation (EEF, 2018, p. 1) state that feedback "can be verbal or written, or can be given through tests or via digital technology. It can come from a teacher or someone taking a teaching role, or from peers".

Formative assessment practices involve elements common to much, if not all, teaching. However, there are also domain-specific approaches and practices which may be enacted differently in different subject areas. For the purpose of this chapter we focus on *direct, short-term, formative assessment in mathematics,* where the practices, including feedback, are deliberate and inform the students' or teachers' immediate next steps. Essentially, this is assessment which "plac[es] instructional decision-making at the heart of the issue" (Wiliam, 2014, p. 2).

Formative assessment: the evidence and impacts

Formative assessment was developed during the 1960s, which makes it somewhat surprising that we are yet to establish a widely accepted definition despite using the concept for 50+ years. While it is the effective use of formative assessment which is important at a practitioner and student level, there is a need to have a common definition if practitioners and researchers are to communicate effectively and if we are to compare 'like for like' across studies. Formative assessment is central to practice in many schools; hence, it is important to hold an overview of the key ideas presented in the literature. Now considered seminal work, the most influential work on formative assessment is *Inside the Black Box* (Black & Wiliam, 1998). Although the research is now dated, evidence from the Black Box series, which includes *Mathematics inside the Black Box* (Hodgen & Wiliam, 2006), and from the EEF toolkit (2018) seems to present a fairly consistent picture (although EEF do note variability in the effectiveness of feedback across studies). In this chapter we draw on a number of key ideas presented across this literature, including the findings that:

- formative assessment shows positive gains but these are more modest than the gains from feedback as a practice in and of itself;
- effective use of feedback can have significant impacts on learning, but it must be used appropriately and be supported with professional development for teachers;
- self- and peer-assessment is challenging for students and they need to be taught explicitly how to do this.

Formative and summative assessment in mathematics: what can we assess?

Beliefs about the nature of mathematics and accountability pressures may have resulted in a greater preponderance of summative assessment in the subject. Summative assessment has been suggested as problematic because it is target-driven, emphasises competition and beliefs about fixed-ability, and only tells the student what they can or cannot do, not what they need to do to improve. However, the issue is broader than saying summative assessment is problematic and should be replaced with formative assessment. It is possible that both summative and formative assessments become target-driven with the result that various forms of assessment exist in our classrooms in a state of confusion and tension. This makes it harder for any form of assessment to work as intended. For instance, some formative assessment practices may be implemented in a way that is only superficially formative, or possibly even summative. Evidence gathered through students' "traffic light" responses – a practice where students use green/amber/red cards and/or dots to indicate their understanding – may not be being used by teachers to inform future learning directions, but instead to record summative levels of understanding. Conversely, summative assessment practices such as written tests may be used formatively, particularly if they are shifted from the end to a midpoint in a teaching sequence and the results inform teaching in subsequent lessons.

Even if used as intended, it would still be wrong to say that one form of assessment is 'better' than all alternatives. We need to consider how we are using assessment and for what purpose. Mathematics is possibly more complex in terms of assessment than many other subjects. While viewing mathematics as a subject of procedures and rules to learn may have supported summative assessment of students' application of methods, we suggest that conceptual understanding, mathematical thinking and mathematical processes are far more complex to assess. By their very nature, key mathematical processes, such as conjecturing, cannot be assessed by screening for errors nor can they be marked as right or wrong. It is necessary instead to make judgements of students' thinking processes. Certain approaches to teaching, learning and assessing lend themselves better to assessing mathematical processes. We examine these later in this chapter. Before that, we would like you to consider this:

Activity 1: Formative or summative?

Identify an assessment activity you have used or seen recently such as an examination question or a question asked to check understanding. List the summative and formative outcomes. How might you make the activity more formative? Revisit your ideas after reading the next section.

Formative assessment in practice

We noted above that formative assessment, and in particular effective feedback, raises attainment. The important term here is effective. There may be multiple barriers to the implementation of effective formative assessment and feedback in practice. In this section, we examine how some of the key features of formative assessment can be used effectively.

The importance of effective feedback

One of the significant findings from the literature is the importance of feedback and the differing impacts of different types of feedback (for example, EEF, 2018; Wiliam, 2014). Feedback to students is a normal consequence of assessment. For example, the screening for errors that occurs when marking a textbook exercise is a form of feedback when the marked work is returned to students. Students are often given feedback in the form of grades or levels. Sometimes they are also given qualitative feedback, either in writing on their work or orally as the teacher circulates the room. The Black Box research found that, rather than quantity, it is the nature of the feedback given that is critical to the success of formative assessment. Feedback can only be considered formative if it guides the students or teachers in the next stages of their work, that is moves learning towards fulfilling the learning objectives and success criteria of the lesson. In practice, this means that the feedback given – written or oral – should not only highlight where the student has been successful, but also explicitly identify what the student needs to do next. It may also be beneficial to plan specific assessment time into lessons in which the formative assessment can be acted upon and a dialogue set up between students and teachers.

The key issue in providing feedback is in its interaction with other types of assessment. We discussed earlier how different forms of assessment may conflict with each other. Feedback is a key area where this can be seen and it is a particular issue within mathematics where giving marks and grades is commonplace. Giving students marks only tells them their achievement on a particular task; it does not tell them very much about what they need to do to improve their work. It would be a reasonable assumption that giving a written comment in addition to the mark would fill this gap, telling the students how well they have done and also what they need to do next. However, the Black Box research identified that where both marks and written feedbacks are given, students tend to ignore the written feedback in favour of the mark: "Where the classroom culture focuses on rewards, 'gold stars', grades or place-in-the-class ranking, then pupils look for ways to obtain the best marks rather than at the needs of their learning which these marks ought to reflect" (Black & Wiliam, 1998, pp. 8–9). What does this mean in the mathematics classroom? This research suggests that to give effective feedback, teachers should only tell the students, in words, what they have done well and highlight the next step(s) to take. Grades and marks should not be given. The Black Box research gives two possible approaches. First, teachers can record marks but provide only written feedback to students; second, they can give students their marks after they have responded to the written feedback.

Discussion, questioning and classroom talk

As indicated above, feedback may involve a dialogue between students and teachers. Beyond this, classroom talk may be engineered to form a formative assessment role. In order to support students in their learning, the teacher needs to know what the student knows. This is not straightforward, particularly with mathematical thinking processes that underpin problem-solving and reasoning. Using formative assessment, the teacher needs to find a way to access what the student knows and assess the nature of their thinking, as well as guiding the student in the next steps of their learning. One strategy that may be useful in supporting this is carefully planned discussion, teacher questioning and classroom talk. This approach requires setting up a classroom environment where interaction is the norm and students are actively engaged in lessons (see Chapter 11 by John Mason in this volume for an extended discussion).

The Black Box research shows that well-planned questions can extend students' engagement. These questions do not need to be elaborate; simply asking students "why do you think…" may be enough (see Way, 2011, for further examples of questions). It should be remembered though that however effective the questioning, the teacher is only one part of what happens in the classroom. It is important that space is given to teacher and student dialogue. Strategies should be implemented to open up this dialogue. These include asking probing questions and being interested in the response, setting up longer wait times (the period between asking a question and accepting an answer) to allow more students to respond with extended answers, and asking students to discuss their answers before responding – or to try and come up with multiple responses. We will see some of these strategies in action in our illustrated example later in the chapter.

Professional development

It is clear from this brief foray into the research and exploration of how this might be enacted in practice that this is a complex and at times contested arena. While feedback in particular produces significant learning gains it is not unproblematic. Panadero (2018) describes formative assessment practices as a difficult discipline requiring sustained practice if they are to be implemented successfully. Across all subject areas, it is noted that teacher professional development is needed to understand, implement and continue to effectively use, feedback practices. The importance of professional development is recognised in the *Improving Mathematics in Key Stages Two and Three* evidence review (Hodgen et al., 2018); while effective assessment is the first recommendation of the review, Hodgen et al. caution that Continuing Professional Development (CPD) is integral to successful formative assessment, feedback and addressing students' misconceptions.

Although the gains may be substantial, individual teachers and schools must consider how they will implement formative assessment – and give time to its implementation – if they are to realise these gains in practice.

Self- and peer-assessment

Self- and peer-assessment is integral to formative assessment but can be difficult to implement effectively. Given that formative assessment and the provision of effective feedback are hard for teachers, it seems reasonable that students also find the processes difficult and need to be taught how these can be applied and used effectively. In particular, students at this initial stage will find it helpful to know what they are assessing themselves or others against, using clear, shared learning objectives and success criteria.

Assessments made by students often focus on extrinsic aspects of the work such as presentation, or have a tendency towards being overcritical. Neither helps the student in identifying the next steps to take. Particular strategies that may support self- and peer-assessment include writing up expected learning achievements in transparent language; extending students' "Traffic Lights" responses by asking them to justify them to their peers and using annotated examples of strong responses to a given task to support dialogue and provide a structure to peer-assessment. Beyond this, as well as learning how to produce or provide self- or peer-assessment, students need to know how to act on their own or others' assessments, much like they must understand how to use – and potentially enter into a dialogue with – teacher feedback.

Activity 2: Implementing formative assessment.

Imagine you're working with a class without giving grades and a parent complains that their child's work has not been marked. How would you respond? While the learning gains resulting from effective formative assessment are well documented, other groups, such as parents, may need to be convinced. Can you think of other possible barriers to its implementation and think about how they might be overcome?

Teachers' use of formative assessment: an illustrated example

We have looked at some factors to be considered in using formative assessment effectively but what would these look like in a mathematics classroom? We are aware that classrooms are dynamic environments. There's always much more going on and much more for teachers to consider in addition to implementing formative assessment practices. In this section, we explore how some teachers manage this in the mathematics classroom.

Our discussion of classroom practices is taken from Barnes' (2017) research on improving students' perseverance in mathematical reasoning. Two teachers of

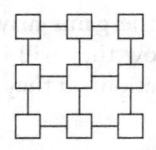

Number Differences
How can you arrange the numbers from 1 to 9 in the
squares on the adjacent grid so that the difference
between joined squares is odd? Why does this work?

Figure 19.2 Number differences.

(Source: adapted from NRICH, 2020)

Copyright statement:

10–11 year olds in different schools in England applied interventions to facilitate the learning of students with limited perseverance in mathematical reasoning. The interventions were designed to enable the students to follow a reasoned line of enquiry that resulted in justified arguments being formed. We are particularly interested in what the teachers did during their lessons and how their practices and interventions illustrate the concepts of formative assessment and the issues raised in this chapter when applied to a non-routine aspect of mathematics; mathematical reasoning. They used the ideas of learning objectives and success criteria to structure their thinking, planning and feedback.

The teachers in this example introduced the activity *Number Differences* (NRICH, 2020) in their classes, explaining the need to work out how to place the numbers and why the arrangement works (Figure 19.2). They provided students with number cards and a recording sheet with multiple blank 3 × 3 grids.

Activity 3: Analysing affordances and barriers to formative assessment.

Try the activity yourself, and consider where the barriers and affordances to formative assessment might lie.

How were the learning objectives and success criterion established?

This lesson focused on the development of students' perseverance in mathematical reasoning and particularly their capacity to pursue a line of reasoned enquiry resulting in the formation of generalisations and why these are true. The first learning outcome was formed from the reasoning aim of the National Curriculum for England and Wales (DfE, 2013), while the second learning objective for this lesson established the concepts that the students would reason about:

1   To form a generalisation and develop an argument about why it is true.
2   To reason about the odd/even property of the differences between numbers.

While the National Curriculum sets out that students first learn about the odd/even properties of number and the concept of subtraction as finding the difference between the ages of 5 and 7, it recognises that mathematics is an interconnected subject in which pupils should make rich connections across mathematical ideas to develop reasoning. Hence, reasoning about concepts that had been learned at an earlier stage of study provides opportunities for students to establish the rich connections necessary for successful mathematics learning.

In forming a success criterion from the learning objectives, the teachers considered the question: 'what will it look and sound like if students meet the learning objectives?' Generalising and forming convincing arguments formed the central focus of the lesson and the teachers translated this into accessible language for their 10–11 year old students to establish the success criterion: I am able to explain how to position the numbers and why this works.

Students' responses

The following examples illustrate the reasoning processes that the students engaged with. In the following section, we look at the teachers' assessments of these processes and their subsequent interventions to support students' work towards the success criteria (see Chapter 20 by Ian Jones for discussion on assessment of processes). As you read these, you might want to consider how you would respond.

Students making trials: Ruby, Alice, Emma and David began by manipulating number cards in a provisional way to create their first trials (Figure 19.3a). Initially their trials were randomly organised and resulted in both unsuccessful and successful solutions. When they found solutions that matched the criteria, they recorded these on a printed sheet. After they had established the odd/even pattern for successful solutions, Alice continued to find more solutions: "One more to go and then we've got 23!"

Students forming and testing conjectures: Michelle and Mary had formed the conjecture that odd and even numbers needed to be in adjacent positions,

Figure 19.3 Students forming and testing conjectures and making trials (a and b).

beginning with an odd number in the top left corner. They tested this conjecture by beginning with an even number in the top left corner. They realised that they were not able to use the remaining number 7 but needed an even number in the bottom right corner to maintain an odd difference between adjacent numbers, so they used a Numicon 2 (see Figure 19.3b). However, they then rejected this solution and conjecture as it did not use the numbers 1–9.

Students forming generalisations: David produced generalisations of the patterns made: "The odd numbers will always have to touch the even numbers. All you have to do is an even number here, an even number here, an even number here and an even number here [pointing to mid position of each side] and then the rest odd".

Teachers' assessments and interventions

So how did the teacher use formative assessment in this lesson? First, they noticed that some students had worked out the pattern to form successful solutions yet had persisted in applying the pattern to create more and more successful solutions. The teacher needed to move the learning forward towards the intended learning outcome, so used a short whole-class discussion as a form of intervention to refocus the students on forming generalisations with convincing arguments. Feedback such as "If you have 10 solutions and a pattern that works, then your job is to explain that pattern and why it works" was used to support students in understanding what was required of them. This is particularly important if students believe that pages of calculations are an indicator of success; they may need regular reminders of the success criteria (explain how to position the numbers and why this works) and guidance to stop creating solutions once they have established a pattern.

With other students, the teacher noticed that they were able to generalise how to find solutions but had not yet formed a convincing argument about why their method worked. Here, the teacher intervened, guiding the students to use sentence starters and reasoning connectives displayed in the class to frame their arguments, for example: if…then, because…, so… and to use diagrams to support their arguments. Further on in the lesson sequence, the teacher assessed that all students were able to form generalisations about how to arrange the numbers. However, while many were able to formulate convincing arguments about why the generalisation was true, not all did this. Therefore, and fitting succinctly with the assessment cycle, the teacher identified that future lessons need to focus on learning outcome 1, adapting learning outcome 2 to match the mathematical concepts within the next unit of work.

These lessons took place within the policy context of the National Curriculum of England and Wales. This policy sets the expectation that students should know, apply and understand the concepts, skills and processes specified in the programmes of study. The learning objectives were selected from these aims and programmes of study, and the success criterion was derived from these. Prior to the lesson, the teachers considered the indicators of partial success and the interventions that could be used when students demonstrated partial success. Planning for formative assessment in this way enabled the students to overcome barriers to success during the lesson.

> ## Activity 4: Integrating formative assessment into your practice.
>
> *Consider a lesson you have recently taught or observed:*
> *How might you construct one or more learning objectives for the lesson?*
> *What learning opportunities were/could have been provided to enable the children to meet the intended learning objective(s)?*
> *What did/could success look and sound like in relation to the learning objectives?*
> *What interventions were/could have been put in place during the lesson to support children to meet the learning outcomes?*
> *How might future lessons be adapted in light of reading this chapter?*

The student and learning at the heart of assessment

In this chapter we have examined some key debates in mathematics education, in particular those related to the nature of mathematics and how it could be taught and assessed. Through the key literature we identified some barriers to, and strategies to implement, effective formative assessment. We end this chapter through emphasising three key – and very much interrelated – concepts.

First, the student is central to effective formative assessment. They are a key player in a process, indeed they may even be enacting the process, identifying the next steps in and maintaining the journey towards the intended learning.

Second, to be able to apply formative assessment to inform students' mathematical understanding, our assessment practices need to extend to mathematical thinking, reasoning and problem-solving processes. While one could argue that thinking processes – alongside acquisition of facts and procedures – *could* be assessed through summative-style assessment practices such as written tests, these may give an incomplete picture of a learner's mathematical thinking, reasoning and problem-solving processes. Formative assessment is necessary to focus on the underpinning thinking processes, such as conjecturing and generalising, something which we argue is hard to capture through written summative evidence alone.

This brings us to the final key concept; it is essential for all parties to know what the intended learning is and what success in this learning looks like. At the same time, teachers need to be responsive to the unexpected, a theme explored by many contributors to this volume. We concur wholeheartedly with Wiliam (2004) that formative assessment is about 'instructional decision-making', but we recognise that this is not an easy or always predictable process; it is one which requires substantial investment of time and thought – sometimes in the moment – to be implemented effectively.

Further reading

While now more dated, we strongly recommend readers engage with the original Black Box series:

Black, P., & Wiliam, D. (1998). *Inside the black box: Raising standards through classroom assessment*. London: GL Assessment. This booklet offers a summary of the extensive research literature into formative assessment. It shows that there is clear evidence that improving formative assessment improves results, and offers evidence showing how formative assessment may be improved.

Black, P., Harrison, C., Lee, C., Marshall, B., & Wiliam, D. (2003). *Assessment for learning: Putting it into practice*. Buckingham: Open University Press. This book gives a fuller account of the earlier booklets: Inside the Black Box and Working inside the Black Box. It discusses four types of action: questioning, feedback by marking, peer- and self-assessment and the formative use of summative tests.

Hodgen, J., & Wiliam, D. (2006). *Mathematics inside the Black Box*. London: nferNelson. This booklet applies the findings in the earlier Assessment Reform Group publications to mathematics. It considers some principles for mathematics learning, activities that promote challenge and dialogue, questioning and listening, peer discussion, feedback and marking, and self- and peer-assessment.

We also point readers to the eight conference talks examining where things stand 20 years after the Black Box publication:

Multiple speakers. (2018). Assessment in Education: Principles, Policy and Practice 25th Anniversary Conference: Assessment for Learning 20 years after the Black Box. Department of Education, University of Oxford, March 13th 2018.

The NRICH Primary Team. (2014). *Reasoning: The journey from novice to expert*. Cambridge: University of Cambridge. <https://nrich.maths.org/11336≥ [Access date 11.02.2020].This article discusses strategies to support students' mathematical reasoning processes and details a suite of sentence starters to support them to communicate reasoning.

References

Barnes, A. (2017). *Improving children's perseverance in mathematical reasoning: creating the conditions for productive interplay between cognition and affect*, Doctoral Thesis, University of Brighton [online] <https://research.brighton.ac.uk/en/studentTheses/improving-childrens-perseverance-in-mathematical-reasoning-creati>[Accessdate11.02.2020].

Black, P., & Wiliam, D. (1998). *Inside the black box: Raising standards through classroom assessment*. London: GL Assessment.

Black, P., Harrison, C., Lee, C., Marshall, B., & Wiliam, D. (2004). Working inside the black box: Assessment for learning in the classroom. *Phi Delta Kappan, 86*(1), 8–21.

DfE. (2013). *National curriculum in England: Mathematics programmes of study*. London: Department for Education.

EEF. (2018). *Teaching & learning toolkit: Feedback*. London: Education Endowment Foundation.

Harrison, C. (2018). The beginning of the assessment for learning reform in the UK (part 1). Evidence Based Education Blog [online] < https://evidencebased.education/kmofap-assessment-for-learning-reform-part-1/> [Access date 11.02.2020].

Hodgen, J., & Wiliam, D. (2006). *Mathematics inside the Black Box*. London: nferNelson.

Hodgen, J., Foster, C., Marks, R., & Brown, M. (2018). *Improving mathematics in key stages two and three: Evidence review*. London: Education Endowment Foundation.

Mittler, P. J. (1973). *Assessment for learning in the mentally handicapped*. Edinburgh: Churchill Livingstone.

NRICH. (2020). *Number differences*. Cambridge: University of Cambridge. [online] <https://nrich.maths.org/2790> [Access date: 11.02.2020].

Panadero, E. (2018). Formative assessment: Where do we go from here? Paper presented to the *Assessment in Education: Principles, Policy and Practice 25th Anniversary conference*, Department of Education, University of Oxford, March 13th 2018.

Way, J. (2011). *Using questioning to stimulate mathematical thinking*. Cambridge: University of Cambridge. [online] <http://nrich.maths.org/2473> [Access date: 11.02.2020].

Wiliam, D. (2014). Formative assessment and contingency in the regulation of learning processes. Paper presented in *a Symposium entitled Toward a Theory of Classroom Assessment as the Regulation of Learning at the Annual Meeting of the American Educational Research Association*, Philadelphia, PA, April 2014.

Wiliam, D. (2018). Formative assessment: Confusions, clarifications, and prospects for consensus. Paper presented to the *Assessment in Education: Principles, Policy and Practice 25th Anniversary conference*, Department of Education, University of Oxford, March 13th 2018.

Acknowledgement

The authors would like to acknowledge Alice Onion who co-authored an earlier version of this chapter.

Chapter 20

The fitness and impact of GCSE mathematics examinations

Ian Jones

The General Certificate of Secondary Education (GCSE) in Mathematics is a course that is assessed by written examination taken by many 16-year-olds in England, Wales and Northern Ireland. Originally GCSE exams were qualifications designed for the end of compulsory schooling, and since school leaving age was raised to age 18 rather than age 16 the relevance of GCSEs as national summative assessments has been questioned (Ratcliffe 2014). The examination papers and the grades awarded are the subject of ongoing debates in the media and among people interested in secondary mathematics education. In this chapter I will explore two central themes of these debates. The first is the contention that the examination papers sat by children are not fit for purpose because they lack 'rigour' and are getting 'easier' over time. This is a widely held belief commonly propagated by some politicians and by elements of the media. The key evidence for this contention is the year on year increase in the number of students getting higher grades, leading to a change in grade structure and moving from letter to numeric grades from 2015. The second debate theme I will consider is that GCSE exams present mathematics as a fragmented discipline made up of isolated ideas, rather than as a coherent body of connected ideas. This is a belief common among teachers, researchers and other professionals who are concerned this fragmentary presentation has a detrimental impact on how mathematics is perceived, taught and learned in many secondary classrooms.

I begin the chapter by providing a brief summary of the history and purpose of GCSE mathematics exams, before describing how they are designed, administered and marked. I then consider the debates around fitness for purpose and fragmentation in some detail. Finally, I reflect on the promise and potential drawbacks of alternative approaches to the current ways of doing things.

Background

In England, Wales and Northern Ireland, GCSE courses were introduced in 1986 as a replacement for the previous system in which children considered to be in the top 20% were entered for 'Ordinary level' exams, intended as preparation for post-compulsory education towards 'Advanced level' exams. The next 40% took the 'Certificate of Secondary Education' (CSE) exams intended as preparation for the world of work and 40% of pupils were not expected to take any examination; therefore, the system was not designed to cater for the full attainment range. This system was increasingly considered unfair, partly due to the perception of CSEs as second rate.

A key GCSE development across many subjects was the introduction of coursework to complement exams. Since then mathematics assessment has often been somewhat out of step with other GCSE subjects. For example, in 2009 coursework was dropped from mathematics, but no other subject, due to overwhelmingly negative responses from mathematics teachers (QCA 2006). Their main concerns were that it was difficult to know if the work was wholly the students, and some coursework tasks assumed a high level of literacy.

Unlike most other subjects, mathematics was offered at three tiers of difficulty until 2006 when it changed to two tiers in line with other GCSEs. Mathematics differed from the two other 'core' subjects, namely English and Science, by only offering a single qualification rather than two or three, despite requiring a similar amount of effort (Smith 2004). For example, many students are entered for two qualifications in English for language and literature. More recently, the linked pair pilot GCSE, offering two qualifications in 'Methods in Mathematics' and 'Applications of Mathematics', was intended to address this perceived imbalance (Vordermann et al. 2011) but has since been discontinued.

> *What mathematical knowledge and skills should we expect of school leavers?*
> *Should GCSE exams assess pure mathematics as preparation for further study, or*
> *applied mathematics as preparation for work and life?*

How exams get made

Unlike national Key Stage tests, commonly called SATs and written by government sponsored agencies, GCSEs and A-level exams have traditionally been produced by several independent organisations known as examination boards or 'awarding bodies' (ABs). Originally the ABs were regional but over time they have merged, resulting in a handful of competing ABs in England, Wales and Northern Ireland. At the time of writing, five ABs produce GCSE mathematics exams.

The ABs work to tight government requirements setting out the percentage of each examination paper that must test content knowledge and problem-solving skills and the percentage of questions that must be set in 'real-world' contexts. Each AB produces detailed specifications of the mathematics students are expected to learn, and these are submitted to the government regulator for accreditation.

A given examination paper and its mark scheme are usually drafted by an individual examiner. Examiners tend to be practising or retired teachers who draw on their knowledge of students and previous exams when producing new papers. They work to very tight deadlines and often recycle old questions, tweaking the contexts and examples used. In order to ensure the paper conforms to government regulations the examination writer completes a tick list known as an 'assessment grid'. The assessment grid contains columns referencing the required content (statistics, algebra and so on), processes (knowledge recall, problem-solving and so on) and difficulty (questions spanning all grades from 1 to 9) that the examination paper must cover. For every question part the writer completes a row of the assessment grid to create an at-a-glance picture of the overall balance across the paper.

Once a paper has been drafted, the writer sends it to other examiners for feedback and then revises it accordingly. The paper is further reviewed and modified at a meeting of a Question Paper Evaluation Committee (QPEC). A QPEC meeting usually lasts a day or two, during which time several papers by different writers are tabled. QPECs are chaired by a Chief Examiner and attended by up to a dozen examiners, including the writers of the tabled papers. QPEC meetings can be intensive events in which papers are picked apart and writers have to decide when to concede and when to defend their work. The committee works through each paper one question at a time, checking everything from punctuation and formatting to mathematical content and coherence.

In addition the QPEC will consider the accessibility of questions to all candidates from a wide spectrum of economic, social and cultural backgrounds. I observed one meeting in which the phrase 'elderflower cordial' was changed to 'orange squash' as it was felt this would make the question more accessible to a broader range of candidates, particularly those from working-class backgrounds. However, ensuring that all candidates are equally well served by the phrasing and situating of questions is an all but impossible task, and research shows that working-class students are systematically disadvantaged by the contexts used (see Cooper and Dunne 2000 and Chapter 4 by Peter Gates and Andy Noyes).

This question proofing is demanding work and takes up the bulk of time and energy in QPECs. The assessment grid is continually referenced and often amended for each question, and then checked again once the paper is complete. Sometimes a paper is signed off for publication at the end of a meeting, other times the writer has to undertake revisions and present it to the committee again at a later date. Interestingly, and perhaps worryingly, GCSE examination papers are never trialled with students before publication.

A given examination paper might be sat by anywhere from a few dozen up to tens of thousands of students. Once complete the scripts are collected and scanned and a sample analysed in order to amend the mark scheme. Marking procedures vary across ABs. Some contract teachers to mark entire scripts, others contract clerics, undergraduates and teachers to mark individual questions. The work is usually done electronically to avoid the costs and inefficiencies of transferring thousands of paper scripts around the country. Examiners moderate the marking, checking the quality and remarking a sample to ensure consistency. Statistical analyses are conducted to check the performance of the examination, and an examiners' report is produced describing how students responded to the questions.

Once every script has been allocated a mark, a great deal of effort goes into assigning grade boundaries. Much of this work is undertaken by awarding meeting panels made up of examiners using statistical data and samples of scripts. Examiners tend to be conscientious people who go to great lengths to ensure that students are treated fairly and given the benefit of any doubt. Nevertheless, the panel is under great pressure to ensure the grade boundaries are consistent with other examination papers, other ABs and, notwithstanding the recent change in grade structure, and from letter to numeric grades, previous years. (See Robinson 2007 for detailed descriptions of the processes involved.)

The final outcome is that every script is assigned a grade. Where a school is concerned that a student may not have received the correct grade an enquiry can be made. The AB investigates to check for errors, and corrects the grade where necessary. If the school is still not satisfied it can appeal against the grade. This is a more serious process that only results in a handful of grade changes every year across all GCSE subjects (Ofqual 2011).

Fit for purpose?

GCSE results are published every August to great media fanfare and, almost inevitably, frenzied concerns about the standards of education compared to previous years. This often leads to claims that GCSE exams are not fit for the purpose of assessing mathematical achievement. This is partly because recent decades have seen increasing numbers of students obtaining higher grades year on year.

For example, in 2001 the number of students achieving a grade C or higher was 50.1%, by 2011 it had crept up to 58.8%. This could be interpreted as implying children's mathematical achievement is increasing in some objective manner. Perhaps students really are improving due to better teaching or higher aspirations and expectations. However, the improvements in GCSE grades over time are not matched by international measures (for example OECD 2010) or independent research (for example Coe 2007).

A common perception is that examination papers are getting easier over time (for example Clark et al. 2010). ABs have been accused of making examination papers predictable, producing textbooks that focus narrowly on tested content (for example Paton 2012) and advising teachers how to gameplay exams (for example Newell and Watt 2011). Others claim that an increased performativity culture is putting greater pressure on students and teachers to ensure high grades (Walport et al. 2010). This is said to have led over time to more cramming and examination training in classrooms, as well as schools directing a disproportionate amount of resources towards borderline students and, up until their abolishment in 2012, an over reliance on resits. Further reasons offered for recent 'grade inflation' are that markers are overly generous (for example Cooper 2012), and awarding meeting panels tend to give borderline students the benefit of the doubt (Cresswell 1986). More generally, the number of qualifications has increased as students are offered more 'pathways' through learning mathematics (see Chapter 21 by Cathy Smith), stretching the capacity of the national assessment system. Some researchers (for example Coe 2010) have questioned the very notion of maintaining a fixed standard from the past, arguing it is undermined by the updating of content to ensure qualifications remain relevant, and by ongoing changes to government regulations such as the introduction and subsequent dropping of modular courses. The recent switch from awarding letter to numeric grades in 2017 is a case in point. The new numeric grades were deliberately calibrated to not map directly to the old letter grades, making it difficult to meaningfully compare standards spanning 2015–2016.

Despite the controversies and differences of opinion about standards over time, there does exist some consensus among educators, researchers and other interested parties that the content of GCSE mathematics exams is inadequate. For example, researchers scrutinised 100 Grade A students' scripts and concluded that the examination papers did not adequately assess algebra (Noyes et al. 2011). Some students had got full marks on supposedly algebraic questions by using purely arithmetical trial-and-improvement techniques. Others had obtained their A grade despite avoiding algebra questions altogether.

> *Is it meaningful to have a single measure or grade for everything that is encompassed by the term 'mathematics'? What would be the pros and cons of measuring and grading different components of mathematics separately?*

The fragmentation of GCSE mathematics

Another widely expressed concern is that GCSE mathematics exams contain too many short questions that test rote learning, and not enough long questions that test sustained reasoning (Vorderman et al. 2011). In a typical examination paper each question part is worth less than three marks on average, and most question parts are worth just one or two marks. Taking a mark per minute as a rough guide this suggests that the average length of reasoning chains expected of students is less than three minutes, including the time required to read the questions. This fragmented nature of mathematics exams stands in contrast to many other GCSEs, and this remains the case despite attempts by government regulators to encourage more substantial questions.

The combination of pressure to achieve high grades and the fragmentary nature of examination papers is reported to have a detrimental impact on the teaching and learning of mathematics in secondary classrooms (DfE 2011). The short questions that make up the bulk of GCSE exams test the recall and application of memorised facts, and so this is where many teachers focus their mathematics lessons to help students achieve high grades. Ofsted (2008) reported that:

> higher order skills underpin what it means to behave mathematically. It is of serious concern, therefore, that national tests do not require students to use and apply mathematics in substantial tasks through which they are able to decide what approaches to adopt, use a range of mathematical techniques in exploring the problem, find solutions, generalise and communicate their reasoning. The importance of these skills is highlighted in the new National Curriculum's key processes and they underpin the recently published standards for functional mathematics. However, unless external assessments reflect these important processes, they are unlikely to influence a significant shift in teaching and learning mathematics. (p. 35)

As such, even those students who obtain high grades are sometimes unable to use or apply their mathematics outside of the narrow constraints of GCSE examination papers. Higher education institutions and employers report that school leavers lack the necessary mathematical knowledge and skills for further study and the workplace (Walport et al. 2010). It is now common for employers and higher education institutions to offer in-house mathematics training and support to compensate for this (Hoyles et al. 2010). Moreover, many 16-year-olds are turned off by the thought of studying mathematics beyond compulsory schooling. Less than 20% go on to study any further mathematics at all, far fewer than most comparable countries (Hodgen et al. 2010).

The causes of fragmentation

Why are the questions in GCSE mathematics exams so fragmented? There are several contributing mechanisms (Jones 2010). As described above, ABs must ensure their exams conform to precise government regulations. The most direct way to achieve this is to use many short questions, each of which corresponds to a specific requirement that can be ticked off in the assessment grid.

Market forces are also considered to be a fragmentary pressure on examination papers. ABs are in financial competition with one another to sell their assessment services to schools, and teachers are in a performativity culture that incentivises them to choose those exams papers they consider the most predictable and passable. It is easier to train students to pass exams containing many short questions that test recall than fewer long questions that test sustained reasoning.

Another fragmentary pressure is the need for exams to achieve acceptably high marking reliability. Marking reliability can be thought of as 'marking repeatability', that is the extent to which each student would have obtained the same grade if his or her examination script had been marked by a different examiner. Marking reliability can be increased by making the examination up from many short questions that have a limited range of 'right' answers. For example, multiple choice tests have perfect marking reliability because there is no ambiguity as to whether each question has been answered correctly or not.

Acknowledgement of this fragmentation has led to regular reforms to increase the amount of non-routine mathematics such as problem-solving questions and applying mathematics to real-world contexts. A recent revision is the tightened requirement for ABs to ensure that 25–30% of the marks available in GCSE exams are awarded for mathematical problem-solving, increased from 15% to 25% prior to 2015. Moreover the definition of problem-solving, known as Assessment Objective 3 (AO3) in the technical jargon, has been updated and extended (Holmes et al. 2017). Prior to 2015 AO3 was defined as students being able to "interpret and analyse problems and generate strategies to solve them" (Ofqual 2009, p. 9). The revised statement for AO3 (Ofqual 2015, p. 6) reads

AO3: Solve problems within mathematics and in other contexts.
Students should be able to:

- translate problems in mathematical or non-mathematical contexts into a process or a series of mathematical processes;
- make and use connections between different parts of mathematics;
- interpret results in the context of the given problem;
- evaluate methods used and results obtained;
- evaluate solutions to identify how they may have been affected by assumptions made.

An analysis of sample assessment materials published by ABs in response to the revised requirements for AO3 found that the new style of problem-solving questions reflected three main characteristics (Holmes et al. 2017). First, there were multiple possible methods for answering a question. Second, and related to the first characteristic, the initial step required to answer a question was not obvious or explicitly stated. Third, there was no standard or preferred way to answer a question, all methods were equally valid in terms of the mathematical knowledge and skills required. Nevertheless, whether such reforms to GCSE mathematics exams result in superficial or substantive reductions of fragmentation is a matter of debate (Noyes et al. 2011).

Alternative forms of *assessment*

Are there alternative ways to assess students that might better match the revised AO3? We don't have to look too far for ideas. As noted above, mathematics is one of the few GCSE subjects to be assessed entirely by written exams. Most other GCSE subjects at least include a 'controlled assessment' component, which typically involves practical work completed under examination-like conditions. Inspiration can also be found around the world. For example, summative mathematics assessment in Sweden includes an oral component.

Many experts agree that summative assessments should be based on a diverse set of evidence including written exams, project work, practical investigations and oral exams (for example Black and Wiliam 2014; Schoenfeld 2002; Swan 1993; The Royal Society 2014). This can help overcome problems that undermine the appropriateness of more traditional assessments. It can also address the detrimental aspects of 'teaching to the test' by providing 'tests worth teaching to'. A broad base of evidence might better assess the intentions of Key Stage 4 mathematics reproduced above, and could include the components shown in Table 20.1.

> *What do you think might be the benefits and drawbacks of each type of assessment listed above? What other types of evidence not listed could be used to assess students' mathematical achievements?*

Table 20.1 Possible components of a broader approach to assessing Key Stage 4 mathematics

Content-based	Recall and application of content assessed using short, structured questions requiring short answers, which might include well-designed multiple choice questions.
Problem-based	Deep understanding of mathematics assessed through problem-solving questions. Examples of such questions designed for use in the United States can be seen on the website of the Mathematics Assessment Project (see annotated bibliography).
Practical	Mathematical proficiency assessed using a variety of mathematical tools to complete a given task. These might be manual, using protractors, compasses and so on, or digital, using, for example, spreadsheets, simulations or graphical calculators. Evidence collected could include the finished artefact as well as multimedia files (photographs, movies, audiorecordings).
Choice	Students choose from a range of questions within a paper. The nature of choice offered would need to be carefully designed. For example, all questions might require similar mathematical knowledge and understanding but focus on applying it to different contexts.
Oral	Students attend a face-to-face interview in which they are asked about the mathematics they have learnt.
Comprehension	A mathematical text is presented followed by a set of questions to test understanding, analogous to a comprehension test in language subjects. Following the example of Nuffield A level Physics (Black, 2008) the text might be about a topic not explicitly taught during the course.
Essay	Students produce a creative piece of mathematical work in response to a short, open prompt. Such a prompt might be "Write everything you know about prime numbers", or a carefully chosen photograph and the statement "Describe all the mathematics shown in the picture".
Portfolio	Samples of work are collated over the two-year duration of a GCSE course and compiled to produce a portfolio of evidence of mathematical learning for each student.

Alternative forms of *assessing*

As discussed above, awarding bodies outsource marking to clerics, undergraduates and teachers who undertake extra work in their holidays. Students and their teachers are not involved in assessing their own work, and some argue that they should be (for example see Chapter 19 by Alison Barnes and Rachel Marks). This might enable learners to feel more engaged with assessment, and teachers to use it diagnostically to help with further learning.

There are understandable concerns about placing the assessment process in the hands of students and their teachers. The system is open to abuse and indeed this was one of the concerns that led to the abandonment of coursework for GCSE mathematics in the late noughties, and any shift must be approached cautiously. However, quality can be checked by independently reassessing a sample of students' work. Moreover, research suggests that peers tend to be fair and are often more consistent than their teachers when assessing one another (Topping 2003). In addition, teacher assessment is used for summative assessment in some countries around the world, demonstrating that it is possible to do (Askew et al. 2010).

Another concern about involving students and their teachers in summative assessment is that it implies a shift away from using standardised mark schemes and towards relying on peer and expert judgement. This is problematic because judgement is based on subjective opinion, whereas mark schemes attempt to set out what should be credited in an objective manner (Laming 2004). Using judgement for assessment has been shown to be consistently less reliable than using standardised mark schemes. Low reliability is not merely a technical inconvenience, in practice it has been shown to introduce bias into the assessment system, to the detriment of students from ethnic minority backgrounds (Gillborn 2008).

Until recently this was perhaps an insurmountable challenge. However, recent technological developments mean that it is now possible to produce rank orders of students in terms of mathematical achievement that are based on human judgement and yet are as reliable as rank orders produced by marking. This is achieved by presenting judges with pairs of students' work and asking them to decide which of the two has demonstrated the greater mathematical achievement. The outcomes from many such pairings can be used to construct a robust rank order (Jones and Inglis 2015; Pollitt 2012). Objections to placing peer and expert judgement at the heart of assessment may therefore weaken over coming years.

Concluding comments

How might an aspiring mathematics teacher respond to the burdens, opportunities and debates around GCSE exams? For many teachers the existing regime is undesirable but real. The only fair thing to do is to train students to obtain the best grades they can, thereby improving their life chances. For others the examination system is a challenge but not a barrier to teaching mathematics in an engaging and conceptually satisfying manner. Some argue that, despite all the problems and debates, the best way to prepare students for GCSE exams, as well as further study, the world of work and life in the modern world, is to teach as well as possible, and in the style most suited to you and your students.

Further reading

Commons Education Select Committee (2018) *Education Committee: Publications*, London: UK Parliament. http://www.parliament.uk/business/committees/committees-a-z/commons-select/education-committee/publications/. What do politicians, regulators, awarding bodies and others in positions of power really think about GCSE exams? The Commons Education Select Committee publish a wealth of candid and revealing minutes and reports that can be downloaded for free from the provided url. It takes a little perseverance to dig through but for those interested in high-level politics it is well worth the effort.

Mansell, W. (2007) *Education by Numbers: The Tyranny of Testing*, London: Politicos Publishing Ltd. http://educationbynumbers.org.uk. Warwick Mansell is a well-known education journalist with a particular interest in the effects of testing on teaching and learning. His book and blog offer a highly readable and somewhat alarming overview of issues and debates surrounding high-stakes assessment across all school subjects including mathematics.

Mathematics Assessment Project (2015) Mathematics Assessment Resource Service. http://map.mathshell.org/materials/index.php. The mathematics education group at the University of Nottingham are well known internationally for producing high quality assessment materials. Sample prototype materials from the "Mathematics Assessment Project" can be downloaded for free from the provided url.

Newton, P. et al. (2007) *Techniques for Monitoring the Comparability of Examination Standards*, London: Qualifications and Curriculum Authority. https://www.gov.uk/government/publications/techniques-for-monitoring-the-comparability-of-examination-standards. This edited book offers an authoritative and detailed overview of how examination standards are monitored and maintained, and provides thoughtful discussions of the debates and limitations of different methods. It can be downloaded for free from the provided url.

Ofqual (2015) *A Comparison of Expected Difficulty, Actual Difficulty and Assessment of Problem Solving across GCSE Mathematics Sample Assessment Materials*, Coventry: Office of Qualifications and Examinations Regulation. https://www.gov.uk/government/publications/gcse-maths-final-research-report-and-regulatory-summary. A technical report on Ofqual's research into the impact of the 2015 reforms to increase the quality and quantity of problem-solving questions in GCSE mathematics exams. By reading this report you can gain an informed opinion as to whether such reforms result in substantive or superficial reductions in the fragmentation of Key Stage 4 assessment.

Research in Mathematics Education (2017) *Special Issue on Summative Assessment*. https://www.tandfonline.com/toc/rrme20/19/2. Recently the UK's top academic journal for mathematics education research published a special issue on summative assessment. The special includes papers on GCSE mathematics, as well as studies from around the world and at other levels of mathematics education.

Swan, M. (2006) 'Learning GCSE mathematics through discussion: what are the effects on students?', *Journal of Further and Higher Education*, 30: 229–241. Malcolm Swan challenges the widespread assumption that teaching to the test is the most efficient way to improve students' grades. Swan demonstrates this for the case of students retaking GCSE mathematics after compulsory schooling. These students are often particularly disheartened and demotivated.

References

Askew, M., Hodgen, J., Hossain, S. and Bretscher, N. (2010) *Values and Variables: Mathematics Education in High-Performing Countries*, London: Nuffield Foundation.

Black, P. (2008) 'Strategic decisions: ambitions, feasibility and context', *Educational Designer*, 1: 1–26.

Black, P. and Wiliam, D. (2014) 'Assessment and the design of educational materials', *Educational Designer*, 2: 1–20.

Clark, L., Harris, S. and Walton, M. (2010) 'GCSE results 2010: Record number pass a year early including a 5-year-old', *Mail Online*. Online. Available at HTTP: www.dailymail.co.uk/news/article-1305902/GCSE-RESULTS-2010-Record-number-pass-year-early-including-5-year-old.html (accessed 4 January 2018).

Coe, R. (2007) *Changes in Standards at GCSE and A-Level: Evidence from ALIS and YELLIS*, Durham: Durham University.

Coe, R. (2010) 'Understanding comparability of examination standards', *Research Papers in Education*, 25: 271–284.

Cooper, R. (2012) 'Generous' examiners to blame for inflated A-level and GCSE grades', *Mail Online*. Online. Available at HTTP: www.dailymail.co.uk/news/article-2088717/Generous-examiners-blame-inflated-A-level-GCSE-grades.html (accessed 4 January 2018).

Cooper, B. and Dunne, M. (2000) *Assessing Children's Mathematical Knowledge: Social Class, Sex and Problem-Solving*, Buckingham, Open University Press.

Cresswell, M. J. (1986) 'A review of borderline reviewing', *Educational Studies*, 12: 175–190.

DfE (2011) *The Independent Evaluation of the Pilot of the Linked Pair of GCSEs in Mathematics - First Interim Report*, London: Department for Education.

Gillborn, D. (2008) *Racism and Education: Coincidence or Conspiracy?* London: Routledge.

Hodgen, J. et al. (2010) *Is the UK an Outlier? An International Comparison of Upper Secondary Mathematics Education*, London: Nuffield Foundation.

Holmes, S., He, Q. and Meadows, M. (2017) 'An investigation of construct relevant and irrelevant features of mathematics problem-solving questions using comparative judgement and Kelly's Repertory Grid', *Research in Mathematics Education*, 19: 112–129.

Hoyles, C., Noss, R. and Kent, P. (2010) *Improving Mathematics at Work: The Need for Techno-Mathematical Literacies*, Abingdon, UK: Taylor & Francis.

Jones, I. (2010) 'Why do GCSE examination papers look like they do?', In *Informal Proceedings of the British Society for Research into Learning Mathematics*, Newcastle-upon-Tyne, November 2010. Newcastle: BSRLM, pp. 61–66.

Jones, I. and Inglis, M., (2015) 'The problem of assessing problem solving: Can comparative judgement help?', *Educational Studies in Mathematics*, 89: 337–355.

Laming, D. (2004) 'Marking university examinations: some lessons from psychophysics', *Psychology Learning and Teaching*, 3: 89–96.

Newell, C. and Watt, H. (2011) 'Examination boards: 'We're cheating, we're telling you the question cycle'' *The Telegraph*. Online. Available HTTP:www.telegraph.co.uk/education/secondaryeducation/8940799/Examination-boards-Were-cheating-were-telling-you-the-question-cycle.html (accessed 4 January 2018).

Noyes, A., Wake, G., Drake, P. and Murphy, R. (2011) *Evaluating Mathematics Pathways: Final Report*, London: Department for Education.

OECD (2010) *PISA 2009 Results: What Students Know and Can Do – Student Performance in Reading, Mathematics and Science* (Vol. 1), Paris: OECD Publishing.

Ofqual (2009) *GCSE Subject Criteria for Mathematics*, Coventry: Office of Qualifications and Examinations Regulation.

Ofqual (2011) *Appeals Against Results for GCSE and GCE: Summer 2010 Examinations Series*, Coventry: Office of Qualifications and Examinations Regulation.

Ofqual (2015) *GCSE Subject Level Guidance for Mathematics*, Coventry: Office of Qualifications and Examinations Regulation.

Ofsted (2008) *Mathematics: Understanding the Score*, London: Office for Standards in Education.

Paton, G. (2012) 'Head attacks 'aggressive commercialisation' of exams' *The Telegraph*. Online. Available at HTTP: www.telegraph.co.uk/education/education-news/9003153/Head-attacks-aggressive-commercialisation-of-exams.html (accessed 4 January 2018).

Pollitt, A. (2012) 'Comparative judgement for assessment', *International Journal of Technology and Design Education*, 22: 157–170.

QCA (2006) *QCA's Review of Standards: Description of the Programme*, London: Qualifications and Curriculum Authority.

Ratcliffe, R. (2014) 'What is the point of GCSEs?', *The Guardian*. Online. Available at HTTP: https://www.theguardian.com/education/2014/aug/19/are-gcses-still-relevant-education-training-age-18 (accessed 27 Dec 2018).

Robinson, C. (2007) 'Awarding examination grades: current progresses and their evolution', in P. Newton et al. (eds.) *Techniques for Monitoring the Comparability of Examination Standards*, London: Qualifications and Curriculum Authority.

Schoenfeld, A. (2002) 'Making mathematics work for all children: issues of standards, testing, and equity', *Educational Researcher*, 31: 13–25.

Smith, A. (2004) *Making Mathematics Count*, London: The Stationary Office.

Swan, M. (1993) 'Improving the design and balance of mathematical assessment', in Miss, M. (ed.), *Investigations into Assessment in Mathematics Education* (pp. 195–216). Dordrecht: Springer-Science + Business Media.

The Royal Society (2014) *Vision for Science and Mathematics Education: The Royal Society Science Policy Centre report 01/14*, London: The Royal Society.

Topping, K. (2003). 'Self and peer assessment in school and university: Reliability, validity and utility', in M. Segers, F. Dochy, and E. Cascallar (eds.), *Optimising New Modes of*

Assessment: In Search of Qualities and Standards (Vol. 1, pp. 55–87). Dordrecht: Kluwer Academic Publishers.

Vorderman, C. Porkess, R., Budd, C., Dunne, R. and Rahman-Hart, P. (2011) *A World-Class Mathematics Education for all our Young People*, London: The Conservative Party.

Walport, M., Goodfellow, J., McLoughlin, F., Post, M., Sjøvoll, J., Taylor, M. and Waboso, D. (2010) *Science and Mathematics Secondary Education for the 21st Century: Report of the Science and Learning Expert Group*, London: Department for Business, Industry and Skills.

Chapter 21

Choosing the future

Which mathematics?

Cathy Smith

In this chapter I look at two questions that concern policy and research in post-compulsory mathematics. The questions are:

- How can we understand and compare different mathematical courses of study?
- How can we understand students' choices to study mathematics?

As in most long-lasting education debates, the answers are not simple: they depend on how you approach – and theorise – education, what you think is convincing evidence, and whether you are setting out to understand mathematics in schools or to change it. I discuss these ideas in the context of academic mathematics pathways on offer for 16-year-olds in England. I then introduce some of my own research, arguing more widely that the ways that we understand and try to change school mathematics are not just about mathematics but also about how we view adolescence and progress. These questions will resonate across other national contexts where, for example, issues of choice, identity and ways of being mathematically are intertwined with the structure and variety of mathematics courses and formal assessments available.

All students in mainstream education in England and Wales study mathematics until they take a General Certificate of Secondary Education (GCSE) examination at age 16. GCSE grades carry high stakes: those who do not reach a 'pass' grade (denoted C–A* until 2017 and 4–9 thereafter) are required to repeat the examination in the subsequent year. Academic-track 16–18 year-olds, preparing for university, then study three main Advanced level (A-level) subjects which may or may not include Mathematics. There is typically time for one supplementary course, which may lead to repeating GCSE Mathematics or English, another A-level, an extended project or a relatively new qualification, Core Maths. England is out of step with other nations in allowing mathematics to be optional at age 16 for those who have reached a threshold level (Hodgen, 2010). This is the rationale that caused the government in 2015 to ask examination boards to produce the Core Maths qualification, filling this gap and setting a goal for near-universal, but still optional, participation in some form of mathematics post-16 (Smith, 2017).

When students get a choice, they use it. Research into students' experiences of learning mathematics suggests that many are profoundly disengaged from their mathematics lessons and simply do not want to continue. As one oft-quoted student puts it, "I would rather die!" (Brown, Brown and Bibby, 2008), while another less dramatically comments "You have done it every year and it just gets kind of tiring" (Murray, 2011, p. 278). A large survey (Noyes and Adkins, 2016) of students who had 'passed' GCSE found strong opposition to compulsory mathematics at age 16 – particularly among those with grades B and C who were precisely the Core Maths target group.

These findings of stable and widespread disengagement might suggest a downturn in studying mathematics post-16. In fact, examination data over the last 20 years has shown a dramatic fall, but then rises in the number of Mathematics A-level candidates (Figure 21.1). It is clear that students' choices do not depend just on past experiences but also involve their future aspirations and society's expectations. Families, schools and governments understand choosing mathematics as a way to brighten individuals' life prospects and the whole country's economic future. One of the roles of mathematics education research is to examine how the curriculum could (or should) meet these economic and political goals in the light of our knowledge about students' learning.

> *Think of an adult colleague who chose to stop studying mathematics at age 16. What arguments might convince him or her that mathematics should have been compulsory post-16?*
> *How would you argue differently to convince a current 16-year-old?*

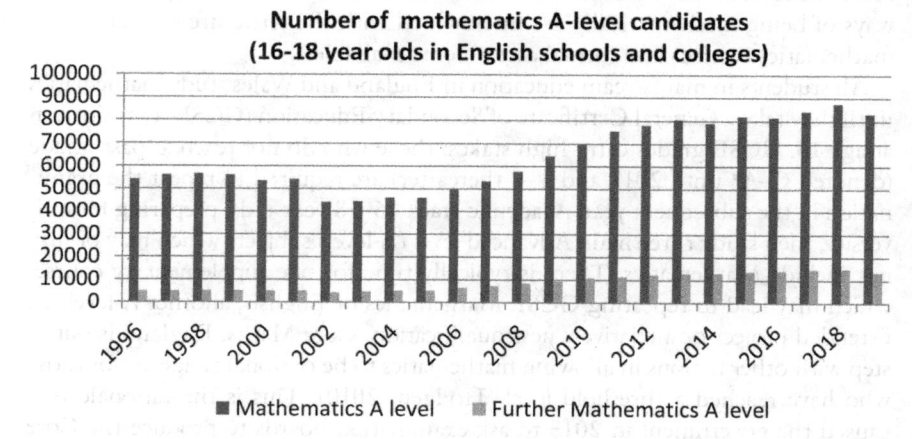

Number of mathematics A-level candidates (16-18 year olds in English schools and colleges)

■ Mathematics A level   ■ Further Mathematics A level

Figure 21.1 Number of Mathematics A-level candidates (16–18 year olds entering A2 in English schools and colleges).

Post-16 study in England is organised by target qualifications. There are three main examination boards in England, which compete for school entries by offering different versions of qualifications based on characteristics specified by the government. New mathematics A-level specifications were introduced in 2017 for first examination in 2019. There are two mathematics A-levels, although (capital-M) Mathematics is by far the most common, with 81,000 students completing in 2016. Representing 11% of all A-levels taken, this was the highest proportion since 1996. It is notoriously hard to match examination data over time, but this is probably just below the 1980s numbers. The major change to its content in 2017 was that all students must study some mechanics and some statistics.

The second A-level, Further Mathematics, is a traditional supplement for students who want to extend their mathematics. It includes topics such as complex numbers and integrating with partial fractions. It has been viewed as an elite option available only in a minority of schools, mostly large or private ones (Matthews and Pepper, 2007). Recently numbers have risen (Figure 21.1) after government-funded promotion among students, teachers, parents and universities. Further Mathematics is of particular interest because of its gateway function for high-status STEM fields of science, technology and engineering and mathematics. This gives it a prominent role in the processes of including and excluding students through mathematics (Smith, 2010).

The new Core Maths qualification was taken by around 6,800 students in 2018. It is intended as a two-year course that strengthens the mathematics students have learnt at GCSE (for example introducing functions that model exponential growth and decay, and tackling rates of change without calculus) and introduces new statistical techniques. It focuses on applying mathematics and statistics in authentic situations: selecting and applying mathematical ideas to represent, analyse and address questions about those contexts.

Potentially then, there are three parallel, academic post-16 pathways in mathematics (Core Maths, Mathematics and Further Mathematics): 'parallel' in their timing but pitched at different conceptions of mathematics and its uses. These particular examples are specific to England, but we find similar stratifications and purposes in other western education pre-university systems, for example Australia, or the European and International Baccalaureates. Of course, in most Baccalaureate systems mathematics is compulsory, while in the United Kingdom (and Australia) students enjoy more autonomy. However, this self-determination comes with the responsibility for students to make – and be seen to make – successful choices and to achieve the grades that prove them. The responsibility to choose instils a combination of freedom and self-scrutiny that follows the contemporary western model of neoliberal governance, through which individuals' will to act is acknowledged and also used to reinforce institutional practices (Rose, 1999, see also Chapter 7 by Anna Llewellyn).

Comparing mathematics pathways

We are used to thinking of mathematics as a hierarchical subject, where each topic relies on knowledge lower down in the hierarchy. When we do recognise strands, we talk of organising them in a spiral curriculum, with mathematical topics building on each other and increasing in complexity and abstraction. So in describing the three courses above, it makes sense to acknowledge their different starting and end points: Core Maths has its roots in GCSE but overlaps with A-level Mathematics, while Further Mathematics extends it. Implicitly, then, we often think of mathematics courses as lying along a single dimension. This hierarchy of abstract content makes them easy to compare and hard to claim as equivalent.

However, it is also common to think about qualifications as equivalent. The institutional structures of schools suggest this by organising the curriculum into timetable slots, in mix-and-match subject combinations. Equivalence is also suggested when the University and College Admissions system (UCAS) awards points to grades regardless of subject. Mathematics and Further Mathematics are both two-year A-level courses with embedded AS-level examinations for exit after one year, and score the same UCAS points. Core Maths has the same teaching time as the AS-level and earns the same UCAS points (slightly less than an extended project). Looking wider, in the classification that extends across academic, technical and vocational education, A-levels and Core Maths are all 'Level 3' qualifications, which means that holders can gain and apply knowledge in situations that are detailed and complex, but well-defined. Assessment researchers argue that similarly named qualifications should be worth the same over time and between subjects, because that is how wider society can understand their meaning and trust in their fairness (Coe et al., 2008).

Against these institutional assumptions, we have the hierarchy of disciplines and the social judgements of employers and universities. In 2011 the self-styled elite Russell group of universities in the United Kingdom published a list of 'facilitating' A-levels. These included Mathematics and Further Mathematics and excluded newer A-levels such as Law. The existence of elite preferences is not surprising; it is part of the 'grapevine' knowledge that sustains middle-class educational privilege (Ball, Maguire and Macrae, 2000).

This list reopened arguments that A-level subjects do have different intrinsic values, and specifically that mathematics needs more recognition and must be defended from innovation. Previous efforts to widen the range of pathways, such as introducing an A-level in Use of Maths, were a particular focus of criticism. The political think-tank Educators for Reform (2009) suggested that "poorly-informed students – in particular those at the weaker schools" – would be distracted by the implied equivalence, choose the wrong pathway and end up excluded from further STEM study. Use of Maths is now discontinued but was in many ways a precursor to Core Maths (for a student-focused evaluation, see Wake, Williams and Drake, 2011). Until the 2017 changes, A-level Mathematics itself included a choice of option modules in mechanics, statistics or decision mathematics. These could be combined to give breadth, or depth, or to reflect teacher expertise. Universities supported this diversity because it allowed the range of applications to flourish, particularly mechanics which is difficult without physics. However, a government review of A-level (Matthews and Pepper, 2007) reported the diversity as a problem and questioned their equivalence. They were particularly concerned that universities may penalise students for choosing an easier option when it was the school that imposed this.

We can see here how the temptingly mathematical notions of hierarchy or equivalence became enmeshed with political significance, and contributed to the 2017 A-level curriculum changes. Arguments for and against equivalence call on ideas of equity and of protecting students from unexpected consequences. For some, the problem lies in subject choice itself, and these arguments support a baccalaureate system and/or compulsory mathematics. For others individual choice is not inherently problematic but requires managing so that students are responsible only for their own decisions, not other people's. This individualisation feels appealing, but we have seen in Chapter 4 by Peter Gates and Andy Noyes how social class inequalities are reinforced by treating students only in terms of their school-based identities.

Comparing questions

I now look at another way of comparing mathematics pathways by comparing the associated examination questions, and I use this method to give a flavour of Mathematics and Core Maths. The analytic framework I introduce here is drawn from studies that compare the demands of examination questions through their structure (Hughes, Pollitt and Ahmed, 1998), their mathematical steps, complexity and familiarity (Kathotia, 2012) and grammatical complexity (Morgan, Tang and Sfard, 2011).

Work through the two questions in Figure 21.2 and consider:
What are their different conceptual demands: how many variables are involved?
How are these represented (algebraically, graphically, in words, in numbers)? Are variables introduced one at a time or together? What numbers and operations are involved? (You might find it helpful to draw on the approach to thinking about examples elaborated in Chapter 15 by Tim Rowland.)
What are their different reading demands: how much text? Is all the information you need in the text? How closely linked are the question and the information? Do students need to devise their own strategy for answering a question? Do they need to organise how they give their responses?

I selected these two questions because their similarities and differences help to characterise the relationship between Mathematics and Core Maths. Given the

Question A (redrawn from AQA 2017a)

Note: Core Maths issues preliminary material before the examination. In 2016–17 this was a 4-page document on Income Tax, National Insurance (NI) and the National Minimum Wage. It contains tables in which student can find the appropriate allowances and basic rates for tax (£11000pa, 20%), NI (£155 per week, 12%) and National Minimum Wage (£6.70 for 21s and over), and a sentence about the National Living Wage for workers 25 and older (£7.20 per hour). The question tells students to use the document.

Q8   At the start of 2016 Samir is 24 years old and works 40 hours each week.
He is paid the National Minimum Wage.
He pays tax and National Insurance but has no other deductions.
His net pay after tax and National Insurance are deducted in £243.15 per week.
The government states,
"New National Living Wage gives you an extra 50p per hour in your pocket."
Samir says,
"When I am 25 the increase in **my** net pay will be less than 35p per hour."
Is he correct?
You **must** show your working.

[6 marks]

Question B (redrawn from AQA 2017b)

Chris claims that, "for any given value of x, the gradient of the curve $y = 2x^3 + 6x^2 - 12x + 3$ is always greater than the gradient of the curve $y = 1 + 60x - 6x^2$".

Show that Chris is wrong by finding all the values of x for which his claim is not true.

[7 marks]

Figure 21.2 Exam questions.

narrow range of questions available in 2018, it would be hard to claim that they are typical of each course, but they come from a mainstream examination board, draw on the compulsory course specifications and there are similar questions in other exemplar material. Both ask the student to respond to a statement that compares two variables. As well as this similarity, you will have identified a range of differences between them. Let's discuss those that are characteristic.

Question A is from Core Maths. It involves six main variables (old net pay, new hourly and weekly pay; tax and NI deducted, difference) and all are numeric.

They are introduced over several sentences, not in the same order as they will be used (for example tax and NI are introduced next to *net* pay). Students must convert between representations as words, numbers and in tables. The question uses three operations (−, ×, ÷) and percentages. Numbers are decimal and involve some rounding. Information is given in the text and preliminary material, which both include redundant information and require some inferences (for example, the relevance of being 25, the need to use tax bands). The context is real and invites a socio-economic opinion. The question does not specify how to start the problem, how to organise the working (which has four alternatives in the mark scheme), nor what is a valid mathematical response.

Question B is from the specimen papers for AS-level Mathematics. It involves six algebraic variables (x, expressions for two curves, their gradients and the difference). The first five are introduced in one sentence, not precisely in the order of use, but with grammar indicating the relationships between them; the last is inferred. Students must convert between this verbal representation and algebraic expressions but ignore the possible graphical representation. The question uses three operations (+, −, ×), differentiation and factorising. Numbers are all integers. There is no redundant information and no context to indicate why Chris speaks about comparing gradients. The text does not specify how to start the problem. It does specify that Chris is wrong and, in words, what will be considered a valid mathematical justification, but leaves the student to organise the form of their response (for example, it does not say 'by writing an inequality in x' although this is required in the mark scheme).

Comparing these two questions shows that they do have distinctive features that reflect the courses' purposes and different classroom practices. There is a hierarchy of complexity: Mathematics A-level is concerned with abstract relationships and algebraic manipulation, while Core Maths focuses on identifying numeric variables and relationships within authentic situations, and using these to support reasoning about that context. There is also evidence here to challenge a unidimensional model of difficulty: Core Maths has weaker links between the question and the information needed to answer it. It demands that students read and use mathematics in a way that is absent in Mathematics.

In a previous edition of this book, I analysed questions from 2008 Further Mathematics and Use of Maths A-levels, and noted how similar they were despite their different purposes. Both used a structure and wording that restricted opportunities for students to select strategies, to move back and forth between representations or to organise their own responses. They signalled a very clear procedure for candidates to start and follow. That is not to say that candidates would find the questions easy: many would not. However, the perception that examinations systematically reduced variation lay behind calls for mathematics curricula to move away from a hierarchy of technical fluency and towards problems that prepare students to think mathematically – and hence the 2017 changes (see Chapter 20 by Ian Jones for further discussions of these debates).

Studying mathematics

Research into student experiences gives another perspective through which to understand different mathematics courses. Studies agree that students most likely to study A-level Mathematics are those who have already achieved well at GCSE, and are thus more likely to have higher socio-economic status (Strand, 2014). Exploring the interactions of gender, ethnicity, class and prior attainment leads to intriguing variations, with one being that students from certain ethnic groups (Chinese, African, Indian and Pakistani) are more likely to choose mathematics regardless of attainment (Noyes, 2009; Reiss et al., 2011).

The Transmaths project (Wake, Williams and Drake, 2011) tracked students with B or C grades at GCSE Mathematics who had chosen one of the A-level mathematics pathways available at the time: either Use of Maths (the precursor of Core Maths) or Mathematics. They found differences between the cohorts: Use of Maths students were unlikely to choose STEM careers and were more diverse in ethnicity, class and prior attainment. Those with C grades made more progress on the Use of Maths pathway than in Mathematics, and were less likely to drop out or get an ungraded result.

Transmaths showed the value to students of providing an academic mathematics pathway that focuses on applying known mathematics rather than preparing for university mathematics. Students found it refreshing to research what mathematics to use, to make and connect meanings for themselves and to explain mathematics to others. They talked about the challenge but also how these lessons increased their understanding. The recent experiences of Core Maths teachers reinforce the value of such a qualification. Teachers report that Core Maths suits both the students who need some mathematics for their career but not at the abstraction of A-level, and those who "were taught to jump through hoops to get enough marks" at GCSE and need to become "users of mathematics rather than just being doers of mathematics" (Golding, Smith and Blaylock, 2018, p. 75). Teachers describe Core Maths as giving students confidence, scepticism and a sense of agency over mathematics, including an emergent belief that mathematics should, and can, make sense.

Comparing the Further Mathematics and Mathematics pathways has been much less controversial. STEM employers, universities and schools largely agree that Further Mathematics should be similar to Mathematics just more extreme: deeper in its abstraction, broader in its applications and sharper in its eventual function of selection. Further Mathematics is even more closely linked with the 'clever core' of high-attaining students, and is popular among students from professional backgrounds and Asian ethnicities (Matthews and Pepper, 2007). My own research has followed the promotion of Further Mathematics in state schools, investigating the accounts of non-traditional students who took up Further Mathematics as a twilight-hours course. Unlike the research above, I use a post-structural approach that considers what identities are offered and formed through these experiences. Students' accounts of doing mathematics have to make sense of the practices they engage in and also the fact that they chose/choose to participate, and because of this reflexivity I consider experience and choice together.

> *Think back to whether you chose to continue mathematics, perhaps to A-level or degree standard. What kind of decision was this? Who influenced you?*
> *Would you describe your choice as rational – weighing up the costs and benefits?*
> *Or as expressive – reflecting who you are, setting out who you want to be?*

Why choose an A-level in mathematics or further mathematics?

Students who describe their reasons for choosing Mathematics A-level usually give one or more of the following:

* Mathematics leads to good careers.
* Mathematics is useful.
* I have always been good at maths.
* I enjoy mathematics.
* Mathematics is hard.

> *Which of these reasons entered into your decisions?*

Calling these 'reasons' suggests that choosing is a practice of weighing up contributory factors, some concerned with mathematics, some with the social world and some the individual chooser. In this approach to theorising choice, the next step is to identify what the relevant factors are, and to investigate how changing the image of mathematics, the practices of society or students' self-perceptions would make a difference to choice 'calculations'. Debate in this area is often quasi-statistical in tone, centred on identifying which factors are significant and how they interact. For example, a political think-tank has suggested that mathematics should have more university-entry points than other subjects so students understand its higher value (Kounine, Marks and Truss, 2008). This would change social practices (university entrance procedures) in order to affect the image of mathematics; it is a 'policy lever' that influences people without constraining them. Another example is often suggested in response to girls' continued lower participation in A-level Mathematics (stuck around 40% since 2001): adopting classroom teaching methods that promote confidence and enjoyment for girls would encourage them to stay on (Brown, Brown and Bibby, 2008, see also the discussion in Chapters 7 and 8 by Anna Llewellyn and Mark McCormack and Luis Morales, respectively).

Nevertheless it seems likely that choice is more complex, because sociological research tells us that choices are both rational *and* expressive (Rose, 1999). Choosing articulates what we think is important, and that gives a message about who we are. In the list above, the first two reasons – 'mathematics leads to good careers', and 'mathematics is useful' – are about the role of mathematics in a western technological society. When students choose mathematics for these reasons, they align themselves with high-status, powerful positions in society and with modernist views of progress and utility. We can see here how easily the qualities of mathematics in society can be read onto the choosing student as showing a self-entrepreneurial spirit.

What about the next two reasons in the list? 'I have always been good at mathematics' and 'I enjoy mathematics' are both qualities of the student. Using knowledge about yourself is a widely accepted rationale for making life choices. Still, for these to be valid factors in choosing mathematics, we need to understand them as stable characteristics, unlikely to change or to become irrelevant as students start their A-level studies. The first in particular suggests that mathematical ability resides in a person and makes that person apt for any formulation of school mathematics. Chapter 5 by Mark Boylan and Hilary Povey interrogates this fixed conception of mathematics ability.

The 'personal enjoyment' rationale also suggests taken-for-granted understandings that there is a kind of person who simply likes 'mathematics', rather than perhaps enjoying solving equations but not sketching asymptotic graphs. It can come as a surprise to students that A-level topics such as statistics and mechanics have very different feels. Although enjoyment may feel quite a trivial reason to continue or discontinue mathematics, it is intricately bound up in how we present ourselves as successful in making choices and in managing the work we need to do. This can be shown by studying the language patterns in data when students are asked to account for their subject choices. We can identify how multiple reasons for studying mathematics intersect for particular individuals, and how the individuals use choosing mathematics to construct themselves as becoming mature, autonomous, disciplined adults (Smith, 2010).

In the extract below, Hayley and Esther have just explained that they chose to study A-level Mathematics because they enjoyed it. Esther contrasts it with biology where she once cried because she couldn't understand her homework:

Cathy: And you wouldn't see maths making you cry?
Esther: Oh it probably could! Stats probably could make me cry.
Hayley: Frustration. I don't cry like with things like that but ... but frustration could make me like ugh! I can't work it out, I can't work it out. I don't know how she has done it!
Esther: Oh, I get like that when I don't understand something. But I still enjoy the subject.
Hayley: Yes. I love numbers.
Esther: I will still come back and try to learn more.

Hayley: I love the fact that if I can't do it I will just do more and more to see how I can get to the answer. Like try different methods and you always know that there is a way that you can do it. And if you haven't done it then you need to work out what it is.

Both girls emphatically describe unhappy feelings in mathematics but still claim to 'enjoy the subject'. They make sense of this tension by separating statistics and things they don't understand from their relationship with mathematics as a whole, which Hayley describes as loving 'numbers'. By returning to primary school mathematics (and emotions), she carries the successes of the past into the present, and positions enjoyment as an expression of an 'authentic' identity. Such repositioning that looks both backwards towards childhood and forward towards accomplishment is part of the self-work of contemporary adolescence (Smith, 2019). Hayley's last sentences repeat her love of mathematics as something established through practice and flexibility and over time, giving her knowledge about mathematics and about herself-in-mathematics. She reworks frustration into something more enjoyable – the certainty of having an answer – and uses it to position herself as someone who is resilient, showing both confidence and perseverance. This is an example of what I mean by working-on-yourself through mathematics. There is an interesting context to this mathematical friendship: Hayley comes from a lower GCSE set than Esther and struggled throughout the first A-level year. Yet in the second year, Hayley continued mathematics and Esther gave up. I suggest that we see in this kind of self-talk how Hayley can justify carrying on with mathematics despite some discouraging results and painful times. She uses the promise of eventual success as a means of feeling happy in her mathematics *and* in her self-work.

I chose this excerpt because it also links to the last of the common reasons: 'mathematics is hard'. At first sight this looks like a reason *not* to study mathematics. If maths is *too* hard, you are unlikely to enjoy it or do well. However it does feature significantly in students' reasoning. Hayley can work towards happiness by working on a mathematics problem, and the acknowledgement that mathematics is hard renders her own self-management even more impressive. Continuing with mathematics helps her demonstrate something special about herself. This notion of *proving yourself* with mathematics has been analysed by Heather Mendick (2006) (and see Chapter 9 by Heather). In 'proving themselves' with mathematics, students align themselves with a powerful authority and reconcile two contemporary discourses of adolescence: knowing who you 'really' are and ensuring that you will make progress.

Closing thoughts

In the discussion above I have highlighted approaches to choice that are relevant to thinking how mathematics courses differ and how students understand mathematics. The approach that is dominant in policy-making has been to consider mathematics and identity as separable, so that any patterns in who chooses mathematics are side effects, treatable as misfunctions of our educational system. Or we can think about reasons for choosing mathematics (or not) as being closely connected with constructing identities of entrepreneurial progress, ability, enjoyment, challenge and masculinity. This is not deterministic; on the contrary, contemporary understandings of selfhood and adolescence place a high premium on managing oneself. Nor is it equitable since we cannot all take up different identities freely. But from this perspective we have another way of understanding and researching different mathematics courses: as contexts in which mathematics, success and difficulty are differently positioned in relation to adolescence and self-work.

Further reading

Mendick, H. (2006) *Masculinities in Mathematics*. Maidenhead: Open University Press. A readable introduction to post-structural perspectives on identity and how they play out in/through mathematics. The main focus is on gender, but the approach is equally influential in thinking about mathematics and social class.

Smith, C., Golding, J. and Bretscher, N. (2018) *Special Issue: Preparing to Teach Mathematics Pathways beyond*, 16. This collection of project papers analyses the challenges and opportunities faced by teachers as they start to teach A-level and Core Maths and some of the connections between mathematics content knowledge and mathematics-specific pedagogic knowledge.

https://www.stem.org.uk/core-maths. The website hosting information and resources for Core Maths qualifications. There are interesting level 3 activities for teaching calculus, decision mathematics and dynamics.

https://amsp.org.uk/. The website of the Advanced Mathematics Support Programme showing teaching resources and events for A-level Mathematics and Further Mathematics.

References

AQA (2017a) *Level 3 Certificate MATHEMATICAL STUDIES 2017 Paper 1*. Available from https://allaboutmaths.aqa.org.uk/attachments/8646.pdf (accessed February 2018).

AQA (2017b) *AS Maths (7356) Specimen Question Paper 1*. Available from http://filestore.aqa.org.uk/resources/mathematics/AQA-73561-SQP.PDF (accessed February 2018).

Ball, S., Maguire, M. and Macrae, S. (2000) *Choice, Pathways and Transitions Post-Sixteen*. London: RoutledgeFalmer.

Brown, M., Brown, P. and Bibby, T. (2008) '"I Would Rather Die": Attitudes of 16-year-olds Towards Their Future Participation in Mathematics', *Research in Mathematics Education*, 10(1): 2–18.

Coe, R., Searle, J., Barmby, P., Jones, K. and Higgins, S. (2008) *Relative Difficulty of Examinations in Different Subjects*. Durham: CEM Centre, Durham University.

Educators for Reform (2009) *The Misuse of Mathematics*. London: Reform.

Golding, J., Smith, C. and Blaylock, M. (2018). 'Learning to Teach Contextualised Problem Solving in a Non-Calculus Mathematics Pathway', *Teaching Mathematics and its Applications*, 37, 69–83.

Hodgen, J. (2010). *Is the UK an Outlier? An International Comparison of Upper Secondary Mathematics Education*. London: Nuffield Foundation.

Hughes, S., Pollitt, A. and Ahmed, A. (1998) 'The Development of a Tool for Gauging the Demands of GCSE and A Level Exam Questions', in K. V. Belfast (ed.), (2012) *Mathematics in A Level Assessments*. London: Nuffield.

Kathotia, V. (2012). *Mathematics in A Level Assessments*. London: Nuffield.

Kounine, L., Marks, J. and Truss, E. (2008) 'The value of mathematics'. London: Reform.

Matthews, A. and Pepper, D. (2007) *Evaluation of Participation in GCE Mathematics: Final Report*, Qualifications and Curriculum Authority.

Mendick, H. (2006) *Masculinities in Mathematics*. Buckingham: Open University Press.

Morgan, C., Tang, S. and Sfard, A. (2011) 'Grammatical Structure and Mathematical Activity', *Proceedings of the British Society for Research into Learning Mathematics (BSRLM)*, 31(3): 113–118.

Murray, S. (2011) 'Declining Participation in Post-Compulsory Secondary School Mathematics: Students' Views of and Solutions to the Problem', *Research in Mathematics Education*, 13(3): 269–286.

Noyes, A. (2009) 'Exploring Social Patterns of Participation in University-Entrance Level Mathematics in England', *Research in Mathematics Education*, 11(2): 167–183.

Noyes, A. and Adkins, M. (2016). 'Studying Advanced Mathematics in England: Findings from a Survey of Student Choices and Attitudes', *Research in Mathematics Education*, 18(3): 231–248.

Reiss, M., Hoyles, C., Mujtaba, T., Riazi-Farzad, B., Rodd, M., Simon, S. and Stylianidou, F. (2011) 'Understanding Participation Rates in Post-16 Mathematics and Physics: Conceptualising and Operationalising the UPMAP Project', *International Journal of Science and Mathematics Education*, 9(2): 273–302.

Rose, N. (1999) *Powers of Freedom: Reframing Political Thought*. Cambridge: Cambridge University Press.

Smith, A. (2017). Report of Professor Sir Adrian Smith's Review of Post-16 Mathematics. Department for Education.

Smith, C (2010) 'Choosing More Mathematics: Happiness Through Work?', *Research in Mathematics Education*, 12(2): 99–115.

Smith, C. (2019) 'Discourses of time and maturity structuring participation in mathematics and further mathematics', *British Journal of Sociology of Education*, 41(2), pp. 160–177. doi: 10.1080/01425692.2019.1697206.

Strand, S. (2014). Ethnicity, Gender, Social Class and Achievement Gaps at Age 16: Intersectionality and 'Getting It' for the White Working Class. *Research Papers in Education*, 29(2): 131–171.

Wake, G., Williams, J. and Drake, P. (eds.) (2011) 'Special Issue: Deepening Engagement in Mathematics in Pre-University Education', *Research in Mathematics Education*, 13(2).

Index

Note: *Italicized* page numbers refer to figures, **bold** page numbers refer to tables.

ability (mathematical) 3, 5, 13, 30, 49, 55, 57–8, 60–3, 89, 93, 95, 125; ability-based teaching 63; grouping 48, 55, 63, 66; thinking 27, 48, 55–63, 66–7
absolutist 83, 95–6
abstract activity 101; *see also* activity
abstraction 36–7, 152, 196, 203, 234, 272, 276
accommodation, reformation, transformation in teaching for sustainability 206–7
achievement 3–5, 7–9, 13, 32, 44–5, 49–50, 52, 61–2, 66, 69, 71–2, 174, 224, 236, 247, 249, 259, 264
The achievement-wellbeing trade-off in education (Sahlgren) 50
Acker, J. 91
activity 43, 57, 60, 122, 148, 152, 178, 213, 221; abstract 101; mental 70–1; neutral 203; rule-breaking and 82; tasks and 144–6, 151
adolescence 269, 279–80
adults 32, 61, 92, 131, 212, 278
affective opportunities 234–5; *see also* opportunities
African-Caribbean students 59; *see also* students/learners
aggregated geographical measures 44
Ainley, J. 149
A-level (mathematics) 210, 241–2, 257, 269–73, *270*, 272–3, 275–9
algebra 33–4, 228–30
algorithms 34, 113, 228–30; for calculation 112; in ICTs 31; mining of

personal data 40; over-reliance on 174; security 179; vertical 178
alienation 67
Al-Khowarizmi's equations *229*
all-attainment groupings 60, 62, 73
all-attainment teaching 58, 66–76; *see also* teaching
Almagest (Ptolemy) 227
Angier, C. 74
Antikythera 230
anxiety 60, 170, 179
approaches 13, **15**, 19, 95; *see also* accommodation, reformation, transformation in teaching for sustainability
Arabia 224
Archimedes 230, 236
Arendt, H. 38
Arithmetic Composition (van Doesburg) 231
Ark (multi-academy trust) 16, 18
artificial intelligence (AI) 159–60
arts 230–2
Askew, M. 20, 152, 176
assessment(s) 5–9, 69, 243–54, 262–3; cycle 243–4, *244*; grid 258; self/peer assessment 249; skills 45; teachers 252–3; *see also* A-level (mathematics); feedback; General Certificate of Secondary Education (GCSE); Programme for International Assessment (PISA)
Assessment for Learning (AfL) 243–4
Assessment Objective 3 (AO3) 262
assistants *see* digital assistants
attainment 46–7, 51–2, 56–9
attending to attention 138–9
attitudes 32–3, 49, 51, 92, 95

augmented reality (AR) 159
Australian students 9; *see also* students/
    learners
authorship of tasks 147–9
Avant-Garde movement 231
Avcu, R. 188
average (mathematical) 3, 6, 7–8, 66,
    84, 157, *158*, 162, 199–200, 202,
    205–7, 260
awarding bodies (ABs) 257, 261–2

Babylonian Algorithm 228, *228*;
    see also algorithms
bags *see* virtual school bags
Banwell, C. 115
Barmby, P. 80
Barnes, A. 249
barriers 60, 93–4, 241, 247
Barwell, R. 105
A Beautiful Mind (film) 103
Becker, J. R. 96
behaviour 38, 71, 82, 91–2, 95, 98,
    143–5, 150–2, 176, 201, 205
Beishuizen, M. 178
beliefs 13, 20, 25, 39, 56, 58–62, 67,
    79, 246
benevolent sexism 92
Bhaskaracharya's Pythagoras
    proof 226, *227*
big data 31
The Big Short (McKay) 103–4, 106–7
binary divisions 81
Black, P. 245
Black Box research 247–8; *see also*
    assessment(s)
Bloom, B. 13, 16, 18
Bloom's taxonomy 80
Boaler, J. 60, 67, 71–2, 81–2, 84, 96
bodies (physical) 90, 93
Bolsonaro, J. 49
books *see* electronic book
Bourdain, A. 104
Bourdieu, P. 44
Boylan, M. **15**
Brazil 49, 214
Bring Your Own Device (BYOD) 162–3
Bring Your Own Technology (BYOT) 162–3
Brunelleschi (architect) 230
Bruner, J. 20
bullying, homophobic 95
Burton, L. 96
Buxton, L. 170

BYOD *see* Bring Your Own Device (BYOD)
BYOT *see* Bring Your Own
    Technology (BYOT)

calculations: approaches 169, 178–9;
    cost/profit 30; Gini coefficient *215*,
    217; global mean temperature 199;
    idiosyncratic strategies 173; mental 169,
    175, 179; speed for 172
calculative reasoning 36–40
calculator *see* colour calculator
Calder, A. 232
capabilities 31–2, 98, 152, 225
capital (economic/cultural/social/
    linguistic) 32, 44–5, 47
Cardano's factors *230*
Cardano's solution *229*
card-matching simple functions *153*
career advancement 30
Carreira, S. 162
Centre for Education Economics (CfEE)
    50, 52n1
Centre for the Study of Market Reform of
    Education (CMRE) 52n1
Certificate of Secondary Education
    (CSE) 257
Chandor, J. C. 103
charter school 16
child-centred pedagogy 80, 170;
    see also pedagogy
China 7–9, 17, 104, 224
choices 34, 83, 122, 151, 183, 225, 233,
    241; lifestyle **220**; subject 269–71, 278
Chongzi, Z. 226
citizenship and mathematics 211, 220; *see
    also* democratic competence
Clarke, D. 146, 153
class 43–8; *see also* social class/classification
classroom 118, 238, 248; *see also* spacious
    classroom
Claxton, G. 68–9
climate change 49, 105, 199–202; chal-
    lenges 155; description, prediction,
    communication 199–200; formatting
    and 204–6; mathemacy and 200–2
Clinton, H. 102
cloze technique 133; *see also* questioning
Cockcroft Report 19–20
coding skills 107; *see also* skills
coefficient *see* Gini coefficient
cognitive opportunities 234–5
Cohen, L. 107

co-learner 74; *see also* students/learners
Coles, A. 146, 153
collateralised debt obligations (CDOs)
103–4
colour calculator 127–8, *128*
comparing questions 273–5;
see also questioning/questions
competence(s) 48, 105, 198–9, 201–2,
204, 206–8, 220, **220**
completing the square (CTS) 185, 187
complex instruction 71
concave quadrilateral *127*
Concept Maps 235–6
confidence *see* self-confidence
Confrey, J. 74
conjectures 116, 118–19, 125, 127–9,
131–2, 135–8, 150, 191, 242, *251*,
251–2
Connolly, P. 43
consumer spending habits 45
Continuing Professional Development
(CPD) 248
controlling questions 132–3;
see also questioning/questions
conversation, culture of 94
costs *see* social costs
counterexamples 118, 190–1;
see also examples
coursework 257, 264
Coxeter, H. S. M. 125
creativity (in/and mathematics) 56, 108,
159, 170
critical literacy 199
cultural beliefs 20; *see also* beliefs
cultural capital 32, 44–5
cultural knowledge 56
cultural stereotypes 59;
see also stereotypes
culture: of conversation 94; family 47;
heritage and 225–32; objectification 38
curriculum/curricula 13, **15**, 20, 59–60,
63, 73, 159–60, 224–38; knowledge-based 83; national 63, 169, 179,
251–2, 261; place of mental mathematics in 174–7; planning 69

Daily Telegraph 82
Dali, S. 232
Das Capital (Marx) 103
data processing 31; *see also* big data
data representation 31
data set *219*
Davies, P. 156, 159

decimal point ignored (DPI) error 189
decision-making 39, 73, **220**, 245, 253
De Geest, E. 62–3
dehumanisation 36, 39
della Francesca, P. 230, *230*
democratic competence 105, 198–9, 201–2,
204, 206–8; *see also* competence(s)
democratic society 31, 33
demotivation 67; *see also* motivation
Denmark 48
Denvir, H. 176
Department for Education (DfE) 47
De Prospectiva Pingendi
(della Francesca) 230
diagonals of regular polygons 126, *127*
dialectical competences **220**
dialogic teaching 20; *see also* teaching
differential diagnosis 4
differentiation 275
digital assistants 159–60
digital curriculum 159;
see also curriculum/curricula
digitally disadvantaged 161
digitally privileged 161
digital technologies (in the classroom)
155–66; access 161–3; artificial intelligence 159–60; fake news 155–8; forms
of 163–5; mobile divisions 161–3
digital tutors 159–60
dimensions of variation 186–7, 189
disadvantaged communities 49
disaffection of students 67
discourses 49, 79, 80–2, 84, 91, 97, 271
discussion 248
disengagement 63, 67, 270; *see also*
engagement
division (operation) 146; binary 81;
chunking 171, *172*; examples used in
lesson on *147*; long division *171*, 171–4;
long multiplication and 169; mobile
161–3
Downfall (film) 102
Duchin, M. 105
Durrell's Algebra 144; *see also* algebra
Dweck, C. 13, 61–2, 75
Dylan, B. 107
dynamic geometry 163–4
dynamic mathematics 163–4

Ebert, R. 106
economic capital 44, 45
economic growth 50
economic indicators 44

economic theory 31
education 4, 8–9, 13–14, **15**, 16, 18–19, 30–1, 33–6, 50, 78, 80–4; of digital technologies 163–5; international comparison 58; normalisation 79; post-compulsory 257; social construction 95–7
educational data mining (EDM) 160
Education Endowment Foundation (EEF) 18, 245
Educators for Reform 272
effective feedback 247–8; *see also* feedback
eight-dot shapes 116, *116–17*, 119, **119**
electronic book 159
elementary schools 31
Elephant in the Classroom (Boaler) 82
elitism, popular culture against 105–8
empty number line (ENL) 177–9, *178*
engagement 69; *see also* disengagement
Engels, F. 103
engineering 230–2
England 3, 5, 7, 10, 13–14, **15**, 16–17, 19–21, 46, 58, 67, 80, 84, 102, 170, 210–12, 224, 242, 250, 252, 256–7, 269, 271
English Department for Education 16
English education 14
English mathematics educators 20; *see also* teachers/educators
enjoyment (of mathematics) 50, 74, 242, 277–80
entrepreneurs 16, 102
equality, perfect 216
equations *see* Al-Khowarizmi's equations
equity (and inequity) 39, 50, 52, 71, 86, 112, 161, 165, 207, 242, 273
Equity in Education: Breaking Down Barriers to Social Mobility 50
Ernest, P. 95, 170
error *see* decimal point ignored (DPI) error
esteem *see* self-esteem
ethical irrelevance 36
ethical judgements 67
ethnicity 45, 71, 96, 276
Euclidean-style proof 234
Euler's formula 233, *234*
evidence 18–19
examination boards *see* awarding bodies (ABs)
examinations *see* A-level (mathematics); General Certificate of Secondary Education (GCSE); tests

examples 182–92; to avoid 189; counterexamples 118, 190–1; dimensions of variation 186–7; experienced teacher in Turkey 188–9; generic 190–1; interlude 190; learner-generated examples (LGEs) 113, 190; quadratic functions 185–6; ways of using 182–4
exam questions *274*; *see also* questioning/questions
exchange 14, 16–17, 31, 74
expectations 49, 57, 71, 92
Experian 45
exposure, pedagogies of 94

failure 11, 32–3, 49, 85, 92, 96, 102
fake news 49, 155–8
Falck, O. 158
family culture 47; *see also* culture
Fausto-Sterling, A. 91–3
Fauvel, J. 238
favouritism 40
feedback 244–5, 247–8; *see also* assessment(s)
femininities 82, 91, 97; *see also* masculinity
finance 17–18
Finland 3–5, 8–10, 48, 58
"Finnish miracle" 3
Finnish students 3
Flatlanders 108
flipped learning 159; *see also* learning
formal education 56; *see also* education
formative assessment 69, 243–54; assessment cycle 243–4, *244*; evidence and impacts 245; learning 250–1, 253–4; in practice 247–9; students 253–4; success criterion 250–1; teachers 249–50, 252–3; *see also* assessment(s)
formatting power (of mathematics) 103, 203–6
fossil fuels 204
Foucault, M. 79, 86
Frankfurt School 35, 38
fuels *see* fossil fuels
functional mathematics 211, 261
funnelling 136–7

Galileo 231
GCSE *see* General Certificate of Secondary Education (GCSE)
geeks 106

gender 89–98; differences 89, 91–2;
   discrimination 92; gap 45; heterosexual
   assumptions 94–5; masculinities/
   femininities 82, 90–1, 97, 107, 280; sex
   93–4; social construction of 90–1, 95–7;
   social factors affecting differences 91–2;
   societal constructions 97; stereotypes 92
gendered behaviours 91; *see also* behaviour
General Certificate of Secondary
   Education (GCSE) 6, 43–4, 46, **46**,
   59, 84, 256–65, 276
generic examples 190–1; *see also* examples
genius 102–3, 105–6
genuine enquiry 133–4; *see also*
   questioning/questions
genuine interest in questioning 137–8
geodemographic segmentation 45
geometry *see* dynamic geometry
Gervais, S. 92
Gifted (film) 102
Gini coefficient 196, 207, 210, 214–17,
   215, 219–20
globalisation 49
global mean temperature anomalies *202*
Gomez, S. 104
Goodman, A. 44
Good Will Hunting (film) 103
Gove, M. 169–70, 177
government policy 3, 13, 156; *see also* policy
grade retention 7
Graven, M. 213
Gray, E. 184
Greene, J. 4
Greenwald, S. J. 108
Gregg, P. 44
Grounding for the Metaphysics of Morals
   (Kant) 38
groupings *see* all-attainment groupings
Guangdong 8
The Guardian 89
Gunderson, E. 92

habits 45, 68, 146; *see also* consumer
   spending habits
Hammond, P. 204
Hansen, A. 149
happiness 33, 50, 279
Hart, S. 62
Hawking, S. 102
heritage *see* culture; ethnicity; history of
   mathematics
Hero of Alexandria 230

heterosexuality 94–5;
   see also homosexuality; sexuality
Hidden Figures (film) 102
higher education 32, 170, 261;
   see also education
Hindu squares *226*
History in Mathematics Education (Fauvel
   and van Maanen) 238
history of mathematics 224–38; classroom research and 238; culture and
   heritage 225–32; evolution and action
   232–5; maps 235–8; narratives 235–8;
   orientations 235–8
Hodgen, J. 245, 248
Holt, J. 137
homophobia 94
homophobic bullying 95
homosexuality 49, 95;
   see also heterosexuality; sexuality
Hong Kong 8–10
horizontal mathematisation 150
hukou 8
hypercube 232, *232*

identity 34–5, 61, 84, 91, 93, 97, 242,
   269, 279–80
IEA *see* International Association for the
   Evaluation of Educational Achievement
   (IEA)
The Imitation Game (film) 102
immigrations 49
*Improving Mathematics in Key Stages Two
   and Three* (Hodgen) 248
income deprivation **46**
Income Deprivation Affecting Children
   Index (IDACI) 44, 46–7
indeterminacy 113, 122
India 214, 224, 226–7
inequality 40; achievement 66; perfect
   216; socio-economic 214; *see also* equity
   (and inequity)
informal education 56; *see also* education
informal relationships 73
information and communication
   technologies (ICTs) 29, 31
innate ability 13; *see also* ability
   (mathematical)
innate biological ability 89
Inside the black box (Black and Wiliam) 245
institutions: higher education 261;
   masculinity-making 91; social 199;
   society and 39; sociological studies of 91

instrumental reasoning 36–40
instrumental understanding 35, 80,
    173–4, 177; *see also* understanding
Intelligent Tutoring Systems (ITSs) 159, 164
interaction *see* teacher-pupil interaction
Intergovernmental Panel on Climate
    Change (IPCC) 197
interlude 190
international assessments 8–9;
    see also assessment(s)
International Association for the
    Evaluation of Educational Achievement
    (IEA) 5
international influences, mastery 17
interrogation of self experience 135–6
intersex 93; *see also* sex
interventions 69, 250–3
irrelevance *see* ethical irrelevance
Issar, K. 106

Jablonka, E. 211
Jackson, M. 102
Japan 8
Jerrim, J. 9
Jiangsu 8
Johannesburg data set *219*
Johnson, H. L. 146, 153
Johnson, K. 102
Jones, D. 6
Jones, K. 156
Jordan, M. 106
judgements 45–6, 67, 246

Kant, I. 38
Kapitoil (Wayne) 103, 106–7
Kelman, H. C. 39
King, R. 35
knowledge (mathematical) 6, 10, 13,
    19, 21, 30–2, 48, 56, 72, 81, 84,
    105, 108, 112, 155, 161–3, 166, 182,
    185, 225–8, 242, 261; subject 244;
    see also teaching
knowledge-based curriculum 83
Korea 3, 8–10
Kullberg, A. 146
Kyoto protocol 200–1

Lakatos, I. 233
language 31, 34, 36, 79, 81, 107, 164, 278;
    abstract 33, 184; competence 48; of
    conjecture 116; gendered nature of 92;
    object-oriented 35; tests translation 6

Lawson, N. 201
learner-generated examples (LGEs) 113,
    190; *see also* examples
learning 5, 13, 18, 35, 43, 47, 51–2, 68,
    71, 73–4, 152, 250–1, 253–4; *see also*
    education
Leonardi, B. 94
lesson content and purposes 15
levels (national curriculum) 63;
    see also A-level (mathematics)
Levenstein, K. 210
life-related competences **220**;
    see also competence(s)
linguistic capital 47
literacy *see* critical literacy; mathematical
    literacy; quantitative literacy
Liu Hui triangles 234, *234*
Lorenz curve 216
low-attaining students 62;
    see also students/learners

Ma, L. 176
Mac an Ghaill, M. 91
Madison, B. 212
The Mail and Guardian 210
Manifesto of the Communist Party (Marx
    and Engels) 103
The Man Who Knew Infinity (film) 102
Maps 235–8; *see also* Concept Maps
Margin Call (Chandor) 103–7
marking/marks 6, 221, 241–2, 247–8,
    258, 260–2, 264, 275
Mårtensson, P. 146
Marton, F. 151, 186–7
Marx, K. 31, 103
masculinity 90–1, 97, 107, 280;
    see also femininities
Mason, J. 187, 190, 234
mastery 13–21, 31, 56; finance 17–18;
    innovation in England 16;
    international influences 17;
    mobilising 'evidence' 18–19; political
    agendas 19; profit 17–18; prospects for
    change 20–1
mathemacy 199–202
mathematical ability 55–6;
    see also ability
mathematical competences 220;
    see also competence(s)
mathematical literacy 196, 210–21
mathematical proficiency 221
mathematical thinking 36–40, 71

mathematician(s) 29, 32, 36, 74, 78, 97, 101, 103–4, 125, 232, 234, 236; ability 125; role of 104; societal constructions of 97; success 36; working in finance 103
Mathematics as a Constructive Activity (Watson and Mason) 234
Mathematics inside the Black Box (Hodgen and Wiliam) 245
Mathematics Mastery 16, 18–19
Mathematics Teacher Exchange (MTE) 18–19
mathematisation 150, 152, 203, 205
maths-gender stereotypes 92; *see also* stereotypes
Maths No Problem (textbook scheme) 16–17
May, T. 17
McCormack, M. 95
McKay, A. 103
meaning-making 67
Mechanica (Hero) 230
Mendick, H. 97, 279
mental activity 70–1
mental mathematics 169–79; empty number line (ENL) 177–9, *178*; English context 169–71; place in mathematics curriculum 174–7; understanding 171–4
meta-questions 134; *see also* questioning/questions
Meyer, E. 94
mindsets 13, 60–2
misogyny 49
misunderstandings 67; *see also* understanding (mathematical)
mobile divisions 161–3; *see also* division (operation)
mobilising 'evidence' 18–19
modelling (mathematical) 35, 74–5, 156, 200; models 15, 21, 30, 36–7, 60, 200, 213, 217, 221
money 17–18, 30
MOSAIC 45
motivation 49, 56, 226
Musk, E. 102

narratives 235–8
National Centre for Excellence in the Teaching of Mathematics (NCETM) 13, 16–18
national curriculum 63, 169, 179, 251–2, 261; *see also* curriculum/curricula

National Numeracy Strategy (NNS) 17, 175–6
Nazism 38
needs 30–3, 50
negotiation 17, 73
neo-fascism 49
neoliberal fiction 83
nepotism 40
Nestler, A. 108
neutral activity 203; *see also* activity
New Labour (political party) 80, 83–4
The New York Times 89
Nine Chapters (Hui) 234
nine-dot shapes 116–17
Niss, M. 211
non-prototypical 111, 121; *see also* prototypical
normalisation 79, 81
normativity 27
Norway 48
NRICH (website) 191, 225
Numb3rs (TV) 103
number differences 250, *250*
numeracy plus 31
numeracy skills 33, 212; *see also* skills

objectification 36–8
objectivity 103–5
obstacle in education 31
occupational indicators 44
Office for Standards in Education (Ofsted) 58, 67, 170, 261
Oil and Gas Authority (OGA) 204
online tasks 149; *see also* tasks
open and closed questions 135; *see also* questioning/questions
open curriculum 73; *see also* curriculum/curricula
open-ended projects 72
opportunities **15**, 33, 44, 59, 61, 63, 71, 73, 95, 137, 145, 161–3, 190, 195–6; cognitive and affective 234–5; employment and life 46; equal 29, 40; higher order thinking 52; mental mathematics skills 175–6
Organisation for Economic Cooperation and Development (OECD) 3, 8, 50, 52, 56, 156–7, *158*, 161–2
organisation of mathematics teaching **15**
organising learners 48–9; *see also* students/learners
orientations 235–8

outcomes 18, 43, 51, 56–7, 59
out-of-school learning 162; *see also* learning
overvaluation 29–41; effects of study on thinking 33–6; mathematical needs 30–3; mathematical thinking 36–40; social costs 32; in and by society 29–30

Panadero, E. 248
parents 44, 49, 92
pedagogy 80, 82, 94, 225; *see also* teaching
peer-assessment 249; *see also* assessment(s)
Pellino, K. 49
perceptions 59, 170, 224–5, 242, 277
perfect equality 216
perfect inequality 216
perseverance 250
personal enjoyment 278
personal traits 68
Phoenix Park (school) 72–3
Piaget, J. 80
Pick's Theorem 115–19, 123–4
PISA *see* Programme for International Assessment (PISA)
planning for unexpected 115–30; Pick's Theorem 115–19, 123–4; role of teacher 128–30; symbolically structured environments' (SSEs) 124–8; triangles 119–24, *120–2*
policy 16, 20, 82–4; *see also* assessment(s); government policy
policymakers 3, 14
political agendas 19
political stability 10
politicians 3, 58
politics and mathematics 108, 197–208; climate change 199–202, 204–6; cyberspace 102; formatting 204–6
polygons, diagonals of regular 126, *127*
popular culture 101–9; *see also* culture
populism 49
post-compulsory education 257
Postgraduate Certificate in Education (PGCE) 211
poverty 44, 52
power, learning 73–4
Pratt, D. 149
primary education 82; *see also* education
primary schools 14, 20, 31, 55–6, 58, 67, 175, 178
private schools 8
problem posing 73

problem-solving 19, 57, 60, 73
procept 184
professional development 13–14, **15**, 16, 21, 148, 248–9
profit 17–18, 31
Profound Understanding of Fundamental Mathematics (PUFM) 176
Programme for International Assessment (PISA) 3–5, 7–10, 14, 17, 48, 58, 156, 161
programming/coding, projects *157*
progression, outcomes and 51
progressive educators 170, 176
progressive theory 50
projects *157*; *see also* open-ended projects
Proofs and Refutations (Lakatos) 233
prototypical 119; *see also* non-prototypical
proxy indicator 44
psychology, education 35
psychopathic 38
Ptolemy 227
public educators 170; *see also* teachers/educators
PUFM *see* Profound Understanding of Fundamental Mathematics (PUFM)
pupil access to curriculum **15**
Pythagorean relation 236

quadratic functions 185–6
quality of pedagogy 225
quantitative literacy 211–12
questioning/questions 131–41, 248; attending to attention 138–9; comparing 273–5; controlling 136; effective usage of 135–8; exam *274*; genuinely interested in 137–8; reason for arising of 131–5; responding to learners 139–40
Question Paper Evaluation Committee (QPEC) 258
Qurra, Thabit ibn 229

Railside School 71–2
Ramanujan, S. 102
randomised controlled trials (RCTs) 18
rationality 30, 39, 97
Realistic Mathematics Education (RME) 149–50
reasoning *see* calculative reasoning; instrumental reasoning
reformation *see* accommodation, reformation, transformation in teaching for sustainability

reification 184
relational equity 71
relational understanding 80, 173;
   see also understanding
relationships 73
relativity of mathematical rigour 232–4
Renert, M. 204, 207
research, education 80–2
restricted curriculum 59–60;
   see also curriculum/curricula
retention see grade retention
Ripley, M. 95
Risman, B. 91
Robbie, M. 104
romantic discourse 81; see also discourses
Rowland, T. 191
rule-breaking, activity and 82
Runesson, U. 146

Sahlgren, G. H. 50
same task 146–7; see also tasks
Sanders, B. 102
Saunders, K. 115
Schoenfeld, A. 221
school(s) see specific schools
school competition 50
Schrub Equities 106–7
sciences 230–2
secondary education 10; see also education
Secondary National Strategy 175
secondary schools 20, 55, 57, 60, 66
Second International Mathematics and
   Science Study (SIMS) 7
Securities and Exchange Commission
   (SEC) 106
segmentation see geodemographic
   segmentation
self-assessment 249; see also assessment(s)
self-confidence 32–3
self-esteem 49, 51, 63
self experience, interrogation of 135–6
self-image 71
self-respect 71
separated values 36–8; see also values
setting 56–60
sex 93–4
Sexing the Body (Fausto-Sterling) 93
sexism 92
sexuality 81, 84, 95–8; see also heterosexuality; homosexuality
sexual minority students 94–5;
   see also students/learners

Sfard, A. 184
Shakespeare, W. 32
shame 60
Shanghai 8–10, 14, 15, 16–21, 58, 83
shapes 116, 116–17, 119, 119
shopping 203
The Simpsons (cartoon) 108–9
SIMS see Second International
   Mathematics and Science Study (SIMS)
Singapore 4, 8–10, 14, 16–21
Skemp, R. 80, 96, 173
sketchpad tools 120
skills: assessment 45; coding 107; habits and
   68; knowledge and 30–1, 48, 261; to
   manage classroom 129; numeracy 212;
   students 175; understanding and 31, 83
Skovsmose, O. 199, 203
social attitudes 95
social beliefs 20; see also beliefs
social capital 44, 45
social class/classification 26–7, 32, 43–52;
   attainment 46–7; class 43–5; defined
   43; judgements 45–6; measurement 44;
   organising learners 48–9; as problematic construct 45; teaching 49–52;
   virtual school bags 47–8
social cohesion 50
social construction 27, 90–1, 95–7
social constructivist 95
social costs 32
social image 39
social institutions 199
social interaction 91
social privilege 49
social reproduction 46
social status 4
social training 34
societal constructions of
   mathematicians 97
society 29–30, 31, 39
socio-economic background of
   students 43
socio-economic capital 44
socio-economic comparator 72
socio-economic disadvantage 49
socio-economic inequality 214
socio-economic status (SES) 32, 45, 51–2,
   162; see also social class/classification
South Africa 210, 212–14, 219
spacious classroom 74–5
Spenser School 69–71
standard(s) 13, 58, 169, 174, 259–61

Standard Assessment Tasks (SATs) 257
Starting Points (Banwell, Saunders and Tahta) 115
Steen, L. A. 211–12
STEM 93–4, 156, 276
stereotypes 59, 92, 97, 102, 104
stretched triangle *121*; *see also* triangles
students/learners 3, 5–7, **6**, 13–14, 32, 43, 45, 48–51, 55–6, 58–9, 60, 62–3, 67, 71, 73–5, 84–6, 95, 138–40, 174–5, 225, 250, 253–4; all-attainment groupings 60; forming and testing conjectures *251*, 251–2; forming generalisations 252; making trials 251; sexual minority 94–5; tasks designed by 150–1; working-class 49, 60, 73; *see also* social class/classification
study skills 70; *see also* skills
subject knowledge 244
success: academic 47; criterion 250–1; expectations of 92; inherited ability 30; mathematicians 36; socio-economic status 32; tests 56
summative assessments 243, 246, 262–3; *see also* assessment(s)
supplementary schools 9
surveillance, normalisation and 81
Swan, M. 146, 152
symbolically structured environments (SSEs) 124–8

Tahta, D. 115
Taiwan 8–10
Tall, D. 184
Task Group 174–5
tasks 143–53; activity and 144–6, 151; authorship of 147–9; designed by learners 150–1; elements of 151–2; nature and role of 143–4; online 149; same 146–7; teaching 146–7, 149–50
teacher-pupil interaction 20
teachers/educators 4, 13, **15**, 16, 20, 21, 50, 55, 59, 71, 78, 92, 128–30, 175, 249–50, 252–3; assessments 252–3; as co-learner 74; exchanges 14, 16–17; expectations 57, 71; progressive 170, 176; public 170; *see also* students/learners
teaching 3–11, **15**, 17, 35, 51–2, 66; ability-based 63; concepts and procedures 183–4; international comparisons 10; prospects for change 20–1; setting practices and 59–60; social

classification 49–52; tasks 146–7, 149–50; *see also* all-attainment teaching; understanding
teaching for mastery (TfM) 13–14, 16, 19–20
Tesseract *232*
tests/testing 4, 6, 14, 17, 32–3, 48, 56, 76, 83, 131, 156–257, 157, 199, 203, 243, 245–6, 251, *251*, 253, 257, 261–3; *see also* A-level (mathematics); assessment(s); General Certificate of Secondary Education (GCSE); Programme for International Assessment (PISA)
TfM *see* teaching for mastery (TfM)
The Theory of Everything (film) 102
thinking: ability 49; effects of study on 33–6; engagement and 69; mathematical 36–40, 71
Third International Mathematics and Science Study 7
Thompson, I. 178
Thomson, P. 47
TIMSS *see* Trends in International Mathematics and Science Study (TIMSS)
Tomlinson, M. 211
Tomlinson Report 212
trainee, teachers 92
trainee primary school teachers 33
trans 93–4, 98
transformability 62, 75
transformation *see* accommodation, reformation, transformation in teaching for sustainability
trans-inclusive 94
translation 6
transmission-based pedagogies 82
trapezium/trapezoid 6
Trends in International Mathematics and Science Study (TIMSS) 5, 7, 10, 58, 156, 158
trial-and-improvement 260
triangles 119–24, *120–2*
Trump, D. 49
Turing, A. 102
tutors *see* digital tutors; teachers/educators
Two New Sciences (Galileo) 231

Um, P. N. 210
underachievement 7, 67; *see also* achievement

understanding (mathematical) 78–87;
discourses of 80–2; functional/
romantic 82, 84–5; instrumental 35,
80, 173–4, 177; knowledge and 81;
mental mathematics 171–4; skills and
31, 83; with/in policy 82–4
unemployment 198
University and College Admissions system
(UCAS) 272
utilitarianism 30

vacuous questions 132;
see also questioning/questions
valuation, education and 30
values: education 18; ethics and 40; needs
18; neutrality 36; priorities and 18, 39;
separated 36–8; societal 39
van Doesburg, T. 231, *231*
Vanishing Point Theorem *230*
van Maanen, J. 238
variable 4, 9, 34, 52, 184, 187–9, 203,
244, 274–5
variation, dimensions of 186–7, 189
Vaughan, D. 102
Vennett, J. 104
vertical mathematisation 150, 152
Vescio, T. 92
virtual environment 235
virtual reality (VR) 159
virtual school bags 47–8

Wafa, A. 227
Wales 84, 224, 242, 250, 252,
256–7, 269
Walkerdine, V. 80–1, 97
Watson, A. 20, 62–3, 70, 187, 190,
221, 234
Wayne, T. 103
welfare, ability and 93
well-being of students 50
Welsh 6, 6–7
West, D. 90–1
Western free-market culture 38;
see also culture
Western school curriculum 224;
see also curriculum
whistle-blowing 39
whiteboard 103
Wiliam, D. 17, 245, 253
working class 44, 48–9, 60, 73;
see also social class/classification
working week 9
World War II 38

Y2K bug 107

Zevenbergen, R. 48
Zimmerman, C. 90–1
Zuckerberg, M. 102